CW00665064

Endorsements

Finally, a new paradigm in compliance and regu[illegible] of what truly matters—values-based and ethica[illegible] leadership. In the 21st century who you are, how you behave, and what you stand for are destined to become the new frontiers of competitive advantage. Success in the future will be all about the culture the leaders create.

Richard Barrett, Chairman of the Barrett Values Centre and Founder of the Academy for the Advancement of Human Values

This book makes an insightful case for business to benefit from being values-driven rather than focussed on short-term profits, and for promoting an open, just culture rather than a blame culture. It also convincingly contends that while business regulators must take closing businesses and deterrence seriously, deterrence can also have counterproductive effects. This is a book rich in lessons about how we can all learn how to build more ethical corporate cultures.

John Braithwaite
Australian National University

In this long overdue, much needed and wonderfully practical book, Christopher Hodges and Ruth Steinholtz have provided a guide for both business practitioners and regulators that lays out the rationale, a mindset and a roadmap for a more realistic, more honest and ultimately more productive working relationship between these two powerful societal players. The book remains remarkably readable and engaging while providing a solid foundation of insights—from both science and real world experience—into the factors that encourage as well as discourage ethical human behavior. The central argument at the book's heart is the simple yet powerful idea that deterrence and adversarialism have not and will not serve to build the trust-based relationships between the public and the private sectors upon which a productive and mutually beneficial functioning of our economy relies—and that cooperation and a mutual learning orientation will. Although their book targets regulators and business practitioners, its lessons provide a critical key for beginning to address the wide-ranging challenges at the heart of our world's current larger spiral of distrust, fear, resentment and retaliation. Hodges and Steinholtz have done us all a great service.

Mary C Gentile PhD
Author of *Giving Voice To Values: How To Speak Your Mind When You Know What's Right* and Professor of Practice, University of Virginia Darden School of Business

After every institutional failure, the cry goes up for more ethical behaviour from more ethical individuals. But where are such people to be found? How would you identify them? Where do they come from—and what militates against them? This book sets itself the ambitious goal of analysing what ethical businesses look like and how they behave. It doesn't dodge the hard questions or promise simplistic solutions but dares to look fearlessly at the most important questions of our age.

Margaret Heffernan
Author of *Wilful Blindness. Why we ignore the obvious at our peril*

Hodges and Steinholtz provide a compelling thesis for an alternative paradigm of ethical based business practice and regulation. It demonstrates the superior outcomes of an ethics-based approach to corporate governance as opposed to rules-based enforcement. Drawing on behavioural psychology, other scientific evidence and many sobering case studies, they explain why regulators achieve their statutory objectives more effectively when they build cooperative relationships with their clients, rather than over-relying on deterrence and thereby failing to influence future conduct. The framework provided here for managing organizational culture includes many practical steps that can be taken to engage and motivate staff to behave ethically and speak out. This is an invaluable handbook for regulators, corporate leaders and ethics practitioners alike.

Peter Massey-Cook
Head of Ethics, EMEA, State Street

Hodges and Steinholtz have done a great service to business. *Ethical Business Practice and Regulation* is a must-read for all leaders eager to drive sustainable social and economic growth by infusing their organisation with value and integrity. The authors' inspirational vision of a better business world—indeed a better society—can be realised with this practical guide.

Roswitha Reisinger
General Counsel Europe, Otsuka Pharmaceutical Europe Ltd

There is a clear and present danger that the economic regulation of utilities becomes ever more invasive and prescriptive. Such a path is undesirable, limiting the discretion and authority of senior management and resulting in a much reduced focus on the needs of the customer.

Chris Hodges' Ethical Business Regulation (EBR) concept has provided the Scottish water industry an opportunity to break out of this pattern of ever decreasing circles. EBR has offered an unique opportunity to explore, constructively and collaboratively, the thorniest of regulatory issues and to do the right thing for customers, our environment and our society.

Alan Sutherland
CEO, Water Industry Commission for Scotland

Regulation is fundamentally about how people in organisations actually behave. This book pulls together the evidence on "what works" in getting the right results. There is a wealth of material here for smart regulators who are pursuing effectiveness through actual outcomes, not compliance with rules for its own sake.

Richard Thomas CBE
Information Commissioner (2002–09),
Committee on Standards in Public Life (2012–17)

In a time where ethical behaviour is increasingly under attack by various governments around the world, Hodges and Steinholz provide a very timely guide to the importance of the culture of compliance in organizations. Hodges and Steinholz consider the essence of ethical and compliant behaviour asking, "*Why do people observe rules? Why do people break them*"? The writers take the reader through a well-organized and compelling journey from biological and physiological influences through to the need for governing agencies and businesses to interact on a relationship of trust. This is critically important because, as the writers clearly articulate in chapter 7, people will not come forward to report ethical breaches if they feel they will be putting themselves at undue personal risk. I truly believe *Ethical Business Practice and Regulation: A Behavioural and Based Values Based Approach to Compliance and Enforcement* is not only essential reading for ethics and compliance professionals, but rather everyone who is engaged in business on some level. Read it and encourage your colleagues to read it too!

Thomas Topolski, CCEP-I
Executive Vice President, Turner and Townsend

ETHICAL BUSINESS PRACTICE AND REGULATION: A BEHAVIOURAL AND VALUES-BASED APPROACH TO COMPLIANCE AND ENFORCEMENT

This book explains the concepts of Ethical Business Practice (EBP) and Ethical Business Regulation (EBR), a new paradigm in compliance and enforcement based on behavioural science and ethics. EBR provides the basis for an effective relationship between a business and its regulators, resulting in better outcomes for both. EBR is attracting extensive attention from regulators and businesses around the world. The UK Government's 2017 Regulatory Futures Review draws on EBR as the foundation for its policy of 'regulatory self-assurance'. EBR draws on findings from behavioural science, responsive regulation, safety and business and integrity management to create a practical and holistic approach. Examples include the open culture that is essential for civil aviation safety, the Primary Authority agreements between regulators and national businesses, and feedback mechanisms provided by market vigilance systems and sectoral consumer ombudsmen. This book provides an essential blueprint for sustainable business and effective future regulation.

Volume 6 in the series Civil Justice Systems

Civil Justice Systems

Series General Editor: Christopher Hodges, Director, Swiss Re/CMS Research Programme, Centre for Socio-Legal Studies, University of Oxford

This series covers new theoretical and empirical research on the mechanisms for resolution of civil disputes, including courts, tribunals, arbitration, compensation schemes, ombudsmen, codes of practice, complaint mechanisms, mediation and various forms of Alternative Dispute Resolution. It examines frameworks for dispute resolution that comprise combinations of the above mechanisms, and the parameters and conditions for selecting certain types of techniques and procedures rather than others. It also evaluates individual techniques, against parameters such as cost, duration, accessibility, and delivery of desired outcomes, and illuminates how legal rights and obligations are operated in practice.

Volume 1: *The Costs and Funding of Civil Litigation: A Comparative Perspective* edited by Christopher Hodges, Stefan Vogenauer and Magdalena Tulibacka

Volume 2: *Consumer ADR in Europe* by Christopher Hodges, Iris Benöhr and Naomi Creutzfeldt-Banda

Volume 3: *Law and Corporate Behaviour: Integrating Theories of Regulation, Enforcement, Compliance and Ethics*
Christopher Hodges

Volume 4: *A Comparative Examination of Multi-Party Actions*
Joanne Blennerhassett

Volume 5: *Redress Schemes for Personal Injuries*
Sonia Macleod and Christopher Hodges

Ethical Business Practice and Regulation

A Behavioural and Values-Based Approach to Compliance and Enforcement

Christopher Hodges

Professor of Justice Systems, and Fellow of Wolfson College, University of Oxford

Head of the Swiss Re/CMS Research Programme on Civil Justice Systems,
Centre for Socio-Legal Studies, Oxford.

Ruth Steinholtz

Founder and Principal
AretéWork LLP

Former General Counsel and Group Security Coordinator,
Head of Ethics, Borealis AG

• HART •
PUBLISHING
OXFORD AND PORTLAND, OREGON
2017

Hart Publishing
An imprint of Bloomsbury Publishing Plc

Hart Publishing Ltd
Kemp House
Chawley Park
Cumnor Hill
Oxford OX2 9PH
UK

Bloomsbury Publishing Plc
50 Bedford Square
London
WC1B 3DP
UK

www.hartpub.co.uk
www.bloomsbury.com

Published in North America (US and Canada) by
Hart Publishing
c/o International Specialized Book Services
920 NE 58th Avenue, Suite 300
Portland, OR 97213-3786
USA

www.isbs.com

HART PUBLISHING, the Hart/Stag logo, BLOOMSBURY and the Diana logo are trademarks of Bloomsbury Publishing Plc

First published 2017

© Christopher Hodges and Ruth Steinholtz 2017

Christopher Hodges and Ruth Steinholtz have asserted their right under the Copyright, Designs and Patents Act 1988 to be identified as Authors of this work.

All rights reserved. No part of this publication may be reproduced or transmitted in any form or by any means, electronic or mechanical, including photocopying, recording, or any information storage or retrieval system, without prior permission in writing from the publishers.

While every care has been taken to ensure the accuracy of this work, no responsibility for loss or damage occasioned to any person acting or refraining from action as a result of any statement in it can be accepted by the authors, editors or publishers.

All UK Government legislation and other public sector information used in the work is Crown Copyright ©. All House of Lords and House of Commons information used in the work is Parliamentary Copyright ©. This information is reused under the terms of the Open Government Licence v3.0 (http://www.nationalarchives.gov.uk/doc/open-government-licence/version/3) except where otherwise stated.

All Eur-lex material used in the work is © European Union, http://eur-lex.europa.eu/, 1998–2017.

British Library Cataloguing-in-Publication Data
A catalogue record for this book is available from the British Library.

ISBN:	PB:	978-1-50991-636-8 (Hart)
	PB:	978-3-406-71911-0 (CH Beck Verlag)
	ePDF:	978-1-50991-637-5
	ePub:	978-1-50991-638-2

Library of Congress Cataloging-in-Publication Data

Names: Hodges, Christopher J. S., author. | Steinholtz, Ruth N., author.

Title: Ethical business practice and regulation : a behavioural and values-based approach to compliance and enforcement / Christopher Hodges, Professor of Justice Systems, and Fellow of Wolfson College, University of Oxford Head of the Swiss Re/CMS Research Programme on Civil Justice Systems, Centre for Socio-Legal Studies, Oxford; Ruth Steinholtz, Founder and Areté Work LLP, Former General Counsel and Group Security Coordinator, Head of Ethics, Borealis AG.

Description: Oxford [UK] ; Portland, Oregon : Hart Publishing, 2017. | Series: Civil justice systems ; volume 6 | Includes bibliographical references and index.

Identifiers: LCCN 2017050984 (print) | LCCN 2017050494 (ebook) | ISBN 9781509916382 (Epub) | ISBN 9781509916368 (pbk. : alk. paper)

Subjects: LCSH: Corporate governance—Law and legislation—Moral and ethical aspects. | Commercial law—Moral and ethical aspects. | Business ethics. | Tort liability of corporations.

Classification: LCC K1005 (print) | LCC K1005 .H63 2017 (ebook) | DDC 174/.4—dc23

LC record available at https://lccn.loc.gov/2017050984

Typeset by Compuscript Ltd, Shannon
Printed and bound in Great Britain by CPI Group (UK) Ltd, Croydon CR0 4YY

To find out more about our authors and books visit www.hartpublishing.co.uk. Here you will find extracts, author information, details of forthcoming events and the option to sign up for our newsletters.

ACKNOWLEDGEMENTS

This book summarises a lifetime's experience and reading, to which many people have contributed and who should be thanked. There are many colleagues and clients from when we both practised law, and since then many academic colleagues and officials who have been very supportive and helpful. Many have been named in previous publications, and we apologise for not repeating a long list here.

People who have been particularly helpful in developing thinking in the past couple of years, and helped with this book, should be named. They are: Graham Russell, Joanna Ivey and colleagues at the Regulatory Delivery Directorate of the Department for Business Energy and Industrial Strategy; Sheena Brown, Lorraine King and Laura McGlynn of the Scottish Government; Jon Round of the Civil Aviation Authority and Captain John Monks of British Airways; Alan Sutherland and colleagues at the Water Industry Commission for Scotland; Douglas Millican of Scottish Water; Ann Bishop and John Hargreaves of Indepen; and Nick Barnard of Corker Binning for permission to include an extract from the firm's blog.

Chris would like to thank, above all, Ruth Steinholtz for many years of happy collaboration and her experience implementing these concepts in organisations, and his wife Fiona for her constant encouragement and material support. He would also like to thank Sebastian Stolzke of Zurich Insurance Company Limited, Eric Schuh and Urs Leimbacher of Swiss Re, Lorenz Ködderitzsch of Johnson & Johnson, Penelope Warne and Guy Pendell of CMS Cameron McKenna, and all their colleagues, plus Arundel McDougall, for providing—scrupulously arm's-length—research funding from the Swiss Reinsurance Company Limited, the European Justice Forum and international law firm CMS, and for allowing him the intellectual freedom to develop the ideas expressed here.

Ruth would like to acknowledge Richard Barrett, Phil Clothier, Tor Eneroth and everyone at the Barrett Values Centre for their wisdom and dedication to cultural transformation based upon values; Sander Mahieu and Pleuntje van Meer for training her in the use of the Cultural Transformation Tools®; David Marks for his encouragement and friendship; and her husband Kjell Folkvord for his courage in moving to London from Norway and adding bright colours and love to her life. Ruth would be remiss if she did not express her deep gratitude to her late parents, Eleanor and Lester Steinholtz, for the example they set and the values and social consciousness they passed on to her. Ruth would also like to acknowledge all those, too numerous to mention, who as ethics ambassadors have humbled and inspired her with their dedication and enthusiasm. Above all, Ruth would like to thank Chris Hodges, for his friendship, confidence and his generosity in inviting her to cooperate with him on this important mission. It is an honour.

The authors would like to thank Sinead Moloney and colleagues at Hart Publishing, Roberta Bassi, Tom Adams, Anna Berzovan and John Hort.

CONTENTS

Appendices

LIST OF FIGURES, TABLES AND BOXES

Figures

Tables

Boxes

LIST OF CASE STUDIES

LIST OF ABBREVIATIONS

ADR	Alternative dispute resolution
ASAP	As soon as possible
ATC	Air traffic controller
ATM	Automated telling machine
BCCI	Bank of Credit and Commerce International
BVC	Barrett Values Centre
CAA	Civil Aviation Authority
CEO	Chief Executive Officer
CIIA	Chartered Institute of Internal Auditors
CMA	Competition and Markets Authority
COSO	Committee of Sponsoring Organisations of the Treadway Commission
CPD	Continuous Professional Development
CSR	Corporate social responsibility
CTT™	Cultural Transformation Tools
CVA	Cultural Values Assessment
DG COMP	Directorate General on Competition of the European Commission
DNA	Dioxyribonuclear acid
DNB	DeNederlandscheBank
DPA	Deferred prosecution agreement
DVLA	Driver and Vehicle Licensing Authority
EBP	Ethical Business Practice
EBR	Ethical Business Regulation
EDMM	Ethical decision-making model
EY	Ernst & Young
FAA	United States Federal Aviation Agency
FCA	Financial Conduct Authority
FCPA	Foreign Corrupt Practices Act (US)
FI	Financial Institution
FLA	Finance and Leasing Association
FOS	Financial Ombudsman Service
FRC	Financial Reporting Council
FSA	Food Standards Authority
FTSE	Financial Times Stock Exchange listing
FX	Foreign exchange
G20	Group of 20 Nations
G30	Group of 30 Nations
GRI	Global Reporting Initiative
HMRC	Her Majesty's Revenue & Customs
HSE	Health & Safety Executive

IAAF	International Association of Athletics Federations
IATA	International Air Transport Association
IBE	Institute of Business Ethics
ICAO	International Civil Aviation Organization
INPO	Institute of Nuclear Power Operations
IOSA	IATA Operational Safety Audit
IN	Influence network
IPSIS	Independent Patient Safety Investigation Service
ISO	International Organization for Standardization
IT	Information technology
LA	Local authority
LIBOR	London Inter-Bank Offered Rate
MHRA	Medicines and Healthcare Products Regulatory Authority
NGO	Non-governmental organisation
NHS	National Health Service
NMAC	Near Midair Collision
NYU	New York University
OECD	Organisation for Economic Co-operation and Development
OFT	Office of Fair Trading
Ofcom	Office of Communications
Ofgem	Office of Gas and Electricity Markets
Ofwat	Water Services Regulation Authority
ORR	Office of Road and Rail
PA	Primary Authority
PBR	Performance-based regulation
PPI	Payment protection insurance
RD	Regulatory Delivery Directorate of the Department for Business, Energy and Industrial Strategy
RBS	Royal Bank of Scotland
SEC	Securities and Exchange Commission
SFO	Serious Fraud Office
SLC	Standards of Lending Conduct
SMEs	Small and medium-sized enterprises
SMS	Safety Management System
S&P	Standard & Poor's listing
TS	Technology services
TSS	Trading Standards Service
UNCTAD	United Nations Commission for Trade and Development

PREFACE

What is Ethical Business Practice and Regulation?

This book explains why any organisation of human beings is more likely to succeed in its objectives if all the people involved aim to, and do, behave *ethically*. There is a considerable amount of solid scientific evidence that supports the idea that joint human endeavours will flourish when people do so. It is now accepted in business management that companies perform best if they have clear ethical values and behave in accordance with those values, involving all stakeholders.

We apply these lessons to the *regulatory relationship* between public authorities and businesses. We propose a model of an ideal regulatory relationship between authorities and businesses: *Ethical Business Regulation* (EBR). Adopting EBR will maximise good outputs for both business and regulators, and their respective stakeholders—society, staff, customers, suppliers and investors. To achieve EBR, both regulators and businesses need to adopt ethical practice. On the business side, we call this *Ethical Business Practice* (EBP).

The Essence of Ethical Business Practice

An organisation in which the leaders consciously and consistently strive to create an effective ethical culture where employees do the right thing, based upon ethical values and supported by cultural norms and formal institutions. EBP requires people who can recognise ethical dilemmas, challenge constructively, speak up if they know or suspect unethical behaviour, and who use mistakes and wrongdoing as an opportunity to learn and improve. Engagement with EBR then requires the organisation to be open with its regulators and provide evidence of EBP.

Ethical Business Regulation

A relationship between a business, or a group of businesses, and a regulator, or group of regulators, in which the business produces evidence of its ongoing commitment to EBP and the regulator recognises and encourages that commitment.

The Need for a New Approach to Regulation

The basic idea is that it makes sense to operate systems that are designed around how human beings actually behave rather than on theories on how they behave. This needs an evidence-based approach relying on good science instead of theoretical assertion. Decisions are made by people rather than by organisations, although the structures, systems, objectives, culture and incentives that operate within organisations can affect the decisions made by the people who work in them. The focus of achieving compliance with laws should therefore be on affecting both the behaviour of individuals and the organisational environment.

Most people want to 'do the right thing' and only a few do not. It is therefore logical to use an approach that is geared towards the majority of 'good' people who want to do the right thing but may go astray in the wrong context. Too much traditional enforcement thinking is based on the minority of people who deliberately break the rules. We need to adopt a fundamentally distinct approach that differentiates between those who try to behave ethically and those who intend not to. Of course, we will make provision for bad and unethical actors, but the entire system should not be built around them. Paradoxically, at present, too many regulatory systems are built around the idea that anyone who breaks a rule is bad and that breaking rules needs to be deterred by strong punishment. This approach, however, is preventing ethical behaviour rather than increasing it.

It is important to focus on values, culture and ethical behaviour rather than on compliance with rules. We think that the current regulatory approach perversely incentivises organisations to prefer 'tick-box' compliance models over efforts to develop and reinforce a strong ethical culture. Unless regulators and businesses can carve out a cooperative approach aimed at continuous improvement based upon fairness, ethical values and open culture, they will continue to focus on compliance, with the predictable results of non-compliance such as we have seen repeatedly. Focusing solely on rules and responding to breaches of rules by deterrence and punishment simply does not work, as we will demonstrate in this book.

Public authorities generally assume that they behave ethically and treat business fairly. After all, they represent the public interest and have power delegated from the legislature. But in fact, sometimes their behaviour may act as a barrier to businesses acting ethically, albeit unintentionally. Even an individual or business that wants to do the right thing may be deterred by the likely attitude of a regulator. Fear that the response to acknowledging a problem will be to impose blame and take strong enforcement action, especially when the business was trying to put things right, will not support a relationship of honest and open communication between business and regulator. If an enforcer's response to a company that shares full information that it has discovered wrongdoing by some of its staff is to impose a large fine on the business, adversely affecting innocent staff, managers and stakeholders, will that be seen as fair? Should the primary focus rather be on jointly identifying the root cause of the problem, then making sure that the risk of reoccurrence is reduced, repairing any damage and seeing whether any individuals have deliberately acted unethically?

An important barometer of a regulatory system is how it reacts when things go wrong. There is now clear science and experience that we only learn from mistakes if we can share openly information on why the mistake happened and identify the root cause. The civil aviation industry and others have shown with outstanding success that this sharing must be in an open trusting relationship that does *not blame* people simply for making a mistake. If we focus solely on blame every time something goes wrong, people become defensive and we will never learn, we will never fix problems and we will destroy the relationships that would allow us to learn and improve.

Every time there is a major scandal, there is a call for more regulation, in the hope that this will solve the problem. However, it has been shown that more rules and hard enforcement just do not work. Deterrence does not work without highly visible and all-pervasive enforcement, something that government cannot afford and which would be democratically unacceptable. An increase in monitoring, reporting and compliance in general can inadvertently *increase* unethical behaviour, as people feel they are not trusted. Companies can spend large amounts of energy on compliance and have little left over for ethics. Focusing on rules crowds out objective thought on whether behaviour is ethical. Focusing on compliance can engender cynicism and disengagement, as the implicit message is 'we are only doing this because it is the law' and 'we don't trust you'. Disengagement clearly feeds unethical behaviour directly and indirectly as disengaged employees are less likely to speak up and report issues.

The purpose of regulation is to ensure that business performs in the best interests of society. We are convinced that the traditional approach to compliance and regulation is failing and that there is a better way for regulators to support organisations to behave ethically and for organisations to strive to do so. Fundamentally, a focus on compliance will not necessarily result in 'doing the right thing'. Conversely, when the focus is on values-driven ethical behaviour, we believe that compliance with just rules will result.

When one starts to look more closely, there are, in fact, many examples of successful ethical and open cooperation in the UK, such as in the areas of safety (civil aviation, workplace health and safety), general business trading (the Primary Authority scheme, data protection, equality and human rights) and regulated sectors (gambling, medicines, medical technology, water and energy). Profound cultural transformation is needed, but has already been shown to be possible. In 2017, the UK government has proposed a general shift across all sectors towards regulatory self-assurance and earned recognition. We believe that these structures can only work if they are based on a further explicit policy of adopting ethical values—as the Scottish government has explicitly done.

We think that the evidence is now clear, consistent and compelling, and that the time is right for a step change in much regulatory practice. But the same is also true of much business practice. Before we look at that, however, we need to look more widely at society.

The Collapse of Mutual Trust in Contemporary Society

Businesses and regulators are made up of individuals, and those individuals generally possess ethical values and the intention to do the right thing in their lives. But it is not enough for an individual to have strong ethical values and good intentions. Forces such as the context, situation and institution or society within which an individual operates can derail the individual. That is why we must focus on the culture of the organisations and societies within which people inter-relate to ensure that ethical behaviour is supported—and not deterred—and that incentives for unethical behaviour are eliminated. As Richard Barrett says:

> If you want to succeed in business in the era we are now entering, your values must be evidenced in every decision you make and every action you take. Furthermore, your behaviours must align with your values—you must be seen to be walking the talk and operating with integrity. This is important; not just for building societal goodwill, it is also important for building the resilience of your organization and finding economic success.[1]

Humans are basically social creatures: we depend on each other for our collective survival, progress and success. We all belong to multiple, overlapping groups (family, work, club, social, nation, religion and sub-groups within all the above). The problem is that there is currently unmistakeable evidence of fractures in and between various societal groupings. This lack of cohesion threatens our social stability and security as well as our ability to prosper economically.

In 2016, trust in business was higher than trust in government and was *increasing*.[2] However, in 2017, trust was 'in crisis around the world'.[3] The Edelman 2017 trust barometer concluded:

> The general population's trust in all four key institutions—business, government, NGOs, and media—has declined broadly, a phenomenon not reported since Edelman began tracking trust among this segment in 2012.
>
> With the fall of trust, the majority of respondents now lack full belief that the overall system is working for them. In this climate, people's societal and economic concerns, including globalization, the pace of innovation and eroding social values, turn into fears, spurring the rise of populist actions now playing out in several Western-style democracies.
>
> To rebuild trust and restore faith in the system, institutions must step outside of their traditional roles and work toward a new, more integrated operating model that puts people—and the addressing of their fears—at the center of everything they do …

[1] R Barrett, *The Values-Driven Organization: Cultural Health and Employee Well-Being as a Pathway to Sustainable Performance*, 2nd edn (Routledge 2017) xxii.

[2] The Edelman Trust Barometer 2016, www.edelman.com/trust2016.

[3] The Edelman Trust Barometer 2017, www.edelman.com/trust2017.

> We have moved beyond the point of trust being simply a key factor in product purchase or selection of employment opportunity; it is now the deciding factor in whether a society can function. As trust in institutions erodes, the basic assumptions of fairness, shared values and equal opportunity traditionally upheld by 'the system' are no longer taken for granted. We observe deep disillusion on both the left and the right, who share opposition to globalization, innovation, deregulation, and multinational institutions. There is growing despair about the future, a lack of confidence in the possibility of a better life for one's family ... only 15 percent of the general population believe the present system is working, while 53 percent do not and 32 percent are uncertain.

This evidence of fracture is visible in many areas of life. We focus on the effects of a series of major incidents of individuals and organisations failing to operate ethically, which has resulted in the collapse of public trust in business. You only need to think of the financial crisis of 2008 and the low esteem in which banks are held by society, the fraudulent behaviour of Volkswagen in 'dieselgate' and bribery scandals involving BAE Systems, GlaxoSmithKline, Siemens and Rolls-Royce to name but a few. In sport, you might think of FIFA, of doping in professional cycling, and of Russia's expulsion from the Olympics due to institutionalised doping. A decade ago in public life in the UK, the issue was a collapse of trust in Members of Parliament as a result of the expenses scandal, as well as phone hacking by journalists. On the international scene, countries too numerous to mention have been racked by corruption scandals that in some cases have brought down governments. Evidence of corruption across the world is extensive—for example, the Odebrecht scandal in Brazil, said to involve paying \$3.3 billion to politicians between 2006 and 2014, the equivalent of 80% of the company's net profits.[4] In February 2017, some 300,000 Romanians took to the streets to demand the scrapping of a law that would have decriminalised low-level corruption and, once they achieved that, demanded the resignation of government figures who they did not believe were committed to fighting corruption.

One of the fundamental points revealed by the Brexit vote and the election of President Trump has been the seriousness of the rift between what Prime Minister Theresa May has called 'the marginalised or overlooked' and those they perceive to be the influential and well-off (depicted as elites). As *The Economist* said, people 'who feel they have been left behind after the financial crisis have turned to populists' for a voice.[5] To this we would add the anger and frustration of the average person when confronted with evidence of corruption amongst the privileged and the lack of accountability that has characterised the institutional response to many of the ethical lapses listed here.

This is also linked to a 'post-truth' period, in which factual accuracy is ignored (examples being the Iraq dossier and the numerous statements by President Trump and his press secretary that the media were deliberately falsely reporting

[4] *The Economist*, 22 April 2017, 39.
[5] *The Economist*, 7 January 2017, 64.

the numbers who attended the inauguration). All of this is evidence of disrespect for ethical values of truth and honesty, and is magnified by the effect of social media. It is particularly worrying when those who are leaders perpetrate it, as they are role models.

British and American people feel that society suffers from an essential inequality; many around the globe worry about resources being wasted; people are unhappy with their governments and the perceived non-responsiveness of state bureaucracy. The results of National Values Assessments conducted in many countries reveal the extent of the problem.[6] The moral psychologist Jonathan Haidt argues that if there is a perception that the group is threatened, it produces retrenchment and withdrawal.[7] Faced with threat, our defensive gene is triggered and may overcome the collaborative, open gene, disrupting trust.

We may wonder how these rifts will be healed. Surely appeals to national solidarity have almost no effect on the ground. The UK Prime Minister has rightly said that: 'The objective of our modern industrial strategy is to improve living standards and economic growth by increasing productivity and driving growth across the whole country.'[8] But how is this to be achieved without addressing the deep rifts that currently exist?

Ethical Values as a Political Manifesto

We think that the answers are readily available when we look at the evidence. The answer lies in basing society and business on *fairness* and *ethical values*. This will build trust and relationships based on a firm commitment to such values. We suggest that societies need to re-state a universal Golden Rule, as their own code of ethics, and to build systems that produce evidence on whether people live up to their shared ethical values or not.

We believe that commitment to ethical values is a force for peace and prosperity through supporting humans working together for the common good. It is this ethical dimension of behaviour that has been largely missing from all previous 20th-century conceptions of what regulation, enforcement and compliance are. Models describing regulatory structures miss the human element. Looking at behaviour through the lenses of psychology and genetics now introduces, first, the social element of relationships into the picture and, second, unavoidable elements of human values, against which almost all of us evaluate rules, actions and

[6] See https://www.valuescentre.com.

[7] J Haidt, *The Righteous Mind : Why Good People are Divided by Politics and Religion* (Penguin Books, 2012).

[8] *Building Our Industrial Strategy. Green Paper* (HM Government, January 2017), https://www.gov.uk/government/uploads/system/uploads/attachment_data/file/585273/building-our-industrial-strategy-green-paper.pdf.

behaviour. If we favour the ethical element in our relationships, everything starts to make sense and drives us towards giving or withholding trust.

These concepts are not new. Polanyi recognised in the 1940s that the basis of compliance with rules and regulation is in fact strongly based on *social* relationships.[9] This type of collaboration that is inherent in EBR operates outside political ideologies, especially models of the past few hundred years that oppose different groups, such as owners of capital against workers or the 'high-flying elite' against ordinary people.

We are intrigued to see the idea of a fair society spreading quickly. At the political level, the Scottish government has a headline policy of a 'fair Scotland', and ministers and officials there have been quick and enthusiastic in their adoption of EBR. UK Prime Minister Theresa May has also based her premiership on building 'a fairer Britain'.[10] At the time of writing, the Scottish government has embraced the EBR approach, whilst the UK government has given several signs of approval of it (see chapter 12), but has stopped short of seeking it as a necessary and integral part of its policy of social and economic renewal. This is promising, since we cannot expect business to focus on building a strong ethical culture based on values if what the regulators require as evidence are tick-box compliance elements. It may be helpful and easy to prove the existence of a speak-up or whistleblowing line, but how much more positive it would be to have an open culture where people are not afraid to speak up to each other and where they are listened to by their managers. This is admittedly more difficult to prove, but far more powerful in bringing about change.

Need for Political Leadership in Basing Society on Ethical Values

We think that broad political approval for EBR will be essential if it is to be fully implemented by all regulators and businesses, and accepted by the public. They can adopt the approach spontaneously, as a number have done, but political leadership is necessary for two reasons. First, political support is needed to defeat the question when something goes wrong of 'who's to blame?' The answer needs to be that we have left the blaming approach behind, as it does not enable us to learn and improve. Instead, we are focusing on fixing the problems and decreasing the likelihood that they will recur.

[9] K Polanyi, *The Great Transformation: The Political and Economic Origins of Our Time*, 2nd edn (Beacon Press, 2001).

[10] T May MP, 'The Government's Negotiating Objectives for Exiting the EU', speech delivered at Lancaster House, 17 January 2017. See also *Corporate Governance Reform: Green Paper* (Department for Business, Energy and Industrial Strategy, 2016) and *Building Our Industrial Strategy* (n 8).

Second, the ethical approach will have a speedier impact if it is adopted holistically and consistently across a society. Only a government can adopt such a holistic policy, even if its implementation requires other steps. The policy can be disseminated through education and information channels, and could transform the operation of public bodies and the relationships between citizens, the state and organisations.

Another player must be mentioned here. The media plays a crucial role in shaping public opinion, although that role is no longer exclusive following the advent of social media. However, if the media focuses on blame and champions punishment and deterrence indiscriminately, both regulators and businesses will be caught in a paradox. It will be necessary to educate the media and the public as to the benefits of EBR, and to take advantage of the many social media avenues available to reach opinion leaders, otherwise regulators will be open to accusations of failing to hold business to account. We outline these benefits in this book and we hope that our message will be taken up by others, who will build on this work and will advocate EBR to the various relevant actors.

The Need for a New Approach to Business

Many businesses treat customers fairly and purport to accept their corporate social responsibility, but do ethical values pervade *everything* that they do? There are too many examples that would argue against this assertion. Individuals who pursue goals based upon their own self-interest (and hence the exclusive maximisation of 'shareholder value', as well as breaking ethical principles) send a message that the person cannot be trusted. It is no longer enough for businesses to focus solely on maximising profits or shareholder value; the interests of all stakeholders must be furthered by the common partnership. This applies to the needs of all employees, including managers and staff, suppliers, customers, investors, regulators, the public, the environment and governments.

The idea of Conscious Capitalism connects *all* stakeholders, and necessarily takes their needs and interests into account.[11] Thus, this represents an important shift from the conception of capitalism driven by maximising owners' profits or shareholder value. Instead, it is based on a holistic concept of how humans might and should inter-relate through the organisations where they work—whether they are owned publicly or privately. When one person in a group is focused more on his or her own success than the group's success, then discord and conflict will ensue, and the group will become dysfunctional. With such a culture, the group will never be able to achieve its full potential. The previous short-term focus on

[11] J Mackey and R Sisodia, *Conscious Capitalism. Liberating the Heroic Spirit of Business* (Harvard Business Review Press, 2014).

shareholder value has distorted the relationship between senior managers and workers, and this, in turn, has resulted in disengagement and decreasing trust.

Whilst many large multinational businesses currently adopt a great deal of what we suggest, and there are many international moves towards aspects of the ethical approach—such as corporate social responsibility, the UN Global Compact, the PACI Principles and the UN Guidelines on Business on Human Rights, together addressing the environment, local communities and people in the supply chain—some relationships in the regulatory space remain old-fashioned and polarised rather than cooperative. In this state of affairs, the full power of the relationship to deliver good outcomes fails to be realised. It is striking how the need to ensure *long-term sustainability* has taken a high priority, from the context of environmental protection and global warming to that of the safety of investing in corporations to maintain long-term growth and pensions.

It is no longer enough for businesses to have perfunctory codes of ethical practice. The organisations that claim to live by such statements of ethical values must be genuine; in other words, the values must be *lived and demonstrated* in the decision-making and behaviours of everyone working for the organisation daily.

A Critical Leadership Role for Business

We think that there is a huge opportunity for leadership by business here. We are struck by the increasing number of commentators who advocate that a culture based upon a firm commitment to ethical values and their application to relationships with all stakeholders—staff, managers, suppliers, customers and investors—is what really transforms business success. Those businesses that have evolved towards a holistic ethical approach achieve outstanding results because they take care to satisfy all their stakeholders' interests and thus gain from their enthusiastic support and energy. But some will see this as a fundamental redefinition of the objective of a business. It is no longer to make profit at all costs; rather, it is to understand that profit comes from a focus on doing the right thing. Put another way, one must take a medium to long-term view of what drives profit. This has been recognised by many in financial regulatory circles,[12] but again requires systemic change and less of an emphasis on short-term results. The transformation comes from applying ethical values to the governance framework required by the Financial Reporting Council. Making this transformation can involve major changes in how businesses operate, but the forces required to drive that change are understood and are summarised in this book. Perhaps what has been missing so

[12] See the work of the Financial Reporting Council on the importance of corporate culture, referred to in ch 9 below.

far is a sense of urgency. The time, however, is now. As Mackey and Sisodia, respectively a leading businessman and a business scholar, have said:

> Capitalism is under attack for several reasons:
>
> 1. Business people have allowed the ethical basis of free-enterprise capitalism to be hijacked intellectually by economists and critics who have foisted on it a narrow, self-serving, and inaccurate identity devoid of its inherent ethical justification. Capitalism needs both a new narrative and a new ethical foundation, one that accurately reflects its intrinsic goodness and virtue.[13]

Richard Barrett says that: 'Values-driven organizations are the most successful organisations on the planet.'[14] He refers to the idea of 'Business as saviour'. Could it be that business provides the critical environment that society has lost through secularisation away from religion, which can be used to re-embed ethical values in society in a way that will unlock mutual re-engagement? It is heartening to see announcements in mid-2017 that Volvo intends to switch its cars from liquid to electric fuels and Swiss Re to switch all its £130 billion investment portfolio to ethical investments.[15]

We suggest that if all those who work in business in any capacity could conceive of their commitment to ethical values not only as a basis on which to do business, but also as a central unifying force to bring about positive change across the societies of the globe, levels of trust in business and government would begin to rise and everyone would reap the benefits.

Overview of this Book

The book is divided into four parts. Part I summarises the scientific evidence for the ideas and hence the basis for the EBR model. Part II sets out the current state of corporate governance and of regulatory policy in the UK, so that we can see what role ethics does—or does not—play on both sides of the regulatory space. Part III outlines the concept of the EBR model, namely how a relationship between a regulator and a business based on ethical principles should operate. In Part IV we set out the essential requirements for EBP, based on two parallel frameworks: first, the cultural and leadership framework and, second, the ethical and compliance framework. This explains how organisations should place values, culture, ethical behaviour and decisions at the foundation of all their activities. We set out at the end a series of checklists that we hope businesses will find useful.

[13] Mackey and Sisodia (n 11).

[14] Barrett (n 1).

[15] Z Williams, 'Is a Carmaker about to Save the Planet?' *The Guardian*, 10 July 2017, https://www.theguardian.com/commentisfree/2017/jul/10/volvo-motor-industry-electric-car-environment?CMP=share_btn_link; J Revill, 'Swiss Re Shifts $130 Billion Investments to Track Ethical Indices' *Reuters*, 6 July 2017, http://uk.reuters.com/article/us-swissre-ethical-idUKKBN19R22Y.

Throughout the book, we include case studies that illustrate good and bad practice. We also refer to some of our personal experiences from the business world. At the end of each chapter, there are conclusions.

Part I. The Ideas

We set out to ask some simple but often overlooked questions. Why do people observe rules? Why do people break them? Answering these simple questions seems fundamental to knowing how we should design and operate compliance systems in businesses and public regulatory systems.

Many compliance and regulatory systems seem to focus on different questions, such as 'How do we increase deterrence so firms will obey the law?' and 'How do we produce a lot of data that shows that we have extensive compliance systems, so that we can argue for lower penalties to be imposed when we break the law?' The latter question seems both less important than the former question and to miss the point.

As we are talking about human behaviour, the logical place to start looking for answers to the first questions would be in the science of human behaviour. There is now a considerable body of convincing evidence from evolutionary biology, behavioural psychology, and sociolegal research into regulation that provides a coherent basis for making a profound change in regulatory practice. The scientific findings have been applied under headings such as 'behavioural economics' and 'nudge', but have not percolated widely into businesses' internal approaches to corporate compliance or public regulators' or enforcers' approaches to maximising observance of law.

Chapter 1 summarises the scientific evidence on what factors affect the brain in producing the behaviour that people observe or break rules. We find that fairness is a critical value for human rule-systems. Research into behavioural psychology has identified important findings on why people observe or break rules. We now know many reasons why people may fail to observe a rule—notably because of inertia, procrastination, the influence of others (especially social groups), misframing of issues, mistakes in assessing probability, not knowing exactly what to do and so on.[16] We often bend the rules and think that we comply when we don't. Biological research suggests that the emergence in humans of an 'ethical gene' is far more recent than the basic defensive or selfish gene that we have long needed to survive. The two genes—protective/selfish and collaborative/ethical—can obviously be in conflict, and when we feel threatened, the older protective one may be

[16] See generally T Gilovich, D Griffin and D Kahneman (eds), *Heuristics and Biases: The Psychology of Intuitive Judgment* (Cambridge University Press, 2002); D Kahneman and A Tversky (eds), *Choices, Values, and Frames* (Cambridge University Press, 2000).

more powerful than the open trusting one. But it is through supporting the open trusting gene that we can create evidence on which we can place trust in others, and hence increase cooperation. Success is so often based on the strength of social relationships, even at work—if those relationships are ethical, this drives good outcomes.

Although it might be depressing to read in chapter 1 that human beings often behave irrationally and may be prone to breaking rules in some circumstances, chapter 2 provides reason for optimism by looking at the many human characteristics that can be developed to build an ethical, cooperative and effective society. We note the importance that most humans place on the value of behaving fairly and being seen to do so. We also note evidence that humans evolve through increasing levels of consciousness, and each level produces the need to develop new means of organising people to improve cooperative action. We believe this to be an optimistic book, built on the shared belief of the authors that positive change is possible if we are conscious of the need for it, open and honest enough with ourselves to learn from our experience and realise the importance of being ethical.

Chapter 3 looks at the traditional approach to making people conform, namely deterrence. We look at examples of where it still applies and note the shift by some public authorities from attempting to deter companies to attempting to deter individuals. We then summarise a growing number of problems with deterrence as a theory, and note that it is primarily based on theory and that there is very little empirical evidence that supports it. We also note that although deterrence remains the fundamental enforcement theory that is applied by some legal systems (such as that in the US) and regulators (competition, financial services), a significant number of regulators and enforcers have left it behind and have adopted a responsive and supportive approach aimed at improving performance and outcomes (and hence improving compliance). We also note the ideas of Maslow, Laloux and Barrett that as humans evolve through different stages, we need to develop new ways of organising ourselves. Laloux thinks that we are going through a new stage and need to replace fear with collaboration.

Chapter 4 notes that adopting a fair approach to wrongdoing involves observing the expectation that the rules will apply to everyone and that if people do bad things, we expect that society will impose a proportionate response. The critical issue is the moral intention with which people acted: was it ethical or not?

Chapter 5 notes that modern business, and hence compliance with the rules and regulation, depends critically on cooperation. The relevant systems depend on constant circulation of information, and everyone has a part to play in this, otherwise the system will not work and we will not be able to operate safely and effectively or be able to improve.

Chapter 6 looks at the critical issue of trust. It is a state of mind based on evidence that we can place trust in others to do what they say they will do, or what we expect them to. People who want their future actions to be trusted need to produce certain types of evidence of past behaviour and present intention, systems and culture on which others can form a judgement. The evidence shows that humans are most productive and innovative when they work together, and base their actions on ethical principles, which creates trust between them.

Chapter 7 introduces the critical point that people will not volunteer information if they fear that they might be criticised—and hence socially ridiculed, disciplined, prosecuted or sued. As such, an organisational and regulatory culture that includes blaming will not support constant learning, improvement and performance. Those responsible for the safety of critical operations, notably in civil aviation, learnt some time ago that 'no-blame' cultures are vital to maintaining safety. Aviation safety is now based firmly, in some countries at least, on an 'open, just culture', which supports people to share all relevant information. Aviation no longer talks about compliance, but performance. It recognises that no human activity is fully risk-free and that we will fail if we simply concentrate on compliance.

Chapter 8 looks at why we should behave ethically. What's in it for others and for us? There is plenty of evidence that organisations that systemically do the right thing, and seek to achieve good outcomes for all stakeholders, are outstandingly successful in their outcomes.

Part II. Where We are Now

In Part II, we take a snapshot of the status of ethical values on the two sides of the regulatory fence, namely in business—specifically in current policy on corporate governance—in chapter 8 and in regulatory policy in chapter 9. We find clear moves to include culture at the centre of corporate governance, as a response to the collapse in confidence in business around the 2008 financial crash, but a reluctance to take the further step of specifying that an *ethical* culture is required. There seems to be a disconnect between those involved in creating corporate governance and compliance frameworks and those who understand organisational change.

Chapter 10 explains the moves towards stronger relationships between regulators and businesses that have taken place both in general UK regulatory policy and in practice by an increasing number of regulators, including civil aviation, water, energy, gambling and equality and human rights. It notes the creation of many structures, arrangements and relationships that support EBR, so that EBR is the logical next step. Indeed, it shows that EBR has been adopted as policy by a number of regulators in 2016–17.

Part III. What is Ethical Business Regulation?

Part III explains what we mean by EBR. It develops the ideas of a relationship between public bodies and businesses based on a relationship of trust, built on suitable evidence that businesses (and public bodies) place ethical values at the core of their activities. The basic concept is explained in chapter 11, and chapter 12 gives a number of examples of where EBR implicitly exists in the policies and practices of a range of UK regulators. It also notes moves in a different direction in the regulation of financial services, where deterrence remains the primary approach. This sector is important to consider, as the lack of a values-driven culture has been identified globally as a fundamental problem that led the financial services sector to behave dysfunctionally, and was a major cause of the financial crisis that began in 2008.[17] These examples together form a significant body of evidence and experience on which future practice can be developed.

Part IV. How to Implement Ethical Business Practice and Ethical Business Regulation

Part IV looks at what businesses and regulators should do to adopt EBR in practice. We explain two frameworks that are required for EBP. Chapter 13 sets out the framework of culture and leadership that will nurture EBP, and chapter 14 sets out the framework of ethics and compliance, founded upon the organisation's values that will anchor and support EBP. These chapters therefore form practical 'how to' manuals. They set out the various essential features that we think are necessary if an organisation is going to operate consistently and sustainably on an ethical basis. The essence here rests on applying ethical values, and this can only be done effectively within supportive frameworks.

The adoption of EBP is a choice by individual businesses and the people who work in them. If they produce evidence of EBP, it will be the responsibility of regulators and other stakeholders to respond by giving them the credit. Convincing evidence of intention and a track record of achievement is the key to EBP and therefore EBR.

Appendices

We include several checklists regarding different aspects of EBP and EBR.

Conclusion

We believe that focusing on ethical values can transform economic and innovative performance. It is good for business and for regulatory performance. We also believe that adopting an ethical approach is currently an essential move for the

[17] *Report of the High-Level Group on Financial Supervision in the EU* (European Commission, 2009); *Toward Effective Governance of Financial Institutions* (G30, 2012); *A New Paradigm: Financial Institution Boards and Supervisors* (G30, 2013); *Report of the Collective Engagement Working Group* (Collective Engagement Working Group, 2013); *A Report on the Culture of British Retail Banking* (New City Agenda and Cass Business School, 2014).

interconnected world we live in, in order to transform globalisation into a force for societal well-being. However, if EBR is to crystallise and support sustainable social and economic growth, as we believe it can, both regulators and businesses need to change. We set out in this book the evidence on the need for change and on how such change can be achieved. It is a vision of a better world—and how to get there.

Part I

The Ideas

1

Why Do People Conform to Rules or Break Them? Piecing Together the Evidence

Why do people conform to rules or break them? This question is fundamental. Humans inter-relate with each other—in families, clubs, social groups, as neighbours, work colleagues, committee members, or in the myriad ways that constitute a society or nation. If we are to live together in situations where we must inter-relate, we base our relationships on our feelings of the extent to which we can trust others to behave in fair or predictable ways. We evaluate the extent to which we can place trust in other individuals or groups from evidence of their past and likely future behaviour. In evaluating others' fairness and predictability, we measure their behaviour against yardsticks of conduct that we call norms or rules. They may be social rules (don't kill people, serve others before yourself, offer an elderly or pregnant person your seat, don't betray the gang) or they may be elevated into laws (don't kill, don't speed, pay your tax on time). Later in this book we will look at the fact that such norms or laws do not necessarily have to be fair to be enforced by those who can exert power. But the first question we should look at is: why do people conform to rules or break them?

In answering this question, we will look at several sources of scientific evidence in this chapter:

— *Behavioural science studies.* What do scientists who study how people behave tell us?
— *Empirical studies on how regulators operate.* What is the practical experience of individual enforcers and agencies on what works and what doesn't work in getting people and businesses to comply with rules?
— *Experience in managing safety-critical contexts.* What have people found about how they need to behave when maintaining safety is vital?

We need to summarise a great deal of science and experience, but we intend this only to be a summary rather than a textbook with extensive details. Instead, we hope that you will be inspired or intrigued to read further. Fortunately, there are several great books that explain the science in greater detail than we have space for, which are listed at Table 1.1. Chris Hodges has summarised much of the evidence in his book *Law and Corporate Behaviour* and the US Internal Revenue Service published an excellent summary of the application of behavioural insights to tax administration in 2017.[1]

Table 1.1: Recommended reading

D Ariely, *Predictably Irrational: The Hidden Forces That Shape Our Decisions* (HarperCollins, 2008).
MH Banaji and AG Greenwald, *Blindspot: Hidden Biases of Good People* (Bantam Books, 2016).
R Barrett, *The Values-Driven Organization: Cultural Health and Employee Well-Being as a Pathway to Sustainable Performance*, 2nd edn (Routledge, 2017).
MH Bazerman and AE Tenbrunsel, *Blind Spots: Why We Fail to Do What's Right and What to Do about it* (Princeton University Press, 2011).
J Haidt, *The Righteous Mind: Why Good People are Divided by Politics and Religion* (Penguin Books, 2012).
M Heffernan, *Wilful Blindness: Why We Ignore the Obvious at our Peril* (Simon & Schuster, 2011).
D Kahneman, *Thinking, Fast and Slow* (Allen Lane, 2011).
F Laloux, *Reinventing Organizations: A Guide to Creating Organizations Inspired by the Next Stage of Human Consciousness* (Nelson Parker, 2014).
J Mackey and R Sisodia, *Conscious Capitalism: Liberating the Heroic Spirit of Business* (Harvard Business Review Press, 2014).
R Sisodia, J Sheth and D Wolfe, *Firms of Endearment: How World-Class Companies Profit from Passion and Purpose*, 2nd edn (Pearson Education, 2014).

How the Brain Produces Behaviour

> [E]ven the most ethical, socially responsible, and law-abiding people are at significant risk of becoming entangled in wrongdoing when placed in an organizational context.
>
> Donald Palmer[2]

Behavioural science has built up to a considerable body of knowledge about how humans behave. This section gives an outline of some of the most important findings. We will see examples of these findings throughout the chapters of this book.

The lifetime's work of two leaders in this field, Amos Tversky and Daniel Kahneman, is now widely known through Kahneman's book *Thinking, Fast and Slow*.[3] This outlines the many reasons why humans might, if they thought about it, intend to do one thing, but in practice do something else. A key concept is that we have fast and slow ways of thinking, so use fast mental short-cuts for situations that we think we are familiar with (heuristics) in order to avoid us having to spend time processing all the information needed to make a logical decision. As an alternative simile, psychologists Banaji and Greenwald use the concepts of the automatic and reflective mind.[4] They show how strongly embedded are our automatic thoughts and impulses, sometimes even acting contrary to our conscious thoughts (such as on race, religion or social status). They record how we rely on unconscious stereotyping to enable us to rapidly perceive strangers as distinctive individuals and create a safe social space.

Much of daily life, from eating to driving, we do automatically, without thinking much about each minute decision. As a result, we might not take the time necessary to make what would be the right decision every time, say when the facts are in fact different from the paradigm and we have failed to realise this. If we get clear feedback soon after taking an action, it can help us to learn whether we are doing well or making mistakes. Sometimes, we are just lazy or fail to think.

People see what they are focusing on: 'they can't find what they're not looking for but they won't find what they're not looking for, no matter how dangerous it is'.[5] This was the conclusion of the famous gorilla experiment: people were asked to watch a video of a game and count how many times the ball was passed between the players. They did the counting fairly accurately. But while they were busy counting, almost all failed to see the figure dressed as a gorilla who bounced onto the pitch from one side, jumped up and down, then bounced off on the other. Our frames influence what we see and what we do not see.

The same traits appear in our reactions to information that we do not want to hear, usually because it challenges our assumptions. We accept things that support our own ideas and ignore things that do the opposite. We consider people who disagree with us to be biased.[6] Margaret Heffernan explains these traits on the basis that: 'The familiar makes us feel secure and comfortable.'[7]

The Need to Check

When decisions involve important consequences, we need to allow ourselves enough time to stop the automatic 'fast brain' short-cut kicking in and to think through the relevant information to allow our 'slow brain' to assess the position more objectively. This might involve thinking, for example, whether we have all the necessary information, whether our initial reaction to a situation is right or whether there might be conflicts between different considerations for which we need to make a balanced judgement.

This is why airline pilots always check all relevant procedures before taking off against a checklist and constantly check facts during flight, asking each other things like 'why are we doing this?' and 'have we got all the information?' as a matter of course. Pilots have a book of checklists to remind them of critical actions that might be forgotten in an emergency.[8] In cultures in which junior pilots cannot question the actions of their seniors, planes can fly into mountains, as has happened historically in Korea and Japan.[9] The introduction of checklists in clinical practice, such as the World Health Organization (WHO) Surgical Safety Checklist, has been shown to improve communication,[10] preparedness,[11] teamwork[12] and attitudes to safety.[13] Introducing checklists in five different medical specialities at each of two hospitals under a randomised trial basis resulted in decreases in post-operative complication rates, patients' length of stay and mortality.[14] Gawande, who was a prime mover in the WHO initiative after studying how checklists are used in aviation and complex construction projects, believes that introducing a checklist can have powerful effects on prompting individuals to work as a team, to communicate with each other, to redistribute authority amongst team members (such as where a nurse permits a surgeon to proceed after all checklist conditions have been satisfied), to get people to take responsibility for finding solutions and actions, as well as to remind people not to overlook steps and to overcome people acting in response to gut feelings instead of checking critical facts (even by fund managers before making investment decisions). He thinks that the common elements for success in teamwork are expectations of selflessness, skill, trustworthiness and discipline.[15]

The need to check basic facts and decisions is important given various other human traits. Humans are hugely influenced by others around them. We usually want to conform to the attitudes of those around us, even when this might be against our own beliefs. The culture of social groups is very important. Individuals with strong personalities can exert huge influence in organisations—from criminal gangs like the Mafia to terrorist cells or religious groups.

People also like the status quo—we don't like sudden change and we procrastinate. So we might be slow to realise that we should do something differently. We are also influenced by how information is presented or 'framed'. Information that is vivid and salient can have a greater impact than information that is abstract, theoretical, statistical or ambiguous. We also tend to be loss averse—we dislike losing something more than we value gaining something. But we might value something as a loss or as a gain depending on how the information is presented to us. Hence, the culture of a group (at work, home or play) can be hugely influential on individuals joining or in the group: it may be benign, ethical and respectful or it may produce behaviour that is selfish, domineering and anti-social.

We are often blissfully unaware of how our response to information is conditioned by how it was framed when we first received it. As a result, we fail to recognise other dimensions that might arise that we should consider. Salesmen know that 'We focus on what we might lose, rather than what we might gain'[16] and market products and services to us accordingly, for example, through sales or advertised reductions in price. If a request or decision is contextualised as a 'business decision', say about advertising or finance, we may fail to recognise that an ethical issue or conflict is raised. A sadly famous example of how framing a decision as a cost–benefit issue can lead to unethical behaviour is the failure to redesign the Ford Pinto, despite its unfortunate habit of exploding when hit from behind. This caused what Bazerman and Tenbrunsel refer to as 'ethical fading', as Ford executives framed it as a business decision based upon the fact that the cost of repairing the problem ($11 per car) was higher than the cost of eventually paying people injured or killed in accidents.[17]

We also think that all we see is all there is, so we fail to check things more deeply. We deduce the general from the specific rather than the other way around. We fudge opposing emotions, especially on other people's behalf rather than our own, or if we think that others are more intelligent or popular than they are. We also try to get around rules—gaming and exploiting ambiguity to our advantage. This is especially true if we think that some rules are not important, and other considerations (such as keeping our job or meeting targets) are more important. Or we might evaluate the substance and interpretation of rules against a deeper matrix of ethical values. As we mentioned earlier, disengaged employees are more likely to misbehave since they do not see why the rules are valid or they feel they have been applied unfairly.

Our fast heuristic also leads to problems because we are not good at assessing probability. Many of us tend to be unrealistically optimistic and discount risks ('It will never happen to me').[18] When strong emotions are triggered, we tend to focus on the outcome and not on the probability that it will occur.[19] Some of these traits can be seen in investment traders who are very active in managing portfolios, constantly reacting to new information: their results are worse than traders who just leave things alone.

Case Study 1: The Ford Pinto[20]

In response to more compact cars produced in Japan, Ford developed a compact car within a short timeframe that was introduced into the US market in 1970. The design parameters were that it was not to weigh over 2,000 pounds and should not cost over US$2,000. In pre-production crash tests, the fact that fuel tanks ruptured was discovered, and hence the risk of explosion was identified, but the danger was not addressed. The pollution control and fuel systems included flaws, and road accidents included some serious fires. The location of the fuel tank appeared to be dangerous, as it could explode if compressed on impact. The authorities proposed increased regulation, which the company resisted. The company carried out a 'cost–benefit analysis', which calculated that a design change of installing an $11 safety valve in each vehicle would cost $137 million, whereas doing nothing would cause 180 deaths, 180 serious burn injuries and 2,100 burned vehicles each year. The company used the same figures as those used by the National Highway Traffic Safety Administration, namely that a life would be worth $200,000, injuries would cost $67,000 and vehicle costs would be $700 per vehicle, making a total of US$49.5 million. Based on this calculation, Ford staff chose not to correct the defect, since the costs exceeded the benefits. The calculation narrowed the focus of relevant costs, excluding reputational issues and the ethical aspects that were obvious to outsiders.

Psychologist Jonathan Haidt believes that humans often make swift moral decisions, based on quick intuitive flashes ('gut feeling'), and then use their reasoning capacity to construct post hoc arguments to support their decisions or actions, whilst discarding evidence or reasoning that does not support the decision taken.[21] In this, he adopts Hume's ideas about pluralist, sentimentalist and naturalist approaches to ethics, and rejects the rationalism, utilitarianism and deontology of Plato and Bentham, who thought that reason was paramount in making decisions. Haidt identifies six moral foundations that he considers to be innate in (non-psychopathic) humans (see Box 1.1).

Haidt argues that those who consider the basic social unit as the individual (liberals) or the family (social conservatives) respond in different ways and to different combinations of the six foundations. Liberals respond strongly to the Care and Fairness foundations, whereas social conservatives can respond to all six and especially Loyalty, Authority and Liberty. Also, these two groups have difficulty in understanding the motivations of each other.

We can see links between Haidt's various foundations and the work of other psychologists like Tversky, Kahneman and Ariely in identifying how we often make decisions quickly—decisions that if we really thought about them are ones that we would probably not make. We can also see the importance of our senses—of fairness, community, self-preservation and so on—in influencing our decisions.

Box 1.1 Haidt's six moral foundations[22]

— The *Care/harm* foundation, which 'makes us sensitive to signs of suffering and need; it makes us despise cruelty and want to care for those who are suffering'.
— The *Fairness/cheating* foundation, which 'makes us sensitive to indications that another person is likely to be a good (or bad) partner for collaboration and reciprocal altruism. It makes us want to shun or punish cheaters'. It also contains a strong element of proportionality. 'The Fairness foundation begins with the psychology of reciprocal altruism, but its duties expanded once humans created gossiping and punitive moral communities. Most people have a deep intuitive concern for the law of karma—they want to see cheaters punished and good citizens rewarded in proportion to their deeds.'
— The *Loyalty/betrayal* foundation, which 'makes us sensitive to signs that another person is (or is not) a team player. It makes us trust and reward such people, and it makes us want to hurt, ostracize, or even kill those who betray us or our group'.
— The *Authority/subversion* foundation, which 'makes us sensitive to signs of rank or status, and to signs that other people are (or are not) behaving properly, given their position'.
— The *Sanctity/degradation* foundation, which 'includes the behavioural immune system, which can make us wary of a diverse array of symbolic objects and threats. It makes it possible for people to invest objects with irrational and extreme values—both positive and negative—which are important for binding groups together'.

— The *Liberty/oppression* foundation, which 'makes people notice and resent any sign of attempted domination. It triggers an urge to band together to resist or overthrow bullies and tyrants. This foundation supports the egalitarianism and antiauthoritarianism of the left, as well as the don't-tread-on-me and give-me-liberty anti-government anger of libertarians and some conservatives'.

Bending the Rules

How many of us comply with every rule all the time? We are humans, not saints. Much 'misconduct' is by good people doing the wrong thing for a variety of reasons. Dan Ariely, James B. Duke Professor of Psychology and Behavioural Economics at Duke University, has found that many people are prepared to cheat a little and do it surprisingly often.[23] He shows that people can cheat and still feel good about themselves by rationalising their bad behaviour. He summarises research that shows that this can happen, for example, when we think that the transgression is small and unimportant, when we are tired, when it doesn't involve money, when we are blinded to the conflict by one or more other goals, or when we are influenced by the behaviour of others. He developed the 'fudge factor theory' to mean the extent to which we can cheat and still feel good about ourselves. Exactly how much we can cheat and still feel good about ourselves depends on our ability to rationalise our behaviour.[24] The central idea is that we are driven by our contradictory desires both to view ourselves in a positive way and to benefit from cheating, and we can rationalise this where we think it is unimportant: 'our internal honesty monitor is active only when we contemplate big transgressions'.[25] Therefore, how a person behaves may be influenced by external factors such as his or her national or organisational culture if these provide a way to rationalise behaviour that would otherwise go against our personal values. For example, an employee who feels that he or she has been unfairly denied a raise or is overworked may rationalise taking company property by telling himself or herself 'they owe it to me anyway'.

There is a lot of research on this and related concepts. Bandura notes the active role that the self plays in allowing people to engage in inhumane behaviour through moral disengagement with the ethics of the organisation in which they work.[26] He suggests eight mechanisms by which individuals are able to convince themselves that their actions are not immoral. Feldman and Smith,[27] relying on work by Moore and colleagues[28] and Ashforth and Anand[29] suggest that exploiting ambiguity in rules is central to people's ability to justify immoral behaviour. People frequently construct self-serving interpretations of the legal and organisational requirements they must follow. Haisley and Weber[30] found that people prefer to take ambiguous risks when this allows them to justify unfair behaviour.

Dana and colleagues found that people are less generous in situations in which they can appeal to moral ambiguity in explaining their actions. Similarly, Hsee found that people make choices that satisfy their preferences, at the cost of best achieving an assigned goal, if they can exploit existing ambiguity about which decision may complete the assignment.[31] Yeldman and Teichman have shown that people use legal ambiguity strategically to formulate a minimal interpretation of what is required from them by laws or contracts.[32] Margaret Heffernan devoted a whole book to the evidence on 'wilful blindness', noting numerous examples of where people ignore the facts in front of them, fail to stand up to institutional opposition, say they were 'just following orders', are led by the prevailing group culture, fail to react if they are among multiple bystanders and work in too many layers of management (out of sight, out of mind).[33]

The 2015 survey carried out by the Institute of Business Ethics (IBE) on the acceptability of common workplace practices shows current attitudes to 'minor' wrongdoing.[34] It commented that attitudes are more lenient towards conducting personal activities during work hours. One could speculate that this may be related to the tendency for work itself to spill out into personal time through smartphones, tablets and laptop computers.

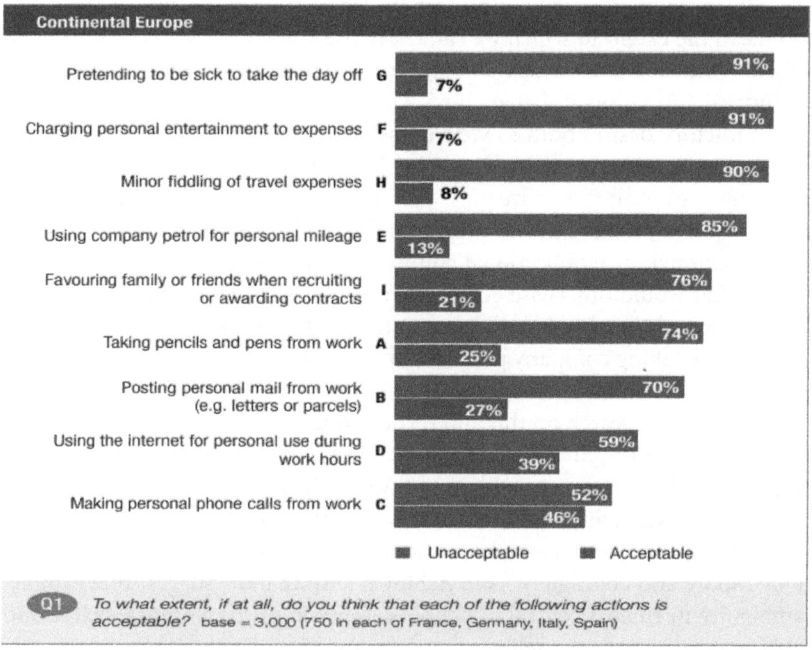

Figure 1.1: Acceptability of common workplace practices, Continental Europe, 2015 (most unacceptable practice first)

People Think They Comply, Even if They Don't

Syed discusses a sobering concept. He summarises research on 'cognitive dissonance' as saying that when we are confronted with evidence that challenges our deeply held beliefs, we are more likely to *reframe* the evidence than we are to alter our beliefs.[35] We feel threatened by this dissonance and our reaction is denial of the evidence, and hence self-deception. Evidence of this tendency is particularly available in the 'post-factual' world we appear to be living in at this time.

So, even if people intend to comply, perfect compliance might not in fact be achieved. Many people think they comply—and think they do so more than others do—but they in fact fall short. Major reasons for this are a lack of expertise, not enough time or resources and unfamiliarity with the rules, complexity and uncertainty as to how to comply.

This is particularly true of small and medium-sized businesses (SMEs), which comprise 99% of all firms[36] and are estimated to produce 60% of all business carbon dioxide emissions, 70% of business pollution, 60% of commercial waste and 43% of serious pollution incidents.[37] It has been said that SMEs often do not get beyond compliance in environmental pollution,[38] whereas large US companies were most likely to be participants in a voluntary compliance programme, driven by gaining public recognition rather than compliance reasons.[39]

As an example of SMEs, Fairman and Yapp studied small hairdressers in different parts of the UK in 2005 and found that they want to be told exactly what to do and *how* to comply.[40] They all believed they complied with the law, even though their formal compliance levels were in fact unimpressive. None of them approached compliance with legal requirements by weighing up costs and benefits. Instead, compliance was more a process of how the SME owner 'made sense' of what they were being required to do. They often failed to recognise that there was a link between how they were operating and the levels of illness in their businesses, and how it ought to be. Improvements occurred as responses to external influence in motivating change, most effectively though face-to-face interventions with an inspector.

Interviews in 2008 with 759 senior managers from SMEs found that the majority (58%) treated complying with regulations as a crucial or very important business responsibility, but as many as 19% considered it neither very important nor not at all important.[41] Significant proportions said that they did not seek guidance on issues of employment (37%) or health and safety (48%). This appears to be related to the fact that they considered health and safety to be the most time-consuming (31%) and costly (33%) aspect of regulation.[42] The researchers identified a typology of five clusters of people: Prepared and established; Guilty procrastinators; Capable but unconcerned; Conscientious but challenged; and Blind-eye turners. Many of these counter-productive attitudes could be addressed by a more cooperative approach to regulation.

A 2010 survey of 482 personnel in businesses with 25 or more employees who were responsible for ensuring that their business complied with consumer law[43] found that 70% claimed to be very or fairly aware of consumer protection law and cases, but actual knowledge was lower.[44] Although 44% claimed familiarity with enforcement cases taken by the (then) Office of Fair Trading, unprompted awareness of specific decisions or cases was low, with just 1% of respondents able to mention any specific cases of relevance.[45] Only 4% of respondents considered that there was a very high risk of businesses in their sector breaching consumer protection law,[46] although 31% believed that they had been disadvantaged by competitors breaching consumer law.[47] The overwhelming majority (95%) of respondents claimed that they had policies and practices in place to ensure that they comply with consumer protection law,[48] but in fact smaller businesses and single-site businesses were less likely to have undertaken these actions.

It is not hard to think of reasons why people find complying with legislation difficult, especially if they work in smaller firms. Many surveys show that businesses find regulation burdensome and time-consuming.[49] The sheer volume of legislation is daunting.[50] Legislation can be difficult to understand.[51] A 2010 survey of 2,009 UK businessmen[52] found that 35% of respondents did not know the sorts of things competition law was supposed to prevent and 34% had no awareness of any competition enforcement action; 41% thought abuse of dominance was happening in their local region and 22% thought there was collusion. Similarly, a 2011 study found that only 57% of large businesses and 35% of small businesses reported that they felt very or fairly knowledgeable about competition law.[53] Very few businesses reported behavioural change as a consequence of hearing about specific enforcement cases.[54]

The need for help and support is especially relevant for micro businesses (those with fewer than 10 employees), where the cumulative burden of regulations, licences and fees is considerable and hampers their ability to stay profitable, grow, invest, hire staff and even pay themselves a wage.[55] A 2010 study found that the level of managerial capability is a key constraint: 'Most frequently we were told that they try to do the right thing, but felt that they were not supported and were unreasonably expected to cope with the same levels of paperwork and regulatory obligations as larger companies.' The study concluded that the move towards more targeted inspection and enforcement meant that fewer businesses were inspected and they had limited if any contact with other local and central government officials.[56]

Targets, Stress and Mixed Messages

Messages that we need to hear and genes that we need to trigger can be overcome or crowded out by other stronger impulses.

Dennis Gentilin argues that fear associated with loss of one's status and title, and the associated financial rewards and lifestyle the position affords, will make people do the wrong things. He ties this to a person's very sense of self and identity being at stake. People will not do the right thing if they are primarily worried about keeping their job, meeting a sales or profits target, having to meet frequent reporting targets, going along with bad decisions by the rest of the group or other influential people or groups. Their attention may also be more focused on problems at home or illness than on making the right decisions in their work. When businesses and hence jobs are threatened, people will mis-sell or mis-report. The Payment Protection Insurance (PPI) scandal in the UK is an illustration of massive herd behaviour in selling inappropriate products to customers.

There are strong conclusions for the design of regulatory and compliance systems. A system that is based solely on inspection, followed by a grading against targets will inherently send inconsistent messages to its subjects. Where inspections are accompanied by criticism, such as 'this hospital/school is low grade and failing', there is little chance that the staff will be motivated or helped to improve. The primary incentive will be to avoid criticism and to cover up inadequacies at the time of inspection or to game the rules to claim performance that is unjustified. The focus will not be on doing the best on a consistent basis. Inspecting and auditing can be an important mechanism for checking the operation of a system and its outputs, but cannot be a primary control mechanism. If inspection is accompanied by criticism or grading, it will drive down performance. Similarly, self-reporting, even when required, is vulnerable to opportunistic behaviour and cherry-picking.[57]

Two of the main drivers of bad behaviour identified by the IBE in 2015 were:[58]

- corporate stress which leads people to take shortcuts; and
- excessive focus on short-term financial targets, which might itself become a source of stress.

The IBE also identified sources of inconsistent cultures coming from a proliferation of corporate takeovers, often followed by poor implementation, and leaving a multiplicity of cultures. The values of these cultures may be in conflict, or poorly understood, and failure to take the time to integrate or at least align the constituent cultures will increase stress and reduce employee engagement. Indeed, the fact that the cultures of the parties to a proposed takeover or merger might be incompatible is now regarded by some as a deal breaker. This was one of the factors that led Unilever to reject the February 2017 offer from Kraft Heinz, for example. The IBE also identifies the fact that complex legal structures or other opacity can make it hard for management to track what is going on. And we will see in chapter 7 below that the inability to determine the root cause of an issue, and to address it is likely to result in mistakes being covered up and bad behaviour perpetuated.

Having a Code of Ethical Practice will simply be irrelevant if people feel that the behaviour that is actually expected of them is to 'make the numbers'. Warren Buffett has said that 'Managers that always promise to "make the numbers" will at some point be tempted to make up the numbers'.[59] Dennis Gentilin's recent review of the evidence on the insidious consequences of focusing on the 'performance' of staff reaches several important conclusions. First, narrowly focusing our attention can cause us to be 'blind' to other events in our environment.[60] Second, obsessive focus on performance targets, plus the use of financial incentives supposedly to incentivise goal attainment, can drive inappropriate behaviour.[61] Third, how incentive schemes are structured affects whether people will engage in dishonest behaviour.[62] Gentilin notes that a study of 90 companies in the Standard & Poor's (S&P) 500 list that had a track record of out-performance versus their peers not only created heightened expectations for future performance, but also displayed an increased likelihood of engaging in illegal activity.[63] He concludes:

> In summary, the research into goals clearly illustrates that when ambitious targets are used in an environment that promotes an obsessive pursuit of these goals, people show a greater preparedness to act inappropriately to hit these targets.[64]

These issues relate to the issue of group culture, which we will examine next.

Group Culture

> Madness is the exception in individuals but the rule in groups.
>
> Dennis Gentilin[65]

> Nearly every ethics issue is a group-level one, because ethics is such an interpersonal process.
>
> Friedrich Nietzsche[66]

The feeling that we belong to a group is very important to us, and we have strong impulses to distinguish people 'like us' and 'not like us', ie, we have a sense of identity.[67] John Just of New York University has produced evidence that people are willing to sacrifice their self-interest for the sake of maintaining the existing social order.[68] People are willing to pay a cost to maintain the difference between 'us' and 'them'.[69]

The slippery slope effect[70] states that implicit biases prevent individuals from seeing gradual changes in their environment,[71] including the gradual deterioration of ethical behaviour.[72] The IBE thinks that one of the three main drivers of bad behaviour is a ready tolerance of small breaches of the rules or accepted best practice, or a tendency to push at the limits of what was permitted, which allowed misdemeanour to become incremental.[73] This can lead to a search for ways to legitimise the behaviour and the excuse that 'everybody is doing it'—in other words, it is accepted behaviour and culture in our group to ignore rules and ethics: these rules don't apply to us. A specific instance of this is lax financial discipline. In a related observation, a US (COSO) framework for Internal Control refers to the

'Control Environment'. It notes that 'late reporting of a control failure or hostility to a critical internal audit report doesn't say anything explicitly about ethics, but it does indicate a state of mind where things that cause discomfort are likely to be swept under the carpet'.

There is, of course, a negative aspect to how groups can reinforce behaviour. Group decision-making can make members of the group willing to accept stupid ideas or hazardous risks[74] that they would reject if they made the same decision alone.[75] The example of how the Nazis were able to dominate the behaviour of a whole nation shows that the effect of a powerful and determined small group can subvert the ethical compass of large numbers of people. That history illustrates how context and situation as well as institutions can override values and intent. Gentilin rightly points out that group dynamics present a paradox. On the one hand, groups can assist and moderate an individual decision-maker, but, on the other hand, decisions can turn out to be wildly unethical. He quotes Nietzsche: 'Madness is the exception in individuals but the rule in groups.'[76]

A vivid example of how a tightly knit group within an organisation can behave in a way that is completely at odds with the organisation's general culture was described by the Financial Conduct Authority in its investigation in foreign exchange dealing:

> [T]raders at different banks formed tight knit groups in which information was shared about client activity, including using code names to identify clients without naming them. These groups were described as, for example, 'the players', 'the 3 musketeers', '1 team, 1 dream', 'a co-operative' and 'the A-team'.
>
> Traders shared the information obtained through these groups to help them work out their trading strategies. They then attempted to manipulate fix rates and trigger client 'stop loss' orders (which are designed to limit the losses a client could face if exposed to adverse currency rate movements). This involved traders attempting to manipulate the relevant currency rate in the market, for example, to ensure that the rate at which the bank had agreed to sell a particular currency to its clients was higher than the average rate it had bought that currency for in the market. If successful, the bank would profit.[77]

It would be facile to imagine that this macho behaviour by traders could be prevented by imposing fines on the bank. It is true that the behaviour was competitive in reaching targets and that individuals stood to achieve large financial rewards and bonuses. But studies do not show that the money itself was the driver of the behaviour. The evidence reveals the *social* competitive element between competing individuals and teams. The real driver of the behaviour was the desire for social recognition as being the team with the best results, the trader with the largest red Ferrari and so on. The money itself was not terribly important to the participants; what was important to them were results and tokens that recognised superior status that came with the best results. Basing their remuneration directly on their financial results—as opposed to the general longer-term results of the organisation as a whole—would inevitably produce behaviour in which ethical values become virtually irrelevant.

The better approach is to change the basis of individual assessment and reward. For example, from 2015, GlaxoSmithKline revised its remuneration scheme for all sales employees, dropping individual sales targets and changing remuneration from being based on targets to evaluation on technical knowledge, the quality of the service they deliver to support improved patient care and the overall performance of GSK's business.[78] The Chief Executive Officer (CEO) said that in providing doctors with information about medicines, 'this must be done clearly, transparently and without any perception of conflict of interest'.[79] Many organisations now look at the means of achieving results and carefully link these to their core values, expecting employees to be able to produce evidence of how their behaviour is aligned with those values.[80] We will look further at these points in chapter 12 below.

Similar points arise from looking at the social aspects of other examples of wrongdoing in sub-groups. We know an increasing amount about cartels, which are secret conspiracies in breach of competition law, such as to fix prices or divide markets.[81] These secret agreements are made by a small group of executives from different companies (an average of 13 in the 1990s and 19 in the 2000s),[82] who act with great care to avoid detection and punishment—including by their colleagues and employers.[83] Cartel meetings are normally disguised,[84] transmitted information is sometimes encrypted[85] and evidence of illegal agreements may be destroyed.[86] A significant number (but not all) involve senior business executives, including marketing and sales managers,[87] although many include 'buffers'[88] who can be 'thrown under the bus' to protect senior management from legal prosecution.[89] The relationship between the individuals in the conspiracy is based on trust and camaraderie, and these features tend to prolong cartel duration.[90] Ashton and Pressey's analysis of all 433 investigations made by the European Commission's Directorate-General on Competition (DG COMP) under EU antitrust laws over the period 1990–2009 (identifying 74 cartels) found that the competitive culture of marketing and sales staff in some organisations might consider team-crime such as price-fixing as an acceptable option in lean times.[91] Such influences may be amplified if sales and marketing managers lack awareness of the illegality of cartels[92] or succumb to narcissism and flattery when being asked to undertake actions that facilitate organisational survival.[93] Lower-ranked managers can be the victim of coercive senior managers when certain management philosophies apply, such as a 'profit-making at all costs' approach.[94] Ashton and Pressey describe the approach:

> Senior managers may focus on quick profits, maximum growth and high levels of managerial remuneration, creating organizational strains leading to criminal outcomes such as cartels. Financial and socioeconomic benefits may also be accrued by the employee for illegal corporate behaviours including bonuses, promotions and the goodwill of colleagues. Alternatively, not participating in cartel activity could lead to lack of promotion, demotion, ostracism or even dismissal.[95] The best predictor of whether a person or firm indulges in cartel behaviour may be past cartel behaviour.[96]

The point about both the above examples—financial traders and cartelists—is that the individuals involved formed their own *social* groups, outside the group structures of their organisations, whose pull to adopt unethical behaviour was so strong as to override the host organisations' cultures. This situation may be an indication that the host organisations' cultures are not sufficiently strong or rooted in ethical values and behaviour. Alternatively, it may be that the individuals are under stress or sociopathic. In any event, we want to emphasise how strong the social element is in affecting behaviour for better or for worse. This is why ethical practice must be a non-negotiable requirement *throughout* an organisation. Board members and senior managers may think themselves to be ethical, but they may not be the ones making the critical decisions on the front line, and they may also be unaware of what decisions are being made and on what basis. They must be acutely aware of the messages they are sending to their direct reports.

One important lesson is that management should pay particular attention to identifying situations and people who may be subject to conflicting values, and should take steps to reduce such conflicts, make them more transparent and thus less likely to influence behaviour.

It is instructive to think about two recent lists of sources of cultural problems. A 2015 survey of businesses in Scotland found the following obstacles and limitations on responsible behaviour:[97]

Can't justify/afford the cost	61%
Lack of staff capacity to get involved	54%
Difficult in being more environmentally friendly	23%
Unclear about the business benefits	22%
Lack of interest from customers/general public	21%
No regulatory requirement	15%
Seen as something for large businesses only	14%
Unsure how to proceed	12%
Never thought about it	10%
Insufficient commitment from company leadership	3%

The Chartered Institute of Internal Auditors recognises that businesses and boards face significant cultural trade-offs, such as the following:

(a) Cultural values as a wealth driver versus cultural values as a protector.
(b) Openness to mistakes versus zero tolerance.
(c) Leadership versus followership.
(d) Independence versus involvement.
(e) Empowerment versus rules and tight rules versus loose rules.
(f) Risk-seeking versus risk-avoiding.
(g) Human capital versus human cost.[98]

How Do We Apply This Knowledge?

Given the scientific lessons set out above, how do we apply this knowledge?

First, we should reinforce the shared understanding of fairness in our society, workplaces, clubs and so on. Part of this will involve including discussions on fairness and ethics in education and continuing education. This is needed in primary, secondary, higher and professional education, and continuous professional development. The UK Financial Ombudsman Service circulates an 'ethical dilemma of the week' to all staff. The idea is not for someone to win a prize by getting a single 'right answer', but to promote thought and discussion amongst all staff on what the right thing to do might be. We need to keep talking—especially to people who see things differently.

Second, we need to ensure that our rules are made and applied fairly. Making rules fairly means having an accepted, fixed and hence predictable process for making formal rules, which involves giving everyone an opportunity to contribute to an open debate through consultation or lobbying, before those who have the power to make the final decision do so in an open, unbiased, honest, independent and fair way. Applying rules fairly is the subject of the next two chapters.

Third, there are various ways in which we can counter our tendencies to take mental shortcuts, follow what others do, underestimate risk, and think we have all the necessary information, rationalise and cheat a bit. Responses include the following.

(a) Stop to think, or having procedures that make us stop before continuing, perhaps making us review if we have all the relevant information and have thought about it.
(b) Checklists, ethical decision-making models, consulting with others, reminders, warnings or gates before taking certain steps will all be useful.
(c) Having reliable information fed back to us on what we do, and what others are doing (rather than what we think we and they are doing), will cause us to think about whether we should change, and whether to follow the behaviour and standards set by others.

Conclusions

1. Human brains are not that good at making consistent and 'correct' decisions—we take mental shortcuts, we follow what others do, we underestimate risk and we think we have all the necessary information. We often break rules 'a bit', such as where we don't think it matters and when we will not be embarrassed.

2. One can look to recent findings in behavioural science to understand the reasons for this and the complex factors that may influence decision-making. Because of this complexity, it is important to be aware of the many pitfalls and to develop mechanisms to guard against the ethical failures that it can cause.
3. Human beings often make fast moral judgements based upon intuition and rationalise their decisions after the fact. This is only one of the mechanisms that may create unethical behaviour.
4. When it is possible to rationalise our behaviour, we are able to cheat a bit and still feel good about ourselves. Therefore, it is necessary to diminish the possibilities for rationalisation.
5. Framing, denial, self-deception and wilful blindness are all behaviours that allow people to believe that they are complying when in fact they are not.
6. Various phenomena influence behaviour in groups, and social pressure is a strong motivator.
7. Science does not support theories that decisions of most people are made as a result of calculations. We accept that some people are sometimes strongly motivated simply by making illicit personal gain, and they can be influenced by a perception that there is high risk that they will be identified/caught. Such motivation usually defines them as criminals.
8. Science suggests that most people make decisions by 'gut feeling', and their behaviour is influenced by multiple factors. It is simply incorrect and missing the point to regard them as acting on the basis of rational calculations.
9. People who make decisions within or on behalf of a group/organisation are influenced by multiple factors, and it is incorrect to analyse 'an organisation's' decisions on the basis that it might (or might not) be a commercial organisation.

2

Characteristics to Build on

Ethics are Innate in Humans

The basic lesson of chapter 1 is that we now know that humans rarely make decisions rationally by weighing up pros and cons, and are, as Ariely says: 'Predictably irrational, most of the time, making many decisions quickly based on emotional and social triggers.' However, despite this, the science also shows positive pointers to how we might support ethical decisions and actions.

We usually achieve more if we work together with others, using the combined power of our efforts and brains. But what enables us to cooperate with others? The answer lies in our 'ethical gene'. The sense of morality—of right and wrong—is inherent in humans. It is present in our DNA. Indeed, evolutionary biologists have concluded that a genetic mutation enabled only particular species to override the inherent drive to self-protection (selfishness) with a drive to perform altruistic acts (selflessness). The distinguished biologist Edward Wilson shows that it was this ability that enabled only *homo sapiens* to collaborate in groups and to divide labour, which enabled our ancestors to break out of Africa relatively recently around 70,000 years ago and dominate the world.[1] However, he notes that the inherent conflict between individualism and what he calls 'eusocialism' remains in us, and our actions can be inconsistent and imperfect. In a modern world where the social world of each human is not a single tribe but a series of interlocking tribes, '[g]roup selection shapes instincts that tend to make individuals altruistic toward one another (but not toward members of other groups)'.[2] Our (relatively recent) collaborative genes can make us want 'our team' to win against other teams. Wilson argues that the inconsistency between genetic responses, and the resultant imperfection, provides the flexibility that is needed in a changing world.

Hence, human nature is, in general, intrinsically moral, as well as moralistic, critical and judgemental. It was this capacity of morality that enabled humans to create sophisticated societies and civilisations. Psychologist Jonathan Haidt follows Darwin in believing that morality is used by humans at both the individual *and* the group level.[3] This produces multilevel selection: he says we are 90% selfish primates and 10% collaborative hivish bees. He thinks that we often act groupishly, rather than selfishly, on moral and political issues, and this can be seen in adhering to the tenets of teams, political parties and religions rather than by acting in our self-interest. Hence, people can vote or act against their personal interests by considering the perceived ethics of their group. Haidt says that only groups that can elicit commitment and suppress free riding will be able to grow.

Levels of Development of Human Psychological Consciousness and Organisations

Fernand Laloux has recently proposed a series of stages in the development of how humans group themselves into different organisations depending on the state of evolution of their ideas and social, economic and political needs. His sequence is: small bands of family kinships, tribes, chiefdoms, small conquering armies, agriculture-based societies, extensive cross-border hierarchical organisations, outcome-based movements such as the Enlightenment and the Industrial Revolution, meritocratic process and project-driven organisations, relationship-based cultures sensitive to individuals' feelings, and structures aimed at reaching consensus among large groups of people.[4] He argues that at each stage, we made a leap in our abilities—cognitively, morally and psychologically—to deal with the world. Each stage therefore invented a new way to collaborate, a new organisational model. He argues that the most recent stage has developed features of meritocratic empowerment, value-driven culture and inspirational purpose, a multiple stakeholder perspective with no hierarchy among stakeholders and the family as the guiding metaphor.

Like many others, Laloux drew on the work of the celebrated psychologist Abraham Maslow, who proposed a hierarchy of human needs, divided into two types: basic or deficiency needs and growth needs. He called the ultimate stage of human development 'self-actualizing',[5] which has these characteristics:

1. *Taming the fears of the ego.* A capacity to trust the abundance of life. A belief that even if something unexpected happens or if we make mistakes, things will turn out all right, and when they don't, life will have given us an opportunity to learn and grow.
2. *Soul searching of who we are and what our purpose in life might be.* Become the truest expression of ourselves. Let go and listen to the life that wants to be lived through us. Don't fear failure as much as not trying. A person who has ambition, but is not ambitious. Life as a journey.
3. *Dealing gracefully with adversity.* Life's way of teaching us about ourselves and about the world. Make frequent small adjustments.

4. *Wisdom beyond rationality.* Rational thinking can be more accurately informed by data. A fearless rationality and the wisdom that can be found in emotions, intuition, events and paradoxes.
5. *Striving for wholeness.* Transcend the opposites of judgment and tolerance. Integrate with the higher truth of non-judgement. This creates a shared space.

Laloux suggests that we are currently engaged in a shift to a new consciousness of collaboration between people and peoples—even if that transformation is not without its upheavals. Against this background about society, it is useful to consider how individuals develop. Kegan and Lahey identified three plateaus of adult psychological development: the socialised mind, the self-authoring mind and the self-transforming mind.[6] Jacques and Clement suggested that we should match a person's level of cognitive complexity (psychological development) to the level of task complexity he or she has to perform.[7]

Richard Barrett also drew on the work of Maslow, extending its application to organisations. He shifted the focus from needs to consciousness and expanded the concept of self-actualisation into three distinct levels by integrating certain concepts from Vedic philosophy into his Seven Levels of Consciousness Model (Figure 2.1).[8] He subsequently realised that specific values could be attributed to each level of consciousness and, therefore, if you could ascertain the values of an individual or an organisation, you could identify which levels of consciousness they were operating from.[9] Whatever values, beliefs and fears are foremost in the minds of the leaders of an organisation, you could determine the levels of consciousness the organisation operates from. This led to the development of a values measuring system based on the Model, which became known as the Cultural Transformation Tools® (CTT). Barrett realised that both individuals and organisations grow and develop by mastering their needs and desires at each stage of development. The seven levels of organisational consciousness are set out in Figure 2.1 and illustrate how this perhaps rather ethereal-sounding concept has quite practical application in organisations.[10] Looking at the seven levels, it is not surprising that the most successful individuals and groups are able to master the needs associated with every level of consciousness.

Also relevant are the ideas of organisational theorist Fons Trompenaars. He proposes that there are five orientations that shape behaviour when relating to others: (1) the extent to which rules prevail over relationships; (2) the degree to which the group is valued over the individual; (3) the range of feelings that are expressed; (4) the range of involvement that is appropriate; and (5) how status is ascribed.[11] He creates a typology of corporate cultures, which need to be distinguished, for example, in reconciling differences between corporate culture and local culture in multinational companies.[12] These orientations again will help us to understand the forces that are operating in organisations with regard to the dynamics of ethical behaviour.

Levels of consciousness		Actions and needs	Developmental tasks
7	Service	Creating a long-term sustainable future for humanity and preserving the Earth's life and support systems.	*Serving*: safeguarding the well-being of the planet and society for future generations.
6	Making a difference	Building the resilience of the organisation by cooperating with other organisations and the local communities in which the organisation operates.	*Collaborating*: aligning with other like-minded organisations and communities for mutual benefit and support.
5	Internal cohesion	Enhancing the capacity of the organisation for collective action by aligning employee motivations around a shared set of values and an inspiring vision.	*Bonding*: creating an internally cohesive, high-trust culture that enables the organisation to fulfil its purpose.
4	Transformation	Increasing innovation by giving employees a voice in decision-making and making them accountable for their futures and the overall success of the organisation.	*Empowering*: empowering employees to participate in decision-making and giving them freedom and autonomy.
3	Self-esteem	Establishing structures, policies, procedures and processes that create order, support the performance of the organisation and enhance employee pride.	*Performing*: building high-performance systems and processes that focus on the efficient running of the organisation.
2	Relationship	Resolving conflicts and building harmonious relationships that create a sense of loyalty among employees and strong connection to customers.	*Harmonising*: creating a sense of belonging and mutual respect among employees and caring for customers.
1	Survival	Creating financial stability, profitability and caring for the health and safety of all employees.	*Surviving*: becoming financially viable and able to meet your physiological needs.

Figure 2.1: Richard Barrett's Seven Levels of Organisational Consciousness

The Importance of Fairness in Observing Rules

After reviewing the findings of behavioural science that are summarised in chapter 1 above, Chris Hodges suggested in *Law and Corporate Behaviour* that there are three key findings on why people will voluntarily conform to rules that are particularly important. People will observe the rules of a family, social group, club, team, business, or nation where:

1. the rule is made fairly;
2. the rule is applied fairly (and that includes evenly, and with a proportionate response, so there should be serious consequences for serious wrongdoing);
3. the rule corresponds to the individual's internal moral values.

The effect of the above three conditions is cumulative. The self-regulatory effect increases the more we think that each of the conditions applies.

The concept that is fundamental to each of these three conditions is *fairness*. Social rules or state laws may say whatever they like (eg, you can only have one child, you can kill elderly people, you can cheat in declaring tax, you can only bathe on alternate Sundays), but in a free democratic society we will only respect and observe the rules if we think they are *fair* and just. The three conditions can be explained like this.

First, rules must be legitimate.[13] They must be made by following fair, agreed, predictable and transparent procedures, which allow everyone to know what is being proposed and, if they wish, contribute to the debate about what the rule should be. This points to the need for fair legislative processes for making laws and consultation for making secondary rules or guidance. This also explains some of our discomfort with the entire concept of compliance. Unquestioning compliance with unethical laws and decrees produced some of the worst injustices in the history of the world. So, the concept of compliance is necessarily incomplete and potentially even dangerous.

Second, rules must be applied consistently and equally for all. There must be no favourites who can avoid them. What's fair for one is fair for all. If we see that some people are being allowed to 'get away with it', we lose faith in the system generally. Therefore, people who deliberately do bad things deserve a proportionate response. People who perceive themselves as having been unfairly treated tend to confront decisions and act uncooperatively.[14] Regulatees have higher compliance where they perceive that inspectors treat them with respect and trust.[15] Employees' ethical values are shaped primarily by employee perceptions of how fairly they are treated by management.[16]

Fair application of regulatory enforcement serves a 'reassurance function' for firms that have made normative commitments to be law-abiding.[17] The importance of procedural justice in shaping legitimacy has recently been confirmed in a large US survey that found lower levels of support for formal authority amongst

Anglo-Americans[18] than Continental Europeans,[19] and that legitimacy is more important than police effectiveness. The researchers suggested that legitimacy is based upon the fairness of the manner in which legal authorities manage their authority, that fair interpersonal treatment is more centrally involved than fair decision-making and that outcome favourability is not a key factor.[20]

Third, the substance of the rule should be perceived as fair.[21] For example, people respond to unjust laws or unfair behaviour that happens not to be illegal (such as successful companies not paying tax in certain jurisdictions). People's views about appropriate sentencing decisions in criminal cases are driven by moral judgements about what is justly deserved.[22] There is much evidence that ethical concerns motivate self-regulatory behaviour in organisational settings.[23]

Many statements have been made by government, regulators and researchers into business regulation that indicate that the majority of businesses wish to comply with the law.[24] There are also academic statements that most business firms in most economically advanced democracies, particularly large ones, substantially comply with most kinds of regulations most of the time.[25] A good commercial reason for people to do this in the business context is to maintain profits by maintaining customers, and doing so through having a good reputation. A 2012 survey found that 'Compliance matters to businesses as it gives a positive message to customers'[26] and that businesses regard compliance with regulation as very important to their brand image: 80% agreed that 'If my business was found to be non-compliant, I would be concerned that it would affect our relationships with customers' and 69% agreed that 'It matters to our business that our customers know that we invest in compliance'.[27]

Conclusions

1. Human nature is, in general, intrinsically moral, and it is the capacity for morality that enabled humans to create sophisticated societies and civilisations.
2. Understanding the development of human and organisational consciousness helps us to identify what motivates human beings and organisations at different stages of their maturity.
3. Most of us have a strong inherent sense of what is right and wrong—a moral compass. We know what's just and fair. We will use this sense to adhere to the rules of the society, club or organisation to which we belong where we think that the rule has been made fairly, is applied fairly and is a fair rule. Therefore, ensuring that we interact on the basis of fairness is critically important in supporting such interaction and, in particular, in achieving conformity to common rules.

3

The Traditional Way of Enforcing the Law: Deterrence

> If only there were evil people somewhere insidiously committing evil deeds, and it were necessary only to separate them from the rest of us and destroy them. But the line dividing good and evil cuts through the heart of every human being.[1]
>
> Aleksandr Isayevich Solzhenitsyn

A great deal of traditional thinking has been that the core purpose of 'enforcement' of law is deterrence—to deter people from breaking the rules. The basic idea is to make people do what you want because if they do not, you will punish them. Thus, a person would obey the law because of fear that a breach will be punished, so it is better to conform than suffer. This approach can often be seen in authoritarian or militaristic societies: deterrence here has a strong relationship to what is called a 'command-and-control' regulatory model. The approach is essentially repressive and based on fear.

The theory that the purpose of enforcement of law rests to a great extent on deterrence has underpinned the civil law, tort liability,[2] and much of the public law of criminal and regulatory law. The idea of deterrence was reinterpreted in the mid-20th century by economic theory, which became widely adopted across the world, especially as economic regulatory agencies were created and expanded as industries were privatised or markets became increasingly subject to economic regulation.

The economic theory of deterrence rests on a series of suppositions.[3] First, markets, and therefore economic actors, base all decisions solely on maximising their net gains (exclusive economic rationality). All decisions are taken on the basis that deciders calculate (objectively, rationally and amorally)[4] the costs and benefits of all their actions.[5] Second, the state should ensure that the costs of wrongdoing by firms exceed the gains. This will be achieved by imposing fines and/or ensuring that damages are imposed for civil liability, because private or public enforcement is interchangeable in terms of economic effect. Third, firms will internalise all costs, so will rationally adjust behaviour to avoid incurring the costs that the legal system will impose on them. The likelihood of having to pay in future for harm or non-compliance will affect the decisions that result in the harm or non-compliance; the threat of sanctions will deter wrongdoing. Firms will be incentivised to take decisions on the basis that the external adverse costs of harm that flow from a decision will be internalised through legal processes,[6] so that the rational calculation will be that it is cheaper to comply than to infringe.[7] Fourth, companies can be considered to be single integrated actors and are able to control the behaviour of all employees. Fifth, the effect of deterrence will increase as penalties get higher and as the likelihood of them being imposed rises (severity and incidence). As a result of this last idea, some authorities multiply fines based on the net harm caused by the supposed rate of non-discovery of the type of wrongdoing (the inverse probability of a fine) and impose punitive sanctions. The rationale is to achieve theoretically 'perfect deterrence'.

Problems with Deterrence

A lot of problems have been raised by scholars with the theory of deterrence, with the economic theory of rational cost maximisation and with the theory of deterrence as regulation.

First, the empirical evidence that enforcement policies based on deterrence have much effect of behaviour is unimpressive, limited and uneven.[8] Decisions by people and businesses are not all made deliberately or solely on the basis of economic costs. Overall, many scientific studies show that people's behaviour *can* be affected if they have a perception that they will be *identified*, triggering a shame response and an adverse effect on reputation, assuming they are susceptible to such emotions.[9] But the situations in which this effect can occur in practice are limited. It could not be an effective systemic approach to affecting behaviour. The scientific studies tend *not* to disclose statistically significant correlations between levels of *severity* of sanctions and crime rates. Increases in the severity or certainty of punishment alone result in only modest (if any) increases in deterrence.[10] In other words, deterrence will only ever have limited effect as a means of affecting future human behaviour.

Second, people sometimes obey norms voluntarily when there is no risk of any sanction being imposed that may flow from decisions in advance of them being made. Third, is it always possible to identify the actor, capture all costs or calculate all costs? Fourth, insurance dilutes the cost-internalisation effect. Fifth, external costs imposed *ex post* are usually just treated as a cost of business and may not have much effect on future decisions. Sixth, if you fine a company, what effect does that have on the individuals who work in it, who make decisions based on a raft of other considerations?

Let us look at these points a bit further. The evidence is that people will not break rules where they perceive that the risk of being identified is high. Contrary to economic theory, increasing penalties will not have much influence on behaviour. The most effective way of making people think that they can 'get away with' breaking a rule is if those closest to them (family or work colleagues, depending on the context) observe the behaviour and then fail to express disapproval. It's really all about social relationships. Compliance is largely *social.* Hence, social embarrassment and reputation are important. Constant surveillance (and enforcement), if practically achievable, would have huge economic and social costs.

The brain can be affected by being reminded that something should not be done, especially if it perceives that the risk of being identified (and embarrassed) is high. So a valid regulatory strategy can be to affect the perception that the risk of being caught and embarrassed is high. But if the risk is in fact low, this strategy will fail. It is not a strategy that will work in many situations, for example, because it is impossible or too costly to guarantee that every wrong act will be identified. Such an approach engenders a culture of constant suspicion and control through fear, which is unacceptable in a contemporary society. Some people are motivated by making money illegally in the belief that they will not be caught, but this does not mean that they will be prevented (deterred) by the risk of punishment or increased punishment.

An example of reminding people of the risk of being identified and socially embarrassed or inconvenienced is to use digital average-speed cameras on roads, making them very obvious and advertising the fact that people are identified and get a penalty if they speed, and that if they go very fast, they will be shamed in the media. The key lever is the perception before the activity is undertaken rather than the sanction that might be imposed afterwards. Alternatively, the more effective sanction is the potential for embarrassment rather than the fine. Another example is students who think that their unattributed copying in exams will be identified by anti-plagiarism software (even if this is untrue). There are many examples of 'nudges' that governments use in similar ways.

A celebrated example of the failure of economic deterrence on social behaviour was the Haifa Day Care Centres experiment, in which the imposition of a fine on parents was simply ignored (an internalised cost) and actually made the undesirable behaviour worse. Furthermore, when the fine was removed, the damage had been done and the previous behaviour was not restored.

Case Study 2: Haifa Day Care Centres

Uri Gneezy and Aldo Rustichini set out to determine the effect of fines on the frequency with which parents arrived late to pick up their children from day-care centres.[11] The study lasted for 20 weeks and was carried out in 10 day-care centres. After merely observing for the first month and sending a notice, they imposed a fine in 6 of the day-care centres on parents who arrived more than 10 minutes late. After the fine was imposed, they noticed a steady increase in the number of parents arriving late. After 2–3 weeks, the number of late arrivals stabilised at a rate higher than in the no-fine period.

The fine was removed at the beginning of the 7th week; however, the rate of late arrivals continued at the higher rate.

Prior to the imposition of the fines, arriving late was perceived as an ethical issue as it was an imposition on the staff of the day-care centre. Once the fine was introduced, the financial penalty allowed the parents to avoid feeling guilty about arriving late.

The researchers concluded: 'The deterrence hypothesis predicts that the introduction of a penalty that leaves everything else unchanged will reduce the occurrence of the behavior subject to the fine. [This] study in a group of day-care centers … contradicts this prediction.'

Experiments have shown that having strong trust between people is far more effective than trying to affect choices by the threat of punishment.[12] There is a strong popular belief in the value of punishment, but it is in fact of little value in terms of affecting future behaviour. Instead, social responses to doing something that one's group will regard as wrong are powerful, such as social embarrassment, disapproval or ostracism.[13] This needs to be more widely understood by the media and the public if ethical business regulation is to succeed.

Experienced academic commentators summed up their views like this:

> Sociolegal research indicates that managers in regulated business firms do not resemble those pictured in the economic model of the firm, carefully calculating the probabilities of detection and the cost of legal sanctions to determine what they can get away with. Amidst the cacophony of information and urgent demands that business managers receive, the deterrent messages sent by legal penalties often do not get through or soon drift out of consciousness.[14]

The Example of Competition Law

It is not hard to find examples of where some people claim to rely on deterrence. Deterrence is the sole theory underpinning the enforcement policies of various regulators and legal systems. It produces very large fines by US and UK financial regulators—in contrast with a far more muted approach by many other regulators, such as the Bundesanstalt für Finanzdienstleistungsaufsicht (BaFin) in Germany. As Roger Miles has said, the 'politics of prosecution' drive the spectacle of blockbusting fines as a form of political theatre and prosecution of individuals to provide 'heads on spikes'.[15] These mediaeval metaphors might themselves cause us to think whether the outcome of such activities is a need for victims or is directed at producing changed behaviour.

An example of where deterrence remains central to enforcement is in relation to competition law. Significantly, with regard to cartels and unlike many regulatory systems discussed in this book, there is no regulatory structure that requires an ongoing (and social) relationship between a regulator and businesses: there is no 'front end', but only a 'back end' of enforcement. The evidence is that cartel conspiracies involve a small number of senior individuals who hide the conspiracy from everyone else, including colleagues. Business may benefit from the cartel, but the company does not formally adopt entering into the illegal agreement, for example, in board or executive meetings or minutes. Cartels typically last 5 to 9 years, so the speed of identification is not high. The record of public authorities of identifying cartels is extraordinarily low. Cartels are usually only identified when businesses themselves find out through compliance or audit functions and self-report to gain immunity from prosecution. Public authorities do not find cartels—companies do and then they tell the authorities.

The question arises how businesses might be helped to find cartels and do so quickly—or more quickly—than at present. Imposing high fines on a business is a curious way of eliciting collaboration between public authorities and firms in addressing what is usually a common problem. How does having to pay a high fine help a business find a cartel? The official answer is that it incentivises businesses to have an effective educational and investigative policy. But again, there are more positive ways of achieving this end that do not risk antagonising the people who work in the business who are innocent and who think that they have been penalised unfairly. Most competition authorities believe that they are angels who are justified by having absolute right on their side, but they are blissfully unaware that the way they go about their work results in them being regarded as enemies by most firms.

Research in the construction industry reported that the 'risk of an OFT [Office of Fair Trading] investigation had not made any impact on the majority of contractors surveyed'.[16] The overall conclusion was that there was a very low level of awareness of any of the OFT's activities directed at the construction sector, particularly the six enforcement cases completed between 2004 and 2006, and respondents did not consider 'that there was any clear message about bid rigging coming from the OFT during this period'. A study published in 2009 to assess the deterrent power of the OFT's penalties regime—which was written on the assumption that deterrence was the objective and that deterrence worked—asserted that 'high fines are a crucially important element of deterrence',[17] but that 'additional deterrence' was needed in the form of individual sanctions,[18] since the levels of fines imposed on firms might not deter individual managers.[19]

Competition authorities typically adopt leniency policies for businesses who inform them of the existence of a cartel.[20] They typically result in the first company to 'own up' (as it is described) being excused from paying any fine—a 100% remission. But, as generally operated, these leniency policies merely incentivise swift reporting by a firm after it has discovered illegality; they do not provide fair incentives to *help* a firm to discover the illegality by individual employees. A serious question arises as to whether it is just to allow the first to own up to escape the fine completely. Surely the fair response should be to work with businesses in incentivising them and their staff to work with the authorities in seeking out wrongdoing and addressing it. It would only be fair to impose sanctions on a business if it has done something wrong. In this context, this means not having or operating an appropriate system to support its staff doing the right thing and wrongly failing to identify illegality. The staff who break the law, their employment contracts, their ethical codes and social agreements with colleagues deserve to be sanctioned in public, professional and business contexts. In fact, in the US, it is usually the case that by the time the authorities have found out about a cartel, the managers who operated it have moved on to work in different companies twice, so they might escape any professional or social censure. At the EU level, no antitrust sanctions can be imposed on individuals. Innocent third parties (such as a business) that have benefited from the illegality should be required to repay gains as a result of unjust enrichment, but not because their actions have broken criminal law.

The above approach can be contrasted with the UK regime for bribery, which includes a clear incentivising of proactive corporate measures. As we will discuss in chapter 12 below, the Bribery Act 2010 specifies that a company that has 'adequate procedures' designed to prevent persons associated with it from undertaking bribery to benefit the company has a defence to a charge against it.[21] 'Adequate procedures' is not defined in detail, although related guidance includes the importance of a culture that does not tolerate bribery and a commitment by senior managers to ethical behaviour.

Incredible Deterrence

The idea behind fining an organisation is that it can control the behaviour of all the individuals who work in it, and imposing a fine on the organisation is the only way of doing that. There is no empirical evidence for this proposition. The approach involves a degree of anthropomorphism—assigning human personality and characteristics to the impersonal construct of a company. Yet the idea remains, although it is diminishing because it has been found to be ineffective. Instead, a shift is occurring to holding individuals responsible, either for their own actions or for the actions of others.

In recent years, the Financial Conduct Authority (FCA) has had an enforcement policy of 'credible deterrence'. This policy is just not credible and could never succeed—in fact, it makes the regulators look incredible, ineffective and foolish.

A simple example is that manipulation of the foreign exchange markets took place long after the banks had said they had sorted out their cultures and approaches, and had been fined very large sums for abusing interbank interest rate benchmarks.[22] The Governor of the Bank of England commented: 'The repeated nature of these fines demonstrates that financial penalties alone are not sufficient to address the issues raised. Fundamental change is needed to institutionalise culture, to compensation arrangements and to markets.'[23]

The US and UK authorities imposed far greater fines on banks than the authorities of any other country. Yet there is no empirical evidence that the behaviour of financial institutions in the US and the UK are better than that of those operating in other countries, or that the regulators are any more effective. If deterrent penalties do not have much effect, it is simply a dead end to imagine that the response to future behaviour is to constantly increase penalties. Where do you stop, especially if scientific evidence is that increasing sanctions have very limited effect? In 2017 the FCA issued a paper that stated: 'A credible deterrence strategy will remain a vital part of regulators' attempts to provide appropriate incentives to improve ɪmpliance, though practical examples from economic regulation suggest that it has some limitations' whilst 'behavioural biases … can affect the way that people take decisions in a professional context.'[24] This view simply fails to grasp the significance of the behavioural science and clings to a theory (deterrence) for which there is at best limited empirical evidence.

We suggest that we need to separate out various issues. First, how can we affect future behaviour and culture? Second, who deserves to be sanctioned for what historical behaviour? Third, should people who have profited from the illegal actions of others pay back the unjust enrichment? Fourth, should they make good any harm they have caused by breaking the rules?

Shifts to Enforcement against Individuals

There has been a recent shift in policy on the questions of who we should hold responsible for what and how. The US Department of Justice made a major shift in its policy in 2015 in the Yates Memo. This policy statement by the former (and now famous!) Deputy US Attorney General Sally Quillian Yates said that the state would enhance its deterrent effect on corporate wrongdoing by prosecuting the individuals who are responsible in the context of resolving cases of corporate criminal liability.[25] In other words, it will focus on prosecuting people and will expect companies likewise to pursue their staff. It will continue to prosecute companies, but will more clearly incentivise self-reporting by companies, based on the carrot of, for example, substituting a deferred prosecution agreement (DPA) or non-prosecution agreement (NPA) for a prosecution.

The Yates Memo gives guidance to prosecutors on the handling of cases involving both companies and individuals in the form of six guiding principles:

1. To be eligible for *any* cooperation credit, corporations must provide the Department with all the relevant facts about the individuals involved in corporate misconduct.
2. Both criminal and civil corporate investigations should focus on individuals from the inception of the investigation.
3. Criminal and civil attorneys handling corporate investigations should be in routine communication with one another.
4. Absent extraordinary circumstances, no corporate resolution will provide protection from criminal or civil liability for any individuals.
5. Corporate cases should not be resolved without a clear plan to resolve related individual cases before the statute of limitations expires and declinations as to individuals in such cases must be memorialised.
6. Civil attorneys should consistently focus on individuals as well as the company and evaluate whether to bring a suit against an individual based on considerations beyond that individual's ability to pay.

Yates explained 'if a company wants any credit for cooperation, any credit at all, it must identify all individuals involved in the wrongdoing, regardless of their position, status or seniority in the company and provide all relevant facts about their misconduct. It's all or nothing'.[26]

A similar approach has been taken in the UK in financial services in order to try to hold 'senior persons' responsible for the activities of people for whom they are supposedly responsible. This is discussed in chapter 12 below. FCA action led to no fines on individuals in 2009 and 2010, but 120 individuals between 2011/12 and 2015/16.[27] Another example is that since April 2015, National Health Service (NHS) directors and 'fit and proper persons' are criminally responsible when care fails in order to 'hold them to account'.[28] In fact, reports of NHS incidents have been deterred. The theory is that sanctions on either organisations or senior individuals will affect the future behaviour of others and are the only means of doing so. The supposed logic behind this is that people may control the actions and behaviour of others. It does not take much knowledge of how organisations operate, and how people behave, to know that that logic does not stand up. Other ideas behind this shift are, first, that a senior person is responsible for the culture of the departments that they lead, and, second, the emotional desire that someone deserves to pay for harming others. We will look further at the culture of groups below. The second idea is at base a desire for revenge.

Shifts from Deterrence

However, a series of shifts away from deterrence as the sole or central approach to enforcement of law can clearly be seen. One example is in the use of the ultimate criminal law sanction for murder, namely capital punishment, which has declined almost to extinction in the US.[29]

UK policy on crime prevention takes a strikingly informed approach.[30] It is based firmly on scientific evidence, behavioural psychology and data analytics. It focuses on what the evidence suggests are the six key drivers of crime—opportunity, character, the effectiveness of the criminal justice system, profit, drugs and alcohol. It also calls for a *collaborative* approach: 'The evidence is clear: where Government, law enforcement, businesses and the public work together on prevention we can deliver significant and sustained cuts in certain crimes.'[31] Although the strategy talks about ensuring that the criminal justice system acts as a powerful deterrent to would-be offenders, it expands the idea by relying on affecting the perceived likelihood of being caught rather than on the severity of sentences. An example is that specific police tactics can increase the perceived likelihood of being caught; for instance, patrolling known crime 'hotspots' has been shown to reduce crime, particularly when accompanied by local problem-solving.[32] 'The evidence suggests increasing the perceived likelihood of being caught, and to some extent the speed with which the sanction is then delivered, has a deterrent effect.'[33]

This approach rests alongside the policy of reducing opportunities for crime, based on the conclusive evidence that crime increases when there are more opportunities to offend and falls when the number of opportunities is reduced.[34]

A major focus of the crime prevention strategy is based on 'Character as a Driver of Crime'. This builds on the finding that a small minority of people commit the majority of crimes:[35] 'for most types of crime, most of us simply wouldn't consider breaking the law to be an option, however clear the opportunity'.[36] The strategy asks why some people become criminals, while others—often from the same neighbourhood or even the same family—do not. In answering this question, it makes some points that are a long way from deterrence:[37]

> The latest research suggests that what this strategy terms `character' is an important part of the explanation.
>
> Evidence increasingly suggests that certain character traits in individuals are related to their propensity to commit crime. Studies following people from a young age have demonstrated that those characteristics—particularly a person's willingness to break social norms,[38] and their levels of empathy[39] and self-control[40]—are strong predictors of whether they offend or not. In fact, researchers at Cambridge University have recently shown that these traits are around three times better at predicting whether a young person will offend than factors associated with their immediate environment, such as hanging around in crime hot-spots, or in the company of delinquent peers.[41]
>
> This is a growing area of research, but we are learning more about the development of these character traits. There are, for example, some aspects of an individual's upbringing which can be very damaging, such as witnessing or being a victim of domestic abuse, or experiencing social deprivation or neglect.[42]
>
> However, the evidence also makes it clear there is nothing inevitable about criminality.[43] The kind of positive character traits which will protect young people from involvement in crime can be learned[44]—someone with low levels of self-control can be helped to improve their decision-making, making them less likely to commit crime—with parents and teachers playing a hugely important role.[45]
>
> The early years are the point where positive character traits are formed making it a key time for intervention.[46] But an important and encouraging part of the growing evidence on 'character' is that, even in adults, the brain can still learn new patterns of behaviour—it is like a muscle that responds to exercise. This means even those with a high propensity to offend can still improve traits such as empathy and self-control throughout their lives.[47]

Deterrence or punishment has quietly disappeared from being a goal or a justification for the law of tort, in British theory if not in American.[48] Lord Bingham, a distinguished Law Lord, said that the primary function of tort law is merely compensation and not behaviour.[49] The British position contrasts markedly with the broad adherence to deterrence in the US, where it is argued that tort law provides a public regulatory function,[50] and 'litigation as regulation' has been extensively developed through economic analysis, assuming that all decisions are made on a calculation of costs and benefits, and an organisation controls all the actions of all its personnel.[51] This approach also encounters difficulties in being based essentially on *ex post* decisions that present difficulties of anticipation by complex commercial enterprises who seek far more detailed *ex ante* clarity of behavioural rules and certainty. It is also argued that fines or damages are just treated by managers and investors as 'a cost of business' and not as leading to behavioural consequences. If there is any deterrent effect of tort liability, it is widely accepted that it is significantly diluted, if not extinguished, by the effect of liability insurance.[52]

Reputation and Identification

We noted in chapter 1 above that most people wish to be seen to be doing the right thing, even if they are not. How others think of us is a powerful driver for our own behaviour. Not many people seek a personal reputation for being *unfair*, unless they are dictators, in thrall to dictatorships, or have no emotional responses (sociopaths or psychopaths). In the business context, maintaining reputation can be important both for individuals and for businesses, not only with customers but also within an industry.[53] As we have seen in chapter 1, most of us automatically assume that our actions are 'the right thing', whether or not they are, because we wish to feel good about ourselves and our reputation.

We also noted the scientific findings that people's behaviour can be affected if they have a perception that they will be *identified*, triggering a shame response and an adverse effect on their reputation, assuming they are susceptible to such emotions. But the situations in which this effect can occur in practice are limited. It could not be an effective systemic approach to affecting behaviour.

A simple illustration of these points is the history of car speed cameras. When fixed cameras were first introduced, people believed that they would be identified and fined if they were pictured driving over the speed limit. But later people were told that the cameras did not always hold film and local drivers would ignore some cameras. In any event, drivers might slow down to pass the camera but then speed up again. However, the introduction of digital average-speed cameras has produced the perception that driving over the average speed throughout the area covered will always be identified.

Reputation has been recognised by some enforcers as a relevant influence on behaviour, but not always correctly. A 2011 survey by economic consultancy London Economics concluded that the three most important factors deterring potentially anti-competitive behaviour were the risk of reputational damage for the company, criminal sanctions for individuals and financial penalties for the company.[54] London Economics noted academic suggestions that reputational damage from competition enforcement is an important deterrent for businesses.[55] It also noted that, contrary to the predictions of the literature,[56] private damages were ranked relatively low by respondents in terms of being an effective deterrent.[57] (We think that this finding was correct!) However, it contrasted this with an earlier finding that sanctions at the individual level are the most important.[58] It seems to us that the findings here were correctly indicating how people felt, but the information was mis-framed within the assumption (which was made in quite a lot of the surveys about attitudes to competition law around this time) that deterrence was the answer—and the only answer—and that assumed belief affected both the questions asked in surveys and the interpretation of the responses.

Enforcement action by authorities may be feared because of the consequential damage to commercial reputation rather than the impact—especially the lasting impact—of any sanction. This fits with the belief that the benefit of enforcement is that it creates a *commercial* level playing field—which is an ongoing consequence.[59] But this does not mean that such enforcement action, if it occurs, will in fact have much effect on future behaviour. The Health and Safety Executive (HSE) found that:

> Prosecution and resultant fines can be argued as an incentive for improving safety, but significant fines are rare, and the deterrents to prosecution tend to be reputational (the shame of appearing in court, the concern to avoid moral condemnation, the fear of bad publicity) rather than financial.[60]

Some studies suggest that 'showcase' actions, which are very focused and well publicised, may have some targeted deterrent effect.[61] The HSE maintains a name and shame website, from which names are never removed.[62] Similarly, an increasing number of scholars have argued that corporate reputation has been an increasingly strong driver of corporate behaviour and has produced self-regulating changes involving increased values-based practice in areas such as labour, environmental, social responsibility, human rights, trading and tax issues.[63]

We think, however, that interpretation of the evidence on reputation has to be framed within the scientific findings on the importance of the perception of the individuals involved. Is the supposed reputational damage to an organisation merely shrugged off as a 'cost of business'? However, American studies show that where a firm is fined or sued for financial fraud, as opposed to other types of regulatory infringements, the stock price falls significantly and remains low for some time,[64] which suggests that the market is reacting to behaviour that goes to the root of whom it can trust.

What Many UK Enforcers Actually Do

Since the 1980s, an increasing volume of academic research has progressively undermined the traditional legal approach that 'enforcement' of law rests on the concept on deterrence. Scholars began to venture out and speak to people 'out there', asking them what they actually did. This led to the discovery that many officials who were responsible for inspecting local businesses to ensure that they complied with the rules spent most of their time *talking* to company managers and staff, encouraging or supporting improvement through education, advice and ongoing support. They only rarely prosecuted people (partly because it took a lot of time and money to do so and partly because whenever they did this, it undermined the relationship between them and the firm prosecuted, making it more difficult to maintain future dialogue and improvement). They responded to people and firms as they found them, and aimed to improve things. In technical language, what they were doing was based on supporting compliance by persuasion and education, which became known as 'responsive regulation', rather than by deterrence through fear of prosecution. They adopted a responsive approach to individual organisations, depending on their situation and willingness to cooperate in achieving compliance, because it worked. Over time, an extensive body of empirical research arose from multiple differing contexts. The leading sectors studied are listed in Table 3.1.

Table 3.1: Research on responsive regulation

—	Care homes for the elderly[65]
—	Water pollution[66]
—	Occupational health and safety and environmental control and also railway safety[67]
—	Environmental protection[68]
—	The mining industry[69]
—	Manufacturing in Thailand[70]
—	Food businesses[71]
—	A range of Australian agencies[72]
—	Danish farming[73]
—	UK fish protection[74]

The two leading scholars who coined the term 'responsive regulation', Ian Ayers and John Braithwaite, also proposed that the sanctions available to enforcers could be viewed as a pyramid. At the top of the pyramid are the most powerful sanctions, such as removal of a licence to operate or imprisonment, but they are rarely used. At the bottom, used frequently, are 'soft' approaches like giving information, persuading and negotiating. As you go up the pyramid, the responses become 'harder' but less frequently used. (It was originally suggested that enforcers would respond to firms by incrementally increasing or decreasing sanctions on a 'tit-for-tat' basis, but this idea has not caught on—responses to particular behaviour need to be proportionate and fair rather than based exclusively on the previous sanctioned action.) The pyramid is widely quoted, and Figure 3.1 shows an example from the Civil Aviation Authority's 2012 *Enforcement Policy*.[75]

Contrary to the legal deterrence model, Kagan and colleagues note that hundreds of large corporations have voluntarily instituted formal, externally certified environmental management systems,[76] participated in industry-run self-regulation systems,[77] joined compliance programmes or undertaken fairly costly environmental and workplace safety improvements that are not required

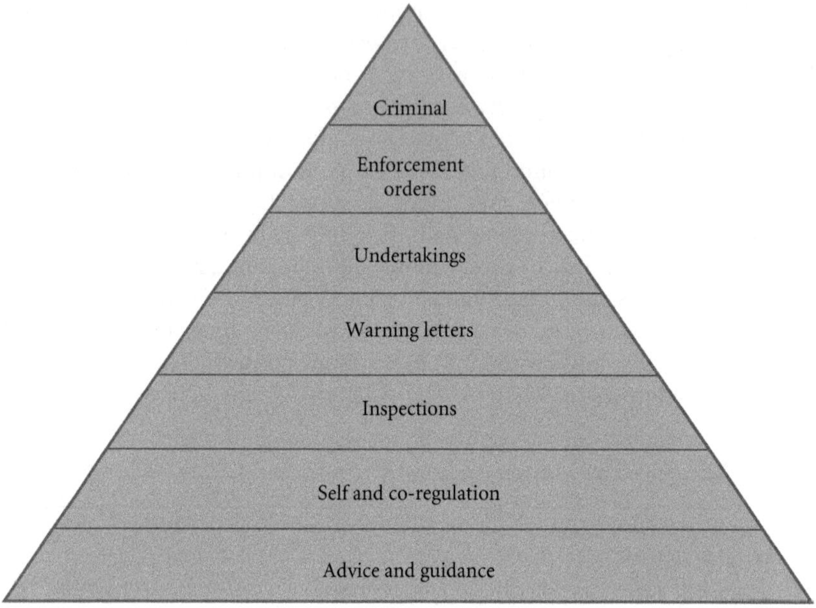

Figure 3.1: Enforcement pyramid of the Civil Aviation Authority 2012

by legal regulations at all, even when these improvements do not clearly save the firm money.[78]

A 2013 government report summarised previous research that there are many social and risk perception factors that influence compliance behaviour, including the following:[79]

— Businesses are more likely to comply with regulations that are seen as fair, appropriate and something that society would expect them to comply with.
— A wish to conform with social norms and the extent to which a business perceives an area of regulation as appropriate (and therefore where compliance would be seen as conforming).
— The extent to which management is aware of a risk, with some evidence that awareness and perceptions of risk vary and may not be accurate. Awareness of risks may vary according to factors such as the presence of professional advisors and the measurability of the risk.
— The extent of business drivers to manage a specific risk (and associated regulations).
— Management perception of the significance of the risk and the effectiveness of risk controls stipulated within regulations.
— The extent of external scrutiny (by inspectors) for a specific risk.

The 'responsive regulators' have found that blaming people, for example, by prosecuting them when they think they are doing their best, destroys relationships and impedes ongoing learning and improvement. In contrast, the way to support ongoing compliance and improved performance amongst honest people is usually by supporting social relationships of trust. Whilst we need to respond to rogues (this is discussed in the next chapter), treating people who are basically honest and trying to observe the rules, even if they are not perfect and could improve, as rogues destroys positive cultures and willingness to comply and share information.

Science Not Theory

The evidence from behavioural psychology and empirical studies noted in chapter 1 has largely undermined the credibility of theories that deterrence and economic rational action in fact produce significant effect on behaviour, whether of individuals or organisations. For example, as noted above, individuals are not skilled at assessing risk and do not make every decision based on maximising personal net gain.

Behavioural psychology supports two key findings that reinterpret older ideas. First, increasing the severity or certainty of punishment alone in fact results in only modest (if any) increases in deterrence.[80] This approach leads to the problem of imposing penalties that are considered to be excessive and disproportionate, and hence unjust, thereby leading to a loss of trust in the imposing authority and the legal system generally. In the criminal sphere, social control strategies based exclusively on a rational choice and deterrence model have had at best limited success,[81] and leading criminologists stress the 'importance of linking the deterrence (or rational choice) perspective with theories that rely on other types of control mechanisms' in society (especially normative attachments).[82]

Scientists are beginning to understand the mechanisms of the brain that operate in different mental states. Different brain states operate when a person acts either 'knowingly' or 'recklessly'.[83] Similarly, responses to rule-breaking and decisions on punishment produce reactions in two parts of the brain that assess the mental state of the offender and the severity of harm caused, which need to be integrated into a decision on the punishment amount.[84] These ideas are a long way from traditional attributions based on assumptions about intention and fault.

Second, the idea that a person will obey a rule out of fear of being punished has been shown to be effective only where an individual *perceives* there to be a *high risk that he or she will be identified*, from which he or she will suffer embarrassment and the loss of reputational esteem.[85] This perception can apply in some situations (where there is high surveillance, such as international nuclear strikes, where average speed limits are visibly measured by digital cameras, or where effective anti-plagiarism software is known to be used). Some criminals may indeed base their decisions to make a fast buck on a cost–benefit calculation, but this involves the belief that they will not be identified, caught and punished.

We can try to base a compliance system partly on getting people to believe that the likelihood of them being identified is high. But the perception of that likelihood will probably have to be realistic, and consistently true to overcome the individual propensity to underestimate risk. This is often unlikely to be the case. Affecting the brain to decide against doing something works in some situations, such as where drivers believe that speeding will be identified by average-speed cameras that are working or where students believe that plagiarism will be identified by software programs. Similarly, in the context of general crime, the 2016 *Modern Crime Prevention Strategy*[86] said: 'The evidence suggests increasing the perceived likelihood of being caught, and to some extent the speed with which the sanction is then delivered, has a deterrent effect.'[87] But achieving this perception consistently in relation to all human—or just commercial—activities and assembling necessary evidence would be impractical to achieve systematically. There will be many situations where it is too expensive or unfeasible to get everyone to believe that they will be caught every time they do something wrong.

The reality is that imposing costs *retrospectively* (to pay for harm caused or as a sanction for doing wrong) does not necessarily affect *future* behaviour.

Behavioural psychology has begun to be accepted as mainstream in some regulatory policy circles rather than as a curious sideshow to deterrence. Reports from the Organisation for Economic Co-operation and Development (OECD)[88] and the World Bank[89] focus directly on the relevance of 'behavioural economics' in understanding how people act and can be influenced to act in desirable ways. There is no reliance in these analyses on deterrence. The language of 'bias' affecting behaviour away from a supposed norm of 'economically rational acting' must give way to regarding 'abnormal' behaviour as not only predictable but also normal.

A Repressive Society or an Open Collaborative Society?

Recall the ideas in chapter 1 above on how human society evolves through stages of development. If we base compliance and enforcement on a system that seeks to identify every breach of rules, or to achieve that perception, as the sole or primary enforcement policy, what would be the consequences?

Do we actually want a society in which everything we do is under constant surveillance to catch us if we do the wrong thing? We would have a constantly mistrustful, even paranoid society—everyone denouncing each other, or suing each other. Kafka and Stalin showed up that way of life some time ago. The resultant uncertainty and mistrust certainly produces a lack of social cohesion, not to mention imposing huge unproductive costs on society.

Surely we need an approach based on personal values and social solidarity. The fundamental cultural values of Anglo-Saxon and European democratic states are based on respect for individuals and social solidarity. These values should be supported by state officers as an approach to behaviour, whether in business, public or social life. Accordingly, ruling by fear in a modern democracy is an unacceptable and arguably unconstitutional policy. Continuous surveillance of behaviour and enforcement by authoritarian regimes tends to be accusatory, confrontational, punitive and coercive, and produces a culture of mistrust and resentment.[90] There is overwhelming evidence from Cold War communist states of cultures involving entire populations living in constant fear of spies, surveillance and informers.[91] As various historical police dramas show, those who wield autocratic power can start to believe that the end justifies the means and that they are 'on the side of the angels' and unaccountable. There is ample evidence that these types of systems actually increase unethical behaviour and drive it underground.

If a repressive and deterrent approach is adopted towards people who think that they are trying to get things right, it will reduce their willingness to comply and collaborate, and there is little evidence that it will induce them to ensure that their future behaviour complies with the rules—in fact, quite the reverse. In contrast, imposing a serious sanction would be both a proportionate response to serious wrongdoing and may also be the right response to psychopathic or sociopathic offenders.

Stages in the Development of Human Society

The idea outlined above of law enforcement as a deterrent reflects a primitive or medieval society in which the head man kept his authority by threatening to kill or hurt people who disobeyed his rules—and actually killing and hurting them when they did (or even if they didn't). This was simply ruling by fear. We have a different conception in a modern democracy. Power lies with the people—that is, with every autonomous individual, who deserves to be treated with respect and who has inalienable rights.

An interesting insight to bear in mind in understanding a lot of what we find about different ideas on how we should 'enforce rules' can be understood in a historical context of the evolution of human stages of development. Quite a lot of the discussion about compliance and enforcement arises because our knowledge of how we work together in society, and how the most advanced collaborative and effective teams work, has not caught up with our understanding of the more primitive way of how we used to work together in earlier times. We saw in chapters 1 and 2 how Maslow and Laloux describe this evolution, and how some people and groups advance more quickly than others, and what Wilson and Haidt say about genetic mutation and the constant conflict between the self-preservative and the collaborative responses. The head of a tribe, or Lord of the Manor, would treat all those under him as his property—a 'command and control' model—and would enforce compliance with his rules or whims through authoritarian means. Society would be stratified vertically, and the leader would rule by exerting power over and punishing those below. Our concept of democratic society now has a flatter structure. Where all citizens are equal and power rests with all citizens, how should people work together in collaboration? How do we give expression to the modern criteria of liberty, equality and fraternity, as memorably stated in the French Revolution? It is reasonable for society to take steps to protect itself, its people and its peaceful order. It is also reasonable to expect citizens to respect others and to work together as members contributing to the common society. Repression and fear are no longer appropriate values. Cooperation, openness and fairness are the relevant values. For one thing, there are just too many people and situations for the authorities to try to control. So citizens have a right to expect that other citizens who live in the same society, from which the members mutually benefit and contribute, should behave in accordance with shared values and norms.

However, Laloux's idea of human organisations moving through phases also hints that various different phases can exist at the same time. This may cause problems, such as confusion and different approaches that are inconsistent. Which phase, which behaviour are we in, and what response is relevant? The answer seems to lie in recognising that the default social expectation is that people will behave ethically, but if some do not do so, then a more punitive approach is justified to protect society.

Conclusions

1. The traditional approach is to 'enforce' the law on those who have broken the rules so as to 'deter' them and everyone else from breaking it in future. Yet historical ideas of 'command and control' regulation and of 'deterrence' as an effective means of 'enforcement' have all crumbled in the face of advances in knowledge about how people make decisions and behave. Deterrence is a theory, but the scientific evidence supports a more responsive approach in most cases.
2. It is unconstitutional in a democratic society to seek to rule people through fear and repression.
3. Empirical evidence shows that deterrence as a law enforcement strategy, that seeks to affect future behaviour has, at best, limited effect.
4. It is right to impose sanctions retrospectively on those who deliberately cause harm to others in society, but doing so does not have much effect on whether the perpetrators or others will break the law in future.

5. The critical question is not 'How can we increase deterrence?' but: 'How can we affect future behaviour of individuals and groups?' We need to separate the backward-looking responses to past behaviour from the forward-looking elements of future behaviour, and approach them in different ways. It is helpful to avoid using the word 'deterrence', since it prevents us from focusing on the mechanisms that actually affect future behaviour.
6. Many UK regulators now operate on the basis of changing the way people and businesses perform through advice, education and support (responsive regulation).
7. Imposing an unfair sanction on those who believe they are trying to do the right thing is likely to be resented and decrease future compliance rather than increase it.
8. These developments make sense against the insight that some societies are evolving into a new stage of development in human collaboration and need to adopt a different paradigm for cooperating.

4

Fair and Proportionate Measures

Fairness in Response to Wrongdoing: We Don't Just Go Soft

An ethical and fair culture, whether within an organisation or in a regulatory regime, must be seen to respond to problems and wrongdoing by distinguishing between people who are basically trying to do the right thing and those who are not—essentially an issue of motivating intention. It is important that enforcement responses should be *fair and proportionate*. This is clearly established by the behavioural psychology referred to in chapters 1 and 2.

If individuals or organisations do *not* behave ethically, people expect to see proportionate responses as a matter of maintaining their belief in a fair society. If individuals engage in criminal activity, people expect to see the law upheld and for there to be a proportionate response by the state. This is an integral response to what we think of as fairness. It is not fair that people get away with behaving badly. It is also bad for a cohesive society. Society is justified in responding to wilful, deliberate or grossly negligent wrongdoing, or repeated unethical behaviour by protecting itself through traditional punitive means. Serious wrongdoing deserves a serious response to protect society and to uphold its values.

But where people have been trying to do the right thing, or have been generally, but not wilfully, ignorant about how to do things, adopting a punitive response would be seen as unfair, and hence would undermine general willingness to comply and suppress the incentive to improve.

Equally, the collaborative basis on which a joint enterprise such as a business operates will be threatened if some people try to undermine it by criminal activity, even if the business receives some gains as a result. The behaviour is essentially selfish and anti-social, as opposed to collaborative and based on mutual respect, and should be against the cultural code of the organisation. That is why the joint enterprise is justified in protecting itself from those who seek to harm it, by taking disciplinary action, and colleagues are justified in responding to a breach of the code of mutual responsibility.

It is fair that society should protect itself from those who intentionally break its rules. But we should have moved beyond a society based on revenge and retribution for all harms. If the primary objective is to maximise *future* compliance, punishing everyone for *past* actions will be unjust if it is ineffective. We excuse those who are not mentally capable.

However, individuals working in organisations may transgress the norms of society and of the organisation because they feel that what 'the organisation' actually wants them to prioritise is not its official ethical policy, but its actual ethic of hitting sales or revenue targets. In circumstances like this, it may be easy to identify who is 'doing the wrong thing', but it also becomes much more difficult to ascribe moral condemnation to individuals on the front line who are doing what their managers expect them to do. If society and organisations recognise this reality, then changes can be made, such as in incentives and in the ability to identify what the real priorities are.

Part of being fair and proportionate is ensuring that the responsibility is attributed to the highest relevant level of management within an organisation rather than the foot soldier who may be a victim of the system or of wilfully blind or 'immoral' management. This approach accords with the concept of 'responsive regulation'.[1]

Proportionate Responsiveness

We need to make sure that we are fair and proportionate in our responses to wrongdoing. A fair society cannot ask or expect its people to obey its rules if it is not itself fair in terms of how it treats those who break the rules.

Both public authorities and commercial authorities need an enforcement toolbox that contains a wide range of powers to be able to respond appropriately and with the greatest flexibility to what is needed to address individual circumstances. The response to unethical actions must be proportionate, and this requires coordinated balance between public, professional, commercial and social sanctions to prevent multiple responses accumulating into injustice. This means that sophisticated coordination is needed between sanctions imposed on persons and organisations, and by responses imposed by different authorities—whilst remembering that it is *social* responses such as ostracism or public reputational effects that are sometimes the most powerful.

What we learned in the first two chapters is that self-imposed and social responses can be enlisted very effectively as both retrospective sanctions and prospective protections. Of course, people need to see those mechanisms at work if they are to have confidence that fairness is being applied. But for people for whom those approaches do not work, we can only fall back on traditional protections. For serious offences, withdrawal of the right to trade is required. Those who engage in armed robbery or systemic financial fraud deserve removal of liberty and the proceeds of crime.

There are many possible responses to unacceptable behaviour. Some are social (eg, embarrassment, ostracism and expulsion), some are disciplinary (eg, warnings, reprimands, termination of membership or employment and removal of professional accreditation), some are private-public (eg, paying compensation and an injunction against doing something) and some are regulatory/criminal-public (eg, warning, undertaking to do or not do certain things, a fine and removal of liberty). Each of these responses should be fair and proportionate to the degree of wrongfulness and harm.

Being proportionate also means that we should not multiply the punitive responses by piling one response on top of another (eg, social shame plus professional and employment expulsion, plus damages plus imprisonment) where this is not appropriate as a response to a historical behaviour or to prevent future wrong behaviour. It may be appropriate to do all these things in relation to some people in some circumstances, but it may equally be unnecessary in relation to future behaviour, and hence disproportionate. So our systems need coordination in their responses. Examples of this are where agreements about future behaviour, paying redress and possible sanctions are all resolved together at the same time, which some regulatory bodies are now doing.

The principle of fairness has several practical applications. People who cause risk or harm should own up quickly so that the potential harm can be minimised and thought can be given to how to avoid the problem happening again. An enforcer should work in cooperation with the relevant level of management of a business to address the risk of the illegal and/or unethical behaviour reoccurring. Credit should be given to a business that cooperates with the authorities, demonstrating a socially cooperative approach. In responding to a breach of the law, enforcers and businesses should first identify what the root cause of the problem is.

People who cause unjustified harm should repair the damage. It is now standard practice for most prosecutors and courts not just to address the seriousness of the behaviour but also to seek to remove any gains from those who have benefited from illegal acts.

Case Studies

The easiest way to illustrate what we mean—and do not mean—is to provide illustrations and let you think about how the fair and proportionate approaches that we have been talking about have—or have not—been applied. Below are various recent cases, which repay thinking about. We think that some approaches were right and fair, and some not. Do you think the outcomes were fair or not? What should have been done differently? How did the defendants and the enforcers or courts focus on affecting future behaviour, and are they likely to be successful? It strikes us that few of them go beyond punishment and therefore will likely be ineffective in preventing future similar behaviour.

In the past few years, many UK regulatory authorities have published enforcement policies and the courts' Sentencing Guidelines have been amended. These policies should be reviewed to see if they are really based on the principles of fairness and proportionality. Many adopt a methodology of a starting point or range of sentence, which can then (rightly) be raised or reduced by considering specific aggravating and mitigating factors. But some are still based solely on 'deterrence', which will simply be ineffective as well as producing unfair outcomes. Many others might be considered to be generally fair in their details, but they are not in fact grounded in the principles of moral fairness and proportionality. They should all be reviewed. A critical issue is to be clear whether and how we are trying to achieve protection of society, fair sanctions, redress for harm done and desired future behaviour.

Case Study 3: Prosecution and Disgorgement of Profits[2]

Duncan Williams of Birmingham illegally sold unlicensed medicines Lipostabil and Ensentiale N, marketed as 'Flabjab' with a claim that they would lead to slimming. Lipostabil worth over £10,000 was seized by the Medicines and Healthcare products Regulatory Agency. On conviction, he and his company were fined a total of £10,000, ordered to pay £19,000 in court costs and ordered to pay £800,000 as disgorgement of profits under section 243 of the Proceeds of Crime Act 2002.

Case Study 4: Dangerous Skin-Lightening Cosmetics[3]

In 2016 London Trading Standards mounted a campaign against high street traders selling illegal and dangerous skin lightening products, in which eight businesses were ordered to pay fines and costs of over £100,000 for their involvement in the supply of cosmetics that either contain banned or restricted substances or failed to comply with safety rules on labelling and traceability. Many of the products contained dangerously high levels of hydroquinone, mercury or corticosteroids, which can result in a host of problems from skin thinning and discolouration to organ damage and even cancer in the long term.

Case Study 5: Manipulation of Foreign Exchange Markets[4]

Traders in various banks manipulated the G10 spot foreign exchange (FX) market between January 2008 and October 2013. The FCA's FX investigation found that the traders:

> Formed tight knit groups in which information was shared about client activity, including using code names to identify clients without naming them. These groups were described as, for example, 'the players', 'the 3 musketeers', '1 team, 1 dream', 'a co-operative' and 'the A-team'.

> Traders shared the information obtained through these groups to help them work out their trading strategies. They then attempted to manipulate rates and trigger client 'stop loss' orders (which are designed to limit the losses a client could face if exposed to adverse currency rate movements). They were attempting to manipulate the relevant currency rate in the market, for example, to ensure that the rate at which the bank had agreed to sell a particular currency to its clients was higher than the average rate it had bought that currency for in the market. If successful, the bank would profit.

Around 20 traders communicated through an internet chat room sending 'comically self-incriminating messages' such as 'If you ain't cheating, you ain't trying'.

Amongst the penalties imposed, six banks were fined a total of £1,409,350,000 for failing to control business practices. No charges were brought against any individual.

Case Study 6: Fraud[5]

On 15 July 2016, Terence Solomon Dugbo was jailed for seven years and six months for defrauding the electrical waste recycling industry out of £2.2million. He had falsified paperwork to illegitimately claim that his Leeds-based firm TLC Recycling Ltd had collected and recycled more than 19,500 tonnes of household electrical waste during 2011, which had never been handled. The judge described the case as a 'sophisticated' crime, involving a huge and complex amount of false paperwork, designed to conceal its intentions from everybody involved. Dugbo was also disqualified from acting as a company director for 12 years on the basis that that he was 'a risk to the public'. The Environment Agency instituted proceedings to recover £2.2 million from Dugbo as constituting the proceeds of crime.

Case Study 7: Cold Callers[6]

In the first six months of 2016, the Information Commissioner's Office (ICO) imposed fines totalling £1.5 million on companies behind illegal nuisance marketing responsible for more than 70 million calls and more than 500,000 spam text messages, frequently to vulnerable people. The ICO received more than 93,000 complaints in the period of nuisance calls and texts. The ICO head of enforcement said: 'Our helpline staff hear first-hand the level of distress cold calls can cause. We have acted on information provided by the public and specifically targeted companies that phone people in the middle of the night, ask to speak to deceased relatives or ring repeatedly after being asked to stop.'

Fines this year include:

- £350,000 for a firm responsible for over 46 million automated nuisance calls;
- £50,000 for a company which sent more than 500,000 texts urging people to support its campaign to leave the EU;
- £250,000 for a claims management company that made 17.5 million calls asking people if they had suffered hearing loss at work.

Case Study 8: Failure to Carry out Standard Safety Work, Failure to Act Swiftly and a Family's Expectation[7]

Benjamin Withers, aged 82, fell 12 feet to his death from an elevated walkway outside Fareham health centre. His mobility scooter collided with a wooden weather screen, which was situated around the main entrance and access-bridge to Fareham health centre. A section of the screen gave way, causing Mr Withers and his mobility scooter to fall through the gap onto a walkway below.

The Health & Safety Executive (HSE) found that the screen had not been constructed to the required standard, no risk assessment had been made to consider the suitability of the screen and the structure had not been adequately maintained. It was also found that the collapsed section was so badly decayed that portions of the wood could be easily removed by hand. Planned maintenance work to replace the rotten wood had been cancelled and rescheduled on more than 20 occasions without ever being carried out.

The NHS Litigation Authority, which had taken on criminal responsibility for two since abolished NHS Trusts responsible for the health centre at the material time, entered guilty pleas to breaches of section 3(1) of the Health and Safety at Work etc Act 1974 (HSWA 1974) and was fined £40,000 and ordered to pay £15,000 costs.

Mr Withers' son said: 'This has been a traumatic event for all my family. Due to these breaches in health and safety our family has lost a devoted husband, father and grandfather. My mother has lost a husband and a major part of her life, this has affected her deeply, she has not been able to visit her local shopping centre or walk past her local surgery where my dad died. The centre is also close to my brother's place of work and he has to see it every day.'

The HSE Inspector commented: 'This tragic incident could have easily been avoided if the barrier … had met the well-known and established standards for design and construction of barriers and if the required maintenance had been carried out as soon as it was identified. Instead a family has lost a well-loved husband and father.'

Case Study 9: Cooperation in Compliance, Self-Investigation and Self-Reporting of Bribery[8]

A US parent company implemented a global compliance programme in late 2011. In August 2012, this compliance programme resulted in concerns being raised within its UK subsidiary, an SME, about the way in which several contracts had been secured to supply its products to customers in a number of foreign jurisdictions. The subsidiary took immediate action, retaining a law firm that undertook an independent internal investigation. The law firm delivered a report to the Serious Fraud Office (SFO) on 31 January 2013, after which the SFO conducted its own investigation. The SFO brought proceedings against the subsidiary alleging conspiracy to corrupt (contrary to section 1 of the Criminal Law Act 1977), conspiracy to bribe (contrary to section 1 of the same Act) and failure to prevent bribery (contrary to section 7 of the Bribery Act 2010) in respect of events from June 2004 to June 2012, in which a number of the company's employees and agents were involved in the systematic offers and/or payment of bribes to secure contracts in foreign jurisdictions. The SFO and the subsidiary agreed a Deferred Prosecution Agreement (DPA), under which the indictment was immediately suspended, and the DPA was approved by Lord Justice Leveson at Southwark Crown Court. Under the DPA, the subsidiary agreed to pay £6,201,085 as disgorgement of gross profits and a £352,000 financial penalty (£6,553,085 in total). A figure of £1,953,085 of the disgorgement was paid by the US parent company as repayment of a significant proportion of the dividends that it received from the SME over the indictment period. In view of the subsidiary's lack of funds, no costs were awarded to the SFO and no compensation order was made.

The SFO Director, David Green, said: 'This case raised the issue about how the interests of justice are served in circumstances where the company accused of criminality has limited financial means with which to fulfil the terms of a DPA but demonstrates exemplary co-operation.' Christopher David, counsel in WilmerHale's white collar crime team, commented: 'The judgment may well give comfort to lawyers and companies that the DPA regime is going to provide a meaningful alternative to a guilty plea in cases of corporate misconduct—not least because the penalty has been carefully designed to remove the benefit of the criminality but not force the company into insolvency. The judgment does ... reinforce the SFO's stated view that companies that self-report and provide full co-operation will be see this co-operation recognised by a favourable resolution.'

Case Study 10: A Sentence for Repeated Failure to Act with a Deterrent Rationale[9]

Thames Water had a permit to discharge treated effluent from Tring STW into the Wendover Arm of the Grand Union Canal. The conditions of the Environmental Permit set by the Environment Agency aim to prevent any negative impact upon the canal itself and activities such as boating and fishing which take place on or in it. Poorly performing inlet screens repeatedly failed, causing equipment at the works to block, leading to sewage debris and sewage sludge being discharged into the canal.

The Environment Agency received complaints from the Canal and Rivers Trust and from the general public about pollution in the canal. Officers attended the site on several occasions; they saw sewage debris including panty liners and ear buds in the vicinity of the outfall. On one occasion, officers worked with Thames Water to arrange for aeration to be installed at the outfall into the Grand Union Canal as a precautionary measure to increase the levels of oxygen in the water.

Thames Water pleaded guilty before Watford Magistrates Court to two charges under the Environmental Permitting (England and Wales) Regulations 2010. The company asserted that there was no financial motivation for or gain from the offences. It had since taken steps to avoid further such incidents, spending £30,000 on replacing the inlet screens at Tring, and there had been a significant improvement in its subsequent environmental performance. It cooperated with the Environment Agency in its investigation. The company was ordered to pay a fine of £1 million, costs of £18,113.08 and a victim surcharge of £120.

Explaining why the fine was so large, HHJ Bright QC stated: 'The time has now come for the courts to make clear that very large organisations such as [Thames Water] really must bring about the reforms and improvements for which they say they are striving because if they do not the sentences passed upon them for environmental offences will be sufficiently severe to have a significant impact on their finances.'

Case Study 11: Corporate Manslaughter by an SME[10]

In 2013, Gavin Brewer and Stuart Meads were walking along Hampstead Road in London after a night out. CCTV footage showed them having an altercation, as a result of which both men fell through a building site hoarding and into an uncovered light well approximately 12 ft below. They sustained head and spinal injuries and died at the scene.

The hoarding was found to be wholly inadequate during investigations following the incident, being only 4 ft tall and made of plywood, and would have given way under only moderate force. The site was found to have been in an unsafe condition for several days, which had exposed members of the public—in particular, children from a nearby primary school—to serious risk. Overall, the company's approach to health and safety planning and training for those on the site was poor.

On 9 May 2016, the small family-run company responsible for the site, Monavon Construction Ltd, pleaded guilty to two charges of corporate manslaughter and a breach of section 3 of the HSWA 1974, which concerns the safety of those other than employees. A charge against director Michael McGowan under the HSWA 1974, which he had denied, was ordered to lie on file following the company's guilty plea.

In setting the penalty, the court applied the Sentencing Council Definitive Guideline on Health & Safety Offences, Corporate Manslaughter and Food Hygiene Offences. The Guideline sets out a process, starting by assessing the seriousness of the offence by reference to the risk posed and the company's culpability in creating or failing to manage that risk. The size of the organisation is then established first by reference to its annual turnover, although other financial factors may be taken into account if the court considers it necessary to ensure that the eventual fine is proportionate.

These factors are applied to a matrix which gives a sentence range and starting point. The range is from £180,000 to £540,000, with a starting point of £300,000 for a 'micro' company committing a Category B offence, to £4.8–£20 million, with a starting point of £7.5 million for a 'large' organisation committing a Category A offence. A 'large' organisation is defined as one with a turnover in excess of £50 million, although the guideline does give discretion for a court to increase fines outside of the suggested range where a company has turnover far in excess of this amount.

Having established the range and starting point, the court should then consider any aggravating (eg, previous relevant convictions, cost-cutting at the expense of safety or obstruction of the investigation) and mitigating factors (eg, no previous relevant convictions, evidence of remedial steps and self-reporting and cooperating with the investigation). Having applied these factors, the court may then adjust the starting point to reach an initial fine.

The court has a general discretion to adjust the initial fine up or down to ensure that the objectives of sentencing are fulfilled. In the case of corporate manslaughter, the particularly relevant objectives will be punishment, deterrence and the removal of gain derived through the commission of the offence. In the words of the guideline, the fine 'must be sufficiently substantial to have a real economic impact, which will bring home to management and shareholders the need to achieve a safe environment for workers and members of the public affected by their activities'.

Finally, the court should undertake a review of the adjusted fine, taking into account the defendant's financial circumstances. In particular, the guideline notes that the court should:

— consider whether the defendant has a small or large profit margin relative to its turnover and adjust the fine accordingly; and
— add any quantifiable economic benefit derived from the offence on top of the fine.

The guidance also requires that the court considers whether the consequence of the fine will be to put the defendant company out of business, but expressly acknowledges that this may be an acceptable consequence.

Monavon's turnover was around £500,000 (reduced from around £2 million at the time of the accident). The seriousness of the accident qualified as Category A. In mitigation, it was acknowledged that Monavon had a good safety record, no previous health and safety convictions, and had acted swiftly to remedy its practices. Monavon also successfully argued that the accident had not been caused as a result of cost-cutting at the expense of safety, thus avoiding a significant potential aggravating factor. The guideline range for a 'micro' company guilty of Category A corporate manslaughter offence is £270,000 to £800,000, with a starting point of £450,000. Therefore, a fine of £500,000, for both offences taken together, represents a slight increase or aggravation on the starting point. Monavon received a reduction of £50,000 against each corporate manslaughter charge for pleading guilty on 9 May 2016, which falls close to the 10% usually allowed for a plea 'at the door of the court', rather than the maximum one-third reduction allowed for a plea at the earliest opportunity.

The company was ultimately fined £500,000 for the two offences of corporate manslaughter and £50,000 for breaching section 3 of the HSWA 1974, and was ordered to pay prosecution costs of £23,653. These costs threatened the financial viability of the company. A publicity order was also made, which will require Monavon to publish a notice in a form directed by the court announcing the conviction and sentence.

Case Study 12: A Shared Approach to Wrongdoing and Resolving Consequences

In the early 2000s, Chris Hodges asked a senior lawyer in a multinational company how the company tried to prevent cartels and how they detected them. He (and many others) said that they have extensive internal education, compliance and checking programmes. He said that, despite their best efforts, they do very occasionally uncover cartels. In his particular industry, it appeared that such illegal behaviour might occur as instigated by the manager of a subsidiary—other sectors appear to produce different behaviour, including some that have very low risk of cartels or foreign bribery. His company had learnt that such behaviour could sometimes be identified by internal due diligence, such as on corporate structure reconstructions or sales. I asked him if the company sacked the managers concerned. He said that they absolutely wanted to do that—the managers' behaviour was completely contrary to company policy and shared morality—but they were in fact *prevented* from doing so because this would result in years of dealing with enforcement authorities over fines on the company (which they thought would have little benefit) and litigation over paying damages, and it was necessary for the company to retain the knowledge of the only individuals who knew what had happened. He was incensed at the injustice of this situation. Things would be better if the authorities could adopt a collaborative approach with the company in finding and responding to wrongdoing, and support swift action in which every aspect was resolved quickly and at the same time. These factors still seem significant in terms of how to support an ethical decision.

Case Study 13: Contrasting Responses to Computer Failures

The RBS Group spends over £1 billion annually on maintaining IT infrastructure. On 17 June 2012, the central Technology Services (TS) of the RBS Group upgraded the software that processed updates to customers' accounts overnight. When it noticed problems with the upgrade, TS decided to uninstall it without first testing the consequences of this action. TS did not realise that the upgraded software was not compatible with the previous version. This caused disruption of the ability of customers of RBS, National Westminster Bank plc and Ulster Bank Ltd to use banking facilities on 20 June 2012. The IT failure affected over 6.5 million customers in the UK for several weeks. Over the course of this period, customers could not use online banking facilities to access their accounts or obtain accurate account balances from ATMs; they were unable to make timely mortgage payments; they were left without cash in foreign countries; the banks applied incorrect credit and debit interest to customers' accounts and produced inaccurate bank statements; and some organisations were unable to meet their payroll commitments or finalise their audited accounts.

The Financial Conduct Authority (FCA) found that banks did not have adequate systems and controls to identify and manage their exposure to IT risks.[11] In particular:

- there were inadequate testing procedures for managing changes to software;
- the risks related to the design of the software system that ran the updates to customers' accounts were not identified;
- the IT risk appetite and policy was too limited because it should have had a much greater focus on designing systems to withstand or minimise the effect of a disruptive incident.

The FCA considered that the incident was not the result of the banks' failure to make a sufficient investment in their IT infrastructure. The FCA acknowledged that since the IT incident, the banks had taken significant steps to address the failings in their IT systems and controls.

On 20 November 2014, the FCA and the Prudential Regulation Authority imposed fines of £42 million and £14 million respectively on the RBS Group.

Case Study 14: Npower Group

Seven companies in the Npower Group upgraded their computerised billing system, as a result of which major problems occurred, including sending incorrect and late bills. Many customers complained, but the company's complaint-handling system was poor.[12] The company acknowledged that its practices fell far short of requirements in relation to its billing and complaints handling, and that it had breached Ofgem's various Standards of Conduct (SLC 25C.5 on treating customers fairly and SLC 27.17 on the provision of final bills) and regulations 3(2), 4(6), 6(1), 7(1)(a)–(b) and 10(2) on complaint handling. Ofgem accepted that Npower had made significant improvements in these areas during the investigation and improved its performance. Ofgem acknowledged that Npower's senior management took action to remedy the contraventions, particularly on the billing issues, and did not consider that its senior management had intentionally contravened the requirements. However, the actions taken were not enough to stop the contraventions from happening, nor did the actions stop them quickly enough to minimise the impact on consumers.

In late 2015, Npower undertook to take a series of improvement actions, to comply with a series of specific targets and to make consumer redress payments totalling £26 million. Penalties of £1 each were imposed on seven companies in the group. (In 2017, Npower raised tariffs by 10.4%.)

Case Study 15: Suppression of Evidence and Making Misleading Statements[13]

Andrew Tinney, the Global Chief Operating Officer of Barclays Wealth and Investment Management (WIM), was chairman of an internal steering committee overseeing a remediation programme that Barclays undertook to correct certain regulatory deficiencies identified by the US Securities and Exchange Commission (SEC) during an examination of WIM's US branch, BWA. The remediation programme included a 'Culture Audit' work stream. As part of that work stream, Mr Tinney received a report from an external consultancy that expressed 'an opinion that BWA had pursued a course of revenue at all costs and had a culture that was high risk and actively hostile to compliance. Its main recommendation is that the firm should replace or consider replacing some members of BWA's senior management':

> Mr Tinney took steps which aimed to ensure that the Report would not be seen by or available to those senior individuals referred to above or anyone else at the Firm, whilst also putting in place a plan (which included briefings and the Workshop) to address the criticisms contained in the Report. He ensured that the Report would not be seen by or available to others by not sharing it with anyone, not entering it into the Firm's records or IT systems, and instructing the Consultancy that they did not need to circulate a copy. Having done so, during the Relevant Period, in breach of Statement of Principle 1, he recklessly made misleading statements and omissions to certain of his colleagues at the Firm as to the Report's nature and/or existence, which he should have been aware would make it less likely that he or the Consultancy would be asked for a copy of it.

The report came to light after a whistleblower had notified Barclays that a report had been buried, and Barclays asked the consultancy to provide another copy. Mr Tinney resigned.

On 14 September 2016, the FCA published a Decision Notice censoring Mr Tinney, who appealed to the Upper Tribunal. The appeal was listed for January 2018.

Case Study 16: Rolls-Royce Systemic Bribery and Corruption Payments[14]

In early 2012, internet postings which raised concerns about the operation of Rolls-Royce's civil business in China and Indonesia came to the attention of the Serious Fraud Office (SFO), which sought information from Rolls-Royce. An investigation was immediately begun by Rolls-Royce itself. From 2013, Rolls-Royce also voluntarily supplied to the SFO reports in respect of its internal investigations into its energy, defence, civil and marine businesses. It gave full and 'extraordinary cooperation' to the SFO over the next 4 years.

On 17 January 2017, a DPA between the SFO and Rolls-Royce was approved by the Crown Court. The DPA ordered the disgorgement of £258,170,000, being the gross profit of the relevant contracts; a penalty of £239,082,645 (paid to central government, a sum reached after applying a discount of 50% for exceptional collaboration) and costs (to the SFO) of £13 million. The judge was 'satisfied that [the total figure of £497,252,645 plus costs] achieves the objectives of punishment and deterrence'. In a coordinated global resolution of the relevant conduct, agreements were also reached with the Department of Justice in the US (covering conduct the energy business in Brazil, Kazakhstan and Thailand and the use of an intermediary called Unaoil) for payment of US$170 million, and with the Brazilian Federal Public Ministry for payment of US$25 million.

The lengthy and complex indictment covered activities spanning 7 countries from 1989 until 2013 (over 24 years). The detailed facts in relation to the 12 counts of conspiracy to corrupt, false accounting and failure to prevent bribery,[15] overall comprising 'extensive systemic bribery and corruption' with a series of aggravating features, were:

1. agreements to make corrupt payments to agents in connection with the sale of Trent aero engines for civil aircraft in Indonesia and Thailand between 1989 and 2006;
2. concealment or obfuscation of the use of intermediaries involved in its defence business in India between 2005 and 2009 when the use of intermediaries was restricted;
3. an agreement to make a corrupt payment in 2006/07 to recover a list of intermediaries that had been taken by a tax inspector from Rolls-Royce in India;
4. an agreement to make corrupt payments to agents in connection with the supply of gas compression equipment in Russia between January 2008 and December 2009;
5. a failure to prevent bribery by employees or intermediaries in conducting its energy business in Nigeria and Indonesia between the commencement of the Bribery Act 2010 and May 2013 and July 2013, respectively, with similar failures in relation to its civil business in Indonesia;
6. a failure to prevent the provision by Rolls-Royce employees of inducements which constitutes bribery in its civil business in China and Malaysia between the commencement of the Bribery Act 2010 and December 2013.

Rolls-Royce had had a Code of Business Conduct (first issued in 1996), which included a prohibition on the payment or receipt of bribes. Over time, amended written policies and committees related to its appointment and payment of intermediaries. In 2007, it issued a Global Code of Business Ethics containing a specific section on bribery and corruption. From the 1996 Code, additional approval was required from a senior Rolls-Royce employee where the proposed payment exceeded 5% of the contract price (in 1996) and Rolls-Royce's CEO (2003). A ban on commissions in excess of 10% of the contract price applied from 2009. The judge found the breaches of the criminal law to be 'devastating and of the very greatest gravity'.

The company undertook a series of compliance actions. In 2013, it appointed Lord Gold to conduct an independent review of its ethics and compliance procedures and to act on an ongoing basis as a 'quasi-monitor' of its compliance programme. Changes pursuant to Lord Gold's recommendations included:

1. Enhanced policies and procedures covering high-risk areas of Rolls-Royce's business divisions.
2. Top-level commitment to ethics and compliance through improved communication and annual manager-led ethics training.
3. Development of a risk assessment framework and implementation of risk assessment procedures into business divisions.
4. Improved due diligence in respect of intermediaries comprising business justification, external due diligence, approval by an Adviser Panel (consisting of Lord Gold and both the Head of Risk at Rolls-Royce and one of its senior external legal advisers), together with ongoing monitoring.
5. Regular compulsory training on compliance issues for all staff with extensive monitoring of anti-bribery and corruption procedures, including regular audits by Rolls-Royce's Audit Committee of anti-bribery and corruption procedures and investigations of issues.
6. Implementation of compliance procedures and training in respect of concessions provided in the civil aerospace industry.

Rolls-Royce reviewed and materially reduced 250 intermediary relationships, suspending 88 intermediaries. It conducted disciplinary proceedings in respect of 38 employees, leading to 11 employees leaving during stages of the disciplinary process, and decisions to dismiss 6 employees; others suffered sanction short of dismissal. These compliance and disciplinary actions cost the company £15,175,331.46. The senior directors and executives of the company were largely new appointments made since 2013. The judge commented:

> The cultural change is evidenced by the steps which I have just described but I have pressed Rolls-Royce to disclose its present constitution and, in particular, the membership of its Board. Had any member of the today's senior management who was implicated or been in a position where they should have been aware of the culture and practices which I have described and were clearly endemic at Rolls-Royce remained in his or her position, this, itself, would have been of real significance and could have affected my approach.

The judge expressed the hope that 'the effect of the DPA is to require the company concerned to become a flagship of good practice and an example to others demonstrating what can be done to ensure ethical good practice in the business world'.

Separate criminal actions were being pursued against individuals.

Case Study 17: The Royal Free Hospital and Data Protection

The Royal Free NHS Foundation Trust provided data of around 1.6 million patients as part of a trial to test an alert, diagnosis and detection system for acute kidney injury to Google DeepMind. The Information Commissioner held: 'Our investigation found a number of shortcomings in the way patient records were shared for this trial. Patients would not have reasonably expected their information to have been used in this way, and the Trust could and should have been far more transparent with patients as to what was happening.' However, she concluded: 'There's no doubt the huge potential that creative use of data could have on patient care and clinical improvements, but the price of innovation does not need to be the erosion of fundamental privacy rights.'

The Information Commissioner concluded that the relationship was one of data controller and data processor. Thus, the data processor had not had free access to patient records for its own purposes. The Information Commissioner resolved the situation by using the opportunity to spread various aspects of good practice, through a blog looking at what other NHS Trusts could learn from this case,[16] and by asking the Trust to sign an undertaking to:[17]

- establish a proper legal basis under the Data Protection Act for the Google DeepMind project and for any future trials;
- set out how it will comply with its duty of confidence to patients in any future trial involving personal data;
- complete a privacy impact assessment, including specific steps to ensure transparency; and
- commission an audit of the trial, the results of which will be shared with the Information Commissioner, and which the Commissioner will have the right to publish as she sees appropriate.

You might like to review the series of case studies above again and ask yourself the questions that we posed just before them on issues of fairness and how behaviour is likely to be affected. You could also debate these issues with colleagues, friends and family. For example, in relation to the Rolls-Royce bribery case, how would you answer the following questions:

- Do you think this penalty will deter the company?
- Will this penalty deter individuals within the company?
- Will the changes to the internal compliance system change the behaviour?
- Will penalties against individual employees (disciplinary or criminal) change their behaviour or the behaviour of others in other companies?
- What will change people's behaviour?
- Why did Rolls-Royce's previous extensive compliance efforts not stop this behaviour?
- What is missing from the measures suggested?
- What will change the internal culture and behaviour within the company?
- Why did Lord Gold recommend 'manager-led ethics training'?

When you have read the rest of this book, come back to your answers and see if they are the same. Do you still think the same about all the other case studies?

Conclusions

1. The basis of a fair society is one that is seen to distinguish between people and organisations that are basically trying to do the right thing and those that are not, and where people who behave unethically are identified and are seen to receive a fair and proportionate response. This predictable visibility and fairness is a foundation of social living.
2. The essence of the fairness of a response to breaking society's rules should be that it is based on unethical behaviour rather than on breach of arbitrary rules that takes no account of whether it was ethical or not.
3. Fair responses need to balance all available responses—by family, social group, state, professional and employer—if they are to be proportionate.
4. Some people just break law deliberately or recklessly, say for personal gain. They cannot be trusted not to continue to behave anti-socially. We must respond to them firmly. The response needs to be fair and proportionate.
5. Actions *after* a problem must be taken into account. People should be encouraged to investigate the root causes of problems and mistakes, and share their actions in putting them right.
6. These conclusions, illustrated by a variety of case studies, are subject to further points made in the following chapters!

5

The Need for Cooperation

The first step in the evolution of ethics is a sense of solidarity with other human beings.
Albert Schweitzer

The idea of humans living together in society means that people work together rather than individually. That is the lesson from evolutionary biology, behavioural psychology and developmental ethics noted in chapter 1. As we saw there, this capacity for collaboration enables the division of labour. We are connected and everyone has a role to play. Cooperating in tasks that involve multiple people, inputs and functions is necessary to achieve effective outputs and efficiency. An obvious example of such a situation is compliance and regulation: multiple people and functions are involved in designing, sourcing, manufacturing, distributing, advertising, selling, checking, auditing, reporting, assessing, feeding back and improving. Barriers between different people involved in those processes—whether they are within groups of people in organisations or between different organisations, such as businesses and regulators—need to be overcome so that the people involved can operate on a cooperative basis if they are going to be effective and efficient. The point was made earlier that Laloux suggests that as humans have needed different forms of collaboration as societies and technologies have evolved, developing different specialisations, we have developed different ways of working together and have developed different organisational structures.

But we need to evolve further to learn to be more effective. The scientific findings demonstrate that it is only those groups that collaborate better than others that will outperform and innovate. This means looking at *how* we can improve our collaboration.

Let us look at what that idea of collaboration means in relation to people working together, first, within an organisation (not just a business, but certainly also a regulatory authority or any other body) and, second, between a business and a regulator. There is a mechanistic imperative: An enterprise will fail to achieve its maximum potential, or will fail completely to achieve its goals, unless everyone plays their part and all the components work as part of the whole. This is as true of success in commerce as it is in regulating markets, prices or safety. There is also a behavioural perspective: if systems are to achieve their potential, the people who operate them must have appropriate relationships based on trust. So what are the best cultures and structures that will support the relationships and behaviours that are needed?

Cooperation is Essential for Business

Cooperation between all those involved in an enterprise is a requirement to achieve a shared or certain end.[1] A mode of organisation is needed to enable coordinated collective action by multiple actors.[2] We will discuss in chapters 13 and 14 how businesses can cooperate most effectively. We will see that business school learning is that the companies that are most sustainable and consistent performers in the long term are those that have clear focus, and where staff have the same core values and goals, which encourage questioning and sharing information and ideas, and hence are innovative; ethical values are good for businesses that value reputation and long-term sustainability and earnings. Individuality and competition are not rejected by this approach. The most successful and visionary companies find that they compete with *themselves* in improving and innovating, and in their behaviour.[3]

An Adult–Adult Relationship

If people are to cooperate fully, they must have mutual respect. This means that the relationship must be *adult–adult*. This may not appear controversial, but does in fact represent a change from how many regulators may see themselves, namely from a position of moral and actual authority over companies. But that relationship is basically one of *parent–child*. The same viewpoint may be present within businesses between owners/managers and employees.

There is now significant evidence that values-driven enterprises succeed because employees are treated with respect. Lynn S Paine recounts that a critical element of the success of global power projects company AES was based on the founders, Roger Sant and Dennis Bakke, seeing people as 'moral, intelligent, socially inclined but individually unique and, at the same time, quite capable of error'. They built their company on the basis that all people would be treated as 'adults' and defined in their terms as:

1. thinking, creative, and capable of making hard decisions;
2. willing and able to assume accountability and responsibility;
3. unique and deserving of special treatment;
4. positively disposed to work in groups;
5. eager to make a contribution or join a cause;
6. fallible, even intentionally so at times.[4]

Treating people as adults means giving them personal freedom to choose how they behave. One example from a growing literature of how employees respond to being given individual responsibility is the story of how an individual operator initiated a personal check at the customer's premises in response to identifying a defect on the production line, recounted by Laloux and summarised in Case Study 18. This action created an invaluable impression in the customer that the supplier cared about him and his business.

It follows that the ideal relationship between regulators and businesses should also be adult–adult, and that the business should have freedom to choose if and how it achieves and demonstrates its ethical business practice (EBP). Business is empowered, but it is also accountable for its actions and it must explain the basis for its choosing a way of achieving EBP. Similarly, this applies within companies—see Case Study 27 on Northern Gas. Companies that try to micro-manage their employees through rules will get people who like to be told what to do. However, Barrett would point out that it is important to consider the stage of development of the employees that are being managed and not to assume that everyone is motivated in the same way.

Case Study 18: The FAVI Brass Foundry[5]

Laloux tells the story of the French family-owned brass foundry FAVI that today makes gearbox forks for the automotive industry and other electrical products. It has an outstanding reputation for quality and on-time delivery. Staff morale is outstandingly high and all take personal pride in the company's achievements and record. The critical change occurred in shifting from a pyramidal management structure to one of teams of 15–35 people, which self-organise with virtually no rules or procedures other than those that the teams decide for themselves. The former human resources, planning, scheduling, engineering, production-IT, purchasing and sales departments have all been rendered obsolete, their tasks having been taken over by the teams. The account manager of, for example, the Volkswagen team shares information with all members of the team on orders, and a shipment date is agreed jointly. There are few meetings, but there is constant communication within and between teams. Workers agree to switch to whichever teams need resources. There are no fights for budgets; there are no middle managers. Workers will stay late to finish jobs and take pride in the fact that everything is done well.

One story from many illustrates this attitude. When an operator on the Volkswagen team noticed a quality problem on a part, he stopped the processing and worked with colleagues to identify any other similar defects in finished pieces. Together with the client's service manager, he drove overnight in a freely available company car to the client and checked if Volkswagen had received any defective items. The client was 'flabbergasted' at this immediate response. No problems were found, but if there had been, a similar issue involving other suppliers would have involved extensive time and paperwork to resolve.

Organisational Structures

In a vertical bureaucracy, power is supposedly concentrated at the top, although elements of power are possibly delegated in decreasing amounts to lower tiers. Crozier set out a classic vertical organisational analysis of the structure of French work organisations (a clerical agency and an industrial monopoly) as existed in the early 1960s.[6] He noted the existence of four basic characteristics.[7] First, there was the creation of a vast body of detailed written and impersonal rules and procedures prescribing what is to be done in all conceivable situations. Second, decision-making was centralised, creating great distance between those who had to decide and those who had the relevant information decisions. This situation led to the adoption of an impersonal decision-making style based on abstract principles of equity, equality and precedent, and was often ill-suited to the problem that the decision was supposed to solve. Third, there was the existence of hierarchical strata insulated from each other and exerting great pressure for conformity on its members. Fourth, there was the 'creation of parallel informal power relations around the groups or individuals capable of coping with residual and unanticipated contingencies and uncertainties affecting the organization's capacity to function in a satisfactory way'.[8] Together, these characteristics created 'vicious circles' of self-reinforcing behavioural patterns. Crozier argued that bureaucracy is a mode of organisation that is incapable of correcting its behaviour in the face of its results. It created self-reinforcing behavioural patterns that reinforced impersonality and centralisation. Change would not be piecemeal or incremental, but occurred after crises.

In contrast to the ultimately sclerotic bureaucratic culture described above, a diametrically opposed mode of business organisation would reflect a flatter structure, in which power is devolved to multiple local groups. This would concentrate elements of information and authority in multiple discrete groups, so that informed, intelligent and swifter decisions could be facilitated, as would innovation. The rapid extension of new technology into all sectors of the economy in the 20th century has meant much greater devolution of responsibility inside organisations, accompanied by an enormous increase in self-employment.[9] The globalisation of labour markets and economies has introduced a raft of culturally related complexities and challenges,[10] and challenges for management.[11]

Peters and Waterman's influential 1982 management text prescribed three key features of a successful organisation:[12]

(a) An emphasis on methods to communicate key values and objectives and to ensure that action is directed towards these.
(b) Delegation of identifiable areas of responsibility to relatively small units, which are encouraged to carry out their responsibilities with considerable autonomy and scope for initiative, but are subject to performance assessments which manifest a preservation of tight central control.

(c) Use of a simple lean structure of management to avoid rigidities of bureaucracy, the complexities of the matrix and the overheads of both.

The lessons are that vertical hierarchical structures have been found to be less effective than horizontal structures; horizontal structures are also far better at supporting ethical cultures and behaviour.

Monitoring Systems: Constant Circulation of Information

Systems for corporate governance,[13] business management, compliance and risk, and regulation involve mechanisms based on the circulation of information to monitor performance, identify risks and make improvements. Examples of regulatory information systems are the pharmacovigilance system for medicines,[14] the RAPEX system for general product safety,[15] the 'safeguard procedure'[16] and post-marketing surveillance system for engineered products,[17] and 'RIDDOR' legislation for workplace health and safety.[18] The European Commission's 2013 'Effective Open Voluntarism' initiative frames effective voluntary multi-stakeholder action, in the context of a wide range of voluntary and self- and co-regulation processes, and 'profound world-wide patterns of change'.[19]

The importance of sharing information and data between regulators and across various risk assessment schemes used by local authority regulatory services has been noted and facilitated by the government.[20] This is in order to enable more accurate targeting of regulatory activities to where they are most needed, in particular to where the risks are greatest, since earlier research had found that if a business performs poorly in a business-critical activity, it is more likely to also perform poorly in other areas of regulated activity. Analysis of different regulators showed that some had information that would have been highly relevant for others, but there was no sharing mechanism or culture, or common approach.

The Cabinet Office better business compliance partnership programme, which started in 2014, was designed to make joint working between national and local agencies more systematic, to strengthen the response to hidden and illicit economic activity, and to improve how agencies support businesses to comply with regulatory and other statutory regimes.[21] The programme comprised five local authority-led partnerships across the country, which included local and national agencies that co-designed a range of innovative ways to make joint working between local and national agencies more systematic. There was considerable prior experience of partnership working with an enforcement focus from police-led programmes such as Operation Challenger (targeting organised crime). The partnership covered a wide range of issues, including misuse of commercial property through to the distribution of counterfeit goods, fraud and money laundering. The partnership combined and reviewed data and intelligence from across partner agencies to target inspections more effectively.

The partnerships developed new ways to share intelligence and compliance data, and also changed how they arranged and targeted enforcement and compliance activities, often using joint visits. Of the range of changes implemented by the partnerships, the following activities were said to have the potential to be transformative:

(a) Combining and analysing intelligence and compliance data from multiple agencies can identify those businesses that are non-compliant in multiple areas. Doing this manually is very resource-intensive. Data science tools that can access and link multiple data sets offer a more effective, accurate and efficient way of combining, comparing and analysing information from a range of agencies.
(b) When agencies combine intelligence and compliance data, and then use the subsequent analysis to target and plan their inspections, these require fewer officers per agency per visit and reduce the number of inspections that result in limited impact on non-compliance.
(c) Well-planned multiple agency visits have the potential to be more powerful than inspections by a single agency, as the full extent of non-compliance can be addressed in a single intervention.
(d) Routine, single-agency enforcement and compliance visits have the potential, with the right training and support, to become a valuable source of intelligence to exchange with the other agencies in the partnership—being each other's 'eyes and ears'.

Further recommendations were published in 2016 on improving information sharing between regulators in order to enable services to work more closely together to deliver better outcomes for business and communities.[22]

Although much of this book is about private businesses, public services are ripe for improvement in joined-up practice. Two surveys around 2015 commissioned by Citizens Advice found that as many as 15 million people who had a poor experience with a public service had not registered the problem as a complaint.[23] Citizens Advice said that complaints not only give providers the chance to make amends for the problem but also offer an opportunity to make sure the poor service is not repeated, yet this valuable feedback is being missed because some people are not complaining. It calculated that in the previous two years, 19.2 million people in England had a poor experience with a public service, such as Her Majesty's Revenue and Customs (HMRC), the Driver and Vehicle Licensing Authority (DVLA), their GP or local authority, yet only 4.2 million of them went on to make a formal complaint. Of the people who had a poor experience of a public service but did not complained, half (52%) didn't think making a complaint would change anything, whereas another 1 in 5 (19%) feared that they could be treated differently after making a complaint, and others were daunted by making a formal complaint or saw the process as too complicated.

A Cooperative Model of Regulation

Most regulatory systems function on the basis of continuous capture, collation, circulation, monitoring and evaluation of information. If a system like this is going to work, it must maximise the input information and enable experts to evaluate it. Regulatory systems are designed to involve two core groups—businesses and regulators. They may also involve others, such as assessors, auditors, ombudsmen and customers (through feedback mechanisms). In some systems, individuals within businesses or private organisations may have regulatory functions, such as qualified persons in the pharmaceutical system and notified bodies in the product certification system. Some trade associations or private bodies may perform inspection and certification functions, such as the British Franchise Association, the Lending Standards Board, the Advertising Standards Authority and the Prescription Medicines Code of Practice Authority.

It follows that if the public, business and stakeholder actors are all going to play their part, they need to work together as part of an holistic system. They might be visualised as co-regulatory or tiered components of an integrated system. But the system will just not work unless there is proper coordination between its component parts. For example, if information is not fed to the right person, incorrect decisions will be taken.

In order to learn and trust, it is important that regulators and businesses *cooperate* rather than having an adversarial and distanced relationship. The approach should be 'Business plus regulator against the problem' as opposed to 'Regulator v business *is* the problem'. Such collaboration needs to be transparent to outsiders, who should see that lessons are constantly being learned as a result of openly sharing and evaluating information and applying the conclusions. The Primary Authority scheme, discussed below, embeds collaboration between local authorities and businesses through individual agreements within which the separate and complementary efforts of business and regulator are recognised.

Tallberg argued a decade ago that what used to be seen as alternative and conflicting perspectives on compliance—public enforcement and internal management—are in fact most effective when combined.[24] This has become ever more true as regulatory systems have become more sophisticated and larger.

Co-regulatory structures can be developed to include commitment to ethical behaviour and mechanisms that generate the evidence to support a relationship of trust. Agreements can include commitments by businesses or their representatives to shoulder responsibility for significant elements of inspection and education, whilst sharing information, so that the regulator is better informed and may act in a supervisory and strategic oversight, whilst retaining the ability to intervene where necessary, backed by the ability to impose behavioural controls and sanctions where necessary. The existence and operation of the collaborative relationship must be fully transparent, allowing workers, customers, suppliers and others to see evidence of how the system operates, to monitor the accurate and reliable performance of each task, and to support earned recognition and hence trust.

Some Examples of Coordination in Regulation

The regulatory systems in which learning and maintenance of performance is critically important—such as civil aviation,[25] pharmacovigilance, and workplace health and safety—approach 'regulation' as a *behavioural* system to support people making the right decisions through constant checking, feedback and learning.

The Pharmacovigilance System: Multiple Actors

The systematic collection of information on the safety of medicines throughout their lifetime of use was developed since the 1960s and is enshrined in EU legislation.[26] The Community Market Surveillance Framework was created for the market surveillance of products 'to ensure that those products fulfil requirements providing a high level of protection of public interests, such as health and safety in general, health and safety at the workplace, the protection of consumers, protection of the environment and security'.[27] Pharmacovigilance is now clearly based on quality system principles[28] over the whole life-cycle management of the product.[29] The pharmacovigilance system is based on identifying *signals*[30] that need to be evaluated from reports in medical literature[31] and reports of adverse reactions that are collected within as large a database as possible,[32] and are then evaluated by an expert committee, the Pharmacovigilance Risk Assessment Committee, based on internationally agreed terminology and formats.[33]

Germany operated a simple system for regulation of diagnostics/biologics in the 1980s. All manufacturers submitted samples to a single test laboratory, which ran two tests on each (to reduce standard deviation).[34] Each manufacturer received its own results and the anonymised spread of general results. This is the Shewhart method of statistical self-analysis. Those who were two grades above or below at the top and bottom received a letter saying that if in the next month's results they remained two grades below or above the average, they would no longer be *reimbursed*. Hence, this system combined regulation and reimbursement. It avoided extensive rules on testing, procedures etc and was just driven by verified data about outcomes.

Civil Aviation: From Compliance-Based to Performance-Based Regulation

The safety of civil aviation rests on a number of techniques, especially the constant checking of procedures and states, and sharing of information. The system can only operate on the basis that everyone whose activities might affect safety, or who might be able to check safety, plays their part within the system. An aviation safety management system (SMS) is defined by the European Commission as:

> [A] pro-active system that identifies the hazards to the activity, assesses the risks those hazards present, and takes action to reduce those risks to an acceptable level. It then checks to confirm the effectiveness of the actions. The system works continuously to ensure any new hazards or risks are rapidly identified and that mitigation actions are suitable and where found ineffective are revised.[35]

In contrast to a quality system, which focuses on output and continuous improvement, a process-based approach focuses on monitoring performance (quality assurance activities) to ensure that the system is capable of reliably producing an acceptable level of output.[36] An SMS requires the documented, repeatable processes of a quality management system. The system is operated by each airline and is overseen by national regulatory authorities. The classic tasks of risk management are involved: hazard identification, analysis of data and risk, and risk reduction activity. An SMS comprises four components: *safety policy*, *safety risk management*, *safety assurance* and *safety promotion*.

Civil aviation safety has evolved from compliance-based regulation to performance-based regulation. The new approach was described by the Civil Aviation Authority like this:[37]

> We know that reacting after an incident or near miss is not the best way to prevent it happening again. We need to examine the causal factors more closely and transform our regulatory activities to follow a more risk and performance-based approach.
>
> Performance-based regulation (PBR) is central to EASA's and ICAO's future plans ... The PBR approach will improve the sharing of risk information and best practice.
>
> *Performance-based regulation may not always mean less oversight*
>
> The development of options to best enhance safety will often involve the identification of poorer performers. Increasing the intensity of our oversight in areas that are most likely to produce an improvement is key to the success of the risk and performance-based approach.
>
> Performance-based oversight will generate the evidence to identify where poor safety performance is endemic, and allow us to focus more regulatory effort in assuring the necessary changes are made. Conversely, we will be able to identify areas where a potential reduction in the intensity of regulatory effort is warranted due to clear evidence of good safety performance.

The Primary Authority Scheme

The Primary Authority (PA) scheme is an outstanding example of a structure that enables and encourages the coordination of multiple actors in different dimensions: at two primary horizontal levels, namely amongst authorities and amongst businesses, and vertically between the public and private sector groups.[38] It started as a means of ensuring that the decisions by over 400 different Local Authority Trading Standards and environmental health enforcers across the country were coordinated and consistent in their dealings with the multiple outlets of a single national business. This responded to the complaint that businesses that traded across the country found themselves subject to inconsistent decisions by different authorities. Thus, the national headquarters of the business group, which is in effect the regulator of all the business' local outlets, enters into a relationship with its own Local Authority, which provides an efficient communication channel that coordinates all relevant actors in the vertical and horizontal limbs (see Figure 5.1).

Importantly, businesses can obtain focused advice and on what they have to do to comply, on which they can rely (assured advice). Compliance with that assured advice would not trigger enforcement action. In other words, they can send requests for advice *upwards* to the authorities, the answers to which they can then apply. If they correctly apply the 'assured advice', their risk of prosecution is almost nil. This approach followed the 2005 Hampton Report on regulatory inspection and enforcement, reinforced by the findings of the 2009 Anderson review of guidance on regulation, which focused on the need for government to give businesses greater certainty over finding, following and interpreting guidance.[39] It encouraged regulators to increase certainty over outcomes, make guidance more accessible, provide clearer guidance, achieve consistent guidance across government and achieve the Hampton vision of a fundamental change in the culture of the relationship between regulators and businesses 'from one of inspection and punishment to one of advice and guidance'.[40] It can be seen that the 'assured advice' element is a striking contrast to the enforcement policy of some other enforcers in other sectors, where a business that admits that it has found something wrong will trigger a serious sanction.

The PA scheme is based on the idea of coordination between regulators and businesses, as an example of collaboration and of tiered co-regulation. Most importantly, it has created a *relationship* between regulators and businesses. They communicate more often and more effectively in solving issues through a collaborative approach, and this in turn tends to generate mutual trust.

Arrangements are overseen by Regulatory Delivery (RD), a directorate of the Department for Business, Energy and Industrial Strategy (RD), which approves PA agreements and their terms, and resolves conflicts in approach. Since neither expertise nor the ability to exert beneficial influence on businesses rests solely with public authorities, PA has been extended to allow certain approved private bodies, such as trade associations, to deliver assured advice (Figure 5.1). PA is currently being extended beyond the local authority community to include some national regulators.

The key components are:

- a written agreed partnership between Local Authority Trading Standards enforcement and a company—or group of companies, or (from 2016) trade associations;
- approval of the compliance plan by the Regulatory Delivery Directorate of the Department for Business, Energy and Industrial Strategy (RD);
- lighter-touch inspection and enforcement;
- direct partnership relationship between single contacts on both sides (group and authority);
- no other authority can take enforcement action without approval of the Primary Local Authority.

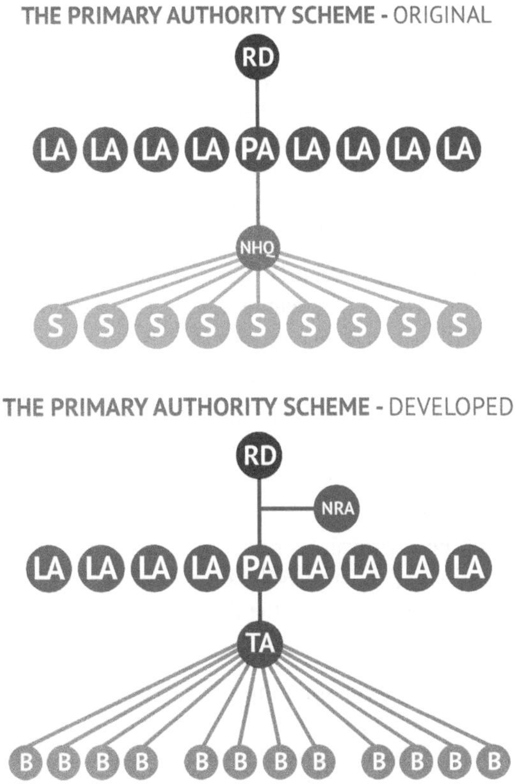

Figure 5.1: The PA scheme

Key:
RD = the Regulatory Delivery Directorate of the Department for Business, Energy and Industrial Strategy
LA = one of over 400 local authorities
PA = Primary Authority
NHQ = headquarters of a business that operates nationally
S = local shop or operation of a national business
NRA = national regulatory authority
TA = Trade association

Health and Safety at Work: Making it Everyone's Concern

EU laws, principally the EU Framework Directive 89/391/EEC,[41] impose a requirement for businesses to adopt a safety management system, appointing designated staff or external advisors to assist them with compliance measures.[42] The HSE set out in 2001 its philosophy for securing health, safety and welfare of people at work and those affected by work activities and the procedures, protocols and criteria that underpin it.[43] This gave an overview of risk and risk management, and considered issues such as the tolerability of risk, how society views risk and the precautionary principle.

The 'ultimate purpose' of the enforcing authorities is 'to ensure that duty-holders manage and control risks effectively, thus preventing harm'.[44] The 'purpose of enforcement' is to:

- ensure that duty-holders take action to deal immediately with serious risks;
- promote and achieve sustained compliance with the law;
- ensure that duty-holders who breach health and safety requirements, and directors or managers who fail in their responsibilities, may be held to account, which may include bringing alleged offenders before the courts in England and Wales, or recommending prosecution in Scotland.[45]

Enforcement is meant to be guided and calibrated proportionately by the Enforcement Manual Model (EMM).[46] The wide range of enforcement tools are selected in an ascending sequence (which corresponds exactly to the approach proposed by leading regulatory scholars John Braithwaite and Ian Ayers) in the following order:

- offering duty-holders information, and advice, both face to face and in writing. This may include warning a duty-holder that in the opinion of the inspector, they are failing to comply with the law;
- where appropriate, inspectors may also serve improvement and prohibition notices,[47] withdraw approvals, vary licence conditions or exemptions, issue simple cautions[48] (England and Wales only); and
- they may prosecute (or report to the Procurator Fiscal with a view to prosecution in Scotland).

Giving information and advice, issuing improvement or prohibition notices, and withdrawal or variation of licences or other authorisations are stated to be the main means that inspectors use to achieve the broad aim of dealing with serious risks, securing compliance with health and safety law, and preventing harm.[49] Guidance was issued in 2015 to assist medium to large employers in their legal duty to consult and involve their employees on health and safety matters, which said that they should 'consider what employees say before you make decisions'.[50]

An Enforcement Code binding on all local authorities (LAs) was issued in 2013,[51] which:

- clarifies the roles and responsibilities of business, regulators and professional bodies to ensure a shared understanding on the management of risk;

- outlines the risk-based regulatory approach that LAs should adopt with reference to the Regulator's Compliance Code, HSE's Enforcement Policy Statement and the need to target relevant and effective interventions that focus on influencing behaviours and improving the management of risk;
- sets out the need for the training and competence of LA Health and Safety regulators linked to the authorisation and use of Health and Safety powers; and
- explains the arrangements for collection and publication of LA data and peer review to give an assurance on meeting the requirements of the Code.[52]

In relation to roles and responsibilities, it said:

> 4. Businesses, regulators, and professional bodies all have a role and responsibility to help prevent work place death, injury and ill health and to apply health and safety at work in a proportionate way ...
>
> *Business*
>
> 9. Health and Safety law in Great Britain clearly sets out that the primary responsibility for managing risks to workers and the public who might be affected by work activity lies with the business or organisation that creates the risks in the first place. This applies whether the organisation is an employer, self-employed, service provider or a manufacturer or supplier of articles or substances for use at work. Whilst the primary responsibility sits with the business, workers also have a responsibility to care for their own health and safety and others who may be affected by their actions. Workers should accordingly be engaged by their employers on health and safety issues ...
>
> *Regulators*
>
> 11. The role of the regulator is to support, encourage, advise and where necessary hold to account business to ensure that businesses effectively manage the occupational health and safety risks they create.
> 12. Regulators should ensure they make best use of their resource and help improve the effective management of health and safety risks in a proportionate way. This is achieved through choosing the most appropriate way of influencing risk creators and by targeting their interventions, including inspection, investigation and enforcement activity, on those businesses and sectors that represent a higher level of risk to the health and safety of workers and the public.

Interventions and enforcement should be proportionate, 'related to the relative level of health and safety risks, including the potential or actual harm, or to the seriousness of any breach of the law', and:

> [C]an achieve this by having trained and competent officers who can exercise professional judgement to:
>
> - Differentiate between different levels of risk or harm;
> - Decide how far short a business has fallen from managing the risks it creates effectively; and

> — Apply proportionate decision making in accordance with the LA's Enforcement Policy, HSE's Enforcement Policy Statement and Enforcement Management Model. …
>
> LAs should maintain a strong deterrent against those businesses who fail to meet their health and safety obligations and put their employees at material risk thereby also deriving an unfair competitive advantage. LAs achieve this by continuing to take proportionate enforcement action in accordance with the Enforcement Management Model. LAs should publicise successful enforcement action to maintain a strong deterrent effect.[53]

The proof of the success of this approach is in the outcomes. Safety performance in Great Britain[54] has steadily improved over the four decades since comprehensive modern regulation was introduced in 1974. The number of workplace fatalities has fallen (from 651 in 1974 to around 300 in 1993/94 and 148 in 2012/13), as has the rate per 100,000 workers (from 2.9 in 1974 to 0.4 in 2013/14).[55] The number of reported non-fatal injuries to employees fell by 70% between 1974 and 2007, and fell to 78,222 in 2012/13, a rate of 311.6 per 100,000 employees (which represented a fall since 1974 of 76%).[56]

A 2016 report told the story of how HSE paid particular attention to the construction industry.[57] This sector had stubbornly high accident rates, with 35% of the national worker fatalities (nearly 900 men) in the 1990s. Traditionally, inspections had been used to intervene on a site-by-site basis, but it was realised that inspections alone by tens of inspectors would never be sufficient to tackle the scale of poor standards across the industry with tens of thousands of construction sites. The HSE adopted a new approach, which was:

> [T]o leverage influence within the industry supply chain in high risk areas, engaging and forming partnerships with parties able to effect widespread change (such as company directors or strategic bodies focused on particular interest groups or sectors).[58] HSE's role was as a catalyst, utilising its unique overview from official data of the harm being caused industry-wide and expertise in understanding reasonably practical controls (but explicitly relying on those who created the risk ultimately to control it) …
>
> The new approach centred on influencing or triggering changes, reliant on the action of others. For the theory to work in practice it was crucial that the risks to be addressed could be recognised by industry as being significant (what), and that the parties engaged with (who) were relevant and influential.

An Influence Network (IN) was created involving four layers of environmental, strategic, organisational and direct influence on construction health and safety. The most significant improvements in the IN factors were observed in organisational and strategic factors, which relate to the management of both companies and sites. In contrast, traditional site-based inspections typically targeted those factors that have a more direct impact on the health and safety of an individual site rather than those that impact on an organisation.

The general approach was identified as the cause of a significant improvement in construction safety as compared to the improvement found in other sectors. The combined rate of fatal and major injury accidents in 2012/13 in construction was 38% of the rate in 2000/01. Over the same period, the number of fatal and major injury accidents fell from 4,410 to 2,161 (a drop of 51%). In 2012/13, the fatal and major injury rate for all other industries, although improved, was still 72% of the 2001/2 figure.

Florentin Blanc has compared the enforcement policies of various countries on workplace health and safety legislation, which all have the same laws, and illustrated clearly that the difference in effectiveness lies not in the rules, but in how the authorities approach the people who have to apply them.[59] The UK's approach noted above has permanently reduced the incidence of serious safety incidents, and this approach was later followed by Germany, with the same outcome. The approach in France, however, relies on inspections and identification on non-compliance, for which penalties are imposed, irrespective of the context. The 'name of the game' in France is for businesses to pass inspections, not to make workplaces safe. Thus, the workplace safety record of France has remained one of the worst in Europe.

Conclusions

1. Advanced human societies are based on advanced forms of cooperation. We need to cooperate to support behaviour, compliance with rules, performance and outcomes. The simple idea is of a quality system that effectively captures and circulates information and allows discussion to enable monitoring, evaluation, feedback, learning and improvement. This means having both systems and channels of communication, and relationships and cultures that are effective in these tasks.
2. Some historical models are based on competition and gaming. But these interactions tend not to demonstrate adequate cooperation. The complexities of modern businesses markets and regulation need to be overcome by building cooperative approaches that cement social relationships. The best results are where members of a team compete with themselves to do better than before, inspired by their and others' achievements.
3. Mutual respect is required if people are to cooperate fully. An *adult–adult* relationship must exist, rather than public officials believing that they are the adults and businesses are children who are not to be trusted, resulting in distant, adversarial on opaque relationships in which information is not freely shared.
4. Organisational structures have repercussions for internal communication and cooperation, and vertical hierarchical structures are found to be generally less effective and not as good as horizontal structures in supporting ethical cultures.

5. Many modern regulatory systems are based on dividing tasks between multiple actors, but it is rarely emphasised that all actors need to work collectively if the system is to be effective. An example of the dispersal of functions is post-marketing monitoring.
6. Effective cooperation can be found in many regulatory systems, often supported by structures that define who does what and that support cultures in which different actors all work together to achieve mutually desired outcomes.

6

Trust Within and in Organisations

Trust is basic for human rights and democracy.

Onora O'Neill[1]

People who do not trust each other will end up cooperating only under a system of formal rules and regulations, which have to be negotiated, agreed to, litigated, and enforced, sometimes by coercive means. This legal apparatus, serving as a substitute for trust, entails what economists call 'transaction costs'. Widespread distrust in a society, in other words, imposes a kind of tax on all forms of economic activity, a tax that high-trust societies do not have to pay.

Francis Fukuyama[2]

Compliance with Rules is Socially Constructed

Compliance with rules is, to a great extent, *socially constructed*. Observing or breaking a rule is primarily a social issue, unless you are a psychopath or sociopath. We have an inbuilt tendency to conform to how our social group behaves, and follow the behaviour of people whose social approval we seek. We usually don't want to break the norms of the social group. This is true of any group—families, work units, social or sports clubs, and larger societies or nations. Each has a social identity. It is equally true of anti-social groups, such as criminal gangs and the Mafia. Solomon Asch's experiments in 1951 showed the extent to which experimental subjects would even ignore the evidence of their own eyes in order to conform. Around one-third of individuals in his study gave an obviously incorrect answer to a simple line judgement task when the others in the room gave that answer.[3]

The research of Brass and colleagues in the 1990s strongly suggested that individuals' social network relationships influence the initiation of misconduct.[4] They concluded that social networks both create opportunities for wrongdoing (when the relationships are asymmetrical, when the actors' statuses are unbalanced and where the network contains structural holes) and constraints (where relationships are strong or multiple, or the actor occupies a central position in the network, or it is dense). These conclusions have been refined somewhat, but the social network theory remains a central idea.[5] This scientifically based viewpoint departs from the viewpoint of philosophy or classical law that individuals have complete control over their actions and are entirely normatively responsible for them.[6]

So if we want to maximise compliance with a group's rules, we should aim to maximise social pressure to behave in conformity with social groups. This means that we need to strengthen working in groups rather than alone, and focus on the identification, support and leadership of groups, but we also need to have a 'value component' to maximise social pressure to behave ethically, that is, in conformity with the generally shared morality of the relevant human society to which we belong. However, let us not forget the lessons of chapter 2 regarding the need for legitimacy and fairness. This applies not only to rules but also to social norms. We need to discuss what the moral values of our group are, whether we all share the same values, and agree on what the values and rules of the group are going to be, so that we can trust each other in working together. The agreed shared values need to be demonstrated in the way we act, reach decisions and react to problems.

In the business context, the most important social groups are those of colleagues who work together. There may be many such sub-groups in a large organisation. There can be different departments spread across many locations, but each should know that the core values are shared. Internal cohesion and trust is increased through a sense of shared values. Each person and group should know that they can trust everyone else to support doing the right thing and not seek to hide or excuse or blame.

All of this fits with the ideas of the economic historian Karl Polanyi in his classic 1944 book *The Great Transformation.*[7] He said that in all human societies before the capitalist industrial market of the 18th century, economic exchange was embedded in social relationships. Since then, economic relations have escaped from social relations and we need to re-embed the economic in the social. Further, economic interests should be understood as informed by social norms and values. The social norms that embed economic activity represent collective rather than 'self-interests', demonstrating the 'primacy of society'. Social interests are not necessarily altruistic, but can serve self-interests.

Polanyi said that regulation should be viewed as an institutional component in the re-embedding of market competition in non-market schemes of coordination, thus redefining the relationship between economy and society in coping with the uncertainty that derives from the dynamics of markets. Markets are always politically embedded in legal rules and institutions. Yet they are also always morally embedded in specific values and norms that support rule compliance and trust within the particular market and social contexts.

All of this also fits with the constitutional settlement in a modern Western society that power lies with the people rather than with a sovereign, as it used to do in earlier societies. Power is de-centred and shared. It makes sense that we should strengthen structures and techniques that enable us to maximise the socially regulating effect of how people think and behave.

The Importance of Trust

> Cooperation is a frequent feature of human society; trust is the very foundation of social and economic life ... Trust is as vital a form of social capital as money is a form of actual capital.
>
> Matt Ridley[8]

This culture of mutual engagement, respect, learning and constant improvement is based on social trust—trust between people and in how people act within their organisations and systems. Philosophers[9] and business scholars[10] have emphasised the critical importance of trust in human and business relations.

The crucial element that underpins both human contracting and regulation is an ability to trust the people one is dealing with. We need trust because 'we have to be able to rely on others acting as they say that they will and because we need others to accept that we will act as we say we will'.[11]

Contracts and regulatory systems are proxies and supports for uncertainty in trustworthiness. Trust gives sufficient confidence to overcome risk and bridge vulnerability.[12] 'Trust is redundant where I have effective guarantees or control of outcomes.'[13] Trust is stronger than mere reliance, the latter being behaviour that is motivated by the pursuit of rewards or the avoidance of punishment is reliable rather than trustworthy.[14] However, it is no longer credible that compliance can be ensured by reliance on formalised structures of accountability and legal duties of accountability. O'Neill argues that:

> *[E]xcept in rare and atypical cases* (the infantile case) both placing and refusing trust is a matter of judging either *truth claims* or *commitments to action (promises)*. Trust in others' truth claims is *well placed* if their words are, or turn out to be, true of the world.[15]

Hence, in order to constitute an intelligent response to evidence of trustworthiness, adequate evidence is needed of non-self-regarding motivation and other-regarding commitment,[16] but this need not be complete evidence, let alone proof.[17] The philosopher Onora O'Neill considers that the benchmarks for intelligent accountability are *informed* and *independent* judgement of performance, complemented by *intelligible* communication of those judgements. She also suggests that we have to know both *who* and *what* we are being asked to trust:[18] the information and issue are personal and transactional. Further, the existence of placing trust invites reciprocal trust, creating a virtuous spiral; equally, a betrayal of trust can trigger a vicious spiral.[19] O'Neill concludes that the real enemy of trust is deception, because deceivers do not treat others as moral equals.

People who deliberately break the law, such as by fraud, or enter into illegal conspiracies such as a cartel, let down all their colleagues. The most important social response to that behaviour should be the one of colleagues who uphold the importance of mutual trust and who respond to the fact that they can no longer trust someone who breaks the rules. If employees are proud of the company, and identify with it and their colleagues, they will not tolerate ethical misbehaviour and are more likely to speak up to either deter or report the behaviour.

Francis Fukuyama's extensive historical study of trust in different societies concluded that: 'People who do not trust each other will end up cooperating only under a system of formal rules and regulations, which have to be negotiated, agreed to, litigated, and enforced, sometimes by coercive means.'[20] Accordingly, this legal apparatus, serving as a substitute for trust, necessarily produces 'transaction costs'. Thus, relationships or societies that are able to operate on trust, as opposed to formality, incur lower transaction costs. Fukuyama concluded that the social capital that is created within a community from the level of trust that it is able to generate, based on shared ethical values like loyalty, honesty and dependability, has major consequences for its economy. Writing in 1995, he contrasted two economic groups. On one side were high-trust societies with plentiful social capital—Germany, Japan and the US—which had the ability to create large, private business organisations and develop large, modern, professionally managed hierarchical corporations. On the other side were relatively low-trust societies like Taiwan, Hong Kong, France and Italy, which had traditionally been populated by family businesses. He concluded:

> A high-trust society can organise its workforce on a more flexible and group-oriented basis, with more responsibility delegated to lower levels of the organization. Low-trust societies, by contrast, must fence in and isolate their workers with a series of bureaucratic rules.

Experiments have shown that having strong trust between people is far more effective than trying to affect choices by the threat of punishment.[21] There is a strong popular belief in the value of punishment, but it is in fact of little value in terms of affecting future behaviour. Instead, social responses to doing something that one's group will regard as wrong are powerful, such as social embarrassment, disapproval or ostracism.[22]

Two distinguished American scholars, Philip Nichols and Patricia Dowden, summarise the importance of trust for businesses:[23]

> Trusted firms have stronger and more productive relationships with suppliers, distributors, and other members of value chains. Trusted firms receive better business terms when working with other entities. Trust enhances the likelihood of innovation and successful entrepreneurship. Trusted firms have more loyal, productive and engaged employees.

The Institute of Business Ethics in London has consistently called for ethical values to be at the heart of business. One of its many useful publications analyses how seven major organisations recovered from a major failure in public trust and how relying on a robust ethical culture was critical to their success.[24]

Evidence for Placing Trust

Trust is essential in relation to future reliance, but it is difficult to measure the likelihood of future compliance or performance and how this might be affected by unavoidable risks. Trust is a state of mind that is based on all the diverse available evidence. Hence, people and organisations should provide ongoing *evidence* that they operate consistently based on ethical values to support the independent judgement of others on whether an expectation of ethical behaviour is warranted.[25] The sources of that evidence need to be reliable and diverse, and the evidence needs to add up to a convincing and consistent picture. The approach is similar to risk assessment, being a *judgement* based on a convincing body of relevant data. The data comes from relationships, especially open relationships. If one is to build trust, one should provide verifiable evidence of past behaviour and of internal culture from multiple sources.

Mere claims by a person or organisation that he or it can be trusted will clearly not suffice. Just because we say we behave ethically is not much evidence of how we behave. But it is a statement of intention.

We therefore need to construct mechanisms by which an independent judgement may be made of whether an expectation of ethical behaviour can apply to counter-parties, regulatory scrutiny, stakeholder expectations and organisations' internal arrangements. Mechanisms producing reliable evidence of trust may include aspects such as: a deep and consistent adherence to ethical principles;[26] measurement and mapping of values and other metrics; a high proportion of satisfied customers; consistent application of compliance systems and audits; transparency; ethical governance structures; belonging to an external professional structure that has high ethical principles and provides ongoing training, helplines, auditing and sanctions; obtaining feedback such as through staff and customer mechanisms or ombudsmen; effective use of internal ethics ambassadors;[27] and structures enabling decisions to be debated to test ethical compliance, evaluated against external views and made transparent. These sources of evidence will be mutually reinforcing so as to provide density.[28] We discuss these points in chapter 14 and provide some checklists in Appendix 1.

People should be encouraged to share information on how to improve things. This will lead to better ways of doing things (innovation, improvement in performance) or learning from mistakes or adverse events (avoidance of repetition, risk reduction and improvement in performance). When determining a response to others' actions, we should differentiate between actions taken with integrity and those that are deliberately anti-social.

People can perceive being subject to 'too many' rules as sending the message 'We don't trust you to do things' or 'We command and control you to make sure these things are done'. Thus, trust is built as individuals are empowered and given space for experimentation, in a relationship in which both the placer and receiver of trust accept the vulnerability of the other.[29]

Experts in management consider that trustworthiness is based on four characteristics: ability, benevolence, integrity and predictability.[30] It has recently been suggested that it is much easier for people to assess and develop trustworthiness when it is associated with ability and predictability. In cases where trustworthiness was mainly about integrity and benevolence, some organisations made use of development tools such as master classes, activity-based learning and case studies. However, assessing these quantitatively was much more challenging and hence there was a stronger focus on making judgements based on personal interactions and having a 'sense' or 'feel' of the person.[31] The ability to measure cultural heath using tools such as the Barrett Cultural Values Assessment (CVA) supplies evidence and therefore diminishes the need for subjective judgement.

One of the underlying factors in the loss of trust in business in recent years may be the predominance of the 'shareholder value' and agency theory of corporate governance, which we will discuss further in chapter 9. It is a requirement for placing trust that a business is not seen to place the self-interest of any of its shareholders, directors or staff above any of other group, or of customers, suppliers or society. The approach is a development of corporate social responsibility, which has itself developed from the need of businesses to engage with internal and external stakeholders.[32] The UK government launched a wider initiative on social responsibility in 2014.[33] We are also seeing a growth in 'mission-led businesses' that have a central purpose of creating a positive social impact whilst still fully distributing profits.[34] The Chartered Institute of Internal Auditors (CIIA) is on the right track in identifying a number of leadership behaviours for building trust (Box 6.1).

Box 6.1 The Chartered Institute of Internal Auditors leadership behaviours for building trust[35]

— Behavioural consistency
— Behavioural integrity
— Sharing and delegation of control
— Communication
— Demonstration of concern
— Consulting team members when making decisions
— Communicating a collective vision
— Exhibiting shared values

How an organisation responds to bad news or adverse events is critical: this is true of both commercial and public bodies. Trust should play a key role here. Do the people and the organisation share the information that there has been a problem or do they try and conceal it? If they share it and work together with others to identify the root cause, then to address effectively the risk of reoccurrence, and to restore and harm done, they deserve trust rather than blame.

Aberrant Personalities: Trust and the Unemotional

We should recognise that some people are not going to respond to concepts of fairness and fair dealing. Margaret Heffernan uses the illuminating description of 'aberrant personalities' for those who are unable to make contact, hide in their offices, seek strategic counsel only from their partners, throw heavy objects at colleagues and so on.[36] Around 1% of the population are individuals who lack empathy and conscience—psychopaths.[37] Psychopaths reason but cannot feel and have limited moral control.[38] Psychopaths are over-represented in the prison population (estimated at 15–25%)[39] and among business leaders (4%).[40] Relying on self-generated emotional responses to maintain a reputation for ethical behaviour, and on social sanctions, will not be enough to influence the behaviour of such people unless they perceive it is in their own self-interest. Gold argues that such people will only ever be weakly trustworthy and that material incentives are needed to affect their behaviour.[41] In order to be ethical and healthy, an organisational culture must exclude such people from certain roles and generally from the organisations entirely. These are the people that Mary Gentile, the author of *Giving Voice to Values*, calls 'opportunists'. They are 'the individuals for whom the recruitment screening initiatives exist in order to try to avoid hiring them in the first place, and for whom the monitoring, reporting and punishment systems are designed in order to deal with them if and when they do make their way into the organization'.[42] These people will likely have a deleterious effect on those around them in a number of ways and they are often apparently successful due to their ability to hide their pathology, and are therefore difficult to let go.

Babiak and Hare point out that 'it is easy for someone—anyone—to confuse behaviour that is psychopathically motivated with expressions of genuine leadership talent'.[43] They therefore emphasise the need for robust recruitment procedures to screen out such individuals and at the same time point out how difficult this is due to the cunning and ability to lie without experiencing feelings of guilt that characterise the psychopathic personality.

Up until now, we have designed our 'compliance' systems around this small percentage of the population and have inadvertently demotivated the far larger group of basically good people who want to do the right thing by indicating that they are not trustworthy and require constant monitoring and micro-managing. We will address this problem in Part IV of this book and will indicate how to right the balance.

Shifts in Corporate Values

It is interesting to note how the relevance of trust and ethics amongst corporations has evolved through important pieces of research. Although Collins and Porras' classic 1995 study of high-achieving companies did not find that any specific ideological content was essential to being a visionary company,[44] things changed on later analysis. In 1995, they thought that the *authenticity* of the ideology and the extent to which a company attains consistent alignment with the ideology counts more than the *content* of the ideology. The highly successful companies all had an all-consuming internal vision that was shared by all staff and drove them to excel.[45] Everyone was pointing in the same direction pursuing the same vision, which, it was then thought, did not have to be ethical.

However, Collins' 2001 analysis of 'great' companies concluded that they all involved creating 'a climate where truth is heard', based on open dialogue and debate, and not on coercion or authoritarian leadership or bureaucracy. Consensus was *not* specifically sought, but discussion and challenge was encouraged. The great firms also selected people who are self-motivated (and not *de*-motivated) to work passionately within a cultural framework of freedom and responsibility to fulfil their responsibilities.[46] We will see in chapter 8 below that the analysis by Collins and Porras turned out not to be the full story, as some of their 'great' firms subsequently failed.[47] In Collins' subsequent analysis of what went wrong in these 'great' companies,[48] we suggest he may have paid too little attention to the possibility that the erosion of positive ethical values was an underlying factor in the stages of decline that he documents.

Since then, Sisodia, Sheth and Wolfe identified that the critical element in business success is an ethical culture that takes into account the needs and involvement of *all* stakeholders in a collaborative approach.[49] Barrett in his latest book focuses particularly on employee well-being as a pathway to sustainable performance.[50]

Since around 2003, a series of books have set out case studies describing companies that have adopted a values basis as their central strategy for doing business.[51] Although some corporate codes of conduct and mission statements first appeared by the 1920s, they spread during the 1980s after the adoption of the US Foreign Corrupt Practices Act and were widely adopted by the 1990s. A watershed, in the context of the Vietnam War, Bhopal (1984) and bribery scandals, was the Defence Industry Initiative on Business Ethics and Conduct, leading to the adoption of the 'Responsible Care' programme by the US Chemical Manufacturers Association, introduced in Canada 1985 and the US in 1988. The transformation can be clearly viewed as a shift away from the sole economic goal of corporations to maximise profits (and hence shareholder value), and to not only take into account but also aim to satisfy the interests of customers, staff, suppliers, local communities, the environment and other stakeholders. The rationale, purpose and hence mode of operations and organisation of an increasing number of businesses quietly changed. As Polanyi would say, social aspects are being reintegrated into the exclusivity of economic interests. Economic and social interests should no longer be irrelevant to each other, but should be integrated within a structured matrix. The next step is to crystallise this transformation in relation to the business world generally and in relation to all aspects of corporate activity—not least the relationships with regulators and the society whose public interests they represent.

Conclusions

1. Compliance with rules is strongly socially constructed. Therefore, to maximise compliance with a group's rules, we should aim to maximise social pressure to behave in conformity with social groups. In a business context, the most important social groups are those of colleagues who work together.
2. Systems that are based on rules and enforcement rather than social trust have higher transactional costs and lower performance outcomes.
3. The crucial element that underpins both human contracting and regulation is an ability to trust those we are dealing with.
4. Trust is built when individuals are empowered and accountable, and where information is shared openly and transparently.
5. If you have complete evidence, you do not need to rely on trust. But in practice, complete evidence is never available, so human, commercial and regulatory relationships need to be based on trust. Deciding whether someone deserves to be trusted is generally based upon evidence of past ethical or unethical behaviour, as the case may be.
6. We can obtain evidence of past behaviour from many sources. If we are looking for evidence of how many people in complex organisations behave, we need multiple sources of information from outside and inside the organisation. The information should show the extent to which past behaviour is ethical and how open the organisation is to improving performance by learning from mistakes, as well as the extent to which we can trust the future behaviour of everyone in that organisation in relation to how they affect people outside.
7. Track record, feedback and systems will be important, but evidence of compliance systems is less relevant than evidence of ethical behaviours that demonstrate the existence of an ethical culture.
8. Compliance and regulatory systems need to be re-focused on how they support, and produce evidence of, an ethical culture, which demonstrates itself in ethical behaviour. There is evidence that leading businesses are basing their modes of operation on ethical values with superior results.

7

How to Learn and Improve Performance: An Open Culture without Blame

We concluded in chapter 5 that in circumstances where safety is critical, it will not be possible to succeed by focusing on compliance; maintenance of performance can only be achieved by constantly checking, feeding back information and learning from errors. Here we need to focus on the difficult truth that if this approach is going to work, it can only succeed in an open culture, that is, one that does not seek to blame people for mistakes. The question in this chapter is how we should respond when things go wrong. How do we respond to adverse events, mistakes, errors, breaches of rules or what we label 'wrongdoing'?

Consider these contrasting responses to adverse events. One approach is to ask: 'Did this happen because a human was the cause, and he should therefore be blamed because he acted deliberately, recklessly or negligently?' This approach sees humans as the ultimate cause of all problems. It assumes that adverse events are only ever caused by humans and can be prevented by blaming people who cause them.

A second approach asks: 'What was the root cause(s) of an event?' Although human behaviour might be involved, the important question is what caused that behaviour to occur? Frequently, several factors will contribute to the ultimate outcome. Only after investigation, when we know what these factors are, can we try to prevent the behaviour happening again, involving the same or different people. The approach is to use root cause analysis techniques to identify one or more factors whose removal will prevent an event from recurring. This is more critical than merely to identify factors that were causal, whose removal would benefit an outcome. The inquiry identifies specifically why a hazard occurred and what factors (environmental, organisational, human, cultural etc) were root causes or causative factors. Only then can root causes be addressed, so as to reduce the risk of a similar event occurring again.

These two approaches should ring bells about what we saw in chapters 1 and 2—that humans have opposing and inconsistent genetic responses (selfishness and selflessness), and that those humans operating in some groups that rely on trust are markedly more effective than those where there is little or no trust. We should not be surprised, therefore, to see responses to adverse events that trigger responses of blame (defensiveness) and forgiveness (collaboration). The first approach is a natural reaction to our 'propensity to simplify the complex and look for associations and inferring causality'.[1]

But the consequence of a blame reaction will impede collaboration and improvement, whereas the consequence of a forgiving reaction will drive learning and improvement. We illustrate the opposing drivers and outcomes in Figure 7.1. Matthew Syed refers to these two deeply contradictory responses to failure, in which some groups have an allergic attitude to failure that produces a knee-jerk reaction of blame, whereas other groups are able to view every failure, however small, as an opportunity to learn and to be a gain in disguise.[2] Unsurprisingly, he makes an impassioned plea for a change in the *attitude* of society towards failure, and he cites a series of examples of where constant learning from failure has produced astounding achievement, ranging from the Virginia Mason Health System in Seattle to David Beckham's dexterity with a football.

The second approach recognises various truths. First, no system will be able to prevent every adverse event from occurring. Both human error and system error are unavoidable.[3] Second, there can be multiple causes of events, some of which are more fundamental than others. Third, multiple descriptions of events are plausible, so finding truth to make changes in how things are done requires multiple inputs.[4] Fourth, humans might have deliberately caused harm in some circumstances, but in (many) other circumstances, the human action might not have been the most important factor, and might be avoidable in future similar situations if changes are made. The focus should be on constant monitoring and learning from events to improve performance and reduce risk. In evaluating information on safety issues, given that humans are the least reliable part of complex systems, the objective is to aim to *design the human out*.

Blaming Prevents People Sharing Information

> [N]o one wants to put on a 'work face' when they get to the office. No one wants to leave part of their personality and inner life at home. But to be fully present at work, to feel 'psychologically safe', we must know that we can be free enough, sometimes, to share the things that scare us without fear of recriminations.
>
> Dennis Gentilin[5]

We have seen that assessment of safety or continuous improvement of performance needs a flow of information.[6] However, at this point, we must confront the fundamental truth that people will not share information if they fear that they might be blamed for something that it reveals. If that is true, it is a powerful reason why we should rethink how we work together and react to accidents.

Evidence that people will not share information if they fear adverse criticism or consequences comes from an increasing number of contexts. Researchers have found that negative experiences are much more memorable and influential than

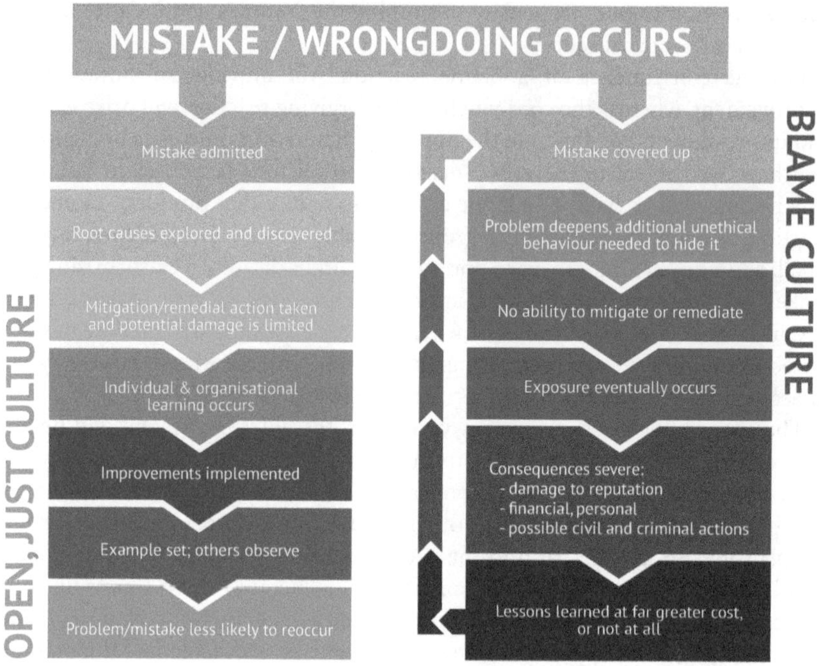

Figure 7.1: Open, just culture versus blame culture: two very different results when things go wrong

positive ones.[7] A person who feels shame may produce distancing from others, resistance and a dismissive, antagonistic stance.[8]

Professionals in generic risk management have also concluded that the flow of information that is vital to assessment of safety or for continuous improvement of performance will be impeded by a 'blame' culture.[9] A nuclear plant manager undermined efforts to promote incident reporting by punishing an employee for his involvement in a near miss.[10] Many statements have been made that individuals in the NHS will not volunteer information if they fear attracting criticism or blame.[11] We mentioned in chapter 5 two surveys around 2015 commissioned by Citizens Advice found that as many as 15 million people who had a poor experience with a public service had not registered the problem as a complaint, in which nearly 1 in 5 (19%) did not make a complaint against a public body because they feared that they could be treated differently after making it.[12]

It is universally accepted in relation to civil aviation that individuals will not share information if they fear potential adverse consequences, whether personal criticism, official investigations, criminal action, employment disciplinary action, social censure, embarrassment or simply uncertainty over what will happen.[13] 'The sheer threat of judicial involvement is enough to make people think twice about coming forward with information about an incident that they were involved in.'[14] The European Commission said in 2012 in the context of aviation safety:

> Individuals may be refrained [*sic*] to report occurrences by the fear of self-incrimination and their potential consequences in terms of prosecution before judicial authorities. In this context Member States should not institute proceeding [*sic*] against a reporter on the basis of its report, except in case of gross negligence. In addition, the cooperation between safety and judicial authorities should be enhanced and formalised by the means of advance arrangements which should respect the balance between the various public interests at stake and notably cover the access and use of occurrence reports contained in the national databases.[15]

The aviation sector has concluded that if safety systems are aimed at using information about risk, it is not enough for them to be based on the maxim 'if you have done nothing wrong, you have nothing to fear'. This approach does not overcome anxiety about a wide range of potential consequences. Instead, the approach has to be based on a 'no blame' culture if sufficient core data is to be made available. The aviation industry has therefore developed the principles of a 'just culture' and an 'open culture', adopting particular approaches to safety and accountability.[16]

The tension is 'between wanting everything in the open, while not tolerating everything', and this has to be based on relationships of trust, so that people will share their mistakes with others.[17] The culture is blame-free but not accountability-free.

The Root Causes of Accidents

We contrasted above two alternative viewpoints for viewing how adverse events are caused—and therefore how to prevent or stop them. Following one approach, adverse events are the product of human behaviour that falls into simplistic categories, such as 'human error', 'at-risk behaviour' or 'recklessness'. The assumption is that these labels are stable categories of human performance, but they can be criticised as in fact being the observer imposing a personal judgement of individual moral accountability rather than applying immutable categorisations. Another viewpoint is that consequences are products of circumstances and systems rather than human behaviour.[18]

Actions judged after the event focus on an adverse outcome that happened to occur, and this framing expands its significance.[19] This approach chimes with that taken in the report into the Clapham Junction rail crash: 'There is almost no human action or decision that cannot be made to look flawed and less sensible in the misleading light of hindsight. It is essential that the critic should keep himself constantly aware of that fact.'[20] Sidney Dekker, an expert in 'just culture', identifies critically contrasting viewpoints:

> Accountability that is backward-looking (often the kind in trials and lawsuits) tries to find a scapegoat, to blame and shame an individual for messing up. But accountability is about looking ahead. Not only should accountability acknowledge the mistake and the harm resulting from it, it should lay out the opportunities (and responsibilities!) for making changes so that the probability of such harm happening again goes down.[21]

Similarly, Syed has recently pointed to the dangers of responding to problems by punishing people:

> In business, politics, aviation and healthcare, people often make mistakes for subtle situational reasons. Increasing punishment in this context doesn't reduce mistakes, it reduces openness, it drives the mistakes underground. The more unfair the culture, the greater the punishment for honest mistakes and the faster the rush to judgement, the deeper this information is buried. This means that lessons are not learned, so the same mistakes are made again and again.[22]

As noted above, accountability comes through sharing information about failures and improvements, and a mutual desire to learn lessons.

Aviation Safety Research

Studies carried out in the US on the behaviour of air traffic controllers (ATCs) and pilots made crucial findings. One analysis found that 25% of all accidents could have been prevented if the pilot had been challenged when making an error.[23] The concept of 'destructive obedience' was found to be dangerous.[24]

We should remember that the background in the US is that violations are prosecuted by the authorities. One study looked at what happened after computerised surveillance was introduced for the performance of ATCs and pilots.[25] When performance was measured precisely (through installation of computerised surveillance), people focused their attention on the activities being measured. The number of reports of easily measured air traffic violations increased dramatically (see Figure 7.2). Further, when ATCs and pilots focused much of their attention on precisely measured activities, it did not distract them from also noticing those situations which were not being measured. Instead, the heightened awareness of the precisely measured events seems to have generalised to other similar situations.[26] Pilots also substantially increased the number of reports they filed about potentially dangerous situations that the new computer system could not detect. It was concluded that when the authority increased scrutiny on ATCs, pilots also perceived that they were more likely to be caught, so there was a dramatic increase in the volume of pilot incident reporting following the implementation of computerised surveillance.[27]

But pilots did not report through the official system and instead reported throughout to the voluntary system (ASAP). The critical difference was that ASAP did not result in any disciplinary action. The ASAP system was established by the US pilots' association and management of American Airlines as a learning-based, non-punitive safety reporting system. Its safety committee reviewed and responded to each report, recommending corrective action if necessary,[28] but did not attempt to determine who was to blame or initiate enforcement action. The Federal Aviation Agency (FAA) was prohibited from prosecuting air traffic violations based on confidential reports gathered by ASAP. It rigorously enforced the law if it discovered a potential violation from another source, such as from computerised surveillance. The FAA did not grant immunity to pilots for reporting air traffic violations to ASAP, but it substantially reduced the punitive measures for those who had inadvertently violated a federal regulation and voluntarily reported it.

A further study compared three aviation safety monitoring systems.[29] One system operated by the FAA changed its policy on whether to prosecute or excuse people who failed to report near-mid-air collisions. It first introduced an offer of immunity from prosecution for pilots reporting, after which reporting increased dramatically (from 559 in 1965 to 2,230 in 1968). It later retracted immunity in 1972, after which reporting dropped (to 231 in 1987) and remained low (see Figure 7.3).[30]

······ July 1983–July 1984, FAA incrementally installed computerised surveillance in air traffic control centres.

●●●● August 1984–December 1995, Air traffic controllers under computerised surveillance.

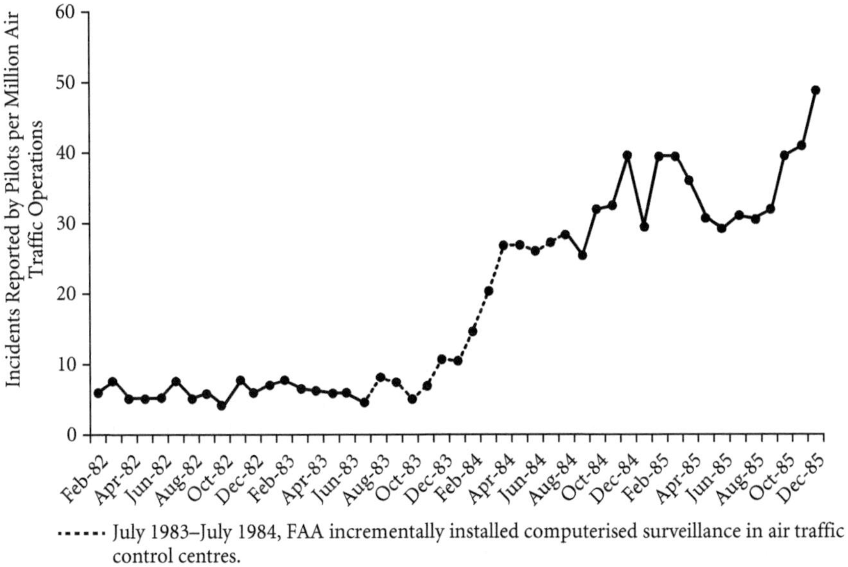

Figure 7.2: Pilot reports of computer-detected events to the aviation safety reporting system (1982–85)[31]

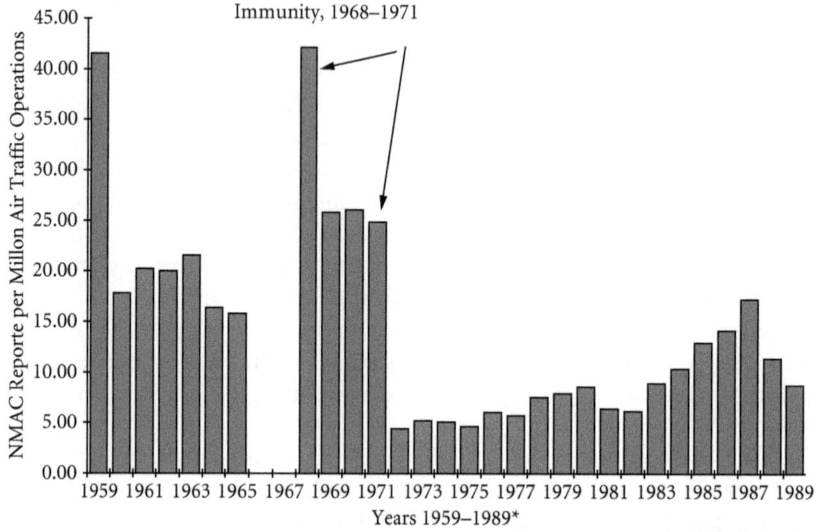

Figure 7.3: Pilot reports of Near Midair Collisions (NMACs) 1959 to 1989 and under federal Aviation Administration Grant of Immunity (in operation 1968–71)[32]

Safety Regulation in Civil Aviation

Safety in civil aviation is critical. It is essential that planes do not crash. Crashes are catastrophic for all those on board and those on whom the debris falls, and the reduced confidence affects business. Pilots do, of course, have 'skin in the game', so are motivated to maintain safety. But ATCs, engineers, maintenance and other staff involved in aviation safety do not risk their own lives. The success record in civil aviation is outstandingly high when compared with many other forms of transport or other activities such as healthcare. Airline members of the International Air Transport Association (IATA) moved 3.6 billion people in 2015 and lost a miniscule number of them. In 2012, there were 10.5 million flights in the EU, involving 925 million passengers and 14.5 million tonnes of cargo.[33]

The regulatory system includes requirements for control systems, approval of operations and key people, and reporting of critical information so that it can be expertly reviewed and key points fed back into practice as swiftly as possible. Important information is learned from speedy investigation into the causes of accidents, but this may only provide sparse learning.[34] But it is the *constant* feedback and review of information on how things work that is how safety is maintained in practice. The concept of 'compliance' has been replaced by focus on *performance*: the approach is constantly to improve how people and the system are performing in a risk-based world.

In order to maintain that flow of information, the issue that is regarded as critical is *a just culture* for all individuals involved, whether they are regulators, ATCs, pilots, corporate management or people who close cargo doors. The critical change in the approach occurred when it was realised that the imposition of sanctions for not reporting information produced the result that no information was reported, since people feared they might be criticised. The terminology has also changed from a 'no blame' culture to an 'open' and 'just' culture, as the former was regarded as too simplistic.

Just culture has now been enshrined in EU legislation:

> The sole objective of safety investigations should be the prevention of future accidents and incidents without apportioning blame or liability.[35]

> The civil aviation system is based on feedback and lessons learned from accidents and incidents which require the strict application of rules of confidentiality in order to ensure the future availability of valuable sources of information. In this context sensitive safety information should be protected in an appropriate way.[36]

> The civil aviation system should equally promote a non-punitive environment facilitating the spontaneous reporting of occurrences and thereby advancing the principle of 'just culture'.[37]

> The information provided by a person in the framework of a safety investigation should not be used against that person, in full respect of constitutional principles and national law.[38]

> ... the difficulty in capturing all occurrences ... raises the need for action in the area of the implementation of a 'just culture'.[39] Further work is required to encourage a culture of open reporting within the aviation industry and to support the development of an environment where individuals feel able to report safety significant events without the fear of reprisal.[40]

The legislation defines 'just culture' as meaning:

> [A] culture in which front line operators or others are not punished for actions, omissions or decisions taken by them that are commensurate with their experience and training, but where gross negligence, wilful violations and destructive acts are not tolerated.[41]

However, just culture draws a line between acceptable and unacceptable behaviour. 'A wilful violation is not acceptable. An honest mistake is.'[42] Standards of behaviour require professional competence, openness, sharing and taking responsibility for one's mistakes by correcting them and improving.[43]

It has also been recognised that the just culture has to apply *everywhere*: if it is not seen to be followed in *all of* the regulatory, professional accreditation, commercial and social spheres, it will not be sustained. If a no-blame culture is to be successful, blame must be removed from *all* of the relevant contexts within which people work: regulation (of entities, systems and professionals), employment, liability and social. A just culture must operate in every context: public system regulation, professional regulation, employment discipline, legal liability for compensating harm and social relationships. If there is a conflict in the approach between any of these groups, then the sharing and learning process will not work.

Full transparency is needed between operators, intermediaries and regulators, but, perhaps counter-intuitively, public confidence can be adversely affected if too much quantitative data is published. Public confidence can be maintained through transparency of qualitative but not always quantitative data.

The Current Approach of the Civil Aviation Authority

The Civil Aviation Authority (CAA) regards itself as being on a 10-year journey in supporting change in processes and systems. It was recognised that compliance with licence requirements and occurrence reporting represented only a minimum foundation for operational safety, but did not necessarily deliver the desired level of safety *performance*.[44] The CAA built on the previous compliance-based approach rather than throwing it away. It found that a rules-based system produces a response of 'How do I get round the rule?' and is backward looking, whereas a principles-based approach tries to be forward looking and encourage people to take responsibility for their cultures. An intermediate step was to create an international standard, in the voluntary IATA Operational Safety Audit (IOSA) Programme and manuals on best practices and an Organization and Management System.[45] The SMS standards were subsequently incorporated into regulatory requirements. This led to the mandatory approach of the International Civil Aviation Organization (ICAO),[46] and was a significant enabler of the performance-based regulation (PBR) approach. The CAA summarised the new approach:

> To achieve our strategic objective and to improve what are already very high levels of safety, we need to do something different. Further regulation and just doing more of what we currently do will not have the greatest effect. We know that reacting after an incident or near miss is not the best way to prevent it happening again. We need to examine the causal factors more closely and transform our regulatory activities to follow a more risk and performance-based approach.[47]

The critical component of PBR is about *building relationships*—from perceiving the regulatory–operator relationship as moving from a parent–child relationship to one between adults who have reason to trust each other. It recognises that responding to events by blaming individuals or organisations will neither improve performance nor support trust relationships. The best airlines regard it as a matter of honour to raise potential issues with responsible regulators swiftly—but also to implement solutions without waiting to be told. The risk lies first with the business, which must address it directly. In this system, it is the regulator's job to challenge, including challenging complacency (such as 'We've always done it this way'). Having a conversation that reveals disagreement is a sign of success in addressing issues. The CAA regards it as essential to talk to airlines about their culture and key personnel. Complacency and turning a blind eye are behaviours to identify and address. It finds that recording concerns expressed in minutes of meetings, which companies have later to confront and may be questioned on, has a significant effect on addressing differences of opinion.

A 2016 paper from the European Commission, based on interviews with senior airline executives, summarised a number of relevant points:

> *Safety first—but not at any cost*
>
> The senior executives interviewed discussed safety as something non-negotiable. However, there are economic and performance pressures on the industry that could soon begin to affect safety—there is less and less 'fat' in the system, and the next cost-cutting exercise could impact safety.
>
> *Maintaining safety under pressure*
>
> Following an event, there is often political and media pressure to react. It is as if a decision must be taken irrespective of whether it is the right decision. Sometimes a quick reaction is clearly the right one to take, but other times it may be better to wait for more information, or not to react. The overriding question is whether the decision or action will actually improve safety.
>
> *Accountability and responsibility at the top*
>
> The senior executives interviewed strongly emphasised their feelings of accountability and responsibility for safety, and this translated into active leadership on safety in their organisations. Regulators in particular need to be clear on their true accountabilities; if they take on too much accountability, this can disempower those they are regulating.
>
> *Searching for evidence*
>
> The rich data sources need to include talking to post holders and the frontline staff, to help detect weak signals. Quantitative data including KPIs are not enough. All the executives are relying on a rich variety of data, much of which is qualitative, in order to make decisions. This rich data flow only works if there is a culture of trust in the organisation, and a strong safety culture that ensures that safety information is fed up to the top.[48]

There is an increasing public emphasis on a 'manifestation of a more open culture'.[49] A similar approach is also spreading in the workplace safety context, although not yet so embedded:

> Leaders should pay attention to the importance of open and trusting safety communications with the workforce. Developing good working relationships characterised by openness, support and mutual respect, behavioural consistency, sharing and delegation of control as well as demonstration of concern are some factors that help promote trust.[50]

Accountability and Responsibility in a Just Culture

The internal culture requires not just sharing of information but also training, listening, prompts, reminders, questioning and the constant mutual support of all staff and managers.[51] This open culture reinterprets responsibility and accountability. Traditional conceptions involve a 'vertical' idea of responsibility being owed to a superior and enforced downwards on inferiors. In contrast, in a 'just culture', accountability is owed horizontally to one's colleagues (and family, friends, customers and so on) to be completely open in constantly sharing relevant information. It will be 'enforced' by colleagues in a social response through the immediate loss of trust on discovering or suspecting that a person has not been open. Accountability is maintained by constantly, visibly contributing to the group. It rests on the following main premises:

> The core Safety Policy is that every employee accepts responsibility and accountability for occupational and operational safety. Everyone must be responsible for and consider the impact on safety of everything that they do. Selection, recruitment, development and training of staff should be aligned with the core policy. Responsibility for implementing the safety management system is delegated to the appropriate level in the organisation.[52]

As we saw in chapter 6, the social contract of trust is broken when people act unethically or when information is not openly shared. Traditional conceptions of 'responsibility' and 'accountability' rely on authoritarian structures, naming, shaming, convicting and punishing. If trust is to be maximised, social accountability is the critical mechanism. Strong social accountability can replace traditional mechanisms of legal responsibility and punishment.

Essentially, blame is replaced by a collaborative approach to problem-solving rather than an adversarial relationship between individuals in the organisation as well as with regulators. Individual accountability is not removed, but means a responsibility constantly and openly to share all relevant information. Where that sharing ethic exists, failure to share is a serious social transgression, which is 'enforced' socially.

An approach based on learning and improvement supports a coordinated intra-company and external-regulatory response to problems that, instead of blaming, proceeds through the following steps: openly clarifying all the facts; full investigation into the root causes to identify what went wrong and how to reduce the risk that any human in a similar situation would repeat the undesired behaviour; implementing such responsive measures by all relevant actors; redressing any harm caused; and imposing professional, employment and public sanctions that respond to the degree of moral fairness. Transparency is one of the features of ethical environments.

One of the current challenges is that whilst some national aviation authorities adopt a just culture approach, some others across the world remain in punitive, blaming and deterrent mode. The latter is a serious threat to effectiveness and performance. Some authorities want to fine pilots and organisations; if they do that, pilot reporting goes down, and the airline's ability to know what its own organisation is doing in harmed.

Case Study 19: You Can Make a Mistake and Be Encouraged to Pick Yourself Up, But if You Consistently Disrespect Colleagues, You Deserve to Be Out

This story concerns a transport company in which two engineers who were working on a high platform fell off and were badly injured. Subsequent investigation found that neither of them was wearing a safety harness, in clear breach of company policy and rules. Further, it transpired that the senior engineer habitually failed to wear a safety harness, since he believed that it interfered with his work. The other engineer was a junior person who was heavily influenced by the more senior colleague. The company was concerned that its internal procedures had allowed the fact that failure to wear safety harnesses had gone unchecked, especially over some time, and 'put its hands up', responding openly in its dealings with the HSE to improve its system and performance in future. It concluded that the senior engineer's attitude was unacceptable and fired him, whilst retaining and supporting the junior engineer.

Boards and Just Culture

The Chartered Institute of Internal Auditors (CIIA) strongly supports a 'just culture' and said in 2016 that the 'just culture' that applies in aviation can be applied to other industries and sectors:

> All industries could benefit front the underlying concepts of 'just culture', namely:
>
> — The need to differentiate between wilful or reckless misdemeanours and well-intentioned mistakes.
> — The importance of applauding messengers. When the messenger is shot, learning stops.
> — Asking what went wrong, rather than who is to blame.[53]

It described the concept that should be adopted by boards of directors like this:

> Boards should try to embed a 'just culture' which distinguishes between: simple mistakes/errors; risky behaviours; and recklessness. A 'just culture' promotes an atmosphere of trust but makes clear where the line must be drawn between acceptable and unacceptable behaviour.
>
> This 'just culture' that only punishes individuals for reckless actions is intended to promote an atmosphere of trust in which people are encouraged, even rewarded, for providing essential safety-related information, but in which they are also clear about where the line must be drawn between acceptable and unacceptable behaviour, An effective reporting culture depends on, among other things, how the organisation handles blame and

> punishment. A 'no-blame' culture is neither feasible nor desirable. Most people desire some level of accountability when a mishap occurs, but they also want to ensure people are not scapegoated for things that were not their fault. In a just culture environment, the culpability line is more clearly drawn. A 'just culture' is, therefore, not the same as a 'no-blame' culture.[54]

It also emphasised that a 'just culture' needs both the employer and the employee to cooperate:

> Organisations need to have clear reporting processes and organisation-wide communication, and to provide all staff with effective training initiatives ... Staff need to feel safe but also to see what they are reporting is not going unheard otherwise they will question why they bother. Individuals can be encouraged to be open and honest about their mistakes but they need to be completely assured that it is safe to do so. Staff perception is critical—they also need to know that what they have reported has made a difference.

The CIIA suggests that 'insightful internal auditors' can assist in supporting and identifying cultures, and that a 'just culture' can be strongly supported by control technologies.[55] It argues that systems and subsequent risk reporting do not allow anywhere to hide, and the 'belt and braces' approach means that problems reported by staff members are likely to be picked up by the technology anyway: 'The technology helps them to be honest.'

An Elusive Open Culture: The NHS

It is interesting to look at a situation where the goal of an open culture has been identified but has proved elusive to establish—and why. The National Health Service (NHS) has been trying to adopt a 'no-blame' culture for over 15 years, drawing on the hugely successful approach in aviation safety. However, making institutional progress in that direction in healthcare has not happened. As major scandal succeeded major scandal in the NHS, almost every subsequent report into the causes of the problems and the actions to be taken has identified a culture of blame and fear as being at the root of bad practice, lack of team-working and failures to speak up about problems. The impediments to establishing a 'no-blame' culture are the continued existence of a 'blame culture' in one or more of the dimensions of public regulation of premises and systems, professional regulation of staff, liability for injuries based on negligence, authoritarian and hierarchical regimes within organisations, a controlling culture within NHS structures emanating from ministers and officials, and the 'blame and shame' approach adopted by the media. To those woes can be added low morale caused by perpetual structural reorganisation and funding crises.

There have been many calls for a new approach. In around 2000, there was a strong push to adopt institutional use of root cause analysis as a means of learning from problems, coupled with addressing a systematic inability to analyse and learn.[56] The 2001 Bristol Royal Infirmary inquiry called for 'a new culture of trust, not blame' and 'the abolition of clinical negligence litigation, taking clinical error out of the courts and the tort system'.[57] The Chief Medical Officer instigated a move away from medical negligence as the sole response to injuries,[58] which led to the NHS Redress Act 2006, but it has not been implemented in England, and its partial implementation in Wales has not proved to be a success.

The 2015 Morecambe Bay hospitals maternity review, despite finding a 'seriously dysfunctional' maternity service at Furness General Hospital, adopted a clear distinction between errors and concealment:

> We make no criticism of staff for individual errors, which, for the most part, happen despite their best efforts and are found in all healthcare systems. Where individuals collude in concealing the truth of what has happened, however, their behaviour is inexcusable, as well as unprofessional.[59]

The overall verdict on Furness General Hospital was:

> What is inexcusable, however, is the repeated failure to examine adverse events properly, to be open and honest with those who suffered, and to learn so as to prevent recurrence.[60]

Similarly, the 2014 report into two Welsh hospitals warned the public, the media and politicians against responding to its critical findings by attributing blame:

> The Review Team is concerned that this Report may be seen by some, and be reported by others, as evidence of failure and incompetence which should result in a search for 'the guilty' and for 'heads to roll'. This is the current bullying language frequently used to vilify those with responsibility for services and care in the NHS and other public services ... in every organisation providing services to the public, there will be lapses in standards and practice in some way ... It is very important to say this, in this report, which is about services provided by local people to fellow citizens in their own community. Local and national governance arrangements should provide the reassurance to the public that care and treatment issues ... are routinely identified and action taken without recourse to one-off external reviews.[61]

The need to view human actions in the context of wider factors was emphasised in 2014 by Professor Norman Williams, President of the Royal College of Surgeons, and Sir David Dalton, Chief Executive of Salford Royal Hospital, when calling for a 'duty of candour' to be re-emphasised in the NHS, through training and supporting staff, improving the levels and accuracy of reporting of patient safety incidents, and spreading and applying lessons learned into practice.[62] These authors commented:

> While there can be a degree of individual responsibility when something goes wrong (and that is certainly how it feels to the practitioners concerned) it is vital for investigations of harm to consider the human factors in the context of team, organisation and system factors. This is not only because it is a fair and balanced way of understanding individual responsibility, but also because it provides a far firmer basis for understanding why harm has occurred and therefore of preventing future harm. Individual cases of

> harm, rightly considered, can provide insights into wider organisational issues that can contribute to harm, such as loss of notes, the poor management of resource pressures, and shortcomings in discharge processes.[63]
>
> A compliance-focused approach will fail. If organisations do not start from the simple recognition that candour is the right thing to do, systems and processes can only serve to structure a regulatory conversation about compliance. The commitment to candour has to be about values and it has to be rooted in genuine engagement of staff, building on their own professional duties and their personal commitment to their patients.[64]

The 2015 Francis Report into whistleblowers in the NHS, arising after the Mid-Staffordshire Hospitals scandal, said that:

> [W]e have seen cases where a culture of blame leads to entrenched positions, breakdown of professional relationships and considerable suffering, utterly disproportionate to the nature of the problem from which this process originated …
>
> The overarching principle is that every organisation needs to foster a culture of safety and learning in which all staff feel safe to raise a concern.[65]

However, the House of Commons Public Administration Select Committee rightly noted in 2015 that:

> An unresolved tension between the desire for an open 'no blame' culture and the demand for the clear accountability the public is entitled to expect from a public service.[66]

In 2016, the 'no-blame' rationale was clearly stated in documents setting out the rationale for introducing a new investigatory body, the Independent Patient Safety Investigation Service (IPSIS), modelled on the airline industry's Air Accident Investigation Branch, on the basis that a 'no-blame' learning culture in aviation had led to dramatic reductions in both fatalities and cost 'and we now need to do the same in healthcare'.[67] The Secretary of State said:

> But if we are really to tackle potentially avoidable deaths, we need culture change from the inside as well as exhortation from the outside. A true learning culture has to come from the heart. And this means a fundamental rethink of our concept of accountability.
>
> Time and time again when I responded on behalf of the government to tragedies at Mid Staffs, Morecambe Bay, Winterbourne View, Southern Health and other places I heard relatives who had suffered cry out in frustration that no one had been 'held accountable'.
>
> But to blame failures in care on doctors and nurses trying to do their best is to miss the point that bad mistakes can be made by good people. What is often overlooked is proper study of the environment and systems in which mistakes happen and to understand what went wrong and encouragement to spread any lessons learned. Accountability to future patients as well as to the person sitting in front of you.
>
> The rush to blame may look decisive. It may seem like professionals are being held accountable. In fact, the opposite can happen. By pinning the blame on individuals, we sometimes duck the bigger challenge of identifying the problems that often lurk in complex systems and which are often the true cause of avoidable harm.[68]

A major justification for the creation of IPSIS was to address the causes of safety incidents, echoing the approach of civil aviation safety:

> Safety issues and related incidents are often the result of complex local, organizational and system-wide processes, with similar events recurring repeatedly in different places across the healthcare system. The purpose of safety investigation is to understand the patterns of causality that produce harm, and to make recommendations that can address those causes across the healthcare system in order to improve the safety of all patients.[69]

Under the heading 'Promoting a just culture', the policy report continued:[70]

> The purpose of safety investigation is to identify and explain the circumstances that lead to harm, in order to develop recommendations to improve safety in the future. This is only possible with the active, honest and open engagement of healthcare professionals. This is essential to ensure that the underlying causes of harm have been fully uncovered, to bring about changes in processes and practices to improve safety, and to provide patients and families with full and truthful accounts of past events.
>
> Securing the trust and confidence of healthcare professionals depends on establishing a 'just culture'. A just culture is one in which healthcare professionals are able to report safety incidents, and participate in safety investigations secure in the knowledge that they will not be inappropriately blamed or penalized for any actions, omissions or decisions that reflect the conduct of a reasonable person under the same circumstances.
>
> The vast majority of safety incidents are associated with inadvertent or unintentional errors on the part of caring and committed staff. These errors are typically provoked by poorly designed systems, equipment, or work contexts. A just culture depends on establishing a clear distinction between the 'honest mistakes' of well-intentioned healthcare workers where punitive responses are neither warranted nor helpful; and the rare acts that involve reckless neglect or mistreatment.[71]
>
> Although it will not be the responsibility of the Branch to deliver this change, which is the responsibility of all NHS bodies, it must promote a just culture across the healthcare system, and contribute to it by ensuring that staff involved in investigations led by the Branch are secure in the knowledge that they will not be blamed for events that involve 'honest mistakes' and have been openly shared. This must include mechanisms to protect staff from unwarranted blame by others on the basis of the information provided during an investigation. This has been described as providing a 'safe space' in which staff can participate fully and without fear.
>
> The creation of a just culture is vital in gaining the trust of healthcare professionals. The trust of those affected by safety incidents is equally vital, and it is important that a just culture also recognises those rarer incidents of individual culpability.
>
> ...
>
> For staff, trust will depend principally on knowing that they will be treated fairly and not blamed for genuine mistakes. They must feel safe from unwarranted blame when taking part in an investigation. We are struck by work that has shown that the most effective learning takes place in conditions of psychological safety, characterised by a shared belief that participants will not be embarrassed, rejected, or punished for speaking up.[72]

The statements quoted above all seem to us to point in the right direction. The difficulty is in achieving the ideals set out here in practice. Some major impediments are: the sheer size of the NHS, which produces the impression in those on the front line that they are run by distant political masters who have no understanding of what is needed to make things work in daily practice; the existence of several hierarchies, such as amongst different professions (eg, surgeons, anaesthetists, nurses, pharmacists and auxiliaries) and managers (eg, administrators, consultants, registrars and others); the continued existence of unrealistic performance targets rather than behavioural targets; and an ongoing fear of criticism and blame, whether from inspectors, employers, the media or lawyers.

These impediments prevent genuine collaborative teamwork in many NHS units. For example, the need for a consistent and comprehensive 'no-blame' culture has implications of fundamental importance for systems that seek to resolve disputes. The application of rules or processes based on blaming people will deter the flow of vital information and will prevent the achievement of safety and improved performance. The insight arises at a point in time when less adversarial mechanisms are spreading in relation to delivering compensation, such as consumer alternative dispute resolution (ADR) or ombudsmen and online dispute resolution (ODR)[73] and 'no-blame' administrative compensation schemes.[74]

An open approach could have been applied in financial services by triggering review of simple questions such as 'Is this practice ethical?', 'Is this product in the best interests of the customer?' or 'Does this customer need this product?' This is an approach that could transform the NHS.

The Importance of an Educated Public Response

The public (media, reputational and regulatory) response to how the organisation has responded is itself critical. Responding to people who are trying to do the right thing by blaming or punishing them is not fair and will itself destroy trust and stifle people being honest and achieving improvements. The response to blame people is triggered by the ancient defensive gene that is in us, but we need to control that response if we want to respond fairly and encourage collaborative learning and improvement. If we are to learn and improve, the blame response has to be resisted and replaced by the trusting response to those who have tried to act ethically. Even in deterrence-dominated US, an influential body of financial associations have advocated reliance on teamwork, helping and relying on one another to solve problems.[75] In responding to adverse events, we should not hide problems, but should share the information, rectify things and seek solutions to improve things in future.

Conclusions

1. Blaming people prevents information flow. People who fear being blamed hide the truth from themselves and others.
2. If we want to learn, improve and maintain performance, we must shift from a blame culture to an open and just culture. Effective root cause analysis is not possible without an open and just culture.
3. Recent pronouncements in the corporate governance field support the notion that boards have a role in supporting the development of a just culture.
4. This shift has been carried out with enormous success in some systems, notably aviation safety. The lessons on how to do it are all there to be copied. However, some institutions are still mired in blame cultures and their consequences.

8

Why Should We Be Ethical? Ethical Business Practice as Sound Commercial Strategy

> When the 'ethical culture' component of a business firm's overall culture is strong—when norms and other things guide people in that firm to make sound ethical and social decisions—the firm benefits in two ways: it enhances the positive and controls the negative.
>
> Philip Nichols[1]

> If you see anything whose propriety or legality causes you to hesitate, be sure to give me a call. However, it's very likely that if a given course of action evokes such hesitation, it's too close to the line and should be abandoned. There's plenty of money to be made in the center of the court. If it's questionable whether some action is close to the line, just assume it is outside and forget it.
>
> Warren Buffett[2]

The Social Licence to Operate

One theoretical approach seeks to balance or reciprocate the receipt by businesses of privileges from society, as part of a social licence to operate.[3] This draws historically on Rousseau's social contract theory, revived in terms of corporate citizenship under the influence of John Rawls[4] and Amartya Sen.[5] Scholars have applied the idea of a social licence to operate in relation to corporate environmental responsibility.[6] For example, the crumbling of trust in financial services as a sector destroys its social licence to operate.[7] Relationships based upon trust incur lower transaction costs, as we said in chapter 6.

The social licence can be seen in the Corporate Social Responsibility (CSR) movement, being the alignment of business operations with social values,[8] driving the increasing importance of a strategic approach to the competitiveness of enterprises. 'CSR in its core is nothing more than decent business, perceived as such by society.'[9] CSR has proliferated through internationally recognised principles and guidelines, in particular the recently updated OECD Guidelines for Multinational Enterprises, the ten principles of the United Nations Global Compact,[10] the OECD Guidelines for Multinational Enterprises,[11] the ISO 26000 Guidance

Standard on Social Responsibility,[12] the ILO Tripartite Declaration of Principles Concerning Multinational Enterprises and Social Policy,[13] and the United Nations Guiding Principles on Business and Human Rights.[14] The United Nations Global Compact adopts an essentially self-regulatory model towards sustainability, with civil society as the corporate watchdog.

An increasing number of companies have adopted clear and strenuously supported policies of 'doing the right thing', on the basis of 'enlightened self-interest' and gaining competitive advantage. Over 8,000 companies in over 160 countries have adopted the UN Global Compact, which is based on operating with integrity in human rights, labour, environment and anti-corruption.[15] The UN Global Compact states: 'Corporate sustainability starts with a company's value system and a principled approach to doing business … By establishing a culture of integrity, companies are not only upholding their basic responsibilities to people and planet, but also setting the stage for long-term success.'[16]

The UK government built on the established foundations of corporate *social* responsibility as part of its response to the 2008–12 financial crisis[17] by launching a generalised initiative on *corporate responsibility* (CR) in 2013. It defined CR as the voluntary action businesses take over and above legal requirements to manage and enhance economic, environmental and societal impacts.[18] The policy issued in 2014 noted that CSR had evolved from philanthropy to a core activity for an increasing number of businesses, and 'from how businesses spread their money to how they earn it'.[19] This transformation had been supported by wider realisation of the economic benefits to businesses, such as: staff recruitment and retention; managing risk in supply chains; driving innovation and productivity; and opening up new markets and new business models.[20] The World Wildlife Fund said in 2017 that self-regulation by large companies through credible standards (such as the MCS standard for fish or the Soil Association standard for organic production) had a key role to play in tackling social and environmental issues in supply chains and wider society in order to achieve official Sustainable Development Goals.[21]

Job Satisfaction, Focus and Efficiency

As we noted in chapter 5, business schools have found that companies do best in the long term if they have a clear focus and are based on shared values.[22] Firms achieve long-term sustainability through adopting core unified ideology and goals, and the ability to change everything else. But the latest research has refined the point and finds that the focus must be specifically values-based, where the values are ethical.[23] Those businesses that are values-based provide clear powerful focus for all employees and produce strong local empowerment. The Chartered Institute of Personnel and Development summarised the position:

> Positive and aligned corporate cultures can motivate employees to perform and engage with their work, align behaviours to common values and purpose, share knowledge and insights, be more productive and responsive, and build trust. However, when toxic,

culture can cause significant issues for the business and its employees, leading to low performance and morale, high levels of staff turnover, and in some circumstances, significant harm to the organisation and to the well-being of employees.

Edmans has pointed out that historical theories of business that focused on the use of capital in which employees performed unskilled tasks[24] led the stock market to undervalue companies that focus on human relations and staff satisfaction.[25] He contrasted this with more recent business models emphasising quality and innovation that rely on human capital and hence need motivation and retention of staff.[26] Edmans found that firms with high levels of employee satisfaction generate superior long-horizon returns.[27] Extensive studies have demonstrated that strong ethical culture increases staff loyalty and commitment, increased job satisfaction and a reduction in bad behaviour.[28]

A study of firms in the Standard & Poor's (S&P) 500 by Guiso, Sapienza and Zingales in 2013 found that high levels of integrity of management as perceived by the employees were positively correlated with good outcomes, in terms of higher productivity, profitability, better industrial relations and a higher level of attractiveness to prospective job applicants.[29] However, there was very little evidence that merely 'advertised' values correlated with performance. Nevertheless, when employees felt that senior managers were trustworthy and ethical, performance was stronger.

Thus, it is not enough for a firm to claim to have values—a company must actually live those values and employees must see this. An interesting finding was that firms advertising the value of integrity and those with a higher principal component of advertised values had a significantly higher customer satisfaction index. This may indicate that customers place greater importance on culture and values than the market. Guiso's team concluded that companies making decisions to maximise the current stock market value will underinvest in integrity, which has a clear short-term cost but only limited benefit. In contrast, maintaining a culture of integrity may have some short-term costs (the forgone profit today), but also many long-term benefits. The study concluded that on average, a culture of integrity adds value and that on average, this culture is weaker among publicly traded companies.[30]

The Financial Rewards of Ethical Culture

In 2016, the Chartered Institute of Internal Auditors quoted a case study of Alcoa (a global steel manufacturer), which focused all its efforts on one routine: reducing days lost through injury. This focus on safety culture was found to have two consequences: first, Alcoa went from 1.86% lost work days (already well better than average) to 0.1%; and, second, profits grew from $264 million to $1.4 billion (with a tenfold rise in market capitalisation).[31] Similarly, the Chartered Institute of Personnel and Development said:[32] 'There is much research evidence that shows that organisations with more positive cultural attributes will perform better over the long term.'[33]

A Gallup study found that organisations with highly engaged employees have 3.9 times the earnings per share growth rate compared with organisations with low engagement in the same industry.[34] Data from 5,000 German establishments demonstrated that firms that adopt trust-based work contracts tend to be between 11 and 14% more likely to improve products.[35] The same positive relationship was found in relation to flexible working time arrangements.

One can easily imagine the underlying reasons for this superior performance. Engaged employees will go the extra mile for the organisation. They are less likely to tolerate misbehaviour by colleagues and are more likely to speak up. Also, a company selling its products and services based on merit will foster innovation. A culture of innovation requires openness and empowerment, and will generate and benefit from the extra commitment from engaged employees.

An ethical value-driven culture is good for business.[36] There is ample evidence of this. In 2003 Lynn S Paine demonstrated that 'ethics and economic advantage often do go hand in hand'.[37] Moreover, she pointed out that 'ethics counts' is a better slogan than 'ethics pays'.[38] An 'ethics counts' philosophy is an 'approach that recognises the intrinsic worth of values and take moral considerations seriously in their own right'.[39]

A company that gains business through bribery is unlikely to have the best product on the market. Innovation will cease to be a priority and the company will likely lose out to others that have focused their resources on continuous improvement rather than corruption. Similarly, such a company is unlikely to hold on to high-performing ethical employees, as they will not wish to risk their own careers and compromise their personal values. A company with a corrupt culture will inevitably be exposed and may even fail and destroy the reputations of those still employed there with it, regardless of whether they were involved in or aware of the wrongdoing.

Economist John Kay observes that the most profitable businesses are not the most profit-orientated and argues that happiness is not achieved through the pursuit of profit ('Happiness is not a red Ferrari').[40] Similarly, Colin Mayer of the Oxford Saïd Business School points out that shareholder value is an outcome, not an objective.[41] Mayer suggests that the reason why senior executives insisted on paying themselves so much was to sustain their sense of their own importance ('bonuses come to matter as much for the kudos they confer as the cash they generate').[42] Wealth creation is a collective effort.[43] Erhard and colleagues think that adherence to integrity acts as a commitment not to engage in economic calculations.[44]

In 2014, Sisodia, Sheth and Wolfe published an analysis of 57 US public and private companies, and 15 companies from other parts of the world, which they identified as operating as 'firms of endearment' that adopt a comprehensive approach of delivering the needs of *all* their stakeholders (see chapter 13 below). It showed cumulative shareholder returns for these 'firms of endearment' over 15 years were 1,681% and 1,180% respectively, as against the S&P 500 companies' rate of 117%.[45] They called culture—and, in our terminology, this is ethical culture—the secret ingredient, and society the ultimate stakeholder.

EY's 2016 survey of 100 board members of FTSE 350 companies found that 92% said that investing in culture had improved their financial performance,

55% believed that investing in culture had increased operating profits by 10% or more, and 86% said that culture is fundamental or very important to strategy.[46] These findings are illustrated in the two graphics in Figure 8.1.

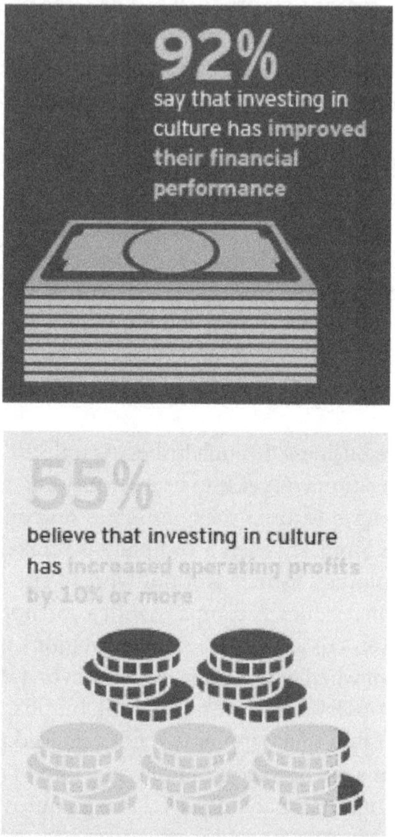

Figure 8.1: Graphics on the findings on corporate culture, EY 2016 survey of FTSE 100 companies' boards[47]

In 2016, the Institute for Business Ethics said that there is a clear correlation between customer satisfaction and financial results. It cited an example from the food sector: firms with a score in the UK customer satisfaction index of one percentage point above the average or more saw their sales rise 17% in the year to October 2015. Those within a point of the average saw their sales rise 3.8%, and those more than a point below the average saw their sales fall by 0.4%.[48]

The most recent evidence comes from a 2017 McKinsey study of 600 firms, which showed that an elite of 27% of them that focused on the long term performed better than the 73% who were short-termist.[49] The former group had an average growth in market capitalisation of $7 billion more than that of other firms between 2001 and 2014, and added nearly 12,000 more jobs on average than other firms from 2001 to 2015. However, it also found that short-termism (analysed as low investment, cutting costs to boost margins, repeated buy-backs, booking sales before customers had paid, and hitting quarterly profit forecasts) is increasing. Across the same period, McKinsey found the following differences between its groups of short-term and long-term companies:[50]

— Average company revenue	47%
— Average company earnings	36%
— Average market capitalisation	58%
— Average company economic profit	81%
— Average job creation	132%

A business that systematically takes decisions on the basis of ethical business practice may inherently involve some cost and loss of profit, at least in the short term. Is it worth it? One could argue that the calculation may depend on whether the business has a short-term or long-term commercial strategy. However, this would be a short-sighted viewpoint. Any short-term gain obtained by corruption is bound to have a myriad of consequences in the organisation.

Ethical Business Practice as a Sound Regulatory Strategy

It follows from what is said above that there is a strong case for ethics in organisational practice as the basis for a sound regulatory strategy, for encouraging businesses to operate and to provide evidence of their profound commitment to all-pervasive ethical business practice, and for regulatory bodies to promote, encourage and reward demonstrable ethical cultures by businesses. It is also a fundamental requirement that regulatory bodies should themselves behave—and be seen to behave—ethically and fairly in all their activities. Indeed, it can be predicted that if there is *not* an alignment between the ethical values of society and those of either or both of businesses and enforcement authorities, not only will (sometimes very serious) problems of non-compliance continue to arise and not be identified quickly enough, but achievable improvements in conformity, performance, innovation and growth will also not be made.

We will build on these points in chapter 11 on the reasons for EBR. A business that aims to live by EBP should inherently have a good relationship with regulators and enforcers. This should lead to sharing and solving problems quickly, and the consequence should be lower fines than for a business whose motivations are not clearly ethical or that hides wrongdoing. Redress should still be paid, but transactional costs should be reduced and corporate reputation should be enhanced rather than damaged.

Bringing activities on *all* relevant aspects of regulatory compliance under a single ethical framework should result in increased efficiency, better compliance outcomes, and lower costs of investigating and rectifying non-compliance.

Being Unethical Causes Damage

Moving to the negative case, a business that fails to behave ethically in a society where such behaviour is expected can expect to suffer serious reputational and commercial damage when its behaviour is made public. In simple terms, ethics are increasingly recognised as required for sustainable business in an increasingly open society. In fact, such organisations may suffer hidden damage even before any public exposure; in addition, qualified individuals who operate on the basis of ethical values become uncomfortable and leave.

There are many recent examples where questionable activities have damaged reputation (recently, for example, phone hacking by journalists, Volkswagen (VW) and fraud in emissions, Rolls-Royce and bribery of foreign purchasers, Tesco and late farmers' payments, various multinationals and fair tax payments, FIFA and the International Association of Athletics Federations (IAAF) and bribery, mis-selling by banks, rate-fixing by financial institutions, and doping in cycling). These cases demonstrate a series of adverse consequences: reputational damage, consequential subsequent difficulty in trading, problems in staff morale, employee engagement and recruitment, direct costs of large fines and damages, followed by increased insurance premiums. The list, sadly, is endless.

Huge companies can suffer significant damage as a result of the actions of one person, or a small number of people, such as at VW, which has resulted in a fine of \$14.7 billion in the US to date, \$10 billion spent on buying cars back from owners and compensating them, and \$4.7 billion spent on environmental projects. Proceedings are ongoing in Europe and the final cost of their behaviour is still unknown. It remains to be seen how many people were involved in bribes paid by Rolls-Royce in a dozen countries over 24 years, resulting in fines and payments under DPAs of £671 million to authorities in the US, the UK and Brazil in January 2017.[51]

The OECD noted in 2015:

> When detected, misbehaviour causes direct and indirect costs for companies, including reputational damage and loss of customers, among others. There indirect losses are harder to measure externally than direct penalties, for which there is more information available. According to Global Investigations Review, of the world's 50 largest corporate penalties imposed since 1990, most of them by US enforcement agencies,[52] 42% of all cases and 64% of all fines were imposed only in 2013 and 2014 (Figure [8.2]).[53] Six of the 41 companies on the top 50 list appear more than once; one appears four times and tops the list of total fines. Meanwhile, those that aim to behave responsibly pay the price by operating in distorted and distrustful markets, as well as by shouldering increased compliance costs caused by some of their competitors' wrongdoing.[54]

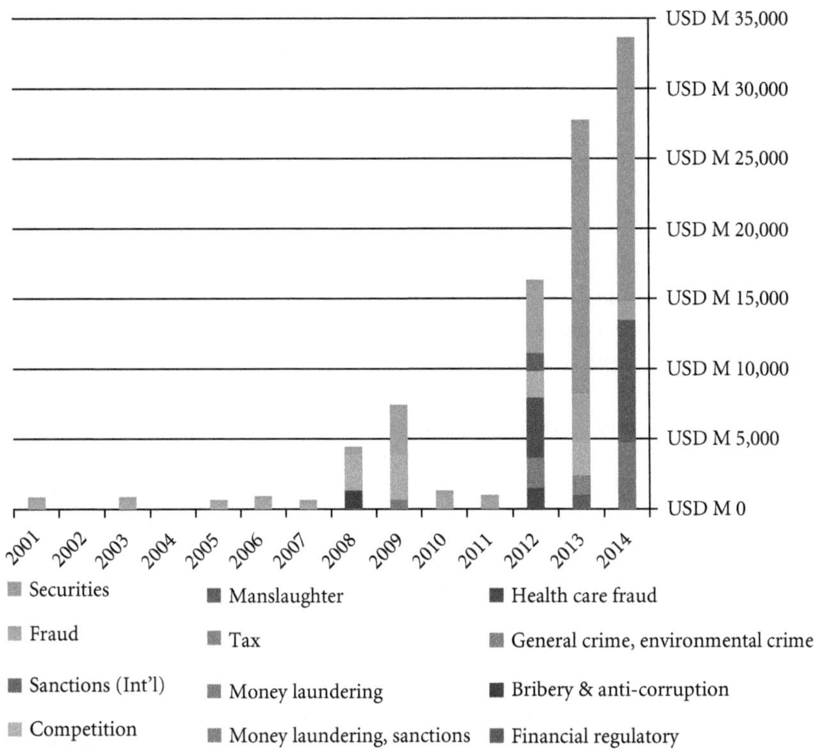

Figure 8.2: Top 50 corporate fines, per type of infraction and year (2001–14)

A 2014 report on by the European Systemic Risk Board shows that penalties applied to banks for misconduct reached €163 billion over the past five years, arguing that they potentially create systemic risks on their own.[55]

... Standard Chartered ... in 2012 paid a $340 million fine for money laundering failings and agreed to a series of remedial actions.[56]

The impact of misconduct and sanctions over firms' valuations is also visible, not always in the form of a clear drop in share price (Thompson Reuters-Accelus, 2014) but via increased volatility (Eccles, Ioannis and Serafeim, 2011) and a change in the landscape of investors, often leading a shift from long-term to more opportunistic and risk-averse shareholders. As stated by a high-profile fund manager in the face of allegations of misconduct in one of the companies in his portfolio, the decision to disinvest was based on this added risk.[57]

Finally, senior managers and board members are also increasingly being held accountable for their company's misbehaviour in some sectors, particularly the financial sector, via personal liability, including the adoption of claw-back provisions to recover corporate bonuses paid for periods where misbehaviour is subsequently discovered, and forced changes to management teams[58] to add skills related to compliance and risk.

According to a 2014 OECD analysis of the 427 foreign bribery cases concluded since the entry into force of the OECD Anti-Bribery Convention, more than half were carried out with the involvement of some level of management—sometimes even the CEO.

Conclusions

1. There is ample and growing evidence that values-driven businesses are more successful and sustainable than others.
2. This is not just because getting caught behaving unethically can severely damage the reputation and financial health of an organisation or even cause it to fail (in the case of Arthur Andersen, the loss of trust resulted in the collapse of the partnership altogether).
3. This is also because values-driven organisations engage the discretionary energy and enthusiasm of staff (as well as all other stakeholders) in achieving the organisation's ethical objectives. It is in everyone's interests to encourage a focus on values, culture and higher purpose.
4. This conclusion has implications for any organisation—public or private—and also for the organisations that inter-relate with them, such as regulators, in relation to their own cultures.
5. Unethical behaviour causes considerable damage not only to the organisation itself, but also to individual employees involved and other stakeholders. We should therefore ensure that we respond firmly to unethical behaviour. Being unethical should be unacceptable and should attract adverse consequences in terms of reputation, responsibility to put right harm caused and relevant sanctions.

Part II

Where We are Now

9

The Status of Corporate Governance

Having reviewed the status of the ideas and evidence on why and how things ought to operate in an ethical business world, we now summarise the status of the thought-leadership within the corporate world on best practice on governance. This will identify the current requirements on culture and ethics for boards of directors and companies. We will find the emergence of a strong focus on corporate culture, but only a tentative focus on ethical values. But first we should ask whether it is possible to balance profits and ethics. Is capitalism inherently incompatible with ethical business practice? No, it isn't.

The Conflict between Ethics and Profits

> Money blinds us to our social relationships, creating a sense of self-sufficiency that discourages cooperation and mutual support.
>
> Margaret Heffernan[1]

The question of the role of business in society underlies much of the change that we are documenting and advocating in this book. A critical issue that we need to confront is whether business can ever be ethical, given the inherent conflict that is faced between doing the right thing and making a profit, so as to hit targets in making returns, and maintaining employment and growth in owners' incomes, bearing in mind the effect that that has on pensions and investments.

If making money is inconsistent with always doing the right thing, then Western capitalism is doomed. However, the shifts in corporate practice and the case studies make clear that it is possible to make money by demonstrating that you care about delivering not just good service but also an ethical service. As we have noted, there has been plenty of criticism of the mantra that has driven businesses operating on the model of 'free world capitalism' for some decades, namely the goal of 'maximising shareholder value'. A new balance has been struck between profits and people, and between capitalism and social issues.

The classic theory runs like this. It is axiomatic that capitalism is a political and economic system in which enterprises compete to make profit. Firms are owned by shareholders, who choose to invest their capital in a firm in exchange for, and with the expectation of, making profit.[2] Avoidance of conflicts between the interests of owners and managers (the 'agency problem') is minimised or avoided where the interests of both groups are aligned and managers are incentivised by being paid by results. This is the model of 'maximising shareholder value', which has dominated corporate theory and practice since the 1970s. It holds that the sole purpose of a company is to 'maximise shareholder value'.[3] It demands that firms should just pursue profits and act in their own self-interest.[4] Extensive pre-occupation with mechanisms that align (only) the economic interests of intermediaries with those of their supposed principals (agency theory)[5] paved the way for a utility-maximising model to become an all-encompassing theory of human behaviour.[6]

It is widely agreed that business behaviour became narrowly focused on maximising shareholder value from the 1980s,[7] linked with a widening of citizens' shareholding (and thus a dilution of external control by individual shareholders) and a political ideology linked with individualism[8] and individual liberty.[9]

The Mirage of Maximising Shareholder Value

Not surprisingly, the 'maximising shareholder value' and its associated 'agency theory' approach led to capitalism being attacked for 'greed, selfishness, exploitation and a crude disregard for any interests but one's own'.[10] The classic model has been identified as the cause of a series of serious adverse consequences.[11] Shareholders have held other stakeholders to ransom.[12] Risks have been misallocated, service providers have extracted huge rents,[13] and pay was significantly higher than was justified by long-term performance.[14] The equity market was overcome by the short-term maximisation of profits.[15] Remuneration structures involved annual performance fees for asset managers, with large bonuses based on short-term profits. Viewing an organisation as a nexus of contracts fails to see how it operates as a social institution.[16] The model of business as a linear process of production and consumption has been revealed as failing to recognise 'the full complexity of the flow of materials, energy and information in the modern economy' and, in so doing, the former version of capitalism 'has mistaken money for value, and growth for development'.[17]

The goal of maximisation of shareholder value has recently drawn strenuous criticism from leading scholars, especially on the basis of having been a root cause of the global financial crisis. John Armour and Jeff Gordon of the University of Oxford and Columbia University argue that the shareholder value norm creates incentives for firms to systematically undermine the efficacy of regulatory internalisation mechanisms, thereby failing to avoid the significant externalities that were thought to be avoided.[18]

Exclusive focus on shareholder wealth creates organisations typically characterised by a culture of compliance and control.[19] Employees, particularly those with high aspirations, are likely to find the culture constraining, and the culture itself tends to stifle innovative thinking from the lower ranks.[20]

In a 2017 article in the *Harvard Business Review*, Joseph Bower and Lynn Paine attack the traditional theory head-on.[21] They argue that the goal of exclusively pursuing shareholder value and its associated theory of agency are flawed in their assumptions, legally confused and damaging in practice. Shareholders have no rights as 'owners', managers are not shareholders' 'agents', shareholders have no incentives to exercise care in managing the company, and shareholder centricity is rife with moral hazard, as shareholders have no responsibilities (as directors and managers do) to protect the company's interests, and are unaccountable for their actions. The result is opportunism in share ownership and trading, in which activist hedge funds have wreaked havoc on the sustainable value of some companies. The average holding period for public company shares in the US has rarely been over one year since 1999 and is often a few months: 'much of what activists call value creation is more accurately described as value transfer. When cash is paid to shareholders rather than used to fund research, launch new ventures, or grow existing businesses, value has not been created'.[22]

Bower and Paine argue that the policy should be company-centred rather than shareholder-centred: 'The notion that managing for the good of the company is the same as managing for the good of the stock is best understood as a theoretical conceit necessitated by the mathematical models that many economists favour.'[23] Their model 'would have at its core the health of the enterprise rather than near-term returns to its shareholders. Such a model would start by recognising that corporations are independent entities endowed by law with the potential for indefinite life. With the right leadership, they can be managed to serve markets and society over long periods of time'.[24] The interests of the corporation are distinct from the interests of any particular shareholder or constituency group. Bower and Paine assert that corporations perform many functions in society and must create value for multiple constituencies. These are powerful arguments and they are central to our concepts of EBP and EBR.

By contrast, UK law adopts an 'enlightened shareholder value' model,[25] under which directors must promote the success *of the company for the benefit of its members* and in doing so have regard to various factors, for example:

- the likely consequences of any decision in the long term;
- the interests of employees;
- the need to foster the company's relationships with suppliers, customers and others;
- the impact of operations on the community and the environment;
- the desirability of the company maintaining a reputation for high standards of business conduct.

We consider that Bower, Paine and colleagues are right, and that even the UK model is inadequate (although better than the US model). The basic idea is that a corporation is a distinct actor in society; not only must its interests be central, but it must also play a responsible role in society by respecting the interests of *all* its stakeholders.

Maximising shareholder value is a valid consideration for business, but it should rarely be the *only objective* of an organisation. We agree with Colin Mayer that shareholder value is an *outcome*, not an *objective*.[26] We argue in Part IV that the real guiding principle of an organisation should be to base all decisions and actions on ethical values, which means taking into account the objectives of all the organisation's stakeholders, and so delivering value to them is also relevant. A commercial organisation must, of course, have a valid commercial plan and value proposition, otherwise it will fail.

In short, it is entirely possible for businesses to be both ethical and commercially successful if they honestly place ethical values unequivocally as the centre of the enterprise and apply them consistently to all decisions and behaviours.

Can Corporate Structures Impede Ethical Behaviour?

Colin Mayer's view of the corporation is that it is a mechanism for providing commitment to others. His analysis of the causes of the 2008 economic crisis was that the Anglo-American models of corporations have destroyed essential trust and commitment, since they have enabled and incentivised short-termism, such that business continuity is systemically disrupted in pursuit of the realisation of instant profit by incentives to create mergers, and asset stripping by hedge funds.[27] He suggested that corporations need to exhibit morality, based on three sets of principles. First, companies need values that are credible, consistent and moral. The values will be those of the corporation's customers, investors and employees. Public and private values can be integrated. Second, since self-restraint, reputation and regulation are ineffective, a corporation needs third parties (trust boards) to restrain it from defaulting on its values. Third, the shareholding structure should allow enhanced control to be conferred on shareholders who commit to invest in the corporation for a long period.[28] Mayer argues for the German corporate model in which a supervisory board regulates the management board's operational decisions against the set of stated values of the company.

Whilst agreeing with the premise that a corporation should be run on ethical principles, we do not see the need for duplication of boards in this way. Such a mechanism would only act as a board controlling another board, and there is mounting evidence that single boards that are committed to ethical values can operate well. Further, a control at board level does nothing by itself to ensure ethical practice *throughout all levels* of the organisation.

At a structural level, Mayer's form of corporate governance and ownership—the 'trust firm'—combines responsibility with power and denies power without responsibility. It therefore defines the notion of a moral corporation and imbues the corporation with a degree of morality which exceeds that of the individual.[29] But ethical governance structures would not stop at the board level. Many publications are now appearing on how to grow an ethical culture within a business,[30] and we will talk about this in chapters 13 and 14.

Donald Palmer concludes in his review of the theories of misconduct in organisations 'that a large number of structures and processes without which organizations could not function can cause a significant number of the good apples to embark on wrongful behaviour or to join the few bad apples intentionally pursuing wrongful courses of action'.[31] While we agree with this conclusion, we do not share his apparent pessimism that structures cannot be changed. In fact, that is exactly what we are advocating.

Ethical Structures Tend to Be Open and Flat

It is striking that different case studies into ethical businesses find that their internal organisational structures tend to be flat rather than hierarchical. Decisions are made by empowered staff rather than by a limited number of managers. These businesses also report strikingly good economic results.

Case Study 20: Conscious Capitalism[32]

John Mackey is the co-founder and CEO of Whole Foods Market. His journey from counter culture to capitalism led him to propose a model of free-enterprise capitalism, grounded in an ethical system based on value creation for all stakeholders, involving four tenets:

A. higher purpose and core values;
B. stakeholder integration;
C. conscious leadership;
D. conscious culture and management.

Mackey and Sisodia defined the qualities of conscious cultures as: trust, accountability, caring, transparency, integrity, loyalty and egalitarianism. They asserted that the approach of traditional businesses in giving their managers hard targets for metrics (like market share, profit margins and earnings per share) merely confuses cause and effect.

In asserting conscious capitalism, they contrasted different leadership styles: first, masculine traits of aggression, ambition, competition and left-brain function; and, second, the rise of feminine values of caring, compassion, cooperation and more right-brain qualities, heralding a harmonious blending of these human values in work and life. It is critical to hire people who align strongly with the purpose of the enterprise.

The key principle is to locate decision-making at the lowest possible level by passionate and inspired team members, unless there is compelling evidence that the organisation would be better off making decisions at a higher level. Without empowerment, there is little innovation or creativity. In the company, leadership is mostly about facilitating change and transformation, and management is about efficiency and implementation.

Corporate Governance and Culture: International Statements

The response to the 2008 financial crisis included several strong shifts in corporate governance. One was that companies should adopt a long-term viewpoint to their activities so as to ensure that shareholders' investments remain sustainable and secure. This sense of stability is vital for any sophisticated market and for institutional investors who are responsible for assets such as pension funds. The second shift was a clear movement to considering the interests of *all* stakeholders in a company, thereby moving away from the previously dominant model that 'maximising shareholder value' was the sole objective. A third shift, integrally related to the other two, was an increased emphasis on the importance of corporate values and culture. Let's look at these more closely.

The OECD issued *Principles of Corporate Governance* in 2015 that include the need for companies to provide for the interests of shareholders, key ownership functions, institutional investors, stock markets and other intermediaries, and all relevant stakeholders.[33] The OECD is promoting better corporate governance as a way to prevent corporate misconduct and to rebuild trust in private business, 'precisely to create an environment of trust, transparency and accountability necessary for obtaining long-term investment, financial stability and sustainable growth. If nothing is done, the very fabric and foundation of doing business in an effective and sustainable fashion is at risk'.[34]

In setting an agenda for the future governance of financial institutions, the G30 issued a notable report in 2012 in which it set out that behaviour 'appears to be key' and that to achieve the right behaviours a shift is required from the 'hardware' of governance (structures and processes) to the 'software' (people, leadership skills and values).[35]

> *Values and culture may be the keystone of FI [financial institution] governance because they drive behaviours of people throughout the organization and the ultimate effectiveness of its governance arrangements.*
>
> Suitable structures and processes are a necessary but not a sufficient condition for good governance, which critically depends also on patterns of behaviour. Behavioural patterns depend in turn on the extent to which values such as integrity, independence of thought, and respect for the views of others are embedded in the institutional culture.
>
> In a great FI, positive values and culture are palpable from the board to the executive suite to the front line. Values and culture drive people to do the right thing even when no one is looking.[36]
>
> ... The following are the specific views and recommendations designed to encourage FI board members, executive leaders, supervisors and shareholders to pay heed to the importance of values and culture ...:

> 1. Honesty, integrity, proper motivations, independence of thought, respect for the ideas of others, openness/transparency, the courage to speak out and act, and trust are the bedrock values of effective governance.
> 2. It is for the board of directors to articulate and senior executives to promote a culture that embeds these values from the top to the bottom of the entity. Culture is values brought to life.
> 3. Well-functioning boards set, promulgate, and embed these values, commonly in the form of a code, so that directors, senior executives, and all other employees in an entity are fully aware of the standards of behaviour that are expected of them.
> 4. Because of their power to influence behaviour and the execution of the FI's strategy, values and culture are essential dimensions of inquiry and engagement for supervisors. Major shareholders or their fund managers should be attentive to the culture of an entity when making their investment decisions and engaging with an investee board.[37]
>
> Absent impeccable personal values—honesty, personal integrity, and motivation—nothing is possible. Honesty and personal integrity are self-explanatory and important in any business, but especially in FIs, where public trust and a reputation for honesty and integrity are essential to the value proposition.

The G30 report regarded a customer-centred focus as driving business behaviours, and to be a strategic choice, not a governance issue, which is then translated into operational discipline. Financial institutions, it said, had societal responsibility, since they are licensed by society to serve the needs of society.

In 2013, the G30 followed up its 2012 report by describing 'a new paradigm' for interaction between supervisors and boards of major financial institutions across the globe, based on interviews with more than 60 senior supervisors and board members of some of the largest global and domestic banks in 15 countries.[38] It noted that much attention had been given to new regulations in areas such as risk-based capital, liquidity, resolution and risk management, but 'not enough attention had been placed on "softer" issues that rules alone cannot address, such as enhancing supervisor-board relations to improve supervisor and board effectiveness, or on the culture of firms'. The G30 said that the approach should be based on mutual respect and trust, and should involve a particular culture:

> Realism is important. The goal is not a partnership. The fact that it is the responsibility of supervisors to assess boards means there will inevitably be occasional tension, and the new paradigm requires a substantial increased time commitment from many board members and supervisors. But the potential payoff is large. What is needed is not more of the same, rather it is a step change in the level and quality of the interaction between boards and supervisors, and having the right people who take the time to make that happen.

The G30 considered that boards remain with primary responsibility for the implementation of effective corporate governance, and it emphasised the leadership role of the chairman, the need for adequate board skill sets, regular board effectiveness reviews, and good visibility on risk/prudential matters for the board. But boards and supervisors should adopt a paradigm of trust-based interaction based on clear mutual expectations, with a focus on examining business model vulnerabilities, governance effectiveness and culture. The goal was effective two-way communication, predictability and no surprises from either party.

> Boards of financial institutions need to welcome interaction with high-quality supervisors, view such interaction as contributing to board effectiveness, and understand that it is the responsibility of the supervisor to seek reasonable assurance that the board is effective and the institution's risk culture is appropriate and to help the supervisors fulfill that responsibility. Boards need to make enhancing supervisory relations a priority and take specific action to support the new paradigm recommended in this report.

In emphasising the importance of culture and ethical standards, the G30 said:

> Boards must understand the culture of their organization, in conjunction with their business model. While an institution's broader culture affects its attitude toward risk taking, it is important to prioritize attention to risk culture since it has the most direct connection to safety and soundness of financial institutions. Boards should identify and deal seriously with risky culture, ensure their compensation system supports the desired culture, discuss culture at the board level and with supervisors, and periodically use a variety of formal and informal techniques to monitor risk culture. Supervisors should share their observations about the institution's risk culture with the board, and should watch for serious culture issues that need rectification. Supervisors and policy makers should be cautious about writing rules or guidance about culture, and should set realistic expectations about what is achievable.[39]

The G30 report noted that systems and messages can reinforce or undermine the culture of understood behaviours and attitudes within an organisation:

> Culture is the internal compass that guides individuals' behaviours when no one is looking. It involves soft features that defy quantitative measurement, but they cannot be ignored.
>
> There is no one culture that is appropriate for a major FI. Any culture can fail ...
>
> Culture is closely aligned with business model. Management, boards, and supervisors should carefully consider whether the business model reinforces a healthy culture. Business strategies and models that focus on sales rather than customers, short-term results rather than long-term value, growth rather than sustainability, and low cost rather than efficiency, can create unhealthy cultures. It can be very difficult to change the culture without also changing the business model.
>
> The risk culture of individual institutions will naturally be embedded in the institution's overall culture and in the financial culture of the country ...
>
> The realistic expectation of supervisors' interventions should be to deal with potentially seriously problematic cultures (outliers) that are not adequately mitigated and that boards have not dealt with. Understanding culture more broadly at major institutions is valuable. But supervisors should avoid attempts to make granular cultural distinctions between one firm and another. There is no one FI cultural ideal. To expect more than this is to ask for the undoable, to waste scarce resources, and to lead to excessive intrusion into how banks are run.

The report recommended that supervisors and boards should use a short list of simple descriptors of culture:

> Useful descriptors of desired culture include: valuing risk awareness across the FI; sustainability; client-focused; integrity; accountability; independence of thought; respect for the views of others; transparency; doing the right thing; balanced decision making; open to constructive challenge, including from subordinates; viewing risk management and compliance as adding value; culture of ownership of risk and compliance in both the business and control functions; collaboration across functional groups; innovation; excellence in execution; learning from mistakes; inclusion of others; conservative; and prudent or cautious.
>
> While these traits appear to be uniquely desirable, they can also be problematic in certain circumstances; for example, too conservative or cautious a culture can lack the dynamism needed for success, which in turn is a key bulwark of safety and soundness. Again, as an example, the organizational culture literature has identified that an excess of collaboration can produce groupthink, which itself can pose risks.
>
> In contrast, various people interviewed for this report suggested elements of culture that can be problematic. Examples include: growth for growth's sake, an excessive sales- or cost-focused culture, an overbearing CEO (or business line head), an unduly deferential culture, an excessively aggressive culture that does not adequately consider whether the identified goal is the right thing to do, cultures that push business while disregarding risks and controls, an ego-driven or star-performer culture, hubris, seeing policies and limits as items to be gamed, siloed cultures, and excessively valuing autonomy over control and adherence to policies.
>
> Aspects of culture that could prove problematic can be mitigated. For example, some bemoan the powerful short-term-performance-driven-CEO culture. But organizations do need active, engaged CEOs who can push change and achieve complex strategies for success (which is important for safety and soundness). The downsides of this culture can be mitigated by an equally strong board, with highly effective challenge, including the counterweight of a very strong chair.

This approach can be contrasted with the policy of focusing on individuals through rules on accountability and criminal sanctions, which was discussed above at chapter 3. We suggest that the latter approach is doomed to failure and will produce inconsistent and ineffective results.

Restoring Confidence in the City of London through Corporate Governance and Culture

The 2008 financial crash caused not only an economic crisis but also a loss of confidence in banks and in the City of London-based corporate world generally. Virtually every subsequent report into the crisis emphasised not only the need to improve the regulatory system but also the importance of the culture of businesses.[40] The Corporation of the City of London was particularly concerned that the ongoing sequence of financial scandals would undermine confidence in the City and would lead to significant deterioration in the ranking of London as a financial and corporate centre.[41]

The starting point is that the UK Companies Act imposes the following duties on a company director:

> A director of a company must act in the way he considers, in good faith, would be most likely to promote the success of the company for the benefit of its members as a whole, and in doing so have regard (amongst other matters) to—
>
> (a) the likely consequences of any decision in the long-term,
> (b) the interests of the company's employees,
> (c) the need to foster the company's business relationships with suppliers, customers and others,
> (d) the impact of the company's operations on the community and the environment,
> (e) the desirability of the company maintaining a reputation for high standards of business conduct, and
> (f) the need to act fairly as between members of the company.[42]

The Lord Mayor of the City of London spearheaded an initiative to restore the City's 'trust and values', recalling the traditional adage 'My word is my bond'. This produced a series of agreements on improving business culture and behaviour, based on the following actions:

— *Leadership with Integrity*. A new research and education programme at Cass Business School.
— *Performance with Integrity*. Recruitment, appraisal and development would be linked to ethics and behavior. A new policy guide and best practice toolkit in performance management was prepared to help employers embed values at three crucial stages: recruitment, performance appraisal and development. The toolkit particularly addresses the needs of the individual who delivers short-term financial results but does not work by the organisation's values and creates excessive risk. The work was cross-referenced to published professional standards, regulatory requirements and internal disciplinary processes.
— *Governing Values*. Designed to enable Boards to ensure that values are observed and 'lived'.
— *The City Obligation*. A personal pledge to be taken voluntarily by those working in the City to uphold the City's enduring values, the highest standards of integrity and professional behavior, with a focus on obligations to clients and other stakeholders. Similar to 'My Word is My Bond'.
— *Integrity Resources*. Defining and sharing best practice, including: next generation leaders; remuneration and regulation; diversity and inclusion; training and development; corporate social responsibility.[43]

The UK has had a principles-based approach to corporate governance since the 1992 Cadbury Report, which introduced a code based on openness, integrity and accountability.[44] The 2009 Walker Review concluded that the UK's unitary board structure and Combined Code of the Financial Reporting Council (FRC), and its 'comply or explain' mode, remained fit for purpose for companies generally and not just financial institutions.[45] New editions of the UK Corporate Governance Code were issued in 2010,[46] 2012[47] and 2014.[48]

The Code calls for 'dialogue which is both constructive and challenging' and states that a key role for a board is to establish the culture, values and ethics of the company.[49] The Stewardship Code was issued by the Financial Reporting Council to enhance the quality of engagement between institutional investors and companies, to offer sharper emphasis on long-term company strategy and to tackle overly complex incentive schemes which encourage short-termism and tend to pay out asymmetrically.[50] Various supportive statements were issued by investors' bodies,[51] including clarifying the principles on 'comply or explain'.[52]

Taking a Long-Term View

When decisions are made in businesses, the profit-versus-ethics conflict discussed above depends on whether the decision is taken in the short term or long term. A short-term decision might easily save or delay spending money on making improvements, or maximise prices, whereas a longer-term perspective might support incurring the cost or foregoing the income now so as to build customer loyalty and reputation. As just noted, all the recent City policies have emphasised the importance of established UK companies taking a long-term view as a matter of supporting trust in investing in and doing business with UK companies.

The 2012 Kay report set out principles to provide a foundation for a long-term perspective in UK equity markets and made recommendations to re-establish equity markets that work well for their users.[53] The 2014 Corporate Governance Code emphasised that the purpose of corporate governance was to deliver the *long-term* success of a company:

> Governance and the Code. 1. The purpose of corporate governance is to facilitate effective, entrepreneurial and prudent management that can deliver the *long-term* success of the company …
>
> Section A: Leadership: Every company should be headed by an effective board which is collectively responsible for the *long-term* success of the company.[54]

The requirements were carried over into the 2016 Code:

> 4. One of the key roles for the board includes establishing the culture, values and ethics of the company. It is important that the board sets the correct 'tone from the top'. The directors should lead by example and ensure that good standards of behaviour permeate throughout all levels of the organisation. This will help prevent misconduct, unethical practices and support the delivery of long-term success.[55]

The 2014 Code update increased the provision by companies of information about the risks which affect longer-term viability.[56] There was also an update in 2016 that focused on confidence in audit.

The focus on the long term can be noted elsewhere, such as in the 2004 United Nations Global Compact on Corporate Sustainability, the 2010 UK Stewardship Code promoting responsible investment and the 2015 UN Global Compact update's six Principles of Responsible Investment.[57] In 2016, the UK Committee on Standards in Public Life also re-emphasised the importance of its seven principles of selflessness, integrity, objectivity, accountability, openness, honesty and leadership.[58]

In 2016, the Investment Association launched an initiative aimed at using long-term investment to promote productivity.[59] This called for a series of actions, including pressing companies to cease quarterly reporting, managing capital in ways that allow for investment, simplifying behavioural incentives, encouraging investment consultants to promote a long-term approach and improving reporting on culture.

Under the FRC's leadership, a package of reports by different institutions involved in the City of London was issued together in July 2016, which emphasised the importance of corporate culture and gave advice on how to support it.[60] The general philosophy was stated in the Foreword to the FRC's document by its Chairman, Sir Winfried Bischoff:

> There needs to be a concerted effort to improve trust in the motivations and integrity of business. Rules and sanctions clearly have their place, but will not on their own deliver productive behaviours over the long-term. This report looks at the increasing importance which corporate culture plays in delivering long-term business and economic success.
>
> A healthy culture both protects and generates value. It is therefore important to have a continuous focus on culture, rather than wait for a crisis, Poor behaviour can be exacerbated when companies come under pressure. A strong culture will endure in times of stress and mitigate the impact. This is essential in dealing effectively with risk and maintaining resilient performance.
>
> Strong governance underpins a healthy culture, and boards should demonstrate good practice in the boardroom and promote good governance throughout the business. The company as a whole must demonstrate openness and accountability, and should engage constructively with shareholders and wider stakeholders about culture.
>
> In taking action on culture, I should like all those involved to consider three important issues:
>
> **Connect purpose and strategy to culture.**
>
> Establishing a company's overall purpose is crucial in supporting the values and driving the correct behaviours. The strategy to achieve a company's purpose should reflect the values and culture of the company and should not be developed in isolation. Boards should oversee both.
>
> **Align values and incentives.** Recruitment, performance management and reward should support and encourage behaviours consistent with the company's purpose,

values, strategy and business model, Financial and non-financial incentives should be appropriately balanced and linked to behavioural objectives.

Assess and measure. Boards should give careful thought to how culture is assessed and reported on. A wide range of potential indicators are available. Companies can choose and monitor those that are appropriate to the business and the outcomes they seek. Objectively assessing culture involves interpreting information sensitively to gain practical insight.

The strong emphasis on culture is notable. However, if we read both the Code and the related documents closely, there is a striking omission. They are peppered with references to the importance of a 'healthy', 'strong' or 'positive' culture and to the problems caused by a 'weak' or 'bad' or 'toxic' culture, but there is no reference to the basis for making an evaluative judgement on the moral value of the desired culture. The FRC hardly indicates that culture should equate to a particular value-system or be ethical. At least the OECD's 2015 *Principles of Corporate Governance* mention that 'the board should apply high *ethical* standards' (emphasis added), even if it is only once in a long document.[61]

A criminal gang, such as the Mafia, has a strong culture, which can drive its commercial success. The precise problem with the corporate world has been that the single-minded pursuit of profits and shareholder value has caused a disconnect between the *ethical values* of the societies in which corporations operate and those demonstrated by many businesses. Public objections to corporate practice are widespread—unfair trading, misleading advertising, exploiting vulnerable consumers, poor service, being ripped off, senior executives being paid huge sums of money, traders selling products that customers do not deserve to be sold, fixing rates, fiddling expenses, paying bribes, hiding fraudulent devices intended to avoid regulatory requirements, covering up bad practice, not paying tax in jurisdictions that produce large revenues, polluting the environment and using slave or underpaid labour. In voicing these objections, people are responding from an innate sense of *fairness*, irrespective of the precise rules of legality.

What people expect to see is behaviour that is fair, just and ethical, based on shared norms and values. If that is so, corporations or trading centres that fail to demonstrate that they also require ethical commercial behaviour will not deserve the trust of their customers, workers, investors or regulators. We suggest that the next step is for the City and the corporate world to focus on the absolute requirement of demonstrating that trust can be placed in its organisations because they demonstrate that they act in accordance with the ethical values that society expects.

Room for Improvement in Ethical Business Practice

There is empirical evidence that ethical values are not currently as strong as they should be in business. Although a 2016 survey of the values most prized by FTSE

100 companies found that integrity was the highest scorer at 35%, responsibility, trust and honesty were all far lower, each only scoring 14%. Table 9.1[62] sets out the percentage of FTSE 100 companies espousing the particular value. These results clearly indicate that more emphasis could be placed on values in general corporate culture.

Table 9.1: The values most valued by FTSE 100 companies

Value	*Percentage of respondents mentioning*
Integrity	35%
Respect	28%
Innovation	24%
Safety	18%
Transparency	16%
Excellence	15.5%
Teamwork	14.5%
Responsibility	14%
Trust	14%
Honesty	14%

The 2015 survey of employees by the Institute of Business Ethics (IBE) found that Britain's attempt to 'move on' from the financial crisis and second wave of corporate scandals has led to higher engagement in business ethics, but the UK is 'drifting in the doldrums', with trust being lost as a result of companies 'not playing fair' with levels of tax and executive pay.[63] The position it reports across Europe is far from satisfactory. In Spain, there was a demand for greater openness and accountability, and management is increasingly focused on social responsibility and good governance. France is preoccupied with improving efficiency, whilst the defence sector has been repeatedly implicated in corruption, and banks are also facing misconduct allegations (a leading instance being Jérôme Kerviel, who lost Société Générale €4.9 billion). French organisations are less likely to have ethics programmes. Corruption scandals occurred in Germany from 2005 to 2010, and business ethics have commonly been perceived as unnecessary. However, the VW emissions fraud shocked the world and a profound response is needed. Italy suffers from a continuing economic crisis, such as the *Mafia Capitale* scandal over contract rigging and embezzlement. Overall, the IBE reports that there has been a major decrease in trust in institutions.

The UK Institute of Directors has concluded in 2016 that 'many FTSE 100 companies see governance in pure compliance terms and it has mainly been reduced to the production of boilerplate paragraphs in annual reports', and that 'good governance isn't a question of meeting minimum requirements but rather it is the consequence of tuning many variables to produce optimal performance'.[64]

It may not be so easy to deliver ethical behaviour in practice, given the current state of the corporate world. Much needs to change and it will take time to deliver the requisite change. After all, mis-selling of payment protection insurance (PPI) was universal in the financial services industry,[65] and convicted traders report that they were basically behaving in accordance with the incentives and expectations of the system.[66] The relevance of values within business is a relatively recent idea[67] and has developed in its sophistication.[68] The IBE report notes that:

> Some investors pointed out that with what would normally be perceived as a bad culture could perform well, at least in the short term, and vice-versa. Their interest in culture was aroused primarily when it was affecting performance, particularly if it was a well-publicised regulatory breach which had affected the share price.[69]

The IBE also noted that only 14% of FTSE 100 companies discussed their corporate culture in their annual reports; 58% make a commitment to generating value for their shareholders and 47% explain value creation in their business model. A 2016 survey by Grant Thornton found that 86% of FTSE 350 companies mentioned corporate culture in their 2016 annual reports, but 48% did not clearly communicate their organisation's values. Despite wide acknowledgement that the tone must be set from the top, only 21% of FTSE 350 CEOs addressed culture in their introduction to their annual report.[70]

The FRC report itself cites research that the values 'most valued' by FTSE 100 companies are integrity (35%) and respect (28%), whereas responsibility, trust and honesty come noticeably lower, each with 14%.[71] The Chartered Institute of Personnel and Development said upfront that 'it is often said that leaders think they know what the culture is, but rarely fully understand it'. The FRC report said:

> **Understanding culture**
>
> There is strong agreement among stakeholders that a determined effort is required to build a picture from various indirect indicators and proxies of the true culture at different levels in the organisation.
>
> Companies report that they struggle fully to understand the complex chain of interactions that drive individual behaviour. Traditionally, management has focused on the mechanisms, policies and processes that make up the operational framework of the company and which establish boundaries, norms and minimum standards of behaviour.
>
> The realisation that management and boards need to understand and address less tangible drivers of behaviour, such as closely held values and attitudes or social and power-driven pressures, that can lead people to make poor choices is changing the conversation in the boardroom. To do this justice boards need to shift focus and seek new ways of understanding what is really going on in their organisations.[72]

Figure 9.1 illustrates the gap between senior managers' acknowledgement of the need to understand culture and their confidence that they know how to deal with it. The data was reported in a series of studies[73] and is illustrated by Tor Eneroth of the BVC in Figure 9.1. The responses to questions asked in the surveys indicate that while managers are aware of the importance of culture, when asked about their own organisational cultures, the perceptions were not encouraging.

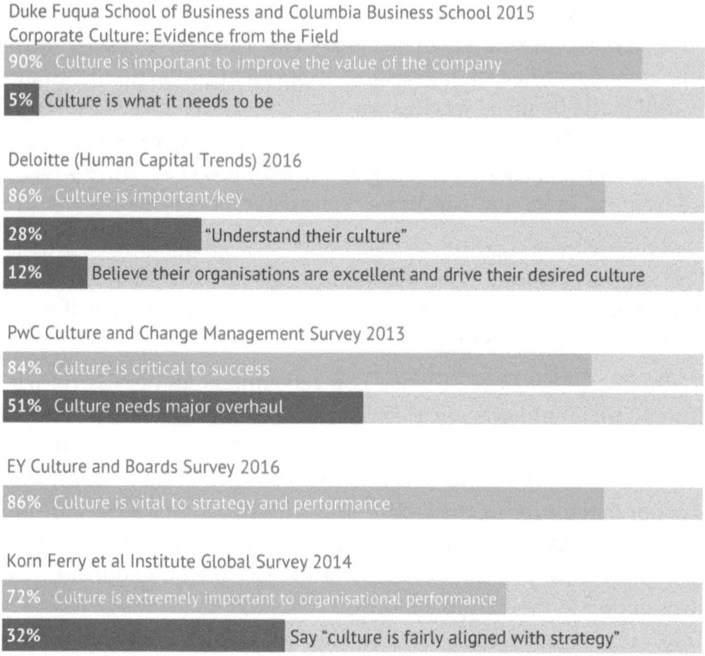
Duke Fuqua School of Business and Columbia Business School 2015
Corporate Culture: Evidence from the Field
90% Culture is important to improve the value of the company
5% Culture is what it needs to be
Deloitte (Human Capital Trends) 2016
86% Culture is important/key
28%
"Understand their culture"
12%
Believe their organisations are excellent and drive their desired culture
PwC Culture and Change Management Survey 2013
84% Culture is critical to success
51% Culture needs major overhaul
EY Culture and Boards Survey 2016
86% Culture is vital to strategy and performance
Korn Ferry et al Institute Global Survey 2014
72% Culture is extremely important to organisational performance
32%
Say "culture is fairly aligned with strategy"

Source: Barrett Values Centre

Figure 9.1: Multiple surveys illustrating the gap between leader's understanding of the importance of culture and their ability to deal with it

Similarly, the IBE report says:

> Dialogue between companies and shareholders on culture and long-term strategy has been improving, but there is a long way to go to open up discussion. Shareholders are heavily focused on performance, often but not exclusively in the short term. Moreover, they do not believe that they can change a 'bad' culture from the outside.[74]

However, the IBE report noted that 'shareholders were not convinced that they had the power or the ability to change a bad culture … Investors generally said a weak culture made them more aware of risk and more likely to sell'.

The OECD's 2015 stocktake of corporate practices found:

> The OECD's results show that even top rank firms struggle with effective implementation and achieving the desired outcomes may take years of dedicated work …
>
> The findings in this report suggest corporate leadership is taking integrity more seriously after the financial crisis. Eighty percent of survey respondents indicated that their company's board was strongly involved in the design and implementation of their company's integrity policy; almost half indicated that the policy was established following a decision by the board. Increased prioritisation of integrity may well have led to an increase in investment in integrity: almost 20% of respondents considered integrity budgets to have increased from 25% to more than 50% over the last 5 years. The way that such budget

> use is perceived speaks volumes about a company's commitment to promoting a culture of integrity, and the results show that 60% of respondents characterised the use of such budget as an investment, as opposed to an expense. At the same time, some companies are exploring cost-efficient ways to a more holistic approach to the business integrity function, to address breakdowns in communication between the various independent business integrity areas in the company.[75]

EY's 2016 Fraud Survey involved interviews with 2,825 senior executives with responsibility for tackling fraud, bribery and corruption from 62 jurisdictions. This survey found that an alarmingly high number of executives continue to justify unethical acts, more than a third said they would be willing to justify unethical behaviour during an economic downturn, while almost half would justify such conduct in order to meet financial targets.[76] A 2016 survey of workers in 13 countries found that in 10 of the countries, 50% or more of the respondents said they had reported observed misconduct. In 11 out of 13 countries, at least one in three respondents had also experienced retaliation, and 90% of this retaliation occurred within the first six months of the initial report.[77]

In April 2017, a parliamentary committee cited evidence that unethical behaviour is 'absolutely embedded' in the culture of foreign aid contractors.[78] In the same month, the House of Commons' Business, Energy and Industrial Strategy Committee reviewed the UK's corporate governance regime and concluded that it is 'a considerable asset which enhances the reputation of the UK as a place to do business', but needs a series of improvements in view of evidence that 'levels of trust in business are lower than in many other countries', given perceptions of unfairness on executive pay levels and payment of tax.[79] The Committee noted with concern various barriers to engagement by investors in influencing corporate decisions and called for increased dialogue facilitated by the Investor Forum.[80]

So, the current position appears to be that although there is wide recognition that corporate culture is important, many businesses have not yet focused on culture as a contributor to success or perhaps even recognised the value of having an ethical culture. Nevertheless, it is clear that an ethical culture is not only the inescapable ultimate goal of a company that aims for sustainable high performance, but that there are also clear moves in that direction by many major companies and business leaders.

A Shortfall in UK Employee Engagement

In 2014, a study of corporations in 34 countries found that only around 4 in 10 employees were highly engaged.[81] The level of 'employee engagement' in the UK is dangerously low. In 2012, only 27% of employees in the UK were 'highly engaged'.[82] This engagement deficit drove output per hour in the UK that was 15 percentage points below the average for the rest of the G7 industrialised nations in 2011; on an output-per-worker basis, UK productivity was 20 percentage points lower than the rest of the G7 in 2011. This represented the widest productivity gap since 1995.[83] We have already discussed the correlation between low employee engagement and elevated culture risk.

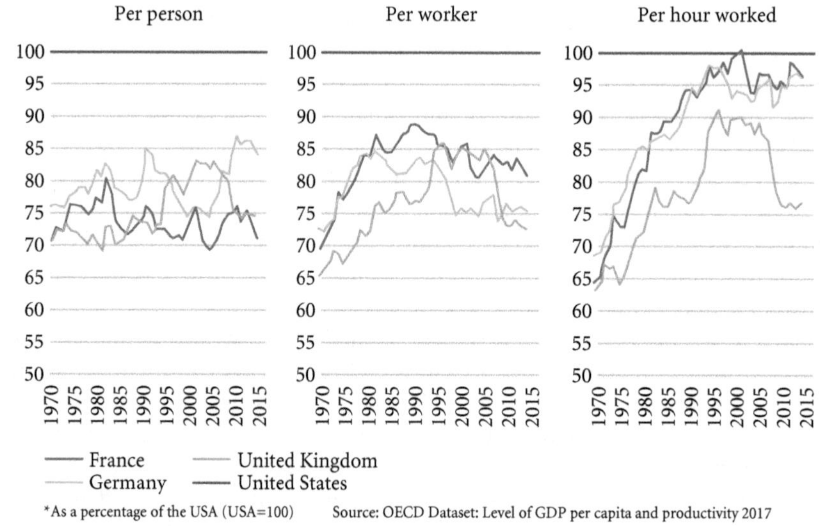

Figure 9.2: Productivity and output in the UK, France and Germany compared to the US

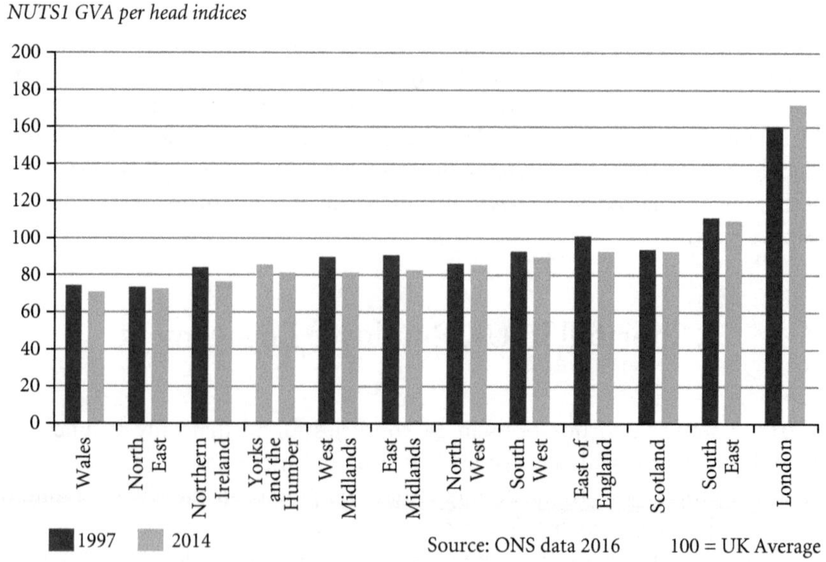

Figure 9.3: Productivity by UK region (1997 and 2014)

The UK government's 2017 Industrial Strategy Green Paper[84] noted that whilst the country had experienced 14% growth since 2010 and unemployment was at its lowest level for 11 years, earnings were still recovering from a substantial decline following the recession of 2008 and productivity was poor, with workers in France, Germany and the US producing on average as much in four days as UK workers did in five (see Figures 9.2 and 9.3). There were significant regional disparities in productivity that were wider in the UK than in other Western European nations, with 61% of people in the UK living in areas with incomes 10% below the national average. Against this evidence, the issue of disaffection by the populace shown in the June 2016 Brexit vote should not be surprising.

The UK National Values assessment by the Barrett Values Centre in 2012 found that the personal values of UK citizens showed that personal relationships were vitally important to them.[85] The values favoured were: caring, family, honesty, humour/fun, friendship, fairness, compassion, independence, respect and trust. However, a far more challenging picture was painted when people were asked about their perceptions of life in the nation. There, people identified bureaucracy, crime/violence, uncertainty about the future, corruption, blame, wasted resources, media influence, conflict/aggression, drugs/alcohol, and apathy as the top ten current culture values.

The Global Level

The latest policy paper by the business group B20, which is attached to the governmental G20 group, does not demonstrate that the importance of ethical values has been grasped by business generally. The 2017 B20 policy paper on 'responsible business conduct and anti-corruption' included a recommendation that compliance efforts by businesses should be 'recognised'.[86] It said:

> **Recommendation 2: Recognize Compliance Efforts – G20 members should be supportive of a company's proactive engagement by providing positive recognition of effective anti-corruption and compliance systems.**
>
> Policy Action 2.1: Acknowledge Adequate Measures—G20 members should recognize corporate compliance efforts when awarding public contracts and when imposing sanctions for breaches, and they should explore additional ways to acknowledge compliance efforts.
>
> Policy Action 2.2: Encourage Self-disclosure and Self-cleaning—G20 members should be encouraged to harmonize their administrative and legal approaches to self-disclosure of compliance breaches, recognize effective and safe internal reporting, and support adequate self-cleaning.
>
> Policy Action 2.3: Promote a Culture of Integrity—G20 should continue its commitment to building a global culture of intolerance towards corruption by reinforcing international cooperation, including the promotion of key international instruments, supporting the provision of capacity building and training for SMEs and in non-G20

countries, as well as improving education on anti-corruption and integrity in schools and universities.

These priorities are the wrong way round. Basing behaviour on an ethical foundation, and hence requiring a culture of integrity, should be the starting point, not the final recommendation. Placing 'recognising compliance efforts' first reflects a US-dominated enforcement policy based on deterrence and large sanctions, based on the assumption that they alone will affect future behaviour. Such an approach will never work. The B20 requests reflect the approach that the authorities incentivise businesses to have a compliance system rather than to act ethically. Hence, the name of the game for businesses is to operate systems to earn lower fines rather than to address their ongoing behaviour.

We suggest that it is time that business leaders and public representatives adopted a fresh approach based on empirical evidence of what works. And this means starting with ethical values.

Conclusions

1. Individuals and commercial organisations can act both commercially and ethically at the same time if they wish to. But if they want to achieve this balanced approach, they need to plan consciously how to balance the competing issues that will arise daily.
2. The classic theory of shareholder value has been criticised and undermined by well-reasoned arguments. New models are company-centred, consider the interests of all stakeholders and facilitate a more long-term view likely to create the conditions for unethical behaviour to diminish.
3. The design of ethical commercial organisations starts with leadership and corporate governance, but also must go further and encompass how everyone in the organisation is going to act and make decisions daily at an organic level. We will discuss these points in greater detail in Part IV.
4. The self-regulation of corporate governance by OECD and in the UK has evolved to be based on the fundamental importance of *values*, by which is meant *ethical values*, but they stop just short of saying so. However, the global debate on compliance is still stuck in an old-fashioned space where compliance systems are thought to guarantee ethical behaviour; they will not and the approach must be modernised.
5. Empirical evidence reveals that employee engagement and hence productivity in the UK are low.
6. Recent reports emanating from the City of London and financial services industry focus on the role of governance in improving behaviour and therefore trust in the sector.
7. The statistics on the extent to which corporate practices and individuals' behaviour is unethical show that there is room for serious improvement.
8. Although senior executives purport to consider culture to be important; in practice they don't seem to pay much attention to it.

10

The Status of Regulatory Policy

Reinterpreting Regulation

Regulation is an attempt by society to *regulate* some of the processes or outputs that commercial or professional actors undertake, but not to completely control it. The essential responsibility for the activity and the risk rests primarily with the business, which takes the risk and the profits by providing outputs that people value in buying. The activity is essentially legal (otherwise it would not be tolerated or licensed), but society's authorities attempt to influence some aspects of it.

Historically, regulatory policy has seesawed between, on the one hand, no regulation (self-regulation) and, on the other hand, strenuous regulation (referred to as 'command-and-control' regulation) and enforcement based on the concept of deterrence. Both these extremes have proved to be ineffective as general approaches for fairly obvious reasons. Most of this book is aimed at finding a happy medium (co-regulation plus ethical business regulation) that is an effective compromise between individual freedom of action and respect for other people.

Colin Mayer has argued that regulation in fact promotes immoral conduct. Regulation leads to gaming against rules to circumvent or minimise their effects, diverts attention from the moral substance to details of rules, is pro-cyclical, and confuses rules with standards, compliance with compassion and obedience with integrity:[1]

> Economics does not recognise the fundamental role of commitment in all aspects of our commercial as well as social lives and the way in which institutions contribute to the creation and preservation of commitment.[2]

Behavioural science looks at regulation, enforcement and compliance through a new lens. If we apply the lessons of chapters 1 and 2, regulation and enforcement are no longer to be visualised as being imposed top-down by authorities, but to be based on agreed values that are shared and demonstrated within a cooperative relationship. Let us remember the idea of compliance as a *social* phenomenon, which can be maximised by supporting social values and relationships, and embedding economic activity in social relationships.[3] Behavioural psychology has been applied by regulators to the actions of consumers (behavioural economics or behavioural insights)[4] and by governments to the actions of citizens ('nudge', such as promoting adherence by advertising statements like 'Most people pay their tax on time').[5] There are many powerful examples of the success of nudge-based strategies.[6] What we are doing in this book is to apply the same science in the regulatory, compliance and enforcement contexts.

Many sectors use the term 'regulation' to describe what they do, whereas the term 'supervision' has been used in the financial services sector partly as a result of its historical 'light-touch' approach. However, the idea of 'supervision' helps by highlighting the point that the primary responsibility for compliance or performance rests with the businesses themselves, and the regulator does not control business activities, but monitors them and takes supervisory action when needed. Whilst some financial regulators continue to adhere to large fines and a deterrence approach, other more enlightened ones across the world have accepted that external regulation cannot be relied on to affect all behaviour, and that what is more important is the personal and group values of the human actors and the ethical culture of their organisational groups.[7]

UK Government Policy on Better Regulation and Enforcement

An ethical business approach already exists in some sectors in the UK, and some others are very close to it, whilst some remain stuck in a deterrence mode that does not produce best results. EBP plus EBR is the next step that can assist right across the board.

There has been continuous evolution in regulatory policy in the UK over the past two decades. We can chart the transformation in enforcement policy of the UK government and regulators from deterrence to responsiveness to support for partnerships based on ethical understandings. It closely parallels the development of academic recognition of responsive regulation discussed in chapter 3. Although the academics were initially only discovering (to general surprise) what certain enforcement officials were actually doing, as time went on, the two communities cross-fertilised each other.

Enforcement in its classical sense is limited to taking formal action against those who breach the rules, such as a prosecution or serving an improvement notice. The concept has expanded 'backwards' to include 'inspection' to determine that compliance is occurring.[8] But the idea is now going further. Just as the idea of *compliance* has given way to that of maintaining continuous *performance* (see chapter 7), the concept of 'enforcing' against people who are trying to do the right thing has given way to more supportive and collaborative approaches. On the other hand, for those who are not trying to do the right thing, traditional enforcement remains relevant.

Several strands of developments have converged to produce change. We can look in more detail at the 'downward' pressure of Better Regulation policy, the 'upward' pressure of experience from local enforcement officers and the 'sideways' evolution of economic regulatory authorities as they realised that their roles were widening. Two important features that these forces produced were increased focus on *behaviour* and in bringing about *redress*.

Recent discussion papers from the OECD have focused on risk-based and responsive regulatory approaches, and omit reference to deterrence.[9] The 2014 OECD recommendations on regulation quietly dropped reliance on deterrence in favour of a responsive regulation approach.[10] A 2014 paper summarised how behavioural economics has demonstrated that there are numerous influences on people's economic decisions, such as the simplicity of information and of the range of available options; the fact that people are drawn towards more convenient options, especially default options; and that the salience of options or attributes can affect how they are weighted in decisions.[11] It also said that: 'Behavioural evidence also suggests that regulatory regimes that are perceived as fair and applied evenly are likely to achieve greater degrees of compliance. Regulators therefore need to build and to prize trust.'[12] The importance of maintaining trust of the regulated by regulators was recognised as an important principle in the governance of regulators.[13]

In 2017, the OECD published a compilation of 129 examples of 60 public bodies applying behavioural insights in 23 countries across the globe. It noted that 'governments are searching for simple and effective regulatory solutions to promote more efficient outcomes without resorting to additional rules or sanctions'. The OECD made two particularly relevant recommendations.[14] First, behavioural insights should be taken into account early in the design of policy (they are usually considered only at a late stage) and, second, they should be applied not just to 'nudging consumers and citizens', but also to regulatory relationships. We fully agree, and suggest that every regulatory scheme and set of rules should have a 'behavioural impact assessment' to confirm how people are going to respond to the rules, and to make sure that the proposals are going to work and will be observed.

Better Regulation

Several governments have applied a policy of 'Better Regulation' in recent years. The idea behind Better Regulation is to be more effective whilst being more efficient: to do more with less and to make sure that what you do is proportionate. This stream of policy made powerful progress in the 2000s by ensuring, first, that new rules were assessed before being imposed to make sure that they should produce greater benefits than the costs they imposed (impact assessment) and, second, that the multiple enforcers to which a business might be subject had a coordinated approach to inspections and to deciding what constituted compliance.[15] The UK has been a leader in Better Regulation and has developed the ideas significantly. The European Commission's Better Regulation policy is based on the need for *evidence*, as well as an objective assessment of such evidence, in addition to costs and benefits.[16]

The first idea of reducing burdens on business and reducing regulatory costs public expenditure led to risk-based regulation, in which regulators' attention was focused on the most serious risks. Many publications by regulators over the past decade refer to the importance of a risk-based approach. A striking example of this is the strategy that the HSE adopted to tackle a very high general incidence of injuries in the construction industry (see chapter 7).

Crucial milestones in the crystallisation of the new UK approach emerged in the mid-2000s. Although the Better Regulation agenda of saving money was important, an equally influential motivation in these developments was a body of research that people often need help and support rather than criticism to comply with regulation. Many official statements were made to that effect.[17] The behavioural research included findings that SMEs believe that they are complying until a person they respect points out that they could improve, in response to which advice they usually follow the advice.[18] Further, SMEs also often lack clarity about *how* to comply.[19] The person who could help them comply and improve need not be a public official, and could be from a Chamber of Commerce, trade association or other expert or adviser.

In accordance with this body of research, both UK government policy and the practice of many regulators have adopted an approach towards regulatory enforcement that is based on differentiating between a supportive approach for most firms and a punitive approach for manifestly wrongful behaviour. Thus, the Hampton Report advocated that regulators should adopt a risk-based approach towards securing compliance and should use advice and persuasion as the first step.[20] The first of the Macrory Penalty Principles for regulatory enforcement for all regulatory enforcement is to aim to *change the behaviour* of the offender.[21] The last Penalty Principle mentioned deterrence, but higher priorities talked of eliminating gain, responsiveness, restoration and proportionality:

- Aim to change the behaviour of the offender.
- Aim to eliminate any financial gain or benefit from non-compliance.
- Be responsive and consider what is appropriate for the particular offender and regulatory issue, which can include punishment and the public stigma that should be associated with a criminal conviction.
- Be proportionate to the nature of the offence and the harm caused.
- Aim to restore the harm caused by regulatory non-compliance, where appropriate.
- Aim to deter future non-compliance.

The duty imposed on many regulatory bodies[22] to observe statutory principles of good regulation is that 'regulatory activities should be carried out in a way which is transparent, accountable, proportionate, consistent, and that regulatory activities should be *targeted only cases in which action is needed*'.[23] Specified bodies are also under a duty not to impose or maintain unnecessary burdens in the exercise of regulatory functions.[24] The 2014 Regulators' Code[25] stresses the need for regulators to adopt a positive and proactive approach towards ensuring compliance, requiring that:

1. regulators should carry out their activities in a way that *supports those they regulate to comply and grow*; and
2. regulators should ensure clear information, guidance and advice is available to *help those they regulate meet their responsibilities to comply.*[26]

Parallel Expansion in Criminal Law

The policies just noted are closely linked with parallel developments in criminal enforcement towards restorative justice and criminals making reparation to victims. The purposes of criminal sanctions were stated in 2003 to be:

— punishment of offenders;
— reduction of crime (including its reduction by deterrence);
— reform and rehabilitation of offenders;
— protection of the public;
— making of reparation by offenders to persons affected by their offences.[27]

Adopting a wider approach to fair response and the expansion of reparative justice in criminal sentencing was pursued by making consideration of Compensation Orders mandatory in every case from 2013,[28] introducing wider use of powers to remove unexplained wealth from criminals,[29] and as a general approach in a raft of new Sentencing Guidelines covering different situations.

In the government's 2016 *Modern Crime Prevention Strategy*,[30] Home Secretary Theresa May only mentioned deterrence in the context of increasing the perceived likelihood of being caught and punished, saying: 'There is good evidence that specific police tactics can increase the perceived likelihood of being caught—for example, patrolling known crime "hotspots" has been shown to reduce crime, particularly when accompanied by local problem-solving.'[31] Greater emphasis was placed on responding to influencing the development of character traits in the small minority of people who commit the majority of crimes.[32]

From Enforcement to Behaviour

Authorities have been given a large toolbox of powers and the ability to use them flexibly to respond to the problems, situations and offenders with which they are faced. The sanctions can be illustrated in 'graded' severity in the 'Ayers-Braithwaite pyramid' of increasing sanctions noted in chapter 3: ultimate sanctions at the top, such as removal of liberty or licence, which are rarely used; in the middle a sequence of responses/sanctions of escalating severity; at the bottom, where most 'enforcement' occurs, informal techniques based on persuasion and negotiation to achieve compliance. It needs to be realised more widely that multiple pyramids apply and should not only be used but also be coordinated to produce a result that is effective, proportionate and efficient. The multiple influencers, who can each exert pressure on future behaviour and also apply their own sanctions, include colleagues, employers, friends and family, local and national media, professional bodies and colleagues, customers, suppliers, consultants, regulators and enforcers, and investors.

There have been various extensions in the approach, not all of which have been consistent. First, whilst businesses may be prosecuted for specified activities and failures, the more fundamental questions relate to whether individuals, systems or cultures were the root cause of the problem. In financial services and the health service, criminal offences have been introduced to pin responsibility for adverse events on senior individuals. This is likely to be ineffective.

Second, the responsibilities of regulators have widened from just enforcing the law to seeing that markets remain balanced and that consumers remain happy and are treated fairly. This has included looking more closely at how firms treat consumers, looking at particular problems of vulnerable consumers, seeing that complaint systems operate well and ensuring that businesses make redress to consumers (hence regulators increasingly use new redress powers or involve ombudsmen).[33] Underlying this is a change in focus for regulators from enforcing safety rules or regulating prices and competition to upholding the values of the society that they serve and represent.

Third, agreements between businesses and enforcers, such as those contained in agreed undertakings, are preferable to prosecutions. The agreements can encompass a complete package that deals with improvements in future behaviour (through improved advice, education, monitoring, feedback, systems and so on, plus specific targets), redress and (if necessary) sanctions or deferment of prosecution.

The current approach is demonstrated in the Consumer Rights Act 2015, which consolidated and extended enforcement powers.[34] It includes powers for specified enforcers[35] to attach remedies focused on behavioural undertakings ('enhanced consumer measures') to Enforcement Orders and undertakings.[36] The government's consultation document when the Act was proposed began by noting that trust was central:[37]

> Markets work best when consumers have trust in the businesses with which they contract. High levels of consumer confidence encourage experimentation, which helps market entry, boosts competition and drives innovation … Consumer confidence is also rapidly eroded by rogue traders.[38]

> An effective enforcement regime requires several elements: law which is clearly understood by businesses and consumers; resources to promote compliance and appropriate enforcement tools to investigate and tackle non-compliance wherever it occurs; and organisation of such resources around the country so that rogue traders have nowhere to hide.[39]

A traditional model was that individual breaches of the law could be prosecuted, punishment imposed, deterrence would apply and the future would be different, without a repetition of that or similar breaches. We no longer think of this approach as being relevant to responding to human or organisational behaviour, or as being effective. The objective is to seek to constantly improve behaviour and performance, ensuring that we are always doing the right thing.

The critical insight is to separate actions that just impose sanctions in response to anti-social behaviour (backward looking) from responses aimed at affecting future behaviour (forward looking). Sanctions imposed for past behaviour should not be seen as being the way to affect future behaviour—one needs a different approach for that.

Changed Approaches by Regulators

Since 2010, all major public regulatory bodies have issued enforcement policies as required by the 2008 Regulators' Code. Analysis of many of these enforcement policies[40] illustrates the notable shift in approach from hard enforcement to support of compliance and performance. We can track the strong influence of responsive regulation, outcomes/redress and disappearing mention of deterrence—with only a small number of exceptions.[41] Figure 10.1 shows the authorities in the right column that cling to deterrence as the central and usually only policy in enforcement: the competition (but not consumer) side of the Competition and Markets Authority, the Financial Conduct Authority, the Serious Fraud Office, and OFCOM. The authorities in the left column adopt a responsive, supportive approach, rarely—and sometimes never—referring to reliance of deterrence. The central column lists the authorities that have shifted over time from an approach based on deterrence to a more open and supportive approach.[42]

It is surprising to realise how few UK authorities currently base their enforcement activities on the deterrence approach and how many authorities adopt a supportive approach as standard. The trend is clearly from 'deterrence' to 'supportive'. This direction of travel for those in the central column is related to the evolution in the functions of authorities that were initially created as 'economic regulators'. Their initial function was just to look at competition and prices in markets (where economic analysis is the core skill) and as time passed, they realised that they had inevitably to concern themselves with broader issues of market behaviour and ensuring the good treatment of consumers (where an understanding of behavioural science is critical). This widening of focus led to the need to ensure that redress is delivered to those who are harmed by unfair trading and that traders' behaviour is effectively addressed. The function includes more than stopping people doing bad things on individual occasions, and necessarily means that they need to look at systemic behaviour and its causes. Responding to individual instances of problems may be necessary, but addressing consistent patterns

Supportive	Mixed: moving from right to left	Deterrence
Effective inspection and enforcement: implementing the Hampton vision in the Office of Fair Trading. A review supported by the Better Regulation Executive and National Audit Office (Better Regulation Executive, Department for Business Enterprise & Regulatory Reform and National Audit Office, 2008). *Toward Effective Governance of Financial Institutions* (G30, 2012). *Civil Aviation Authority Regulatory Enforcement Policy* (Civil Aviation Authority, 2012). *Statement of Consumer Protection Enforcement Principles* (Office of Fair Trading, February 2012). *Meat and Poultry Processing Inquiry Review. Report of the Findings and Recommendations* (Equality and Human Rights Commission, 2012). *National Local Authority Enforcement Code. Health and Safety at Work. England, Scotland & Wales* (Health and Safety Executive, 2013). *Standards of Conduct. Treating Customers Fairly. Findings from the 2014 Challenge Panel* (Ofgem, March 2015). *Corporate Plan June 2015–March 2018* (Revenue Scotland, 2015). *Competition Policy: A Better Deal: Boosting Competition to Bring Down Bills for Families and Firms* (HM Treasury, December 2015). *Corporate Governance and Business Integrity: A Stocktaking of Corporate Practices* (OECD, 2015).	*The Bribery Act 2010. Guidance about Procedures Which Relevant Commercial Organisations Can Put into Place to Prevent Persons Associated with Them from Bribing (Section 9 of the Bribery Act 2010)* (Ministry of Justice, 2011). *The Prudential Regulation Authority's Approach to Banking Supervision* (Prudential Regulation Authority, April 2013). *Enforcement and Sanctions—Guidance. Operational Instruction 1356_10, Version 2* (Environment Agency, 2014). *Enforcement Guidelines on Complaints and Investigations* (Ofgem, June 2012). *Economic Enforcement Policy and Penalties Statement* (Office of Rail and Road, 2012).	*The Financial Conduct Authority: Approach to Regulation* (Financial Services Authority, June 2011). *OFT's Guidance as to the Appropriate Amount of a Penalty* (Office of Fair Trading, 2012), OFT423. *Changing Banking for Good: Report of the Parliamentary Commission on Banking Standards: Volume I: Summary, and Conclusions and Recommendations HC Paper No 27-I, II* Parliamentary Commission on Banking Standards, 2013. *The FCA's Approach to Advancing its Objectives* (FCA, July 2013). FCA's Decision Procedure and Penalties (DEPP) Manual ('credible deterrence').

Supportive	Mixed: moving from right to left	Deterrence
Better Business for All and Growth (Better Regulation Delivery Office, 2015). *Statement of Principles for Licensing and Regulation* (Gambling Commission, 2015). *Food We Can Trust: Regulating the Future* (Food Standards Authority, 2016). *Consultation on Ofwat's Approach to Enforcement* (Ofwat, March 2016). *Farm Regulators' Charter* (DEFRA and Others, 2016). Scottish Government Response to the Working Groupon Consumer and Competition Policy for Scotland (March 2016). *Monetary Penalties for Breaches of Financial Sanctions—Guidance* (Office of Financial Sanctions Implementation, HM Treasury, 2017). *Enforcement Policy* (Regulatory Delivery, 2017). *Information Rights Strategic Plan 2017–2021* (Information Commissioner's Office, 2017).	*Enhancing Consumer Protection, Reducing Regulatory Restrictions: Summary of Responses to the Discussion Paper and Decision Document* (Legal Services Board, April 2012). *The Future of Retail Market Regulation* (Ofgem, December 2015). *Enforcement Policy* (Care Quality Commission, 2015).	*Prioritisation Principles for the CMA. Consultation Document* (Competition & Markets Authority, 2014). Serious Fraud Office (see codes and principles at https://www.sfo.gov.uk/publications/guidance-policy-and-protocols/codes-and-protocols). *Penalty Guidelines: s 392 Communications Act 2003* (Ofcom, December 2015).

Figure 10.1: Classification of the UK authorities' enforcement policies

of behaviour, why it occurs and how it can be changed or avoided is far more important under a risk-based system. This inevitably includes helping people to do the right thing. Thus, trust is increasingly regarded as critical by many regulators[43] and by companies.[44]

The shift illuminates the point that the concept of enforcement in regulatory systems has been misdirected for too long by being designed for the estimated 1–2% of bad actors (psychopaths, sociopaths and criminals)[45] rather than the overwhelming majority of people, who are essentially trying to do the right thing. Of course, it is difficult to estimate how prevalent psychopaths are in the ranks of senior management, though various people have attempted to do so, and the estimates seem to cluster around 3–4%.

All regulators and businesses are on a journey and all are also at different stages of that journey. Not all regulatory bodies are moving at the same speed and some are considerably more advanced than others. Importantly, the OFT/CMA argued that it was not a regulator and thus was exempt from this approach, which is why it remained in an old-fashioned world while other public bodies developed new and more effective approaches. The world of economic theory, which in its classic form produces only deterrence as the policy for enforcement, has been gradually undermined by the spread of behavioural science under the title of 'behavioural economics'. A 2016 paper applies the same science as is discussed in this book, but still starts from the position that consumers are deviant rather than human: 'there is compelling evidence that consumer decision-making systematically strays from what would be expected from a "rational actor" within economic theory. These systematic deviations, termed "behavioural biases", can result in "behavioural market failures", leading to poor outcomes for consumers.'[46] We suggest that the correct approach is that consumers do not 'deviate' from a norm of being rational: as noted in chapter 1, the norm is that people are predictably irrational.

The situation revealed by Figure 10.1 above, showing different public bodies at different stages in terms of their attitudes towards those they regulate, also reveals the following observations about the current state of evolution of different regulatory spaces.[47] First, economic regulators preside over sectors where companies' behaviour is not as good as it should be because the regulator may still believe that its relatively recently endowed extensive powers enable it to control the behaviour of all the banks/energy companies/telecom companies that it regulates, whereas it may not yet have realised that its ability to affect business behaviour is in fact fairly limited and its focus on 'compliance' will not succeed. It is its own self-restricted approach that is the essence of the problem.

Second, if authorities were to treat companies as equal adults, they would respond. As we saw in chapter 1, this point is expressly referred to by both sides in civil aviation. But if you treat companies as naughty children who deserve to be punished, they will act accordingly.

Third, the approach to enforcement and compliance based on deterrence can be contrasted with the approach in safety sectors. In the latter, the adult–adult relationship is widespread, even if it could sometimes be improved—examples are civil aviation, medicines, medical devices and workplace safety. The same mature approach to ethical behaviour is also true of areas such as general retail and supermarkets, where basic trading activity is *not* controlled by sectoral regulators, but where consumers and competitors in competitive markets exert significant control over behaviour through commercial and reputational effects. The adult relationship exists there between businesses and their customers and the market, undistorted by public bodies. This context has enabled businesses to build a strong sense of alignment with their customers' values. It is well-supported in the UK through the Primary Authority structure, which is expressly based on fair ongoing relationships. Similar good outcomes are being achieved by authorities in relation to food standards, equality and human rights, environmental protection and others. However, if an individual consumer protection, environmental health or competition authority adopts a different approach, it will jar and will not tend to support a continuing adult relationship.

Regulatory Pluralism: Multiple Influencers

In businesses of any size, many people influence the decisions that are taken. The influencers can be both internal and external. So, in a society that aims to influence business decisions and behaviour, it makes sense to harness not just governmental bodies to exert regulatory influence, but also business structures and third parties who can do this. Leading scholarly development of the idea of a regulatory system in which multiple influencers or stakeholders influence behaviour ('regulatory pluralism') includes Gunningham and Grabosky's concept of 'Smart Regulation',[48] Black's 'decentred regulation'[49] and Parker's 'open corporation'.[50] In 'management-based regulation', agencies require companies to formulate and implement their own plans and procedures for reducing hazards (and to report on progress), perhaps overseeing or approving plans, or inspecting systems, premises, records or reports.[51] This holistic approach is mirrored in developments in economics, such as 'ValeNet',[52] which 'sees the economy as a network of interactions and value exchanges between many different actors, including millions of businesses, and millions of individuals acting in various capacities and contexts—as consumers, employees, professionals, friends, and so on'.[53]

The people who might influence the behaviour of the people in a business, and hence the behaviour 'of the business' itself, can be located both within and outside a firm, including trade associations, professional advisers and auditors, standards and certification bodies, banks requiring certification with International Organization for Standardization (ISO) standards, insurers imposing pre-contractual requirements and policy conditions,[54] investors, commentators, rating agencies and customer or consumer bodies,[55] as well as employees, even acting as whistleblowers.[56] In terms of political and constitutional theorising, 'power comes from everywhere'.[57]

Contractual governance through networks is being extensively used along supply chains, both nationally and internationally.[58] It is well established that pressure from (usually large) purchasers on (often smaller) suppliers can assist in specifying service levels and quality standards, and quality systems to achieve them.[59] Commercial consequences follow for a firm that is found to have produced goods that do not meet the mandated standards of quality, or to have been at fault in accidents in which it was involved, or to have issued false advertising or financial statements.[60] Potential customers may refuse to trade or may impose more onerous conditions, such as less generous terms.[61]

Cooperative enforcement[62] fosters regulatory compliance through cooperative governance, bargaining and persuasion methods.[63] Bridget Hutter, who has looked at railways in great detail, argues that the growth of trust systems has replaced the function of surveillance that a 'command and control' regulatory system would require.[64] Cooperative enforcement is argued to have advantages of being able efficiently to overcome deficiencies in ambiguous or inefficient regulations,[65] and to facilitate information sharing, especially on risks and how to avoid them. Its disadvantages can include an internal laxity or complacency in terms of the observance of standards, a tendency to delay or avoid beyond compliance so as to avoid incurring costs, and in involving insufficiently strong incentives or forces to induce compliance.[66] In the worst cases, it may involve too close a relationship between regulator and regulated that may involve 'capture' of the former[67] or even corruption. The informality of individual relationships may provide little externalised general deterrence.

However, the UK Committee on Standards in Public Life looked at the standards of behaviour and practice to be expected of regulators in 2016 and concluded that conflicts of interest are essentially a fact of life and have to be recognised and managed, especially though transparency.[68] A regulator who has no understanding of how a business operates, and of the pressures faced by the business and the people in it, will not be doing his or her job. Such a regulator will not be able to intervene in order to achieve effective outcomes, especially at the lowest cost.

Supporting Self-Assurance by Business

An important UK report on regulatory structures was published in 2017, which concluded that the future direction of travel across all regulatory sectors was and should be towards 'regulated self-assurance'.[69] The report was the product of a wide-ranging discussion involving a range of 31 regulators from different sectors amongst the 70-plus that operate, led by the Cabinet Office. The rationale for 'regulated self-assurance' was like this. Effective regulatory delivery models should focus, as far as possible, on outcomes rather than on a rules-based approach. Organisations should be able to find the best way to *self-assure* that they are meeting their legal responsibilities and should earn recognition that they are doing this. Where this occurs, the role of regulators should be mainly to provide information and advice to ensure that organisations assure themselves effectively and reliably, and intervene when they do not. Examples of this approach already exist, such as in various safety areas (civil aviation and the gas safety register), in supply chains (in the food sector, the Red Tractor scheme and egg and poultry schemes), in the Primary Authority scheme and in some aspects of schools and hospitals. The report speculated that significant savings could be made in terms of public sector costs with this general approach.

Regulators Supporting Business Growth

A logical development of the Better Regulation idea has been that regulators need to 'have regard to the desirability of promoting economic growth'.[70] The Statutory Guidance explaining this 'growth duty' specifies that regulators need to ensure that they:

> [H]ave a level of understanding of the business environment, their business community, individual businesses, and the impact of regulator activities on them that is appropriate to their duties and responsibilities, enabling them to deliver a risk-based, proportionate approach in their day-to-day activities.[71]

In explaining the importance that 'regulatory action is only taken when needed', the Guidance says:

> Simple, clear and timely guidance and advice is often the most important contribution that the regulator can make to supporting compliance. It can provide businesses with clarity and certainty, minimising the cost to them of complying with regulatory requirements. Good guidance and advice provide assurance for businesses that gives them and others, such as their customers, confidence that what is required is being delivered. It supports investment in new products, processes or markets and can help businesses to grow.[72]

In relation to proportionate decision-making, the Guidance says:

> 4.2. Regulators have a range of interventions at their disposal when responding to non-compliance, from those designed to incentivise and support compliance to those intended to tackle the most serious or persistent non-compliance. In some circumstances, they may also refer a matter to an organisation, such as another regulator, that is better suited to dealing with it. *Certain enforcement actions, and other activities of the regulator, can be particularly damaging to the growth of individual businesses*. These include, for example, enforcement actions that limit or prevent a business from operating; financial sanctions; and publicity, in relation to a compliance failure, that harms public confidence.
>
> 4.3. Regulators, therefore, should ensure that their enforcement policy sets out clearly the hierarchy of their enforcement actions and the factors that guide their use, so that their interventions are deployed in a proportionate manner on a day-to-day basis. Indicators that a regulator has regard to the growth duty in making decisions on how to respond to non-compliance involve recognition in their enforcement policy of relevant factors including:
>
> A. the nature and level of risks to regulatory outcomes associated with the non-compliance, including the risks to economic growth;
>
> B. the steps taken by the business to achieve compliance and any clear reasons for the failure;
>
> C. the willingness and ability of the business to address the non-compliance;
>
> D. the likely impact of the proposed intervention on the business, both in terms of remedying the non-compliance and in terms of economic costs; and
>
> E. the likely impact of the proposed intervention on the wider business community, both in terms of deterring non-compliance and in terms of economic benefits to legitimate businesses …

4.5. Regulators should, where appropriate, follow the principle that enforcement action is a last resort and they should help businesses first. In particular, businesses that are in the 'start-up' period, for example, require a specific style of intervention to enable them to meet the particular challenges that they experience in achieving compliance in all areas, whilst becoming established in their business. A regulator's response to identified noncompliance by start-up businesses should recognise these challenges. (Emphasis added)

Regulators and Others in Authority: Hindrance or Help?

We cannot lose sight of the sheer quantity of regulation that businesses (especially SMEs) have to cope with, which can crowd out a focus on values and how to achieve compliance with the relevant rules. A large corporation may have thousands of employees spread across 50 or more countries, who have to comply with thousands of different laws on many subjects. It should not be surprising that mistakes occur. Commercial and legal leaders of multinational companies see law as a constant threat and source of instability rather than a provider of stability and order.[73]

A second issue, raised in a post-Brexit vote audit of UK businesses by the Confederation of British Industry, is the 'constant iterative regulatory change that entrenches uncertainty in their strategy, breeding an overly cautious and an overly prudent nature of decision-making'.[74]

The conclusion here is that regulators and enforcers can support or hinder those who create jobs and wealth, and need to think about the consequences of their actions to ensure that they are supporting those who need it.

Conclusions

1. Regulatory policy in the UK has firmly moved away from 'command and control' styles to 'responsive' styles. The 'enforcement' approach associated with these approaches has similarly shifted for most UK regulators in relation to their responses to most businesses (apart from the unethical) from deterrence to supporting compliance.
2. The object is to *support* businesses to satisfy themselves that they are doing the right thing (self-assurance). When they make mistakes, the goal is to assist them to make changes to ensure that they will not repeat the error and that their performance will improve. This approach is intended to support business success and growth.

Part III

What is Ethical Business Regulation?

11

Ethical Business Regulation

Part III of this book puts all the evidence in Part I to work, in the practical context of business regulation as identified in Part II. How should we design and operate a system for the regulation of business activities based on what we know about how people make decisions and behave, both individually and in groups? How should the regulatory and enforcement system work? What should the relationship be between businesses and regulators, and vice versa, and everyone else?

The basic proposition, as we have discussed, is that the system should be based on expecting businesses to adopt EBP, and thus to do the right thing, and should assist and support them to do that. Each business must strive to behave ethically and show that it does. Where evidence of such commitment to ethical behaviour can be seen, businesses should be treated as adult members of society by equally adult public bodies. Businesses should know that where the evidence of their ethical behaviour is less convincing, the level of trust and of response by regulators will reflect this situation. Where a business demonstrates that it cannot be trusted or is a straightforwardly criminal enterprise, it will be treated accordingly. So, the essential choice rests with businesses and the people who work in them, but the attitude of public bodies and their staff is equally important.

Thus, Ethical Business Regulation (EBR) is an open relationship of trust between businesses and regulators built on evidence that both sides can be trusted and that each will, unless evidence to the contrary occurs, treat each other with respect in openly and fully cooperating to regulate risk and commercial behaviour in accordance with the fair rules of their society. This adult–adult relationship is based on the scientific knowledge set out earlier on how to support human behaviour in constantly monitoring and improving performance.

The design and operation of a regulatory system will be most effective where it adopts the following principles:

1. *A policy of supporting ethical behaviour.* The regulatory system will be most effective in affecting the behaviour of individuals where it *supports ethical and fair behaviour.*
2. *Ethical regulators.* Regulators should—self-evidently—adopt unimpeachable, consistent and transparent ethical practice.
3. *Ethical businesses.* Businesses should be capable of demonstrating constant and satisfactory evidence of their *commitment to fair and ethical behaviour*

that will support the *trust* of regulators and enforcers, as well as of employees, customers, suppliers and other stakeholders.

4. *A learning culture.* A blame culture will inhibit learning and an ethical culture, so businesses and regulators should encourage and support an essentially *open* collaborative 'no-blame' culture, save where wrongdoing is intentionally or clearly unethical.
5. *A collaborative culture.* Regulatory systems need to be based on collaboration if they are to support an ethical regime and to *maximise performance*, compliance and innovation.
6. *Proportionate responses.* Where people break rules or behave immorally, people expect to see a *proportionate response.*

Establishing EBR

People and organisations that demonstrate that they can be trusted on a consistent basis deserve the response of being trusted. One of the objectives of EBR is to support commercial activities by providing ongoing and consistent evidence that businesses can be trusted because they behave ethically in all that they do. Having a reputation not just for delivering good service and products but also for respecting customers, staff, suppliers, investors, neighbours, local communities and the society within which one operates should be good for commercial results. But, in addition, it should be good for the outcomes that public regulators and enforcers and internal management and compliance officers aim to produce. A further objective is to enable both business and regulators to benefit from a relationship based upon mutual trust. The regulator will benefit by having a cooperative and trustworthy partner and therefore being able to devote its resources to businesses that are at greater risk of non-compliance. Business will benefit by devoting time and resource to activities that will also enhance its commercial success. Thus, regulators should *enable* firms to enter into EBR arrangements and should *remove barriers* to them doing so, but should not require this: consumers, society and the market should drive the spread of EBR. One would hope that businesses would see the benefit and would encourage their regulators to consider an EBR approach.

The aim in the regulatory context is to do this by a business establishing a body of convincing evidence that it can be trusted to observe regulatory rules, to strive to exceed the standards that they set, to identify the root causes of problems as soon as possible and to take steps to rectify them. It will do this by nurturing an internal culture of doing the right thing and speaking up—an ethical culture. The evidence will be reliable, verifiable, transparent, consistent and constantly produced.

In an ethical business culture, the objectives of internal compliance and external regulation are the same. Accordingly, they should operate together by being integrated and fused, delivering not only effectiveness but also efficiency.

Measures of EBP

A regulator will ask: 'How can I tell if a business is being ethical—if it practises ethical business or not?' Traditional compliance and regulatory systems are based on systems that measure and produce metrics, so we understand that some form of quantification will be desirable. Although measuring culture may combine elements of art as well as science, useful tools are available and have been used to do so for the past 20 years in thousands of organisations. We do not agree with the following conclusion by leading City of London bodies:

> The conclusion that culture matters is a problematic one for regulators because it involves a qualitative approach. They cannot force companies to have a 'good' culture because they cannot define exactly what that means and measure compliance on an objective basis.[1]

Instead, we agree wholeheartedly with the second part of the assertion that: 'Good company culture does not lend itself to easy measurement and cannot be enforced via a tick box exercise.'[2] The components of good company culture can increasingly be measured and described based upon empirical research as the presence of certain characteristics and the absence of others, despite there not being only one combination of these characteristics that produces good outcomes.[3] For an individual business, it is a question of the accumulation of different pieces of evidence, ideally over time. It will by necessity involve examining a range of indicators, both quantitative and qualitative, rather than focusing on one 'objective' standard.

We still must be careful not to approach culture by means of a 'tick-box' approach with one list of requirements, such as might be included in an 'international standard on culture'. Ethical cultures do not all share the same exact characteristics; each business has a unique culture and its own values based, as we have seen, on many factors. Even organisations in the same industry sector will have their own personality and despite this may all be ethical. It is not possible to try to score businesses' 'comparative ethicalness'. In practice, one might say, in general terms, that a business is more ethical in its decisions on some subjects than others (such as staff safety or treating customers fairly) or that some businesses are more ethical overall than others, but these are value judgements and do not lead to a 'one-size-fits-all' definition of 'good' culture.

We suggest that evidence of a 'good' culture can be seen from the existence of systems that encourage certain behaviours and discourage others. There are many indicators and sources of information about culture, including leadership behaviour and communications, cultural values assessments, internal audit reports, anti-corruption risk assessments, employee and customer surveys, exit interviews, turnover rates, performance management discussions, etc. Looking at the number and type of staff, customer or supplier complaints or feedback of any kind can tell you a lot about the extent to which a business is respecting and respected by those groups. The state of an organisation's culture and parts thereof can be measured by established cultural assessment tools that survey employee values and the views of employees and other stakeholders on the values lived in the culture and on managerial behaviour.

In addition to specific cultural values assessment tools, there are other ways that one can collect information about the culture of an organisation, though we believe cultural assessments based upon measuring values are a powerful way to turn qualitative input into quantitative data. No one source of information will be adequate, so it is wise to look at all possibilities. For example, the FRC's 2016 report contains a series of questions and actions for board members to use to identify the culture of their organisation.[4] In addition to a list of questions to ask management, the report suggests board members should get a real feel by talking to the 'front line'. Board members, including non-executive directors, have a role to play in raising the tone of an organisation and their knowledge of the organisation should extend beyond the balance sheet. Therefore, these questions relate to the alignment of human resources processes such as performance reviews and incentives, as well as the risks that the corporate culture may create for the organisation and the ethics and compliance programme. The FRC report notes the employee engagement survey as a very widely used human resources tool for gauging culture. While employee surveys can be useful in this regard, they do not tell the whole story and can be complicated to interpret.

New cultural measuring tools for use in this area are being developed in response to the need to gain specific insights into the so-called compliance culture of an organisation as well. Increasingly, companies are communicating with the public about their values, their aspirations with respect to ethical behaviour and the means that they use to accomplish their goals. The Sustainability Reporting Standards of the Global Reporting Initiative (GRI) are an example of this trend. The GRI was created to promote transparency and drive concerns regarding sustainability into the decision-making processes of organisations globally. Although the standards cover a broad range of topics, they include numerous topics relevant to an organisation's commitment to behaving ethically. The point is that companies are generally becoming more willing to open themselves up to scrutiny in this regard. This is a trend that will facilitate the adoption of EBP.

As mentioned earlier, we do believe that it is possible to identify the general elements of the systemic adoption of EBP by a business. We set out some of our own ideas in chapters 13 and 14. Evidence of EBP could be indicated by external bodies such as the Good Corporation, Investors in People, or British Standards Institute or ISO certifications, but could also be through arrangements with regulatory bodies on the Primary Authority model. However, we emphasise that it is critical to avoid falling into the trap of specifying one rigid description or certification standard of or for EBP and insisting that all companies that aspire to it look alike. This is tick-box compliance by the back door. That is why we advocate a smorgasbord of indicators from which a company can choose those that best fit their culture and risk profile.

The evidence that will be necessary to establish ongoing trust may differ depending on the particular sector, type and size of business, and stage of development of both individual businesses and regulators. Hence, approaches will both differ and develop. In accepting that a business is trying to behave ethically, or to improve its behaviour, the judgement is one of whether the regulator—or any other observer—ultimately trusts that the business is genuinely making a serious and competent effort. Such trust should ideally be based on a relevant spread of evidence of different metrics, outcomes, experience and behaviours, including adherence to the items mentioned in the frameworks set out in chapters 13 and 14, and in whether there is a formalised relationship between the business and the regulator, such as under a Primary Authority-type model in which responsibilities and sources of evidence will be set out.

An EBP approach should start from basic ethical values that govern all actions, decisions and behaviour. In this respect, it equates to a regulatory regime comprising a tiered structure that has basic principles at the top, with secondary principles underneath, followed by rules that have greater granularity. This is the system proposed by Ofgem in 2016. The result should be that the complexity of a regulatory system can be reduced or avoided. The basic principles (do the right thing, check, ask, speak up) should guide conduct in unfamiliar situations. A large body of rules should be avoided, possibly replaced to a considerable extent by less formal guidance on what to do in certain situations (similar to the Primary Authority scheme's 'assured advice' arrangement explained in chapter 5 above, and the Bribery Act's 'adequate procedures' to prevent bribery approach, which will be discussed in chapter 12).

We wish to emphasise that adopting EBP is a voluntary choice by businesses. Regulators cannot require it; adoption should be consciously chosen by individual firms and individually demonstrated. Small or entrepreneurial businesses that are testing concepts or innovations might not be expected to be able to adopt complete ethical systems or frameworks, although mechanisms to ensure compliance with legal requirements would be required. Proportionality is key: are the values, norms and policies adequate in proportion to the risks the organisation is facing? Thus, the steps required to achieve EBP might not be universal, and it may take time for them to spread to some sectors. But it should be possible for those outside a business to be able to identify where a firm stands in relation to ethical practice. The Corporate Governance Code requires a board to establish the business' ethical values, and both these and the extent to which they are achieved should be transparent. We should be able to choose whether we want to work in, with or invest in a business based on its ethical track record. To do so, we need evidence.

EBP should be recognised by enforcers without a formal arrangement necessarily being in place. However, an EBR arrangement can go further than just providing information. It should ideally be a cooperative co-regulatory agreement aimed at delivering the shared outcomes of compliant and constantly improved performance. It should also do the following:

1. Identify who is going to perform which *tasks* in relation to the monitoring and improvement of regulation functions, such as checking, educating, evaluating, feeding back, producing change and so on. The objective is to produce an integrated and efficient system, avoiding unnecessary duplication but providing verification. The delineation of responsibility for specific tasks should be established.
2. Identify what type of *evidence* is going to be produced that will demonstrate not just compliance and performance but also ethical culture.
3. Agree a joint *commitment* to ethical practice to include openly discussing issues that arise and responses to them.

The existing Primary Authority scheme involves constructive, legally recognised partnerships between a business and a nominated local authority, enabling the provision of reliable advice to business and arrangements for coordinated and consistent enforcement.[5] Some Primary Authority arrangements are now being extended to include other regulators and trade associations or others.

The objective will be to find a way to balance conflicting needs: regulators and society want to know who to trust, and companies must be involved in a genuine attempt to express their best ethical culture.

Appendices 1 and 2 contain various lists of actions for businesses, regulators and governments that would support the adoption and spread of EBP and EBR. These lists are intentionally generalised, so they can be applied in differing specific contexts. Making EBR work starts with a state of mind. The objective is to incentivise entities to adopt ways of being and doing that create the conditions for ethical decision-making and behaviour to thrive.

While we must emphasise that there is no one way for an organisation to be ethical or to arrive at ethical business practice, we have set out in chapters 13 and 14 our ideas in the form of a cultural and leadership framework and a values-oriented ethics and compliance framework that, if adopted, we believe would allow an organisation to create, assemble and share relevant evidence with its regulator(s).

The EBR Relationship

The essence of EBR is the *relationship* between a business and a regulator. It is a relationship within which both business and regulator are incentivised to do the right thing and behave openly and fairly because trust takes time to build, but only moments to destroy. It must be adult, open, ethical and just. The Civil Aviation Authority refers to an *adult* conversation between airlines and others and itself, based on mutual respect, in which relevant information is openly shared, discussed and recorded. The parties would usually agree on action to be taken, but can disagree, and recording this usually assists in resolution. A straightforward example of this relationship approach is that of Revenue Scotland, which begins its 'standards and values' with the simple statements set out in Case Study 21. The first requirements on both sides are to be, and to be treated, honestly.

Evidence of trust has to flow from both sides—it is axiomatic that a body and its officials who represent the public should behave ethically. It is necessary to devote enough resources to having this type of relationship and conversation. It is axiomatic that all regulators need to ensure that they themselves demonstrably and consistently adopt the highest ethical standards. This follows inevitably from the well-established criteria of integrity and independence that are essential to maintain the legitimacy of their mandate. Public authorities represent the state and the public. A society that claims to be based on ethical principles should be able to trust that its agents act in accordance with its values.[6] Therefore, it also follows that the higher their standards, the better able public officials should be to encourage businesses to embrace ethical conduct as a route to compliance, and the greater the perception of acceptability of their regulatory and enforcement actions. In other words, if the reputation of a regulator falls below acceptable standards, there is far less hope that businesses will take seriously either the authority of that regulator or ethical conduct in general.

The requirement for regulators to be accountable leads to the need for them to welcome feedback and complaints to help them improve. This means that robust mechanisms need to be in place in relation to how to build trust and listen to feedback, and businesses need to trust that they can use them. Further, applying the concept of fairness to a system of risk-based regulation requires that a regulator should focus its efforts on those who deserve it.

An EBR relationship involves a culture of sharing full information and not hiding or delaying it. The ideal is a relationship jointly focused on achieving the shared ends. It will involve understanding the other's position and priorities. It will involve respect for the unique positions of each side: the regulator represents the public interest (rather than that the regulator is able to exercise power) and the business represents the interests of all its stakeholders and customers.

A regulator will need to adopt a basis and culture of distinguishing between ethical and unethical businesses and responding to each accordingly. A regulator should respond to a business that is ethical and deserves the regulator's trust by adopting a supportive approach. Precisely this distinction is at the heart of the approach to citizens of Revenue Scotland and the Scottish Environmental Protection Agency (see Case Study 21). It is striking how Revenue Scotland's basic covenant is: 'We will treat you as honest, and we expect you to be honest.'

In the context of a relationship between a business and a regulator, the point is that issues should be discussed between them rather than hidden. The EBR relationship should expect openness on both sides. This is the basis of the relationships in the civil aviation sector and the Primary Authority scheme outlined in chapters 5 and 12. If a business is unsure about how to interpret and apply legislation, the 'assured advice' mechanism in the Primary Authority scheme provides a mechanism for it to ask the regulator for a view on which the business may rely. Crucially, making such a request will be highly unlikely to trigger enforcement action.

Case Study 21: Revenue Scotland's Standards and Values[7]

Revenue Scotland will:

- Treat you as honest (unless there is reason to believe otherwise).
- Bring to account those who act dishonestly and try to evade paying tax, and challenge those who seek to avoid paying tax.
- Treat you courteously and with respect.
- Recognise your right to confidentiality and keep your data secure.
- Act with integrity and fairness, comply with relevant laws and regulations, and provide a prompt, accurate and professional service.
- Use our powers reasonably, consistently and proportionately.
- Provide you with guidance and support, helping to make it easy for you to comply with your obligations, pay the right amount of tax and claim reliefs to which you may be entitled.
- Work with you to minimise your costs in dealing with us, respond promptly and conclude matters as quickly as possible.
- Respect your right to complain if you are unhappy with our service, and your right to appeal if you disagree with a decision we have made on tax liability.
- Respect your right to be represented by someone.

Taxpayers and their agents and representatives (paid or unpaid) will:

- Be honest, cooperate fully and take reasonable care to ensure you provide all relevant information.
- Accept the responsibility to understand your tax compliance duties and seek assistance where necessary.
- Respect our staff and treat them courteously.
- Keep accurate records of all activities that may be taxable.
- Make accurate returns and claims with care and on time, to the best of your ability, knowledge and belief.
- Let us know promptly if you think you have made a mistake.
- Let us know promptly if you might have difficulty making a payment.

Responding to Adverse Events: Resisting the Impulse to Blame

When adverse events occur, the temptation to default to a blame culture must be resisted if learning and improvement are to occur. A natural response to problems (but one that Laloux would say comes from an earlier stage of development) is to ask 'Who's to blame?' rather than taking care to find out what the real cause of the problem is—and hence what the real solution is—and then reducing the risk that the problem recurs.

This is not to say that appropriately strong sanctions and responses should not be applied to those individuals who deliberately or recklessly break the law. It is important that proportionate consequences are applied to morally anti-social behaviour. The key issue here is the intention of the individuals: was it ethical or not? Were they wilfully ethically blind? Did the organisation take steps to minimise the risk of ethical blindness? Those with disciplinary and enforcement powers should distinguish between people who are intrinsically legal or illegal, responding to criminals with strong enforcement and supporting learning and improvement by those who were unfortunate or just unintentionally got things wrong. However, even for the latter, their response to having caused harm should be to apologise, explain and repair.

But the EBP and EBR paradigm is to support an open and just culture of sharing information. Adopting a punitive response for people who did not intend to cause harm will destroy that. The enforcement strategies and practices of legislators, regulators, prosecutors and courts—as well as businesses internally—should promote and recognise business commitment to an ethical approach. A considerable amount of work has been done on furthering this approach in various contexts, as we will note in chapter 12.[8]

The paradigm also involves a business doing the right thing by proactively seeking to prevent problems from arising, seeking to identify problems as soon as they arise, disclosing the problem, investigating the problem and identifying its root cause, analysing the means of reducing reoccurrence, making changes so as to reduce the risk of it happening again, putting right any damage caused and continuing to monitor the situation. Enforcement policies should incentivise this behaviour. The approach of the Bribery Act 2010 (see chapter 12 below) to exonerating companies that have adequate procedures in place is on the right track. Enforcement policies that are based on taking into account aggravating and mitigating factors are also on the right track, but they may take into account factors that are irrelevant to the essential issue of whether the perpetrator was behaving ethically or unethically. They are not acceptable if they still impose a high penalty in response to people or organisations that have tried to do the right thing. EBP should also be recognised and supported irrespective of whether a formal arrangement is in place between regulator and business.

If the 'blame game' is not going to be pursued, it will be necessary for people to know that this is the case and that the reason for this is that trying to blame someone for events prevents learning, improvement and prevention of reoccurrence. This will need a clear and consistent public statement of the policy, and political leadership over its adoption. The importance of this cannot be overstated. Both business and regulators will be concerned not to be seen to be adopting a self-serving shift in policy, and the public must therefore understand how they will benefit and how companies will be held accountable for improvements and mitigation of the risk of reoccurrence.

'Deterrence' as a term should be dropped. It involves connotations that are ineffective and describes an earlier style of society that believed that fear and punishment produced good behaviour. We should talk instead about 'affecting future behaviour'. Influencing future behaviour has to be addressed specifically and separately from responding to historical behaviour

The scientific evidence is that 'deterrence' has at best a limited effect on future behaviour in many circumstances. It is possible to influence the brain by reminders not to do something. But constant surveillance of every activity by others is not possible or affordable. A society based on mutual surveillance and accusation is unattractive and constitutionally unacceptable. In contrast to the deterrent approach to *enforcement*, there is now a significant body of evidence that influencing behaviour by maximising actors' internal controls can be highly effective, can apply to multiple behaviours/actions and can be efficient. Further, enforcers in a wide range of regulated environments seek to maximise *compliance and performance* based on supporting rather than blaming. An unfair 'deterrent' response will prevent the voluntary flow of information, prevent learning and undermine an ethical culture.

The basic question in investigations and deciding on sanctions is to identify whether the people who caused the offence were intending to act ethically or not. Are these people and organisations ones that you can trust consistently or ones that do things for unethical motives, such as making money illegally? The Anderson review divided people who break laws into a typology of five clusters of people: prepared and established; guilty procrastinators; capable but unconcerned; conscientious but challenged; and blind-eye turners.[9] A similar segmentation approach has been used by HMRC and the Scottish Environmental Protection Agency, whose model is given in Figure 11.1.

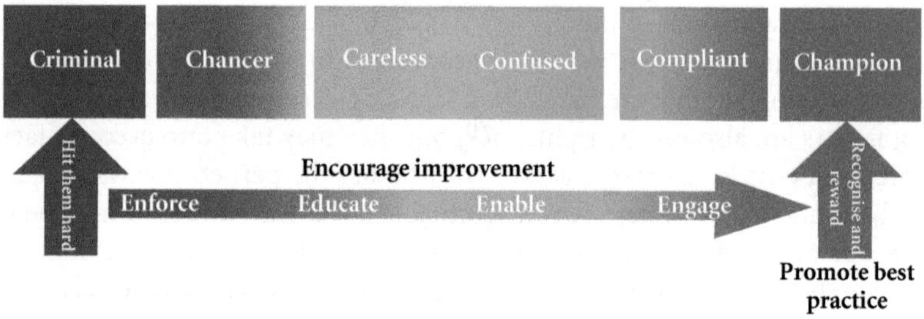

Figure 11.1: Segmentation of offenders: the Scottish Environmental Protection Agency's spectrum of compliance

Case Study 22: Relations between a US Regulator and a Major Company

In the mid-1990s, Hodges attended a large internal conference in an American drug company, at which one of the speakers was a senior official of the Federal Drug

Administration (FDA). He began his remarks by congratulating the company on its close working relationship with the FDA. At that point, an in-house lawyer leant over and said: 'We escort them onto the campus and we escort them off. They only get to see and discuss what is agreed in advance. We don't share things with them unless we have to.' This approach contrasts with what Hodges had observed in numerous different contexts of the relationship between the UK regulator (now the Medicines and Healthcare products Regulatory Authority (MHRA)) and firms in the UK (even the same firm as that just mentioned in its US context). The relationship was based on professional respect and trust, since most of those taking part on both sides were qualified in medicine or pharmacy. They had no difficulty in sharing and openly discussing the technical information, and agreeing the right course of action. The problem that both sides faced was more to do with the inexpert attitudes of politicians and the media, and how best to explain their technical decisions to such non-experts. The first question that these interlocutors would ask was: 'Who is to blame?' To those who were grappling with complex technical issues, lack of complete data, and a serious gap in comprehension and communication, a simplistic framing of an issue in terms of blame was simply irrelevant and did nothing to aid public understanding, reassurance or protection.

There must be better ways than this!

Conclusions: Reasons to Adopt EBR

There are various reasons that support adoption of EBR. For government, the major considerations are:

— to implement economic policy based on both promoting business by reducing burdens whilst also improving outcomes;
— to save public resources in stretched public authorities by extending greater self- and co-regulation that has a significantly higher likelihood of avoiding the historical problems of less than ideal compliance and behaviour associated with self-regulation, by supporting business;
— to seek shared outcomes, growth and innovation;
— to reduce 'compliance' and 'enforcement' activity and to make it more effective, given the growing realisation of the drawbacks of enforcement based on economic or individual deterrence rather than on behavioural science and thus maximising the outputs through motivating and encouraging voluntary ethical practice. This allows enforcers to concentrate resources and hard enforcement on high-risk and criminal activities.

For business, the advantages are:

— to achieve increased performance in terms of compliance and risk reduction, since this supports profitability and innovation;
— to improve relationships with some regulators and enforcers, since an open relationship is more productive in terms of achieving desired outcomes than an adversarial one;

- to address a lack of consistency between different enforcers now that some widely different approaches have become apparent. Inconsistency of approach applies not just within countries but also between states. The different culture of regulators raises challenges and costs for businesses;
- to reduce uninformed political influence on balanced and fair regulatory decisions. This is seen as a real problem in responding in a logical way to reducing risk, especially in responding to a crisis. It distracts from addressing the real issues. The over-reaction of asking 'who's to blame?' leads to a witch-hunt and the imposition of excessive and irrelevant extra regulatory burdens;
- to reduce the level and imposition of fines and to divert expenditure to remediation, although this involves spending on ethical culture and putting things right;
- to benefit from the likely strengthening of the company culture and hence financial performance.

12

Developing Examples of Ethical Regulation

The nature of regulation differs depending on its context and the nature of what is being regulated (safety, prices, standards and so on), and the practice of regulation has also evolved at different speeds and ways in every context. Developing EBP and EBR is a journey, and will differ depending on the sector and context. We look here at some examples of developments that can be seen as supporting EBR (or not). We have already seen in chapter 5 examples of regulatory cooperation, in the pharmacovigilance system (and similar product safety systems), civil aviation safety, the Primary Authority scheme and workplace health and safety. When one starts to look, one can find many diverse examples of current practice that adopt aspects of EBR.

Civil Aviation

A strong illustration of the flexibility and collaboration that is possible within the new approach is that of the Civil Aviation Authority, which has for some years adopted an open approach with most major airlines (but reserves deterrence for some other operators or situations). Figure 12.1 shows that its direction of approach starts with 'collaboration and facilitation', moving to 'advice' and ending with an escalating series of formal enforcement tools.

The Primary Authority Scheme

The coordinated approach of the Primary Authority scheme has been hugely successful in delivering assured advice to support consistent good practice. For trusted businesses, it reduces the need for inspections or enforcement action and instead supports communication within an established relationship so as to identify and swiftly resolve issues as they arise. It has spread quickly, and now involves 10,000 businesses, 90% of which are small. Most of the benefits of Primary Authority for a business have come from the ability to talk to a regulator (paying for the

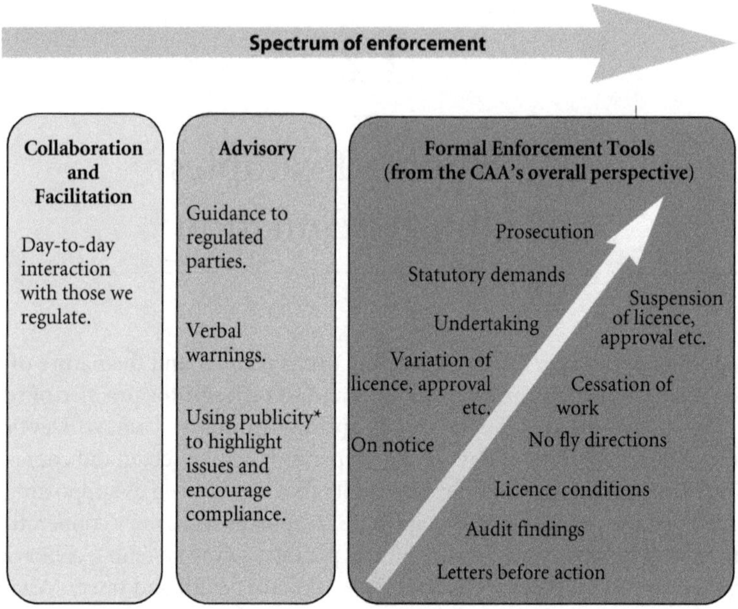

Figure 12.1: ***Civil Aviation Authority Regulatory Enforcement Policy*** **(2012)**[1]

consultancy time). There has only been one dispute to resolve in 8 years, whereas there have been many previously.

Some success stories from the Primary Authority scheme are as follows:

- At a Northamptonshire local authority, savings to businesses in 2014–15 were estimated to be £80,000, with improvements in business compliance and satisfaction.
- Imperial Cars' partnership with Portsmouth City Council reduced complaints to Trading Standards by half and increased turnover by £27 million.
- A care home group (HC-One) made savings of £1 million as a result of agreeing single best practice that was applied consistently across its multiple homes in different geographical areas across the country.[2]

From 2016, the Primary Authority architecture has been extended in two directions: vertically to include trade associations within the relationship structure and horizontally to be able to include some national regulatory authorities.[3] From October 2017, 'every UK business can access advice they can trust from one place'.[4]

The government's Regulatory Delivery Directorate published its service standards in 2017 on what businesses can expect of it, which emphasise that it carries out all its activities 'in a way that supports those we regulate to comply and grow' and includes the following statements (which, it will be seen, are a long way from an approach based on deterrence):

Helping you to get it right

We want to work with you to help your business to be compliant and successful and it is important to us that you feel able to come to us for advice when you need it. We won't take enforcement action just because you ask us a question or tell us that you have a problem …

Responding to non-compliance

Our aim, when dealing with non-compliance, is to deliver fair and objective enforcement in a manner consistent with the intentions of the legislation and the necessity of delivering a robust and credible enforcement regime. Where we identify any failure to meet legal obligations, we will respond proportionately, taking account of the nature, seriousness and circumstances of the offence, including taking firm enforcement action when necessary.[5]

As can be seen from the discussion in chapter 5, the architecture of the Primary Authority scheme, as extended in 2017, is expressly designed so as to enable trade associations and other bodies to be able to influence—and partly regulate—their members. Other stakeholders such as NGOs can also have a huge potential to influence organisational behaviour.[6] Historically, it has proved difficult for external stakeholders to influence, or be interested in influencing, SMEs.[7] Similarly, we noted in chapter 9 concern by investors that they are not able to exert adequate pressure on behaviour. SMEs, by definition, are small groups of people and are more likely to be influenced by the ethics of their owner-managers, which are in turn influenced by market values and revenue-based activities.[8] Equally, there is plenty of evidence that SMEs can be responsive to advice, education and 'rehabilitative' approaches.[9] The Primary Authority scheme has been successfully built on that premise and there are signs of new feedback mechanisms emerging that may assist the responsiveness of SMEs towards customers and wider agendas.

Food Standards

The Food Standards Agency (FSA) has adopted a strategic goal of 'Food We Can Trust' and published the following five principles that form the core of discussions with stakeholders in 2016:

1. *Businesses are responsible* for producing food that is safe and what it says it is, and should be able to demonstrate that they do so. Consumers have a right to information to help them make informed choices about the food they buy—businesses have a responsibility to be transparent and honest in their provision of that information.
2. FSA and regulatory partners' decisions should be tailored, proportionate and based on a clear picture of UK food businesses.
3. The regulator should take into account all available sources of information.
4. *Businesses doing the right thing for consumers should be recognised*; action will be taken against those that do not.

5. Businesses should meet the costs of regulation, which should be no more than they need to be. (Emphasis added)[10]

The FSA's 'Regulating Our Future' policy[11] adopted an 'open policy-making' approach that involves multiple stakeholders: expert advisory groups from industry and from professions, a consumer panel, 'hot house' groups to resolve particular issues (such as national inspection strategies), tailored stakeholder engagement, feasibility studies and pathfinder trials. Potential assurance streams that are anticipated for the future include: audit by independent accredited third parties, internal checks by first and second parties, official controls by a competent authority, and certified regulatory audits, the last introducing competence assessment.

Studies published in 2017 that compared the approaches to assessing compliance and scoring of the public authorities and of two major businesses showed consistent similarities. This supported the policy that audit data collected by food businesses could be used by local authorities to check food hygiene standards and decide ratings.[12] Hence, the authorities could rely on businesses that they trusted. This approach was seen to be logical when it was realised that a major supermarket employed 800 people collating and scrutinising supply chain data.

A programme involving the FSA working *with* the major retailers and processing plants in relation to the incidence of campylobacter on chickens led to a 17% decline in the number of laboratory reports of the bacteria—the most common cause of food poisoning—in 2016, which was estimated to have led to 100,000 fewer human cases of campylobacter, with a direct saving to the economy of over £13 million in terms of the cost of days off work and NHS costs.[13]

Workplace Health and Safety

The good work of the HSE in relation to improving the safety of construction work has been referred to in chapter 5 above. In 2011, the Institute of Directors and the HSE published advice that the basic principles in maintaining health and safety in workplaces were:

1. Strong and active leadership from the top:
   a. visible, active commitment from the board;
   b. establishing effective 'downward' communication systems and management structures;
   c. integration of good health and safety management with business decisions.
2. Worker involvement:
   a. engaging the workforce in the promotion and achievement of safe and healthy conditions;
   b. effective 'upward' communication;
   c. providing high-quality training.
3. Assessment and review:
   a. identifying and managing health and safety risks;

b. accessing (and following) competent advice;
c. monitoring, reporting and reviewing performance.[14]

The advice stated that company boards typically fall short in not leading effectively on health and safety management; they should all consider the following issues: competent advice, training and supervision, monitoring and risk assessment.

A 2012 meta-review of 40 papers, of which 35 were quantitative studies and 5 were qualitative studies, found the following consistent associations between specific leadership styles and safety outcomes:

— *Transformational leadership* (e.g. acting as a role model, inspiring and motivating employees to work safely and showing concern for employees' welfare) enhances a number of safety outcomes including fostering perceptions of a positive safety climate, promoting higher levels of employee participation in safety activities, compliance with safety rules and procedures and safety citizenship behaviours (e.g. participation in safety committees, looking out for workmates' safety).
— *Transactional (contingent reward) leadership* (e.g. clarifying performance expectations, monitoring and rewarding performance) is associated with perceptions of a positive safety climate, positive safety behaviours and reduced accident rates.
— *Passive leadership* (i.e. turning a blind eye to safety) is associated with lower levels of safety consciousness, negative perceptions of safety climate and an increase in safety-related events and injuries.
— The effects of transformational and transactional leadership are both direct and indirect. In the latter case, positive effects are achieved through the promotion of a positive safety climate. In addition, transformational leaders can influence safety by enhancing employees' levels safety consciousness (i.e. knowledge).
— The benefits of transactional leadership are enhanced when safety is valued across different levels of management. Transformational leadership styles combined with trusting relationships between management and employees enhance employee safety performance such as safety citizenship behaviours.
— *Trust in management* influences perceptions of safety climate as well as accident involvement. Behavioural consistency, honesty and integrity, sharing and delegation of control, openness and accuracy of communication, and demonstration of concern are qualities that influence the development of trust in leaders.
— The quality of relationships between employees and management, particularly supervisors, impacts on safety. *High quality leader-member exchanges, characterised by mutual trust, and openness* are associated with higher levels of upward safety communications, safety citizenship behaviours and reduced levels of safety-related events. Safety citizenship behaviours in particular, are pronounced when, in addition to high quality leader-member exchanges, leaders emphasize the value of safety and promote a positive safety climate.[15]

The review noted that those studies that focused on specific safety management attitudes, behaviours and practices (and all of these things could be said of ethics) have consistently shown that:

— *Management commitment to safety* is associated with a reduction in risk-taking behaviours and violations, lower levels of self-report incidents and higher levels of learning from safety events.

- *Perceptions that safety policies and procedures are enforced* and consistently implemented are associated with lower levels of incident under-reporting, self-report injury incident and higher levels of satisfaction with the organisation.
- *Leader support for safety and openness to safety suggestions* is associated with higher levels of employee willingness to raise safety issues, lower levels of self-report injuries, higher levels of satisfaction with the organisation and can lead to a long-term improvement in safe working practices.
- *Safety communication* between management and the workforce is associated with a reduction in the levels of risk-taking behaviours, promotion of positive safety behaviours and reduced levels of self-report work-related pain.
- *Active involvement in safety* helps promote perceptions of a positive safety climate and fosters increased levels of employee accountability and responsibility for safety.

In fact, one of the salient points we have observed is that effective approaches to safety and ethics are remarkably similar.

Case Study 23: Ethics as Analogous to Safety[16]

While reviewing the Borealis Code of Ethics and 'ethics excellence programme', we learned many lessons from the step change in safety that was ongoing at the same time. Messages such as 'you are looking at the person responsible for your safety' posted on the mirrors in the lavatories equated to our mantra 'ethics is everyone's responsibility'. Also, by discussing the relationship between the two concepts, we found it easier to gain employees' attention and commitment to ethics. Safety was more intimately associated with the well-being of the average employee, and it was a not difficult to show how ethics and integrity could affect them in similar ways. This analogy is useful in manufacturing companies that can relate to safety concepts but have not yet matured in their approach to ethics.

Energy

Ofgem, originally created as an economic regulator, broadened its approach and introduced Standards of Conduct (SoCs) in 2014. A principal objective was to produce supply licences that were much shorter, more accessible and clearer about what is expected of suppliers.[17] One of the main objectives was emphasis on a culture of 'treating customers fairly':

> Under this proposed new regulatory approach, there will be a much greater onus on suppliers, right up to board level, to work out what's right and fair for consumers rather than following a list of prescriptions from Ofgem. This requires a significant culture change where suppliers place consumers at the heart of their business, watch carefully for any areas where they may not be getting things right for consumers and, if this happens, put things right quickly. Suppliers who do this will face fewer burdens and have flexibility and space to innovate. Those suppliers who do not take this seriously will have a much more difficult time.

The objective is to 'put responsibility on suppliers to deliver good consumer outcomes'.[18] The Standards of Conduct require suppliers (amongst other things) to:

1. ensure that they behave in a fair, honest, transparent, appropriate and professional manner (SLC25C.4(a));
2. provide information that is complete and accurate and not misleading and provide information which is otherwise fair both in terms of content and in terms of how it is presented (SLC25C.4(b)(i) and (iv)); and
3. act promptly and courteously to put things right when suppliers make a mistake and otherwise ensure that customer service arrangements and processes are complete, thorough, fit for purpose and transparent (SLC25C.4 (c)(ii)–(iii)).

This broadening of focus raised the challenge of how to enforce the SoCs. It has started to engage in dialogue with operators in a Challenge Panel, which is making progress, and is pursuing an initiative on Future Retail Regulation that aligns closely with ethical retail principles, outcomes and conduct.

The change in Ofgem's approach to sanctions is truly dramatic. Its enforcement notices typically set out detailed arrangements on what businesses are going to do in generating change in their behaviour, usually with specific targets, which can be monitored. There has also been a transformative shift between imposing fines to overseeing payment of redress from 2010 to 2015, as shown in Figure 12.2.[19] In 2014/15, redress represented 92.5% of the volume of remedies imposed, with £26.4 million being paid or made available to customers, £15 million in penalties and £19.3 million in payments to charities or other third sector organisations in lieu of financial penalties.[20]

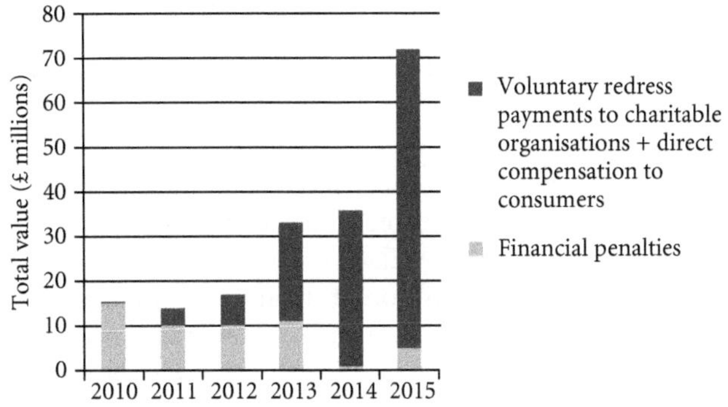

Figure 12.2: Financial penalties and voluntary redress resulting from enforcement actions by Ofgem 2010–15

Equality and Human Rights

The Equality and Human Rights Commission identified extensive legal infringements in the meat and poultry processing sector after an inquiry commenced in

2008. The sector employed 67,500 people. The Commission had a choice between adopting traditional 'hard' enforcement, prosecuting some offending companies, or a 'softer' approach aimed at achieving more widespread and permanent change across the sector. It chose the latter. Reviewing results in 2012, it reported significant progress:

> Rather than taking expensive and confrontational enforcement action, we decided to work with, and support, the industry to improve their recruitment and employment practices. We began by writing to processing firms setting out the main findings of the inquiry, relevant recommendations and encouraging them to draw up an action plan to tackle the challenges the industry faced. We also set up a representative industry taskforce chaired by the Ethical Trading Initiative. The aim of the taskforce was for the industry to take the lead and work together to tackle the challenges it faced, supported by the Commission. The solutions for business came from business.
>
> The supermarkets and industry bodies identified and agreed management practices and key performance indicators (KPIs) to deal with many of the problems identified in our inquiry. These have already been adopted by meat and poultry processing firms supplying most of the major supermarkets.[21]

The Commission continued to work with the industry to embed good practice. As with the similar approach adopted by the HSE, a sea change in attitudes occurred across the sector. Supermarkets and other major influencers were enlisted to support and procure good practice. The Commission has adopted the same approach in relation to other issues, such as employers' attitudes to maternity rights. The basic approach is to work *with* people rather than *against* them.

Water in Scotland: Prices and Wider Issues

In Scotland, both the water regulator, the Water Industry Commission for Scotland (the Commission), and the sole undertaking, Scottish Water, are publicly owned. The principal focus of the regulatory function is to control prices and levels of service for customers. In setting out its methodology for the next regulatory control period in 2021–27,[22] the Commission expressly accepted the principles of EBR set out in *Law and Corporate Behaviour: Integrating Theories of Regulation, Enforcement, Compliance and Ethics.*

The regulatory philosophy of the Commission is that Scottish Water should 'Seek Trust But Expect Verification' and that 'the onus is on Scottish Water to demonstrate both now and on an on-going basis that its customers and other stakeholders should trust it to deliver the right levels of service for an appropriate price'. The Commission said:

> We were very encouraged to learn of the work of Christopher Hodges, Professor of Justice Systems at the University of Oxford. His work on ethical business regulation appears to be closely aligned with the practical steps that we are taking. For example, we agree strongly with his conclusions that a constructive relationship—backed by

strong incentives to 'do the right thing'—will maximise performance, compliance and innovation.

The Scottish Government has adopted the work of Professor Hodges as the basis for their thinking of how best to use their new consumer powers and, more generally, how regulation should work in the interests of customers.

There appear to be several steps required to reduce the potential for information asymmetry, ensure there is no regulatory capture and empower customers and communities to the maximum extent possible. These steps seem to us to include:

Engagement

— Greater trust and openness between regulators and the regulated, which will act as a catalyst for a far more productive relationship and the ability to take forward joint solutions to address the challenges ahead;
— Direct engagement between the regulated company and its customers to agree a detailed business plan that will meet the needs of the full range of its customers;

Managing risk

— An opportunity to agree how uncertainty and risk should be handled: helping drive improved performance and greater innovation;
— An opportunity to provide revenue certainty beyond a particular regulatory control period if this could reduce costs or improve levels of service;

Monitoring and reporting

— Fully transparent reporting of performance—with appropriate evidence—and progress towards meeting agreed service levels and other targets by the company—with further detail being available to those who wish it;
— A mechanism to monitor financial performance and ensure that returns are fair and not excessive but also that a company is insulated from unexpected costs;

Governance

— An expectation that a regulated company will identify the extent of out-performance and discuss how to share the benefits with its owner and other stakeholders (including the scope for immediate improvements or by putting the money away for the proverbial rainy day);
— Scottish Water to take full responsibility for its capital expenditure and be directly accountable to its customers and to the Quality Regulators. It should be able to evidence why it has taken the steps that it has; and
— A strong regulatory body that is able to comment authoritatively on performance. The regulator would produce a high quality and accessible monitoring report—with further detail being available to those who wish it. This would include an expectation that negative comments from the regulator should have a material impact on the management of the regulated company and its reputation.

The Commission proceeded to address 'what needs to change' under this approach of 'Collaboration: Seek Trust But Expect Verification'. It started by accepting that *all* key stakeholders—owner, company and regulator—would be required to change. The owner (the government) would need to 'think long term and recognise that maintaining the legitimacy of water charges in the eyes of customers is the critical challenge'. The company would need to 'demonstrate how and why it is acting in the best interests of its customers—both now and into the future. It has to recognise that its approach will be subject to detailed scrutiny and comment and that its customers will, in future, have ever higher expectations'. The economic regulator would need different skills to focus 'less on econometric modelling and the design of incentives and more on scrutiny of analysis, forensic questioning and rigorous performance monitoring'.

The Commission also accepted that 'embedding trust among stakeholders will be a key enabler to improving the quality of decisions taken in the Scottish water industry and driving benefits for customers', as this is the 'principal foundation' of the concept of EBR.

In relation to the risk of 'regulatory capture', the Commission said:

> There is the potential for 'regulatory capture' when the regulator becomes unable to make appropriately independent judgments about a regulated company. The Commission's experience suggests that it has to be alert to any such accusation. The political process is quick to spot and seek to criticize any failures of governance or performance of a publicly owned company or its regulator.
>
> Regulators should therefore be cautious about working with a regulated company. It is right and proper that economic regulators guard their ability to make independent judgments and avoid being pulled unnecessarily into management detail. It is not surprising that economic regulators generally prefer market solutions—effective markets do, after all, empower customers.
>
> The Commission's experience is somewhat different. It designed and implemented the first 'in the market' framework for competition in the water industry. To ensure that this framework was successful, the Commission understood that it would need to have an understanding of the costs, capital requirements and risks of the business activity that was to be made competitive. It worked, therefore, with Scottish Water and potential new entrants to ensure that non-household wholesale prices and retail margins were appropriate such that an efficient entrant would find it attractive to enter the non-household retail market. This joint working was, in our view, essential to the success of the non-household retail market opening. It largely eliminated the potential impact of information asymmetry. Doubtless prior to that experience, the Commission would have seen collaboration as inimical to effective regulation. It is not. Better information and improved understanding actually significantly reduce the risk of capture.

Nuisance Calls in Scotland[23]

A consistent body of research shows that people in Scotland are disproportionately affected by nuisance calls compared to people elsewhere in the UK. For example, an analysis of 9 million calls received over a 3-year period conducted by the consumer group Which? and call-blocking technology provider trueCall[24] concluded that 3 of the top 5 cities receiving the highest volumes of nuisance calls were Scottish. While for some these calls are simply an annoyance, for others whose circumstances make them particularly vulnerable, they can act as a gateway for unscrupulous actors to cause substantial emotional or financial distress.

The Scottish government does not have devolved powers to regulate this area, but recognises that the principles of EBP and EBR could still be used to take action. In fact, the lack of regulatory power makes it an ideal opportunity to increase collaboration and work to change business behaviour by raising standards and, in so doing, to make it easier for enforcement agencies, regulators and those receiving calls to identify and tackle the worst offenders.

Key to this work is bringing regulators, consumer groups, businesses and academics together to develop a joint programme of work with three linked but distinct strands: empowering those who can to protect themselves; improving business behaviour by emphasising best practice; and encouraging partnership working actively to protect those who are at most risk from serious harm.

All of this rests on the knowledge that there will always be a need to tackle bad actors who prey on vulnerable citizens, but that the vast majority of businesses want to do the right thing and are themselves harmed by abusive practices. Successfully identifying and tackling these actors requires a flexible approach that targets resources where they are needed most and supports businesses that make mistakes rather than intentionally doing wrong to improve and raise standards.

By placing a strong emphasis on collaboration, the Scottish government and its partners are developing a holistic strategy that combines protection, prevention and behavioural improvement. In particular, this will focus on improving business behaviour by developing best practice principles and a forum for shared learning, especially as it relates to identifying and protecting vulnerable customers, and creating mechanisms to ensure that a wide range of organisations, for example, social workers and healthcare practitioners, are linked with enforcement agencies to better identify both those who may need extra support to stay safe and the offenders who seek to exploit their vulnerability.

Bribery and 'Adequate Procedures' to Prevent it

The UK Bribery Act 2010 departed from previous anti-bribery legislation and, among other provisions, established a new corporate offence of 'failure to prevent bribery by associated persons'. It came into force in 2011 and has already motivated many companies doing business in the UK to rethink their approach to compliance. It is a strict liability offence and there is no need to prove that the company intended to commit the bribery. All that is required is that an employee or other 'associated person', basically anyone doing business on behalf of the company, commits active bribery. However, the 'adequate procedures' defence was provided—if an organisation can prove that it had adequate procedures for preventing bribery by associated persons, it may escape liability under the corporate offence.

Although there is no one definition of 'adequate procedures', the UK Ministry of Justice did publish guidance at the time that the Act came into force.[25] During the lengthy consultation period, many people argued for a focus on culture and values and a move away from a tick-box compliance approach. The Six Principles set out in the guidance clearly point to the importance of culture, particularly in Principle 2, Top-Level Commitment, which says: 'Those at the top of an organisation are in the best position to foster a culture of integrity where bribery is unacceptable.' Therefore, top-level management must be committed to preventing bribery and must foster a culture in which bribery is never acceptable.

In addition, the other Principles encourage a thoughtful, tailored approach for each organisation subject to the Act:

(a) *Proportionate Anti-bribery Procedures*; meaning policies and procedures proportionate to the risks that the organisation faces, that are effectively implemented.

(b) *Periodic, Informed and Documented Bribery Risk Assessments*. In addition to assessing the external risks to which an organisation might be exposed, the Guidance recognized that the risks might come from within.

(c) ... a bribery risk assessment should also examine the extent to which internal structures or procedures may themselves add to the level of risk. Commonly encountered internal factors may include:

A. deficiencies in employee training, skills and knowledge
B. bonus culture that rewards excessive risk taking
C. lack of clarity in the organisation's policies on, and procedures for, hospitality and promotional expenditure, and political or charitable contributions
D. lack of clear financial controls
E. lack of a clear anti-bribery message from the top-level management.

(d) *Due Diligence* proportionate to the identified risk, acknowledging that third parties operating on behalf of an organisation pose a high risk of corrupt behaviour.

(e) *Communication*, including training about relevant policies and procedures but also conveying the 'tone at the top'. Included in this concept was the need for 'a secure, confidential and accessible means for internal or external parties to raise concerns about bribery on the part of associated persons, to provide suggestions for improvement of bribery prevention procedures and controls and for requesting advice.' To be considered effective, there needs to be protection from reprisals for reporting concerns.

(f) *Monitoring and Review*: Since corruption risk will change over time as the business evolves, it is important for organisations to monitor and evaluate the effectiveness of their procedures and ensure that they remain fit for purpose.

The tone and content of this Guidance makes it clear that organisations are responsible for having a clear understanding of their business and culture, and of that of their business partners in order to design procedures that are adequate and effective for them.

There is no 'one-size-fits-all' or tick-box solution. There are suggestions and principles that serve as guidance. We believe that this approach encourages companies to think more deeply about all aspects of their culture and continually review their progress.

Product Manufacturers

The importance of balancing economic, technical and ethical considerations was highlighted in a survey of those involved in European product safety and surveillance, published by the European Commission in 2017.[26] Respondents comprised manufacturers (49%), importers/distributors (21%), users (8%), conformity assessment bodies (5%), online intermediaries (1%) and others (16%). No less than 89% of respondents considered that their products were affected by non-compliance with EU product legislative requirements. Of the businesses, 80% thought that non-compliance has a negative effect of sales and/or market shares. Of all respondents, 33.47% thought that the most important reason for non-compliance was a *deliberate* choice to exploit market opportunities at the lowest cost, followed by a lack of knowledge (26.78%), a technical or other type of inability to comply with the rules (10.88%), ambiguity in the rules (10.46%) and carelessness (9.62%).

Financial Services: Regulation Will Be Inadequate Without an Ethical Culture

> The regulatory response to the crash of 2008 has been to fight the symptoms instead of the cause.
>
> Joris Luydendijk[27]

By way of contrast with the sectors noted above, in which elements of an ethical behavioural approach have been adopted with success, it is instructive to consider examples of sectors where establishing behaviour based on ethical values has been identified as important, but has proved to be a challenge. The closed world of competition enforcement has been noted in chapter 3 above. Here we look briefly at the financial services sector. The focus on imposing rules, compliance and legal accountability seems to have crowded out understanding on how to support the spread of ethical behaviour.

Before the 'Big Bang' expansion of the City of London in 1986, informal rules were applied through 'club regulation', gentlemen's agreements based on the principle that 'my word is my bond', self-policed by social responses and ultimately by exclusion.

The financial sector has experienced a series of crises:

- The collapse of significant institutions, such as secondary banking crisis in the 1970s, BCCI in 1991,[28] Barings in 1995[29] and Equitable Life.[30]
- Repeated cycles of mis-selling consumer products and persistent failures to comply with suitability rules,[31] such as pension transfers and opt-outs,[32] PPI[33] and endowment mortgages with interest-only loans.[34] PPI products were mis-sold to over 12 million consumers, and firms paid over £22 billion in compensation between April 2011 and May 2016. This was mirrored in the EU context, where a 2011 trawl of 1,200 mystery shoppers conducted across 27 EU Member States found that only 43% of retail investment products were deemed to be broadly 'suitable' under a relatively simple rubric (i.e. they basically fulfil shoppers' needs in terms of investment liquidity and risk level), while the remaining 57% were assessed as broadly 'unsuitable'.[35]
- Mis-selling of interest rate hedging products, especially to businesses and particularly SMEs.[36]
- Systemic manipulation by banks of the London Interbank Offered Rate (LIBOR).[37]
- General business practices (various banks, including Barclays),[38] such as allegations of intentionally putting business customers into default so as to reap increased fees (RBS).[39]
- The payment of excessive remuneration to employees, especially through bonuses or selling incentives.[40]

One striking feature of this long series of serious failures is why lessons were not learned and changes made earlier. As a result of the emergence of this succession of failures, general confidence in this vital industry fell to an extremely low level, and remained so,[41] fuelled by popular perception that bankers continued to fail to grasp the public's lack of trust in them, as evidenced by the continuing award and receipt of large bonuses, often against overall loss-making results.

Political responses to the financial crisis focused on introducing a massive increase in rules and attempts to impose 'accountability' on individuals in the financial industry, in the belief that would control future behaviour. In contrast, one imaginative academic proposal was to incentivise self-regulation of the financial sector to prevention of systemic risks by relying on meaningful incentives for firms:

- establishing a separate regulatory regime for financial institutions that deal and trade in complex instruments of risk transfer;
- eliminating those institutions' access to federal deposit insurance and other forms of public subsidy;
- mandating mutual self-insurance against the systemic risk which these institutions' activities create.[42]

The proposal was based on the idea that the nuclear industry's self-regulatory response to the disaster at Three Mile Island through the Institute of Nuclear

Power Operations (INPO) and the chemical industry's response to the Bhopal disaster through its Responsible Care programme were based on a 'community of fate'.[43]

Over and above various mechanistic explanations for the series of major failures in this sector, such as a regulatory system that contained numerous technical gaps, and a politically inspired policy of leaving the banks alone ('light-touch regulation'), all major reports on the financial crash emphasised the crucial importance of addressing culture. In other words, the issue raised was the absence of self-regulatory value-based control on behaviour.[44] Three fundamental aspects of the prevailing culture have been identified:

— Maximisation of shareholder value: exposure to short-term value extraction by takeover and asset stripping; focus on short-term performance fuelling spiralling remuneration.
— Incentives: maximisation of personal gain and business profits; bonuses, macho culture, sales targets.
— No other-regarding ethic: pure selfishness.[45]

These aspects have been discussed in chapter 9. For now, we should note some comments on culture. In relation to PPI, the House of Commons Committee of Public Accounts has said:

> The cultures of firms and the nature of their sales incentives have been identified as key factors behind mis-selling. The FCA has taken some action to deal with these root causes, for instance by promoting changes to firms' incentive structures and better training of financial advisers. The Senior Managers Regime, which the Government is introducing for banks from 2016, aims to get senior people to take greater responsibility for the actions of those they manage. But the risks of mis-selling remain, for example pensions freedoms reforms are a potential trigger for future mass mis-selling. Middle managers in financial services firms were often promoted on the basis of achieving sales targets, making it hard to embed more customer-focused approaches.[46]

Statements by the FCA from the same time also emphasised the fundamental importance of a firm's culture.[47] Clive Adamson, the Director of Supervision at the FCA, noted that it was difficult to set criteria for an acceptable culture, but it was possible to observe outcomes and actions that indicated this, and to identify the key drivers of culture at a firm, which include:

— setting the tone from the top;
— translating this into easily understood business practices; and
— supporting the right behaviours through performance management, employee development and reinforcing through reward programmes.[48]

A 2013 report by Anthony Salz into the business practices of a major bank, in the light of the emergence of ongoing scandals, noted that:

> A bank's licence to operate is built on the trust of customers and of other stakeholders, such as its staff, regulators and the public as a whole. Trust is built from experience of reasonable expectations being fulfilled—a confidence that an organisation will behave

> fairly. Successful banks acquire a reputation for being trustworthy. This can take decades to build. Yet it can be destroyed quickly and, in global organisations, by events almost anywhere in the world. Some companies have greater reputational resilience than others. They get the benefit of the doubt when things go wrong—partly because of the far greater number of things that go right and partly because of the way they respond to problems. Public opinion also tends to be more generous to those organisations that seem to be trying to do the right thing, or that have an appreciable social purpose.[49]

The bank had itself noted that trust in banks had been 'decimated and needs to be rebuilt' and that its own behaviours had elicited significant criticism.[50] The bank's culture had favoured 'transactions over relationships, the short term over sustainability, and financial over other business purposes'.[51] Salz found that that culture had predominantly shaped the unacceptable business practices. He laid the responsibility for leading a transformation in culture with the Board and the Group Chief Executive.[52] He recommended that the design and operation of the ways in which the bank managed and developed its people was crucial to supporting a desirable culture, and that the human resources function should be given sufficient status to stand up to the business units on a variety of people issues, including pay. Pay had been seen as the primary tool to shape behaviour, and insufficient attention had been given to personal development and leadership skills (as opposed to technical training).[53] Salz said that the bank must improve its openness and transparency in order to facilitate trust, but this would involve a fundamental change in attitude and mindsets rather than mere reporting[54] Fundamental change was also in relationships with key stakeholders, including moving from a confrontational approach with regulators to one that is more open and cooperative.[55]

Leading scholars also noted a shift in the analysis of financial markets from economics to a social conception.[56] This would necessitate a shift in the style of regulation from rules to a social dimension. A major group of investment firms noted:

> The Group is unanimously and firmly of the view that beyond our formal recommendations, the greatest need is for deep cultural change.[57]

A group of interested parties issued a report in late 2014 that identified culture as the cause and solution of problems for retail banking.[58] It stated that an aggressive sales culture was a major driver of bank failure, that policy interventions addressed structural issues but left culture change to the banks and that all banks had some kind of culture change process under way, but that change remained fragile and many expected bad practices to continue. Culture was said to be better in the new, smaller challenger banks. It called on banks to commit themselves to continuous and consistent delivery of culture change.

In 2016, the incoming head of the FCA identified culture as a key concern:

> There is a reasonable debate about what is culture, but that is not a debate about whether it is important. In my view, culture is a product of a wide range of contributory forces: the stance and effectiveness of management and governance, including that well used phrase 'the tone from the top'; the structure of remuneration and the incentives it creates; the quality and effectiveness of risk management; and as important as tone from the

> top, the willingness of people throughout the organisation to enthusiastically adopt and adhere to that tone. Out of this comes an overall culture. It is not something that has a tangible form. As supervisors, we cannot go into a firm and say 'show us your culture'. But we can, and do, tackle firms on all the elements that contribute to defining culture, and from that we build a picture of the culture and its determinants.
>
> Culture has a major influence on the outcomes that matter to us as regulators. My assessment of recent history is that there has not been a case of a major prudential or conduct failing in a firm which did not have among its root causes a failure of culture as manifested in governance, remuneration, risk management or tone from the top ... As regulators, we are not able, and should not try, to determine the culture of firms. We cannot write a regulatory rule that settles culture. Rather, it is the product of many things, which regulators can influence, but much more directly which firms themselves can shape.[59]

Individual Accountability: The Dead End of a Legal Approach

In 2013, the UK's Parliamentary Commission on Banking Standards considered that a key problem lay with a lack of individual responsibility of bankers and that the answer lay in punitive accountability:

> *The problem*
>
> Too many bankers, especially at the most senior levels, have operated in an environment with insufficient personal responsibility. Top bankers dodged accountability for failings on their watch by claiming ignorance or hiding behind collective decision-making. They then faced little realistic prospect of financial penalties or more serious sanctions commensurate with the severity of the failures with which they were associated. Individual incentives have not been consistent with high collective standards, often the opposite.[60]

In order to improve standards across the banking sector, the Parliamentary Commission inspired a package of legislative reforms 'intended to create a new framework to encourage individuals to take greater responsibility for their actions, and [would] make it easier for both firms and regulators to hold individuals to account':[61]

1. A new 'Senior Managers Regime' (SMR) for individuals, who are subject to regulatory approval, requiring firms to allocate a range of responsibilities to these individuals and to regularly vet their fitness and propriety. The intention was that the most important responsibilities within banks should be assigned to specific, senior individuals[62] so they could be held accountable.
2. A 'Certification Regime' requires relevant firms to assess the fitness and propriety of all employees who could pose a risk of significant harm to the firm or any of its customers.
3. A new set of 'Conduct Rules', with far wider application than previously, sets expectations about standards of behaviour, so as to provide a framework for regulators to make judgements. The key new rules are 4 and 5 in Table 12.1.

4. A new criminal offence for senior managers of reckless misconduct in the management of a bank.[63]

Table 12.1: FCA conduct rules

First tier—individual conduct rules	
Rule 1	You must act with integrity.
Rule 2	You must act with due skill, care and diligence.
Rule 3	You must be open and cooperative with the FCA, the Prudential Regulatory Authority (PRA) and other regulators.
Rule 4	You must pay due regard to the interests of customers and treat them fairly.
Rule 5	You must observe proper standards of market conduct.
Second tier—senior manager conduct rules	
SM1	You must take reasonable steps to ensure that the business of the firm for which you are responsible is controlled effectively.
SM2	You must take reasonable steps to ensure that the business of the firm for which you are responsible complies with the relevant requirements and standards of the regulatory system.
SM3	You must take reasonable steps to ensure that any delegation of your responsibilities is to an appropriate person and that you oversee the discharge of the delegated responsibility effectively.
SM4	You must disclose appropriately any information of which the FCA or PRA would reasonably expect notice.

The Parliamentary Commission's approach of increasing accountability by creating criminal offences for individuals was supported by the PRA and the FCA.[64] The FCA wanted to identify who was 'responsible' for what actions, but was unable to be clear about which senior managers held which responsibilities. The FCA therefore supported making banks identify this so that individuals could then be prosecuted for the deeds of people for whom they were 'responsible'. The FCA also felt it was responding to public anger towards those the public felt 'got away with it'.[65]

Practitioner lawyers criticised the notion of sanctioning senior managers of failed banks on the basis that it failed to address two key problems: a lack of clarity about who was responsible for failure; and the absence of an agreed standard to which key roles should be performed.[66] They criticised the criminalisation of individual conduct when key decisions are usually taken on a collective basis (board responsibility) and they argued that it was unjust to reverse the burden of proof, if a regulator could not satisfy a court that an individual had broken the rules, by making an individual prove the opposite.

Will this attempt to hold some senior people criminally responsible for the behaviour of others supposedly under their control affect the behaviour of the latter? Is it fair?

Case Study 24: The Culture of a Global Industry

The well-known story of the financial services industry over the past decade needs little elaboration. Many have questioned how a whole industry can lose contact with the morality of the society in which it is embedded, such that so much everyday practice (systematic behaviour, such as lending mortgages that could never realistically be repaid, then selling and buying such worthless securities; selling payment protection insurance products to those who did not need them; fixing foreign exchange and other dealing rates; claiming that culture had been 'fixed' when it had not and serious infringements were still being carried on) that was internally regarded as normal and laudable was what external society viewed as being blatantly immoral. Further, how did such practice escape both internal and external attention, and add up to behaviour that was so risky as to endanger the integrity of the global financial system?

The response has to include strengthening the regulatory system, but that is not enough to affect the day-to-day behaviour of so many workers in an entire industry. How can regulators or others affect mass behaviour? Will it be adequate for global regulatory bodies or an impressively large group of judges[67] to insist that bankers adopt an ethical culture? Will preaching at bankers be enough? Will establishing a professional institute for bankers be enough? Will the morale of those involved in the industry be undermined by an extended period of public vilification, such that the quantity and quality of recruitment will suffer, and bankers will drown under a regulatory burden and prefer to take the low-risk option of not lending? There are signs that all these problems remain unresolved in the financial services sector.

Case Study 25: UBS Rogue Trader[68]

Kweku Adoboli booked fictitious trades to cover up gambles and set up secret funds. At one stage, possible losses were $10.6 billion, which would probably have brought down his employer, UBS. When he was caught, he lost UBS $1.4 billion. He was sentenced to seven years in prison. After his release, he gave an interview to the BBC's Economics Editor. He unreservedly apologised for what happened, admitted he had failed, had been dishonest and had made mistakes. He did not think of himself as a criminal and thought that his 'intentions were always in the right place'. He claimed that others at the bank knew of his actions, although UBS denied this and no other charges were brought against others. He said that: 'People are required to take risk to generate profit, because yields in the industry are consistently compressed.' If investment banks continue to push for the same level of profitability as in the past, he expected that traders would continue to be pushed to make profits 'no matter what' and that it could 'absolutely happen again'.

Case Study 26: The Amoral Financial Sector

The journalist Joris Luyendijk interviewed approximately 200 financial services personnel working in the City of London and concluded that the entire system was based on a culture in which amorality was endemic and unavoidable by individuals.[69] Everyone was focused on business ('revenue responsibility') and on making their allocated budget so as to keep their job. Bonuses could be large, but were entirely based on financial results. The traders whose revenue figures were lowest were regularly 'let go' ('a brutal hire-and-fire culture') and individuals' figures could even be publicised daily. Managers were equally focused on their figures and had no time or incentive to consider any long-term or ethical issues. Traders were not immoral; they had no time or opportunity to be either moral or immoral in daily behaviour, as the system unavoidably required them to act amorally in order to make money.

Bankers were quoted as saying: 'I know banks where admitting you got things wrong is not a smart thing to do.' 'The trouble is', he said with a perfectly calm smile, 'a bank's internal management often don't know what's going on themselves because banks today are so vast and hugely complex.' Such organisations 'continue to be governed by a system of incentives that seem almost designed to encourage short-termism'.

Luydendijk concluded that the City was a 'heartless place' that is out of control ('an empty cockpit') and where the culture is incapable of producing ethical behaviour without fundamental changes in how targets, remuneration and careers operate.

Success in Delivering Redress

One area in which the FCA—and various other regulators—has achieved a significant shift concerns the delivery of redress to customers. The traditional approach is that there is a clear distinction between public and private law and actors: public officials deal with regulation, ultimately relying on fines and convictions, whereas private actors must use other intermediaries (lawyers, litigation funders and civil courts) to seek damages. However, regulators have realised that it is part of their job to see that firms treat their customers fairly, that markets that are unbalanced by illegal activity are rebalanced, that illicit gains are not retained by those who have broken rules, and hence that consumers and customers are paid the redress they are due. Thus, regulators in some countries have been given powers to see that redress is paid. These 'regulatory redress' powers form one element in their enforcement toolbox. These redress powers have been used highly effectively by the consumer authority in Denmark (called the Consumer Ombudsman) and various sectoral regulators in the UK. The result is often that businesses' agreement to pay redress is agreed as part of a wider and comprehensive settlement of all regulatory infringement matters. Hence, payment of redress is achieved very swiftly and efficiently, and far more so than if those who have lost out had to instruct lawyers and sue, perhaps in lengthy and costly collective litigation.

The FCA has a number of powers to secure redress to consumers and has been increasingly active in doing so since 2000.[70] Between April 2014 and November 2015, the FCA established 21 informal redress schemes, which it estimates have provided £131 million in compensation to consumers.[71]

The Financial Sector in 2017

From 2014, the Banking Standards Board (BSB) set out to examine how far a firm demonstrates characteristics that it expects to be associated with any good culture in banking, namely, honesty, respect, openness, accountability, competence, reliability, responsiveness, personal and organisational resilience and shared purpose. The BSB's first report in 2017, from the views of 28,000 staff in 22 UK banks and building societies, found 'many examples of good practice', but also identified 'areas where change is needed, and where deep-rooted attitudes and behaviour detrimental to the interests of customers and clients' as well as workers.[72] It highlighted that 'responsiveness, accountability, personal resilience and openness are all areas where ... progress needs to be made'.

In a perspicacious speech in 2016, Minouche Shafik, then Deputy Governor of the Bank of England, analysed five factors that had driven misconduct in the sector and led to fines and redress costs paid by UK banks since 2009 of almost £35 billion:

> A combination of factors caused 'ethical drift' across the industry where bad behaviour went unchecked, and became progressively more widespread and accepted as the norm. Market structures (such as poorly designed benchmarks, unmanaged conflicts of interest, and possibilities for collusion) presented opportunities for abuse. Systems of governance and control focused on second and third lines of defence that were weaker than highly profitable and powerful trading desks. Weak market discipline, particularly from the buy side, meant that poor market practices were allowed to continue. Remuneration and incentive schemes stressed short term returns over longer term value enhancement. And finally, a culture of impunity was prevalent because of a perception that the likelihood of being caught was low.[73]

Emerging Collaboration

We have been critical of both industry and regulators in the financial services sector. We do not believe that an ethical culture can be imposed on people or organisations, whether by regulators or employers.[74] But there is recent evidence of adoption of more collaborative approaches, which are proving to be effective. First, the existence of the BSB itself is something to be encouraged. Second, leading financial regulators around the world are experimenting with a 'regulatory sandbox', which permits banks to test innovative products, services, business models and delivery mechanisms.[75] The technique appears to be successful. The Dutch Financial Regulator DNB has been focused on behaviour and culture for over five years, and although its approach is based upon inspection, it is informed by the conviction that these aspects are key to successful regulation.[76]

Third, the FCA has quietly taken a notably fresh approach to regulating the credit sector, which comprises over half of the firms that the FCA regulates, moving away from the traditional approach of simply imposing rules. The change in style was first seen in relation to credit cards (a sector worth £68 billion), where a market study took an unusually soft approach.[77] It gave examples of good practice, areas of concern and key risks to consumers, and noted that the FCA had worked with industry in developing agreed new approaches. The FCA did not use its enforcement powers, nor did it proceed by proposing a lot of new rules, which would have taken years to introduce. The discursive and consensual approach delivered effective change swiftly. The approach involves transparency, dealing with problems and low key reporting. The same approach is now apparent in relation to the motor finance sector (worth £53 billion). In 2017, the FCA announced a review (not a Review).[78] The Finance and Leasing Association (FLA) responded by contacting the FCA to confirm that it was already working on various initiatives, such as on improving training and competence, and the outcome was that the FCA joined the FLA working group.

Fourth, a partnership between central banks and market participants has produced a Global Code of good practice in the foreign exchange market in 2017.[79] This Global Code is organised around six leading principles (see Figure 12.3), the first of which is 'ethics'.

- *Ethics*: market participants are expected to behave in an ethical and professional manner to promote the fairness and integrity of the FX Market.
- *Governance*: market participants are expected to have a sound and effective governance framework to provide for clear responsibility for and comprehensive oversight of their FX Market activity and to promote responsible engagement in the FX Market.
- *Execution*: market participants are expected to exercise care when negotiating and executing transactions in order to promote a robust, fair, open, liquid and appropriately transparent FX Market.
- *Information sharing*: market participants are expected to be clear and accurate in their communications and to protect confidential information to promote effective communication that supports a robust, fair, open, liquid and appropriately transparent FX Market.
- *Risk management and compliance*: market participants are expected to promote and maintain a robust control and compliance environment to effectively identify, manage and report on the risks associated with their engagement in the FX Market.
- *Confirmation and settlement processes*: market participants are expected to put in place robust, efficient, transparent and risk-mitigating post-trade processes to promote the predictable, smooth and timely settlement of transactions in the FX Market.

Figure 12.3: The FX Global Code: Guiding Principles

Conclusions from the Evidence across Different Sectors

The main themes that emerge from this brief review, which is limited to just a few sectors and some recent developments, are as follows. First, there has been a shift in the goals and rhetoric—and in some cases the practice—of regulators in relation to how they see their roles and what they expect from businesses. Second, those authorities that have widened their approach are increasingly engaging with the *what* and *how* of actions that businesses are planning to take to improve their performance and to reduce the risk of future infringement. To do this, an authority has to shift from operating remotely at a desk, assuming that a monetary penalty will magically induce all desired changes, and engage with how businesses actually operate on the ground, in order to understand what changes can and will be made, and in what sequence, when and by whom. This extra level of understanding necessarily requires the authority to get closer to business practice (through visits and discussions, rather like how a non-executive director should operate in getting around and talking to people). Equally, it requires an open and transparent response to the authority by the business at all levels. This means that the two need to have a *relationship*, and one of trust, based on an open, full and frank basis.

Third, there has been a significant shift by some regulators in the practice of how they respond to businesses who break the rules—in other words, their enforcement practice. A striking example of this is the shift made by Ofgem in the past five years, reducing fines significantly whilst promoting a huge increase in redress paid by infringing companies to consumers, trade customers and charitable causes. (Ofgem is not alone amongst authorities in this shift in emphasis, and various others can be applauded for similar actions, such as the many charitable payments produced by the Environment Agency under its civil sanctions powers.)[80]

We do not suggest that all the sectors or authorities in the following examples have achieved the ultimate vision that we advocate, but we commend them as examples of a significant shift in approach in the right direction. We add a contrasting example of financial services, where some of the rhetoric on culture fully accords with our vision, but much of the practice does not, and seems unable to shift away from a traditional policy of credible deterrence. Therefore, the final point that these examples illustrate is that all authorities and sectors exist largely in their own silos, do not communicate with each other and have not realised what a transformative shift is quietly occurring or that it is one that they could achieve.

The financial services sector stands out in this review by seeming to demonstrate a schizophrenic nature (although the sectors reviewed are selective, and financial services are not completely alone in this, even if they seem now to be in a minority). The BSB pursues the laudable aim of assisting the industry to 'demonstrate to … customers and to others that it is trustworthy'.[81] Meanwhile, leading regulators make statements about the importance of culture in banks, but these statements are then undermined by inconsistent messages over the approach to compliance being based roundly on 'credible deterrence' and the introduction of a criminal regime for senior managers who are to be held 'responsible' for things that might occur in their divisions. This approach is simply not going to work. It is not credible and scandals will continue. The deterrence policy can only go in the direction of increasing penalties, whether on firms or individuals, which will ultimately be seen as unfair and ineffective in achieving behavioural change in behaviours. Customers may receive redress through the welcome intervention of regulators, and the Treasury may benefit from the large fines, but such costs merely serve to increase customers' costs and reduce employees' and investors' benefits, without affecting behaviour for the better. There appears to be no evidence of a holistic relationship of trust, and an absence of blame, between industry and the regulatory community.

In contrast, the energy regulator has made a dramatic switch from imposing fines to starting to address behaviour directly. Authorities dealing with civil aviation, workplace health and safety, trading standards, gambling, equality and human rights, and various others have been moving in this direction for some time.

Harnessing Self-Regulation

The idea that people will change how they behave if someone they respect suggests how they should do things differently, noted in research in how people follow others and in how SMEs need and react to advice, has driven the extension of the Primary Authority scheme to include company headquarters and trade associations as intermediate tiers in the vertical hierarchy. This is merely the old idea of self-regulation in a new guise.[82] But the problem with self-regulation is that people cannot be trusted to act altruistically all the time. The current economic climate of stringency of public resources has also driven the return of interest in self- and co-regulatory structures, as can be seen in the identification of 'earned recognition' and 'regulated self-assurance' in the *Regulatory Futures Review*. This model opens the door to social groups such as colleagues and customers supporting 'doing the right thing' through collective engagement and maintaining individual and collective reputations for ethical behaviour.

EBR offers the answer to this conundrum. It examines the circumstances in which an actor may be trusted by society (and regulators), because he produces constant evidence that supports placing trust in him. Hence, if businesses can be trusted, regulation may be complemented—or might even be replaced in some situations—by actors' commitment to doing the right thing. This was in fact what OECD said in 2011:

> Develop and apply effective self-regulatory practices and management systems that foster a relationship of confidence and mutual trust between enterprises and the societies in which they operate.[83]

In regulatory terms, the trick is for the regulatory system to harness businesses' wish to 'do the right thing' and their actions in doing so, and regard suitable evidence of that as being an integral part of the regulatory, surveillance and enforcement system. The UK government adopted exactly that policy in 2017 for future regulation.

After the publication of *Law and Corporate Behaviour* in late 2015, what is now the Regulatory Delivery (RD) Directorate of the UK Department for Business Energy and Industrial Strategy published a paper summarising the evidence for EBR.[84] These two publications were noted by the European Commission as supporting its strategy for innovation.[85] The Scottish government indicated its intention to include EBR as a consistent core policy in delivering its political goal of a fair Scotland[86] and held a series of meetings with regulators on implementation of this approach. The approach was noted and approved of in the draft *Manual on Consumer Protection* by the United Nations Commission for Trade and Development (UNCTAD).[87] In September 2016, a slightly longer version of the RD paper was commissioned by the UK's Committee on Standards in Public Life as an annex to its report on ethics in regulatory bodies, in which it examined how the seven (Nolan) principles of public life applied to a range of such bodies.[88] This paper set out a number of actions that could be taken by businesses, regulators and government to encourage and support an ethical approach to commerce and regulation, which have been incorporated into this book. The Committee's report concluded that, in accordance with the principle of providing external leadership, 'regulators should actively engage with those they regulate and take a leadership role by encouraging positive attitudes towards compliance'. The Committee recommended that such promotion of an ethical approach to compliance would be supported by a suitable amendment to the Regulators' Code.

The 2017 policy statement by the UK government on 'Future Regulation' recommended that all regulators should aim to move towards a model of 'regulated self-assurance' and 'earned recognition'. This policy statement supported and built on the EBR ideas of an open, no-blame relationship between regulator and business, in which business was supported by assurances from its staff, suppliers, customers, investors and professional auditing and accreditation bodies and personnel.[89] This policy document adopted the proposition that regulators should allow other stakeholders to hold organisations accountable. It expressly extended the regulatory model to encompass a potentially wide range of stakeholders, since they can provide evidence of ethical or unethical behaviour by businesses. It is recognition that regulators are not the only people who represent the public interest.

But more is changing here than just a regulatory structure, from a binary regulatory–regulatee relationship to a 'regulated self-assurance' model involving potentially multiple actors. The implicit acceptance is that rules and models cannot guarantee behaviour. Hence, *ethical* business practice has to be a requirement and cannot be ignored. The government said:

> In practice this means that businesses who 'do the right thing' should be regulated with a very light touch. As part of this, regulators should encourage more ethical business practices. However, where regulated entities do not 'do the right thing' and do not follow ethical business practices, redress should be sought.

What is needed now is a very strong focus on demonstrating the absolute non-negotiability of ethical values in conduct. Thus, fairness—ethics—is inescapably at the centre of both a fair society and of the maximisation of all social (and hence commercial) interactions. Accordingly, the next steps in both corporate culture and regulatory relationships should be towards a norm of ethical behaviour.[90]

Conclusions

1. Cooperative frameworks, relationships and structures, as well as reliance on ethical values, can be seen developing in regulatory regimes across a wide range of sectors. The shift to EBR would be merely a formality in many instances. Elements that can be relied on in EBR regimes can be cross-fertilised from good practice in diverse sectors.
2. The UK government's high-level policy of 'regulated self-assurance' provides a framework within which to embed EBP and EBR. Indeed, the framework may well not work effectively without these ethical and behavioural elements.

Part IV

How to Implement Ethical Business Practice and Ethical Business Regulation

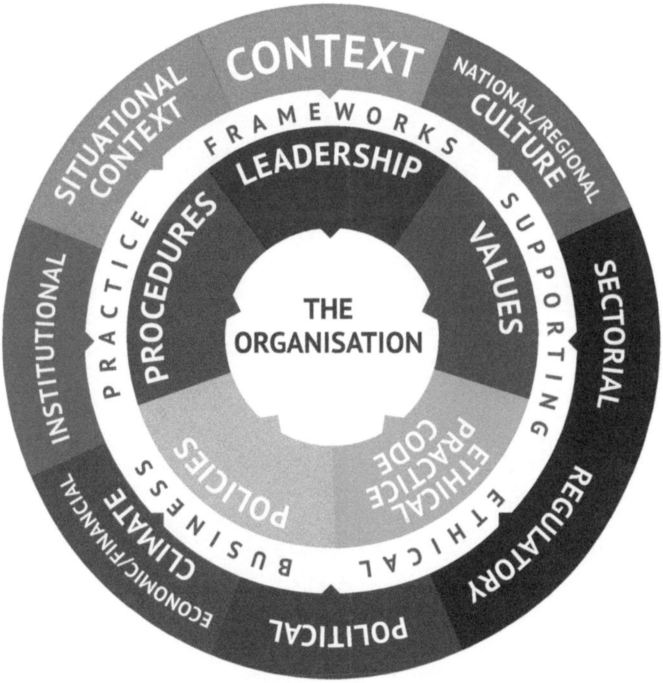

Figure 13.1: EBP and EBR frameworks

As illustrated in the above diagram, every organisation is at the centre of a multiplicity of forces shaping its characteristics and performance. Some of these are outside its control, but many of them are within it, and it is those to which we turn in this part.

A business that chooses to make a commitment to EBP and engage with regulators in an ethical business relationship must clearly demonstrate that the increased trust that it is asking the regulator to place in it is justified.

Depending on the starting point of each organisation, it will take time for an effective and comprehensive culture to develop and for the establishment of the norms and formal institutions that firmly anchor EBP. So, part of the EBR journey may take place in the imperfect state of striving for EBP, and that is acceptable. The advantage is that it will create an incentive for the organisation to strive for effectiveness and to learn from its mistakes. It will be for the regulator to judge whether those mistakes arise out of a sincere desire for improvement or are the result of nonchalance or deliberate decision. We can imagine that this will cause some people to believe EBR is unworkable in the absence of perfection. Evidence chiefly from experience in the safety arena shows that this is not the case.

13

The Cultural and Leadership Framework for Ethical Business Practice in Organisations

Culture, more than rulebooks, determines how an organization behaves.

Warren Buffett[1]

Introduction to EBP

Having set out the ideal of EBR as a relationship between private and public sector organisations in the regulatory context, we now turn to a discussion of the importance of organisational culture as a prerequisite for EBP and suggest certain aspects of how an organisation can establish and nurture an effective ethical culture, such that the organisation deserves recognition that it can be trusted to behave ethically. This chapter focuses on the framework of culture and leadership that will nurture EBP, and the following chapter sets out the framework of ethics and compliance, founded upon the organisation's values, that will anchor and support EBP.

To a considerable extent, these chapters are practical 'how to' manuals. They highlight the various essential features that we think are necessary if an organisation is going to operate consistently and sustainably on an ethical basis. The essence rests on consciously shaping culture by identifying and applying ethical values and the norms and institutions that support them, and this can only be done consistently and effectively by conscious leadership and within supportive frameworks. It should be clear that creating an effective ethical culture is not something that the CEO and executive committee can simply delegate to a compliance function and forget about; they must remain visible and fully involved. The concepts discussed in these chapters apply equally to public and private sector organisations, subject to the obvious distinction that the latter have economic and commercial goals that are generally absent for the former.

The adoption of EBP is a choice by individual businesses and the people who work in them. If they produce evidence of EBP, it will be the responsibility of regulators and other stakeholders to respond by giving them the credit for that. Further, we should not expect perfection. The objective is to aim to behave ethically on a constant basis, but genuine mistakes will occur. Convincing evidence of intention, a track record of achievement and a learning mindset are the keys to EBP and therefore to EBR.

We set out in Figure 13.2 what we believe are the desirable attributes that will establish EBP and help it flourish. We expand on some of the points below, although not all, as some are largely self-explanatory.

The Foundation, People and Ethos, Systems and Processes

The Foundation

— A belief that ethics is everyone's responsibility.
— An articulated and inspirational social purpose.
— Thoughtfully identified core ethical values, whose meanings are clear to all employees, and continuous communication and training for all (including the board) to reinforce the values.
— A public commitment by leaders and managers to EBP, including some form of a public statement.
— Conscious commitment to continuous improvement, curiosity about the organisational culture and demonstration of the basis for placing trust in the organisation, involving listening and feedback from a wide range of internal and external stakeholders.
— Dedication to fairness in all aspects of the business and relationships.

People and Ethos

— Leaders who are fully committed to ethical values and understand their role in creating an ethical culture, and who set a strong, positive example.
— Employee involvement and engagement in fostering ethical business practice, such as using ethics ambassadors.
— Management with the personalities and skills required to promote open communication, ethical decision-making, deep listening and to hold others to account.
— Tolerance and encouragement of constructive conflict with no fear of reprisals for raising difficult issues.
— A collaborative atmosphere—work across functions, business units and cultures with curiosity and respect, and the ability to learn lessons and continuously improve.

Aligned Systems and Processes

— Processes and systems in alignment with ethical values and supporting ethical business practice, embedded in the business, not separate from it.
— Performance management systems and incentive schemes that reward good leadership and ethical behaviours, not just results, and that do not foster unethical behaviour.
— Provision of clear and adequate information and professional assistance to support all aspects of EBP.
— Honest auditing, measurement and monitoring to enable the organisation to demonstrate the existence of a strong ethical culture and the basis for trust.

Figure 13.2: EBP Cultural and Leadership Framework

As we have already seen, many factors influence the extent to which people behave ethically in organisations. There is no perfect formula; however, there are certain components that can be identified as part of the toolbox that will favour effective ethical behaviour and deter unethical behaviour. We will examine some of them, but before we do, it is useful to consider what we mean when we talk about culture in the organisational context.

The Primacy of Culture

> I came to see, in my time at IBM, that culture isn't just one aspect of the game, it is the game. In the end, an organisation is nothing more than the collective capacity of its people to create value.
>
> Louis Gerstner, IBM[2]

The authors of a recent article based upon a 2016 'CEO Success Study' by consultants PwC have joined the growing consensus that an organisation's corporate culture is 'the single most important force for preventing fraud and other misconduct and withstanding regulatory scrutiny'.[3] A study conducted in 2015 found that 85% of the executives who participated believe that 'a poorly implemented, ineffective culture increases the chance that an employee might act unethically or even illegally'.[4]

So what do we mean by corporate culture? There are many definitions. It is often described as the way things are done in an organisation that differentiates it from all others. Culture includes the values and norms widely shared and strongly held throughout the firm that help employees understand which behaviours are and are not appropriate.[5] Corporate culture is made up of the cultural values and norms or 'informal institutions' of an organisation. John Graham and colleagues' Duke and Columbia study defines cultural values as 'the ideals that employees strive to fulfil, while cultural norms are the day-to-day practices that attempt to live out these values'.[6] Companies are made up of these informal institutions, together with the more tangible 'formal institutions', which include corporate policies such as corporate governance and incentive compensation, as well as corporate leadership, the finance function, and recruitment and promotion.

Kotter and Heskett base their concept of culture on Schein[7] and think of organisational culture as having two levels:[8] 'At the deeper and less visible level, culture refers to values that are shared by the people in a group and which tend to persist over time even when group membership changes.'[9] At the more visible level, culture represents the behaviour patterns or style that new employees are automatically encouraged to adopt by their fellow employees. These two elements are in constant interaction and influence each other.

Barrett states that organisational culture is determined by many things, most importantly the personal values of past and current leaders: 'The culture of an organisation is defined by the values that are lived by the leaders, managers and supervisors.'[10] Values are a 'shorthand' way for describing what is important to us individually or collectively at any given moment in time.[11]

There will be many sub-cultures in most organisations depending on its size, geographical spread, history, structure and whether it has grown organically or by acquisition or merger. Most multinational companies today, for example, have grown by acquisition and have integrated the unique cultures of each new component to a certain extent. In some organisations, these constituent parts can remain distinct for years, even decades. In others, they will be integrated into the dominant culture and will gradually blend together, creating a new corporate culture. As a result, when we talk about measuring and understanding culture, it is important to recognise that the culture of an organisation may contain considerable variations according to location, business unit or origin.

Both sociological studies of organisations and recommendations by leading business consultants have focused on the fact that a business is comprised of multiple *individuals* operating within multiple localised *cultures*.[12] The importance to business of culture and of recognising the existence of a diversity of cultures has been recognised at least since the 1950s.[13]

The EBP approach includes focusing on the *individuals* who work in organisations, and how they can each be supported to act ethically, and then widening the focus to the cultures of the groups within which they work. Any individual may behave differently as he or she moves from one group (or meeting) to another, depending on the personalities and subject matter of the discussion. Managerial intervention can never totally control outcomes or expect that complete consensus is normal within organisations.[14] It is not possible to anticipate every possible situation an employee will face in the course of his or her work. However, even though cultures may vary across a multinational company, for example, local subsidiaries being influenced by their national cultures, the firm's values can still be unified.[15] In fact, core ethical values are an important unifying force and may operate while still maintaining cultural differences and local autonomy.

It is entirely the wrong approach to think that one can bring about lasting improvement in an organisation's culture from outside, for example, by imposing on an organisation a moral duty, or criticism or a penalty. The extent to which a culture can be described as ethical depends on the actions of the people *inside* the organisation. However, the context and the society in which an organisation operates can have a profound effect on the culture of the organisation, and must not be ignored when considering the risks to which the organisation may be exposed and the challenges it may face in bringing about change.

Corporations are not static bodies; their cultures and 'DNA' evolve. Organisations are susceptible to *cultural drift*.[16] Mandis, in recording organisational drift in the financial industry, warns of firms incrementally moving away from their intended culture.[17] He also warns that this slow drift often goes unnoticed unless direct and deliberate control is taken to guide that evolution. Therefore, conscious attention to culture must be sustained over time. Experience also shows that a sudden shift away from a strong ethical culture can occur if care is not taken in executive recruitment, for example. Therefore, cultural fit must be taken into consideration in recruitment, as well as when considering an acquisition, otherwise either decision may destroy value and degrade the existing culture.

Schein argues that culture as a concept is an abstraction, and that abstractions are only useful if they are observable and increase our understanding of events that might not otherwise be well understood.[18] Schein also says that 'culture is to a group what personality or character is to an individual. We can see the behaviour that results, but we often cannot see the forces underneath that cause certain kinds of behaviour. Yet, just as our personality and character guide and constrain our behaviour so does culture guide and constrain the behaviour of members of a group through the shared norms that are held in that group'.[19] We would argue that the values held and demonstrated by the (past and present) leaders and shared by members of the group are the strongest force underpinning those norms.

Kotter and Heskett found that culture can have a significant impact on a firm's economic performance.[20] Similarly, culture can, and will, have a significant impact on a firm's ethical performance and therefore its compliance with law and regulation.

More recently, John Graham and his colleagues at Duke and Columbia found that corporate culture provides intrinsic motivation, that is, the desire to perform a task for its own sake, which is more likely to have its strongest effect when employees face choices that cannot be fully regulated beforehand. In these situations, the cultural values and norms of the organisation guide the employees' actions. They state: 'The reason that cultural values and norms may influence business outcomes is that they reduce employees' moral hazard as it arises.'[21]

It is useful to introduce one additional concept from this research—that of an 'effective culture'. Graham and colleagues say that 'an effective culture is one that promotes the behaviors needed to successfully execute the firm's strategies and achieve its goals'.[22] The research found that an effective culture depended on the alignment of and the interaction between the values, norms and formal institutions of an organisation.[23] This is a more academic way of saying that in order to be effective (and, as we shall see, ethical), an organisation must have ethical values that are lived on a day-to-day basis through a variety of norms and that the systems, processes and leadership of the organisation must be behaving in alignment with these values and norms.

As many as 85% of respondents in that study indicated that an ineffective corporate culture can lead to unethical (or even illegal) behaviour.[24] One of the variables that the authors of the study focused on was 'BeingCompliant' as a specific ethics outcome. They concluded: 'Consistent with theory and intuition we find significant evidence that firms with an integrity value accompanied by cultural norms that express integrity (willingness to report unethical behavior, trust among employees, etc.) are likely to have a cultural effect that is significantly greater for compliance.'[25]

Therefore, for the purposes of EBP, it is critical that leaders understand the culture(s) of their organisations and how to increase their effectiveness. As we have seen in the summary of recent studies and surveys mentioned in (Figure 9.1), this is frequently not the case today. The Duke and Columbia study asked the question: 'What is preventing your firm's culture from being exactly where it should be?' Given that 91% felt that culture was important to their firms and 79% placed culture as one of the top 3 or 5 value drivers of their company, the authors wanted to understand what was getting in the way of them having an effective culture. A total of 69% of respondents felt that 'leadership needs to invest more time in the culture' and 48% mentioned 'norms that produced inefficient workplace interactions' as a factor. Other factors were policies that got in the way; focus on short-term objectives and incentive compensation attracting the wrong type of people to the firm.[26]

Perhaps to be able to talk about organisational culture, one must overcome the common misconception that culture is difficult to measure and is therefore purely subjective. We know that various tools can in fact be used to measure culture and to enable leaders in organisations to understand the values that are influencing the behaviour of their employees, and the culture risk they face as a result. The management guru Peter Drucker may have said 'what gets measured gets improved';[27] however, W. Edwards Deeming actually did say: 'It is wrong to suppose that if you can't measure it, you can't manage it—a costly myth.'[28] In fact, leaders have of course been managing organisational culture ever since organisations have existed—they just didn't call it that. And, although useful, as we shall see, quantitative measurements of culture are not the only sources of information about culture.

Consciously Managing Organisational Culture

> Organizational culture is ... a continuing process of articulating contested versions of what the organization should be doing, who it should be responsible to and who does what for reward.
>
> Matthew Parker[29]

Cultural measuring tools support the development of an *ethical* consciousness and improve the organisation's sensitivity to ethical issues by providing insights that can be used as part of an internal conversation addressing both the positive values in the culture and any issues that may be getting in the way of employees behaving ethically.

One of the reasons why we favour the use of Barrett's Cultural Transformation Tools®[30] is their ability to measure the extent to which values are being lived in the organisation as well as what forces may be getting in the way of a healthy or effective culture. *Cultural entropy* is a measure of the amount of dysfunction or wasted energy being expended by individuals in an organisation that can be assessed through a Cultural Values Assessment (CVA), which is one of the tools. It is represented by the presence of potentially limiting values as a percentage of total values identified by those participating in the CVA. Conversely, the proportion of votes for positive values could be said to be a measure of the cultural health of an organisation.[31] This type of information helps leaders to understand the forces that may be increasing risk within their cultures.

Experience shows that the higher the cultural entropy, the lower the level of employee engagement. This correlates to an increased level of 'culture risk' potentially leading to unethical behaviour, as employees find it easier to rationalise bad behaviour because they are unhappy or alienated from their employer. Similarly, disengaged employees are less likely to speak up when witnessing others behaving unethically. Employees who feel undervalued or underpaid may feel justified in using company time to carry on a separate business or in taking company property for personal use. In addition, job insecurity (a form of cultural entropy) increases emotional exhaustion, which subsequently impairs an employee's ability to activate self-regulating processes to avoid engaging in unethical behaviour. But the link is weaker for employees who have high adaptability an stronger for employees who are highly embedded in their organisation.[32] In general, high levels of dysfunction lead to high levels of stress.

Cultural entropy or dysfunction can come from many sources: incompetent (especially fear-based) management, inefficient or misaligned systems, lack of opportunities for employees to express their full potential or bring their values to work, among others. Knowing the source of any serious dysfunction allows management to focus on the issues rather than casting about for general solutions that may or may not address the true underlying problem. In this way they may be able to prevent unethical behaviour from occurring. Prevention in this context is infinitely better than cure.

Cultural measuring tools allow us to 'see' culture in a far more honest and tangible way than was previously possible, and therefore they can also assist third parties in forming judgements as to whether an organisation is deserving of trust. Various types of data on culture can be used as supporting evidence during a conversation with a regulator as part of an EBR relationship. Indeed, the very willingness to look openly at company culture, and share that panorama with a regulator, would give the regulator greater confidence in the ultimate judgement they must form about the business.

The UK government's 2017 guidance on management of risk by public sector bodies includes the point that in creating 'positive risk management behaviours and culture', boards should ask 'How has the organisation set its desired values towards the effective management of risk?' and 'How have you assured yourself that desired behaviours are encouraged and inappropriate risk behaviours are discouraged?'[33]

As the importance of culture becomes more widely accepted, information on how better to measure, understand and manage it has begun to emerge. We share our experience here. However, we wish to emphasise that EBR should not become about gaming the system with particular metrics, standards or methodologies. In terms of ethical and compliance frameworks, certain basic foundational elements do seem to be required, not least because most anti-corruption regulatory regimes mandate them to one extent or another. Often it is not just what is done, but how it is done, and that is the case here. We will now examine some of these foundational elements and discuss how they may be most effectively created and embedded.

Establishing the Organisation's Core Ethical Values

An organisation's true values, which form the foundation of its culture, have a profound influence on whether its members will do the right thing or not. Businesses have increasingly produced statements of corporate values and have emphasised the 'tone from the top', both of which are essential. Barrett acknowledges that the purpose of 'espoused values is to provide a set of common principles that define how people in the organisation should interact with each other and the outside world'.[34] This is important as relationships between people can support or hinder ethical behaviour. Moreover, it is important that these values are supported by the behaviour of leaders and managers, and that the strategy and other formal institutions of the organisation are aligned with the values.

Studies on the causes of sustained long-term business success have concluded that it is critical to establish clear *core values*, which are shared by all members of the workforce, form an ideology that is enduring and able to be applied consistently in different trading and geographical circumstances, whilst operational goals are constantly examined and develop.[35]

A global visionary company separates operating practices and business strategies (which should vary from country to country) from core values and purpose (which should be universal and enduring within the company, no matter where it does business).[36] Values are universal; they transcend contexts. Behaviours, on the other hand, which are the outward manifestation of our values, are context-dependent.[37] This type of culture will generate ideas for improvement (innovation), in which complaints are treated as welcome feedback or gifts,[38] lessons are applied and things are put right when they have gone wrong.

The idea is that companies should set a high standard of values and performance that its people feel compelled to try to live up to.[39] We prefer to think of it as establishing an inspiring purpose and values that can be shared and that will bring people together to do their best for the organisation, to inspire them to contribute their discretionary effort. Systems and processes should prevent individuals from production-line contamination or sabotage, or from hidden cartel arrangements, or from acceding to bribery. But they should also facilitate, and not inhibit, making the right decisions in every commercial and social action.

The ability to measure culture allows management to work consciously to change it by working to instil appropriate core ethical values as the mechanism for improvement and by reviewing their progress over time and adjusting their efforts accordingly. Establishing (or refreshing) the true core ethical values of the organisation is therefore critical. The key point is that the core values must be *ethical* if they are to deserve the support of society's stakeholders. In addition, the chosen values must meet the needs of employees, the organisation and other stakeholders, and must express the unique character or function of the particular organisation.[40] To meet all of these disparate needs, many organisations identify operational values as well as core values.

There should only be a small number of core values, say three to five, if they are to be easily remembered by everyone. These should reflect as many different areas of focus as possible from those illustrated in the Seven Levels Model (Figure 2.1) to ensure that the organisation is aware of all of the areas it must attend to in order to prosper. The way in which the values are chosen is extremely important if they are to be effective. Too often values are chosen by a group of senior executives sitting around a board room table and are based upon their impressions of the organisation or because they 'sound good'. This method is unlikely to result in optimal, enduring values. The employees (and other stakeholders) should be involved in the process of settling on the true core values of the organisation.

Knowing the top personal values of those employed in the organisation, which they believe currently drive the culture and which would improve both the culture and the success of the organisation, gives management a solid foundation and a useful roadmap to follow in the conversations leading to this critical decision. There is no point choosing core values that are not important to a significant proportion of employees; for one thing, they are unlikely to be adopted. Similarly, having the benefit of the wisdom of those experiencing the culture will minimise the tendency towards wilful blindness and or group think to which management teams sometimes fall prey. Values chosen without such an analysis and consultation are unlikely to be unique to the organisation or to 'speak' to its employees. In addition, the very act of surveying employees using a mechanism such as a CVA and using the results as the basis of a consultation will give employees a voice and reinforce the importance of values to the company.

The *process* of discussing and agreeing the values of an organisation will also strengthen the relationships that will make these values real in people's decisions and behaviours. Such discussions also raise awareness of the complexity of ethical decision-making.

In addition, the process of agreeing the values involves defining what the words actually mean. To illustrate this, we picked eight FTSE 100 companies at random and discovered that they shared two values: integrity and respect. However, as Table 13.1 illustrates, each company defines these words differently.

Table 13.1: Examples of companies' value statements on integrity and respect

Company	Integrity	Respect
Barclays	We act fairly, ethically and openly in all that we do.	We respect and value those we work with, and the contributions that they make.
GlaxoSmithKline	We are committed to performance with integrity. Doing what is right for our patients and consumers must be at the heart of every decision we make. In doing so, we demonstrate integrity in action, at every level, every day.	Respect for people: we support and inspire our colleagues to help them be the best they can be and to achieve great things.
National Grid	Demonstrate integrity and openness in all relationships.	Respect others and value their diversity.
Old Mutual	Act and behave according to the highest ethical and moral standards.	Demonstrate, through actions and attitude, care for the feelings and rights of others.
Rio Tinto	We foster a culture of honesty and fairness—to our colleagues, customers, suppliers and the communities in which we operate.	We look out for the health, safety and well-being of our team-mates, and aim to recognise each other's contribution to the success of the enterprise.
Unilever	Always working with integrity: conducting our operations with integrity and with respect for the many people, organisations and environments our business touches has always been at the heart of our corporate responsibility.	
Wolseley	Our 'RESPECT' values guide us in everything we do at Wolseley UK: the way we work, the decisions we make, and how we treat each other: — Results: we deliver on our commitments with fairness, honesty and integrity.	

Although there are common themes, each company expresses its values in its own words. This is as it should be.

The chosen values should be aspirational; in other words, it is not necessary that everyone in the organisation is living up to them from the start. However, they must be feasible. By feasible, we mean that they are values that the organisation's employees can and will (perhaps with some extra effort) live by. If the organisational values are not aligned with the employee population, it will be necessary either to change the employees or change the values.

Full and Consistent Commitment to Ethical Values

> Managers that always promise to 'make the numbers' will at some point be tempted to make up the numbers.
>
> Warren Buffett[41]

Since organisational culture is determined by the values and behaviours of the leaders, both past and present, it is only possible to create and maintain an ethical culture if those leaders are personally committed to ethical values and understand their role in creating the desired culture. Unfortunately, as we have seen in the past, many leaders have tried to appear ethical without actually being ethical. Groucho Marx was incorrect when he said: 'The secret of life is honesty and fair dealing. If you can fake that, you've got it made.'[42] Even leaders whose personal values are ethical may not realise how much time and effort it takes to cultivate consistent ethical decision-making and behaviour in an organisation. Putting a photo of the CEO in the code of ethical practice together with an admonition about the importance of the code is a good start, but it is just that—regular engagement with employees on the subject is required, and behaviour consistent with those personal ethical values must be on display at all times by all levels of management, especially in challenging situations.

A major issue for corporations is to ensure that the chosen corporate values that are claimed in mission statements or speeches by leaders are consistent with the behaviour that occurs 'on the ground'. If not, cynicism and disengagement will inevitably result and may instead lead to an increase in unethical behaviour. John Kay criticised the American model of lightly regulated capitalism and liberal democracy that supposedly controlled large financial institutions, when in reality the floors beneath were occupied by a rabble of self-interested individuals determined to evade any controls on their own activities.[43] Many managers or salespersons may believe that they are expected to produce profits or meet targets or avoid expenditure, and that fine highfaluting statements in corporate codes are of little or no relevance to them. This expectation may be reinforced by the behaviour of their seniors and by the incentives and requirements that apply.

The leaders therefore should be fully committed to ensuring that the values chosen by the organisation are supported by corporate norms and institutions, that is, that the actual day-to-day behaviour that results from the totality of the incentives, pressures, systems and other aspects of the culture is ethical. Praise and reward should be given not just for good work and success, but also for honesty, integrity and openness. Dealings between all staff, supervisors, stakeholders and the public should be fair, honest and open. Information should be appropriately shared, on a continuous feedback basis, with the objective of constant learning rather than blame. When things go wrong, one should not be afraid to apologise, share all relevant information and make redress when harm is caused to others.

In a values-driven organisation, it is not unusual to hear employees ask each other: 'Is that in accordance with our values?'

Leaders influence culture and they often do so unconsciously, without thinking about the wider ramifications of their actions. Too much emphasis on results, profit and targets without reminders about ethics can inadvertently drive misbehaviour. Insight into the values that senior leaders consciously and unconsciously communicate is necessary. In an effectively ethical business, leaders are highly self-aware and know they are being watched and their example followed. They balance their messages regarding the achievement of financial goals with ethical messages and consistent action. And they are more likely to think carefully about how they respond in a difficult situation, based upon what behaviour they are trying to promote. Therefore, leadership is a key element of EBP.

All systems and messages from any part of the organisation should be consistent with the organisation's values. This will require a hard look at current systems and communications strategies as part of a commitment to EBP.

The problem of making decisions against a complex matrix of potentially inconsistent messages and imperatives may be one of the major causes of unethical behaviour. It is one thing to have a Code of Ethical Practice, but if the real message that a salesperson or manager feels is being imposed on him or her is 'make the numbers this month', then the Code may as well not exist. It will be forgotten or 'crowded out' of the decision-maker's consciousness. This is what we mean by living the values—or not.

The basic question is: are the ethical values of the organisation paramount? Do they govern all decisions and behaviour? Or do we just pay lip service to them and remember to invoke them only when it is convenient? We have seen various illustrations of problems in this book.

An Articulated and Inspirational Social Purpose

> A core issue raised by the Green Paper is the question of what should be the purpose of corporations. It is no longer sufficient to say their role is to generate returns for shareholders. To justify their social licence to operate they need to deliver something which society wants and values
>
> Institute of Business Ethics.[44]

There is now extensive evidence that those organisations that see their mission in social terms, and then live up to it, gain the support of staff, suppliers, customers and investors, and attract a reputation for ethical service to humanity and hence commercial success. This point was clearly stated by Dr George G Merck, who founded his company in 1891:

> We try never to forget that medicine is for the people. It is not for the profits. The profits follow, and if we have remembered that, they have never failed to appear. The better we have remembered it, the larger they have been.[45]

If an organisation is to operate effectively in society and deserve its social licence to operate, it has to start by defining its purpose *in society*. Why does it exist; what is it going to do? But viewed in social terms, what value does its existence deliver to society? If it is a public body, it may, for example, deliver benefits to citizens (such as healthcare or social security), represent the public interest, or regulate the behaviour of citizens or businesses. If it is a commercial enterprise, its purpose in this context is not its selfish maximisation of profit, but the value that it delivers to society as a whole. As John Kay says:

> Business exists to serve social purposes and enjoy legitimacy in the short term and survival in the long term only to the extent that such business meets these purposes. Profit cannot then be the 'defining purpose' of a business.[46]

A social mission should energise the commitment and enthusiasm of those working in the organisation—it should be inspirational. It should help them understand and remember that the function of the organisation is more than its commercial function (to produce a regular return for its investors) or other commercial functions (to provide employment or to innovate) or its public function (to collect taxes or to regulate prices).

Many large businesses have impressive mission statements—some of them stretching back many decades.[47] Mackey and Sisodia talk about an organisation's purpose being its 'higher purpose' or 'mission in life', 'the difference you're trying to make to the world', which then drives its mission ('the core strategy that must be undertaken to fulfil that purpose') and vision ('a vivid, imaginative conception or view of how the world will look once your purpose has been largely realized').[48] They concluded that there is no 'right' purpose for every business, and quoted Plato as having articulated the following transcendent ideals:

The Good	Service to others; improving health, education, communication, and quality of life.
The True	Discovery and furthering human knowledge.
The Beautiful	Excellence and the creation of beauty.
The Heroic	Courage to do what is right to change and improve the world.

Some examples given by Mackey and Sisodia, to which we have added, are featured in Table 13.2. We should ask ourselves if all of these really state the organisation's social mission.

The point is to see the essence of how the organisation contributes to the social collaboration between humans in joint endeavour. For example, an intermediary should never regard the furtherance of its own interests as an end in itself (to maximise profits). An intermediary is by definition acting between others, so it needs to define its social function is terms of what it does for those others. For example, the social purpose of a bank is to safeguard customers' assets entrusted to it whilst (providing customers with a fair return) putting the money to good use by lending it wisely and fairly to others who need funds to further their legitimate social objectives.

Table 13.2: Examples of core social purposes

Barclays Bank plc	Helping people achieve their ambitions in the right way.
BBC	To enrich people's lives with programmes and services that inform, educate and entertain.
BMW	To enable people to experience the joy of driving.
Charles Schwab	A relentless ally for the individual investor.
Disney	To use our imaginations to bring happiness to millions.
John Lewis Partnership	The Partnership's ultimate purpose is the happiness of all its members, through their worthwhile and satisfying employment in a successful business.
Johnson & Johnson	To alleviate pain and suffering.
Merck	To discover, develop and provide innovative products and services that save and improve lives.
Old Mutual	Our vision is to become our customers' most trusted partner—passionate about helping them achieve their lifetime financial goals.
Southwest Airlines	To give people the freedom to fly.
Tesco	Serving Britain's shoppers a little better every day.
Thames Water	A water and sewerage services business, delivering the highest-quality water and recycling it safely back to the environment.
Unilever	To make sustainable living commonplace.

Ethics is Everyone's Responsibility

Employee Involvement and Engagement in Fostering Ethical Behaviour

Ethics Ambassadors

Bad men need nothing more to compass their ends than that good men should look on and do nothing.

John Stuart Mill[50]

Sometimes your associates will say 'Everybody else is doing it.' This rationale is almost always a bad one if it is the main justification for a business action. It is totally unacceptable when evaluating a moral decision. Whenever somebody offers that phrase as a rationale, in effect they are saying that they can't come up with a good reason. If anyone gives this explanation, tell them to try using it with a reporter or a judge and see how far it gets them.

Warren Buffett[51]

The likelihood of unethical conduct being raised internally is significantly enhanced when in addition to having ethical leaders, people are surrounded by ethical co-workers and peers.

Dennis Gentilin[52]

Whilst much attention has been devoted to 'the tone from the top', values need to be applied *throughout* an organisation in multiple discrete sub-groups.[53] Staff at every level need to see evidence that the values are applied in practice by senior staff and their immediately superior managers and colleagues. The 2012 UK Engage for Success Task Force identified the importance of 'organisational integrity—the values pinned to the wall are reflected in day-to-day behaviours'.[54]

Often the informal culture is more powerful than the formal visible culture. Often behaviour in organisations originates outside the managerial structure, an example being how a salesperson or minor official inter-relates on the 'front line' with customers or members of the public. The behaviour of peer colleagues is as relevant as the example of senior managers in affecting behaviour and culture. Employees should feel their managers trust them; the converse will provoke misconduct.[55]

Empowering people throughout the organisation makes a difference. Corporate decisions can be immoral, illegal or just bad because no one feels personal responsibility for the ultimate outcome.[56] Encouraging individuals—in private or public employment—to feel responsible for behaviour and outcomes is sound policy. One of the ways of doing this is to involve them in the identification of the core values and the creation and maintenance of the shared norms that will govern behaviour in the organisation. For example, employees make excellent 'ethics ambassadors' and are capable not only of contributing to the creation of training and communication materials, but also of delivering training and awareness-raising messages directly to their colleagues. Much of the knowledge that is required to negotiate today's business landscape from an ethical perspective is reducible to concepts that are readily understood by 'lay people', particularly when the approach is values-based.

While working with organisations to create networks of ethics ambassadors since introducing the concept in 2004 at Borealis, Ruth Steinholtz found that many employees embraced the opportunity to perform this function. Being an ethics ambassador (sometimes called champions, coordinators, stars, officers etc) gives additional meaning and purpose to their working lives and involves other advantages such as increased visibility across the organisation. With proper training and assistance, ethics ambassadors can be more effective at delivering ethics and compliance messages than a lawyer from head office, as colleagues may identify more closely with them and they can exert social pressure by their continued presence. In addition, ethics ambassadors help senior management avoid mistakes created by ignorance of the local culture and language, and are part of the continuous learning loop that is required to keep messages fresh and relevant. As a mechanism for increasing employee engagement, ethics ambassadors are invaluable.

The IBE's recently issued Business Ethics Briefing on Ethics Ambassadors provides encouraging evidence. Among the findings are that 'companies which have established a network of ethics ambassadors tend to put in place a more comprehensive ethics programme than those that have not'. In addition, companies with ethics ambassadors 'appear to place a stronger focus on embedding ethical values to strengthen their ethical culture in general'.[57]

There are other ways of creating engagement and empowerment. Fundamentally, employees should be treated like adults and expected to avail themselves of all opportunities to learn what is expected of them and ask when they are not certain. Opportunities for reflection, introspection, seeking advice and open discussion are preferable to authoritarian decision-making.[58] Working with devil's advocates, Cassandras and multiple advocacy[59] can counter a tendency for conformity in groups that have strong internal cohesion.[60] This chimes with recent political theory on widening of democratic involvement in governance and deliberation.[61]

People and Ethos

Personalities and Employing the Right People

We have already discussed some of the reasons why 'good people do bad things'. But an organisation needs to take care that the right people are doing the right jobs. A key observation by the FRC is that: 'Dominant personalities can be disruptive.'[62] Gentilin notes that power corrupts,[63] although there are contradictory findings.[64] So, the question is how does the performance management system deal with these individuals, particularly if they are apparently successful? Are individuals evaluated on how they achieve results as well as the results themselves?

It should not need repeating that sociopaths and psychopaths do not work well in environments that should function on ethical collaboration between team members. If psychopaths are allowed to remain in such environments, they will distort the behaviour of those around them, with the result that good people leave or become ill due to the stress of trying to cope, and there is general downward spiral in ethical behaviour. It is a vicious circle. An example of this was management style in which the CEO could behave charmingly, especially to investors and the board, but habitually criticise and sarcastically denigrate senior staff in front of their peers (earning the nickname 'Fred the Shred' for Fred Goodwin when he was CEO of RBS). A consequence of this was that voices were not raised questioning the wisdom of the CEO's decisions, with disastrous consequences for both the bank and the stability of the entire UK economy, over the proposal to acquire ABN Amro in 2007, in pursuit of the overriding goal of constant growth to be a global bank based in Scotland.[65]

As the findings from the early investigations into the underlying causes of the VW diesel emissions scandal begin to emerge, it is clear that the dominant personality of Ferdinand Piëch, driven by ambitions for VW to become the world's largest automobile company and managing through fear, were a major contributing factor to this debacle.[66] According to Ewing, 'Ferdinand Piëch, head of one branch of the dominant family, was a dominant presence in management for more than two decades. He created a company culture that allowed fraud to fester'.[67]

Unfortunately, it appears that the percentage of individuals with psychopathic personalities is higher in senior managers (CEOs)—just the group that must be setting a good example to nurture an ethical culture. Recruiting and hiring of senior executives should be carefully done to minimise the risk of getting the wrong people 'on the bus'.[68] Employment policies should seek to identify non-psychopaths,[69] since they are trust-responsive,[70] and to minimise the chances of individuals with psychopathic personalities getting promoted.

Although only 18 CEOs of the world's 2,500 largest public companies were forced from office for ethical lapses in 2016, the trend is rising.[71] The rate of dismissal for ethical lapses was 3.9% of all successions in 2007–11, but rose to 5.3% in 2012–16, a 36% increase. In the BRIC (Brazil, Russia, India, China) countries, it was as high as 8.8% in 2012–16. It may very well be, as is suggested by Karlsson, Aguirre and Rivera, that it is not unethical behaviour by CEOs that is increasing, but rather that investigation techniques have made it easier to prove and social media has made it more difficult to hide.

Collaborative Atmosphere

Working Together with Stakeholders

The ethical imperative involves respecting the legitimate needs of all stakeholders, such as in delivering safe staff working conditions and fair pay, fair dealings with suppliers and customers, providing a fair return for investors and respecting the rules set by society, for example, through regulators—note the repeated use of the word 'fair' in this sentence.

A business has many key relationships with its stakeholders. Stakeholders are not just investors but also include staff, staff representatives, suppliers, customers, local communities and regulators. Relationships need to be established with these groups that go beyond merely one way in terms of information or consultation and demonstrate effective partnership.

Strong recent empirical evidence is produced by Sisodia, Sheth and Wolfe, who have illuminated the fundamental importance of full involvement of *all* stakeholders in a collaborative approach that respects the interests of all (ie, a socially cohesive approach), which they describe as a humanistic model, simply involving *love*.[72] 'Good management is largely a matter of love.'[73]

Case Study 27: Supplying Gas with Love

Northern Gas Networks used to be a status-orientated organisation, but created a customer-focused and safety-focused organisation. It found that internal culture developed quickly, from expecting to be told what to do to building trust based on honesty, transparency and authenticity. Like various other companies,[49] it found that a hierarchical structure prevents trust. Workers who dig up roads love the idea that their most important corporate value is *love*!

Like an increasing number of commentators, Sisodia and colleagues supersede Collins' earlier analysis by highlighting the commercial success of companies that focus on ensuring that every stakeholder (all levels of staff, suppliers, customers and investors) achieves the fair and effective outcomes that he or she needs ('firms of endearment'). They set out diverse examples of such endearing practice from companies across the world. They suggest that the approach produces a distinctive set of behaviours and outcomes shown in Table 13.3.[74] An additional outcome is increased commitment to the organisation and to a high standard of ethical behaviour.

Table 13.3: Examples of endearing practice identified by Sisodia

—	Executive salaries that are relatively modest.
—	Managers with an open-door policy.
—	Treating staff as a source, not a resource.
—	Employee compensation and benefits that are significantly greater than standard.
—	More employee training than that offered by competitors.
—	Employee turnover that is far lower than the industry average.
—	Empowerment of employees to make sure customers leave every transaction fully satisfied.
—	Hiring people who are passionate about the company and its products.
—	Consciously humanising the experience for customers and employees.
—	Assisting suppliers to improve their quality, cost-effectiveness and environmental impact rather than just squeezing them on price.
—	Projecting a genuine passion for customers and emotionally connecting with them.
—	Marketing costs that are far lower than those of competitors, while customer satisfaction and retention are far higher.
—	Viewing suppliers as true partners and collaborating with them.
—	Honouring the spirit of laws rather than merely following the letter of the law.
—	Considering corporate culture as the greatest asset.

Since the launch of the UK Stewardship Code in 2010, which raised the importance of external collaborations, the quality of the dialogue between companies and their shareholders and investors is generally thought to have improved, although the numbers of shareholders engaging actively has not increased greatly.[75] In relation to staff relations, the FRC quotes BAE Systems as building a relationship of trust with organised labour:

> BAE Systems and the unions describe their relationship as one of trust. This is based on a culture of openness, a structure which allows potentially serious issues to be escalated and addressed before they become critical, and a recognition that, in many areas of public policy, the unions and management have common interests.
>
> The central element is the Corporate Consultative Committee that allows BAE Systems to engage with its own union officials at convener level. This has about 30 members and meets quarterly. It discusses issues of mutual interest to the unions and the group. This allows the company to engage with unions at every level throughout the group, while giving individual sites and businesses the freedom to conduct their own bargaining on wages and other specific local issues.[76]

Almost all the reports of different bodies involved in the FRC's 2016 initiative on reform of corporate governance refer to the importance of good relations and communications with all relevant stakeholders: investors, suppliers, staff, customers and regulators. This wide approach to the responsibilities of directors, and an 'enlightened shareholder value' model, is set out in the UK Companies Act.[77]

In relation to customers, the IBE says:

> Delivery of value to the customer is a vital requirement for corporate success and an essential indicator of trust. A positive culture is one that seeks to put the customer first, backed up by incentives, communicates this clearly to staff and provides training which promotes the delivery of value.[78]

A different kind of example is a Local Enterprise Partnership (LEP), which is a voluntary partnership between local authorities and businesses to determine local economic priorities for investment in infrastructure and job growth in an area.[79] LEPs were established to bring together business and civic leaders across a functional economic area to prioritise investment to where it will most effectively drive growth, and to bring a strong business voice to local decision-making to drive sustainable private sector-led growth and job creation. LEPs have established *growth hubs* as a local public/private sector partnership to bring together public and private sector partners to promote, coordinate and deliver business support. Growth hubs provide a mechanism for integrating national and local business support so that it is easy for businesses to access and to support them to start up, scale up and thrive.

Moreover, approximately 75% of the prosecutions reported by the OECD in its 2014 bribery report involved third-party intermediaries, illustrating the importance of sharing one's ethical stance with all those who do business on behalf of the company.[80]

Performance Management Systems and Incentive Schemes that Support EBP

> Money blinds us to our social relationships, creating a sense of self-sufficiency that discourages cooperation and mutual support.
>
> Margaret Heffernan[81]

> Compensation systems can generate perverse economic incentives as well as psychological and social responses that motivate a wide class of counterproductive behaviours ranging from lack of cooperation to explicitly illegal misconduct.
>
> Ian Larkin and Lamar Pierce[82]

The *IBE Good Practice Guide on Performance Management for an Ethical Culture* concluded:

> The annual performance appraisal has a strong impact on subsequent (un)ethical behaviour, and needs careful handling.[83] The way that people are assessed, compensated and rewarded has ramifications for what an organisation achieves and how it achieves it. The purpose of businesses paying staff or suppliers—or of customers paying businesses—is as a fair reward for services or goods rendered or exchanged. Focusing on the words 'fair' and 'reward' pays dividends.[84]

Two problems arise here. First, paying people too much, compared to others, is unfair, and will be seen to be unfair by staff and other stakeholders, whose trust and therefore behaviour will be adversely affected. Second, giving people certain incentives may produce unethical behaviour. In practice, this raises the following problems:

— Do the financial incentives (paying bonuses, commission or just too much, especially where there is too great a differential between top and bottom pay levels) override ethical behaviour?
— Does the pressure that people feel to meet or compete in financial or sales targets override ethical behaviour?

The second issue is straightforward to understand. If you are paid entirely on commission, or you stand to receive a large bonus by hitting certain targets, this will inevitably influence and drive your behaviour. Some financial salespersons were reported as taking out PPI policies for themselves and their families just to meet their targets. At Wells Fargo, millions of fake bank accounts and credit cards were created without the knowledge of customers to satisfy the CEO's exhortation that 'eight is great'.[85] Managers who have constantly to hit unrealistic reporting or profits targets may take many decisions that are neither good for the longer term of the business nor ethical.

Denis Gentilin, who has personal experience of a major scandal in National Australia Bank and subsequently thought deeply about the causes of ethical failures, identified the major factors that drive bad behaviour as money, performance, reward, power and fear.[86] Maybe we need to expand this? All these factors can drive out ethical considerations, and we must find ways to ensure that they do not. He concluded that since environments that promote wealth can magnify unethical behaviour, transparency might be necessary, but is not sufficient. He notes research by Dan Ariely that illustrated how monetary incentives appear only to be effective in inducing increased performance for tasks that are repetitive and mundane in nature.[87] For tasks requiring intellectual effort, such incentives will diminish performance, as the individual has too much at stake and is under pressure.

Bonuses tied to performance are not well suited to inducing honest and trustworthy behaviour.[88] Paying executives on the basis of performance has attracted strong criticism as a practice.[89] In fact, whilst experience from the Enron and WorldCom crises underlined the risks which flawed incentives can pose to market efficiency (and was not adequately learnt),[90] and various theoretical arguments on how particular schemes *might* induce particular behaviour,[91] there is very little empirical evidence on how different bonus schemes affect traders' propensity to trade and which bonus schemes improve traders' financial performance. Recent studies suggest that bonuses may be detrimental for performance, at least when threshold and linear compensation schemes are compared.[92] However, those involved in markets appear not to favour regulation of remuneration.[93]

Some may think that the first issue is less important than the second. Does it matter what key executives earn? Lord Mandelson, when British Secretary of State for Business in 1998, famously said that he was 'intensely relaxed about people getting filthy rich as long as they pay their taxes',[94] although he recanted in 2012, noting rising inequality and stagnating middle-class incomes.[95] The issue is less about absolute levels of income than comparative levels. If the degree of differentiation between workers is unfair, this does not support an ethical culture. The 2014 Governance Code said that executive directors' remuneration should be designed to promote the long-term success of the company, and that the level 'must be seen by all stakeholders, including employees throughout the business, to be fair'. Frances O'Grady, General Secretary of the TUC, said in 2016:

> Many workers and the public remain angry about the level of top pay and the lack of accountability. There is clear evidence that inequality in pay leads to poor decision-making. Management is incentivised to produce short-term results ... there is a dwindling sense of ownership.[96]

In a 2014 report, which found that increases in executive pay between 2000 and 2013 were far greater than the increase in company profits or market value, Simon Walker, Director General of the Institute of Directors, said that 'in some corners of corporate Britain pay for top executives has become so divided from performance that it cannot be justified. Runaway pay packages, golden hellos, and inflammatory bonuses are running the reputation of business into the ground'.[97]

The behavioural rationale underlying such anger and lack of trust is that paying some people vastly more than others in an organisation demonstrates the selfish pursuit of personal gain that is a clear indicator that the individual who benefits and the organisation that permits excessive remuneration cannot be trusted.[98]

Pay differentials have risen dramatically. Bonuses in the City of London tripled between 2002/03 and 2007/08, from £3.3 billion to £11.6 billion.[99] A 2016 academic study into US businesses noted that executive pay was modest from the 1940s to the mid-1970s, controlled to a significant extent by pressure from trade unions and by egalitarian norms,[100] after which a period of unrestrained self-indulgence set in.[101] Addressing the disparity in remuneration between employees at the top and bottom of organisations, and between the levels that apply outside and inside an organisation, remains a serious issue if businesses are to be trusted.

The issue of remuneration has received significant attention. A number of changes have been made in remuneration practice and its controls, including increased reporting,[102] allowing shareholders to vote on aspects of remuneration, longer timescales for evaluation of bonuses and delaying payment of remuneration, and permitting claw backs. These changes seem to have helped, but only to a limited extent. In 2015, it was reported that there had been an increase in the number of companies where longer time horizons had been incorporated in remuneration packages: 51% of FTSE 100 plans in 2015 included a further holding period for at least part of the award compared to 37% in 2015 and around 20% in 2013.[103] Arrangements enabling companies to recover or withhold variable pay, and to consider appropriate vesting and holding periods for deferred remuneration, were in place in 2015 in relation to both annual and long-term incentive plans in around 90% of FTSE 100 companies and 85% of FTSE 250 companies. Companies outlined that long-term share awards may be clawed back in over 70% of FTSE 100 companies and malus may be applied in 84% of companies.[104] The binding shareholder vote on directors' remuneration is thought to have increased the number of interactions between companies and their investors.[105]

Despite these changes, the 2016 FRC report accepted that:

> Pay is a sensitive issue in the UK and affects the standing of business in society. Unfortunately, the continuing inconsistent alignment between executive remuneration and company performance and between the remuneration of senior executives and employees has led to a lack of public confidence. This has taken place despite increasing regulation to improve transparency and accountability. Remuneration practices are often cited as a driver of poor behaviour. The incentives created by performance-related pay, and the corresponding impact on employee behaviours, is something that should be of utmost concern to boards and remuneration committees, which could do more to apply a cultural and values lens to the design of remuneration policies and individual remuneration decisions.

The Investment Management Association proposed a policy in 2016 that pay practices should be simplified, aligned with corporate performance,[106] that shareholder engagement should be improved and focused on the strategic rationale for remuneration structures, and that the board should explain why the chosen maximum remuneration level as required under the remuneration policy is appropriate for the company using both external and internal (such as a ratio between the pay of the CEO and median employee) relativities.[107] Its final policy included a requirement that pay ratios between the CEO and the median employee should be disclosed, and guidance that shareholder consultation should be improved.[108]

In 2016, Theresa May's government proposed shareholder influence over executive pay,[109] following mounting calls for mandatory publication of pay ratios, annual binding shareholder votes on executive pay, and mandatory shareholder committees, attended by an employee representative.[110] Although forced by subsequent political events to abandon these proposals, these reforms were solidly supported by the Business, Energy and Industrial Strategy Committee, which also called for the FRC's corporate governance code and its enforcement to be strengthened.[111] It criticised the fact that two-thirds of FTSE 100 CEOs were paid over 100 times the average national salary and reported that many considered the current system to be broken.[112] It concluded that 'overall pay levels have now been ratcheted up to levels so high that it is impossible to observe a credible link between pay and performance'.[113]

Some businesses have moved to a radically different approach. In 2016 Woodford Investment Management LLP scrapped bonuses. By 2016, reports of shareholder revolts against excessive executive remuneration were appearing regularly: in April 2017, the top managers of Credit Suisse 'agreed' a 40% bonus cut after planned awards totalling SFR 78 million.[114] Models of ethical appraisal are being developed. One such model of appraisal of ethical performance of salespersons examines how performance dimensions (such as sales ability, product knowledge, customer orientation and innovativeness) are carried forward in terms of moral and legal values (including deception, falsification, padding expense accounts and bribery).[115] The IBE advocates incorporating the assessment of ethical behaviours and competencies into performance management systems and sets out various approaches taken by companies to ensure that results are achieved in accordance with their values. Some companies have identified specific values-driven competencies and behaviours and require employees to provide evidence of having exhibited these behaviours during the relevant review period in their work. Examples of such competencies are as follows:

- Take time to really understand the values and discuss what they mean with your team and peers.
- Role model the values.
- Build trust with others though real relationships.
- Deal honestly with difficult issues.
- Be accountable for failure—do not blame others.

Having identified whether an employee has performed with integrity or not, a company has a choice of how to respond. In some cases, the identification of a deficit in this area may preclude the receipt of any discretionary remuneration. In others, it may result in a diminution. This is what happened to Barclays CEO Jes Staley, who received a large cut to his £1.3 million bonus in 2017 because he broke the rules by trying to identify a whistleblower. Other sanctions may be applied depending on the seriousness of the issues. Wherever possible, good practice is to understand the root cause of the employee's failure and develop a plan to address it. Was the employee lacking the knowledge or skills to live the value? Is his or her attitude the problem? Until the reasons for the failure to live the values are understood, any action taken may be ineffective.

Sisodia's research has noted that successful firms that operate based on endearment demonstrate modest executive salaries, above-average remuneration and benefits for employees, and fair prices for suppliers and customers. Transparency International has urged companies to avoid paying staff for performance based purely on output measures, and instead encourage the pursuit of intrinsic reward.[116] They base this recommendation on academic research that, with the exception of repetitive and routine work, it is better not to pay for performance, and found that:

— contingent pay only works for routine tasks;
— extrinsic motivation crowds out intrinsic motivation;
— contingent pay leads to cooking the books;
— all measurement systems are flawed;
— fixating on performance can weaken it.[117]

Transparency International concludes:

> The evidence suggests that it is better to pay people fixed amounts instead of variable pay. Once the rate for a job has been agreed, staff should be left to pursue the intrinsic rewards which accrue from doing a job well, working with others, pleasing customers, etc. It may not be realistic for many companies to abolish variable pay altogether, but it is worth bearing in mind that the risks may outweigh the rewards. Companies should take care that they—and their employees—are not too heavily reliant on financial incentives that fixed pay is sufficient and that consideration is given to intrinsic rewards.

Remuneration at all levels of an organisation should demonstrate to those inside and outside a commitment to fair practice. If that demonstration is absent, internal and external stakeholders will not trust the people who walk away with too much and will not believe in any official statement that the organisation lives by an ethical code. This is a nettle waiting to be fully grasped.

Conclusions

1. Adoption of EBP/EBR is a choice by individual businesses and there is no 'one-size-fits-all' method for achieving it, though it relies on corporate leaders consciously shaping culture by identifying and applying ethical values and the norms and institutions that support them. Adopting EBP will require clear formal adherence by management in statements and policies and informal adherence through consistent demonstrable action, and will also need the support of the workforce, the cooperation of stakeholders, and be underpinned by systems that will anchor it and allow the company to demonstrate its commitment.

2. Corporate culture has increasingly been recognised as the most important determinate of ethical (or unethical) behaviour in an organisation; therefore, it is the foundation of EBP. An effective corporate culture consists of cultural values and norms, and is supported by the formal institutions of the company as well.
3. Cultural measuring tools such as the CVA enable the identification of core ethical values, the management of the culture to decrease 'culture risk', a focus on the sources of cultural entropy and the achievement of ethical consistency across the organisation. Regular use of these tools provides evidence of the effectiveness of these efforts and progress over time.
4. Leaders must be fully committed to a sustainable ethical culture and not create contradictory incentives or send mixed messages. A collaborative atmosphere where constructive challenge is possible without fear is needed, and therefore choosing the right people and ensuring they possess the skills and personality for the job they do is critical.
5. Performance management, incentives and comparative pay levels all contribute to the type of culture that will develop.
6. Having an inspiring social mission, a higher purpose and appropriate values creates high levels of employee engagement and therefore motivates people to devote their discretionary effort to the organisation, take pride in it and be more likely to want to safeguard the organisation by behaving ethically themselves and speaking out if they detect anyone doing otherwise.

14

The Ethics and Compliance Framework: Values Orientation

Focusing Mainly on Compliance is Not the Answer

Compliance is an Outcome, Not an Approach

Ruth Steinholtz[1]

Complying with rules, even the external rules of society or of its laws, starts *within* an organisation and its people, rather than by external imposition through 'enforcement' by state authorities. Lord Thomas of Cwmgiedd, Lord Chief Justice of England and Wales, affirmed this in a speech in 2017: 'it is quite impossible to devise a legal or regulatory regime that can supervise the conduct of another party to a bargain'.[2] Companies manage all their activities through *systems*. For example, financial and output performance is measured by reporting and quality systems, based on constant circulation of information. But having a system does not address the issue of whether the behaviour of people who work in the organisation, and operate the system, will be ethical. Compliance can be defined as 'the action or fact of complying with a wish or command, excessive acquiescence or the state or fact of according with meeting rules or standards'. It is exactly this connotation of excessive acquiescence that puts us off the concept of compliance. History is strewn with examples of people complying with orders and behaving unethically.

The growth in regulation has produced concepts, systems, programmes and personnel focused on risk and *compliance*. Key elements for the success of compliance systems are widely agreed and are mainly the result of pronouncements by US regulators in response to the Foreign Corrupt Practices Act (FCPA). Some of the factors are:[3] the support of senior management[4] and status within the organisation,[5] the existence of 'an internal constituency advocating and working for compliance',[6] communication of the policy and practical implications to all staff, including by training and regular refreshers, auditing and employees' internalisation of the values and practical actions involved in carrying out daily procedures, operations, reward and performance review systems.[7] An updated summary of questions that US authorities may ask was published in 2017 (see Appendix 3).[8] Faced with such a long list of questions about a *system*, we should not be surprised that company compliance departments might fail to focus on values. Regulators, historically those in the US, have driven the development of 'tick-box' compliance, perhaps inadvertently.

Recent pronouncements recognise that compliance systems are not effective without an ethical culture. However, in practice, a company that cannot provide extensive evidence of such a programme when a violation occurs will tend to be treated harshly. This begs the following question: how can a company focus on its culture and values, and still be recognised as attempting to comply? By contrast, the Guidance regarding 'Adequate Procedures to Prevent Bribery' issued by the Ministry of Justice in connection with the UK Bribery Act provides another useful framework. The Guidance is briefly discussed in chapter 11 and is far less detailed, while still providing in our opinion adequate indications of what is expected of companies, and in the process implicitly acknowledging the importance of culture and values.

But a compliance system will not itself produce compliance. In fact, it will fail, whether as an internal means of control or an external means of public regulation. There are three reasons for this.

First, compliance systems do not focus principally on ethical decision-making or behaviour; they tend to focus on processes. They assess whether people have received training, but often not whether they understood it. They involve tick boxes for checking compliance with rules (a process issue), but they do not assess the ethics of what is done or the outcomes (behavioural and ethical issues). They discourage challenge and thought, and therefore may inadvertently result in bad outcomes. Compliance systems rely on the creation of a complex set of rules in the form of policies and procedures rather than on intrinsic values and principles. They are susceptible to being gamed, are difficult to understand if written in legalese and are often presented without regard to the context, so people do not understand why they are being asked to perform what to them seem like wasteful and irrelevant actions. The difference between compliance and integrity is well illustrated by Florian Beranek of the United Nations International Development Organisation in Figure 14.1.

Characteristics of compliance:

- Conformity with externally applied rules
- Prevention of crime by limitation of options
- Based on the assumption that humankind is opportunistic and egocentric
- Implemented by instruction, surveillance, control, threats ...

Characteristic of integrity:

- Self-control on ethical-moral convictions
- Creation of open spaces for responsible, integer [*sic*] decisions
- Based on the assumption that humankind is social, adaptive and idealistic (good)
- Implemented by dialogue, human resource development, role models, appreciation and long-term organisational provisions (must eliminate black sheep)

Business and values:

- Basic and sustainable economic responsibility: necessary to survive
- Legal responsibility: necessary to operate
- Ethical responsibility: necessary to succeed

Figure 14.1: What are the differences between compliance and integrity programmes?[9]

Second, excessive focus on these complex programmes is part of the problem because they erode trust. The existence of a large compliance department, which is often viewed as an internal police force, sends a signal to staff that they are not trusted. The message is that they are being monitored, measured, observed and judged. Compliance may also be viewed as 'them', so they will not trust the compliance staff by sharing full information on what is going on or sharing a problem with them. Staff will suspect that 'compliance' is out to get them. Employees will respond badly to indications that their managers do not trust them and may become disengaged. As we saw in chapters 4, 5 and 6, disengaged employees are more likely to behave unethically or fail to report others behaving unethically.

Third, many compliance departments and consultants create compliance programmes that are largely for training people in complicated policies and monitoring their behaviour to be able to report that the compliance system is in place and is producing data that says it is working. This large amount of data about a large amount of activity can then be produced as evidence that a system is in place in the event of a non-compliance occurring. Much of the effort is directed at producing material evidence that can be placed before a prosecutor or court that the enterprise deserves a lower penalty after something has gone wrong because it has a compliance system, and therefore is doing a great deal to promote compliance. This approach sends the message to the organisation that 'we are only doing this because it is the law. We don't really believe it'. The result is cynicism, perfunctory compliance and disengagement. It is therefore imperative for regulators to understand how their requirements affect the approach that organisations take.

The existence of a large internal compliance department begs the following question: who is responsible for doing the right thing? Finally, compliance approaches tend towards negative communications, such as 'if you pay a bribe you will go to jail'. As discussed in chapter 2, we know that deterrence does not work. Finally, a focus on rules misses the context and is challenged by new situations that were perhaps not envisaged when the rules were developed.

Instead, we need to look at how culture and values coupled with a sensible and proportionate ethics and compliance framework produce ethical behaviour. We need to find ways to increase trust, accountability and engagement. One objective is to encourage people to think before they make decisions and to seek help when they need it. Another is to find ways to enable an organisation to produce evidence of ethical business practice without overwhelming it with compliance bureaucracy.

Instilling the Ethical Approach: A Shift in Emphasis

A Values-Orientated Framework

The core ethical values and the code of ethical practice lay the foundation for all decision-making and actions of the organisation. But they need to be capable of being applied and in fact be applied in practice, otherwise they are merely window-dressing. Having espoused values is important, but is only part of creating and maintaining an ethical culture. They need to be embedded, woven into the DNA, until they become consistently a part of 'how we do things around here'. This takes time and persistent communication, as well as other action so that everyone who works on behalf of the company adopts them in practice. Thus, an organisation needs an ethical framework, and that framework must be adequately resourced and brought to life in a variety of ways.

The IBE considers that ethical values are embedded into the culture of an organisation and influence behaviour through four elements of an effective ethics programme, which each create feedback loops for learning and improvement:

1.	Code of Ethics	Written standards of ethical business conduct
2.	Speak Up Line	Means of reporting misconduct confidentially
3.	Advice or Information Helpline	Advice about behaving ethically at work
4.	Ethics Training	Training on ethical standards of conduct[10]

Treviño and Weaver talk about two different types of formal ethics programmes. They characterise them as either oriented towards compliance with rules and punishment for non-compliance (a 'compliance orientation')[11] or as focusing on ethical values and the 'potential for employees to be committed to a set of ethical ideals embodied in the organisation' (a 'values orientation'). They point out—and we agree—that the two orientations need not be mutually exclusive. We believe that some elements of a compliance orientation are necessary as well as desirable; however, we believe that values and culture should be the primary orientation, as this is more likely to produce the desired outcomes: reduced unethical behaviour, openness and transparency, increased likelihood of reporting violations, and compliance with law and regulation. The converse, as we have already stated, is less likely to be the case. Treviño and Weaver rightly point out that a values orientation based upon creating a sense of shared values will have other positive consequences for the organisation.

We therefore caution against mistaking the existence of a compliance programme for ethical behaviour and encourage business to aim for a values orientation with a backbone of just rules and policies as well as sufficient controls to deter and/or detect wrongdoing on the part of that small percentage of the population who are sociopaths and for whom values represent an unintelligible foreign language and concept.

It is telling that the aviation sector does not use the word 'compliance' and instead talks of 'performance'. This language enables them to concentrate on constantly maintaining and improving. Rather than looking at 'compliance', what we need to look at is the motivation, behaviour, performance and outcomes. And we need to do this all the time. A snapshot may be useful, but it is constant monitoring and feedback, within a positive ethical culture, that will drive performance. Compliance is an outcome, not an approach.[12]

We have tried to make the case for the proposition that having a compliance department responsible for 'compliance with rules' will be insufficient and possibly even detrimental. Indeed, we hope we make the case for keeping a small central function designed to support the business and all other functions in their responsibility for ethics and regulatory compliance, rather than separating the risk from the responsibility by placing it in a large central compliance department. In other words, we are advocating the breaking down of barriers between the support functions in organisations and cooperation among them to support ethical behaviour across the business.

Case Study 28: L'Oreal

L'Oreal has focused on driving ethics into and throughout the business rather than building a large and centralised compliance department. Several practices contribute to L'Oreal's multi-year recognition by Ethisphere as one of the 'world's most ethical companies'. For example, since 2009, the chief executive has made himself available one day every year to answer questions on any ethical matter of concern from staff worldwide through a live web stream. This is followed by a similar session conducted by each of the country managers. In addition, L'Oreal has a network of 67 employee 'ethics correspondents who are charged with bringing ethical leadership to all parts of the business'.[13]

Enumerations of the means of creating—or of the characteristics of—an ethics or compliance framework are not lacking. We do not propose to outline a 'one-size-fits-all' approach here; however we felt it was important in the context of EBP to give the reader a summary of those elements which we believe are fundamental to a framework for ethical business practice.

As part of an EBP framework, we would suggest the elements described in Table 14.1.

Table 14.1: An EBP framework

1. A written code of Ethical Business Practice, developed from within, based upon the organisation's values and aligned with the culture, forming the cornerstone of the organisation's approach to ethics and compliance.
2. Regular ethical/anti-corruption risk assessments, done by the business, with expert support as necessary and the implementation of mitigation measures in response to the risks identified.
3. Clear, succinct policies and procedures that are easily accessible and kept updated.
4. Regular pattern of communications at all levels of management, including regarding demonstrable behaviour in line with ethical principles, publicised sensitively.
5. Training aimed at informing those doing business on behalf of the organisation as to what is expected of them, mainly conducted face-to-face and supplemented by training delivered online or by other technological means, such as apps.

(continued)

Table 14.1: ***(Continued)***

6.	A network of employee ethics ambassadors to assist in embedding ethical values and to help with communications and training.
7.	Development of ethical decision-making skills, including how to recognise and resolve ethical dilemmas and how to effectively implement solutions once they have been determined. This would include ethical decision-making models and scenario-based training using realistic scenarios developed internally (scenario bank).
8.	Adequate resources, including people to develop and deliver the necessary materials for training and awareness raising, to carry out proper investigations of ethical lapses and to capture and communicate lessons learned.
9.	Effective due diligence of third parties, conducted by the business, with support as necessary.
10.	Involvement of relevant third parties and strategic partners in the commitment to ethical business practice, including the supply chain and anyone acting on behalf of the organisation.
11.	An appropriate mechanism for speaking up, catering to the language and cultural characteristics of the organisation, supported by a skilled approach to investigations and discipline, as well as a climate of 'psychological safety' in which to do so.[14]
12.	Monitoring, measuring, tracking and reporting elements of ethical business practice by various means.

Whatever approach is taken; it is fundamentally important that responsibility for doing the right thing remains with the business and that management at all levels are walking the talk, spreading the message and raising awareness. As we have said, ethics is everyone's responsibility and is not the purview of a central compliance department separate from the business unit. Everyone must feel a sense of responsibility to themselves, the company and their colleagues to protect the ethical nature of the culture. We have noted that companies that are more mature in their approach tend to realise that the compliance department is not on the 'front line' and therefore cannot assume the responsibility for compliance from those who are.

Codes of Ethical Business Practice

Once they have been identified, an organisation needs to make its ethical mission and core values transparently available to all stakeholders. Everyone doing business on behalf of the organisation must know what is expected of them. Codes of ethical business practice or business principles are the cornerstone of an ethical approach; a unifying force for many policies and procedures that regulate different aspect of the organisation's ethical life. To be effective, the code must be founded on the company's values and developed in genuine consultation with employees rather than just rolled out from the headquarters. Codes must be visually attractive, carefully translated into all company languages, clear and concise and easy to access and read, fit the culture of the organisation in tone, look and feel, and be available in many formats.

Developing a code internally in consultation with people throughout the organisation will ensure that it reflects the unique culture and risks it faces. It will also create a sense of ownership. A code that is developed at headquarters and is imposed on the organisation is doomed to failure. Questionnaires, surveys or interviews can be used to determine what issues are of most concern to employees so that these can be given prominence in the code. In addition, it is useful to understand how people interact with company information—do they look for everything on the intranet? Would they prefer to have a hard copy of the physical document? What about an app? By the time a code is launched, it should be possible for numerous people to say 'I helped create that document'. Their contribution needn't be so extensive as to bog down the drafting process forever, but employees' views should be actively solicited and considered. Dan Ariely and Mike Norton identified the 'IKEA effect', which is the fact that our sense of ownership and value for something is higher if we have made even a tiny contribution to its creation.[15] Finally, it is obvious that the process of soliciting input and feedback offers an opportunity to begin to educate employees on the subjects contained in the code.

Statements on how ethical values apply to the activities of the organisation should give examples of how the values apply to tasks that may be faced by staff at all levels. They need to be relevant and real for everyday tasks and decisions. Companies often include realistic scenarios or ethical dilemmas and provide guidance about how they believe an employee should behave in these situations. It is also important to include links to additional information rather than trying to include everything in the code. Drafting codes properly is a demanding task; they must be concise and at the same time contain sufficient information and guidance. This points to one of the strengths of values over rules. For example, a statement such as 'treat company property with care and respect' can replace a long list of rules that could never be exhaustive. Granted, it may be necessary for leaders and managers to have a conversation about what the value of respect means in this context; however, this conversation itself is helping to build an ethical culture.

Case Study 29: A Question of Ethics—Borealis Code Development

In late 2003, the task of revising the Borealis Code of Ethics was delegated to Ruth Steinholtz, then General Counsel. Being new to the company and with limited resources, she requested permission to create a temporary team as part of a bespoke programme run with IMD Business School, called 'Courage to Lead'. One of the aspects of the programme was for employees to work together in small groups to develop something of value to the company. The 'ethics excellence programme' that was designed by that team exists to this day. It outlined all the elements of the new approach to ethics. The members of the team came from many disciplines—most had no specific prior exposure to the subject beyond having read the previous code. After an introduction to the subject, the team created a questionnaire, sent it to 50 people throughout the company and proceeded to conduct interviews. They also researched the codes and approaches of peer companies. The input was collected and a massive exercise to collate and organise all the input produced numerous useful insights and much information that was first used to design the new approach and then by the legal department in the subsequent drafting process. At this point, the 'Courage to Lead' team was disbanded and responsibility returned to the legal department. Several rounds of drafts were circulated to managers across disciplines, business units and locations, as well as to certain external advisors. A visual design process was undertaken in parallel. The Code was translated into several languages, the translations were reviewed internally individually and by language groups, and the final product was presented to the Works Councils, the Executive Management Team and the Supervisory Board. The Code was launched in November 2005 at a senior leaders' conference, and ethics ambassadors were trained and asked to return to their units and train 85% of the employee population in the first 12 months after its launch. By the second year, virtually all employees had received face-to-face training. This was the beginning of embedding the ethical principles contained in the Code, entitled 'A Question of Ethics'. Other resources followed, including a Sharepoint site, training modules, a QuestionLine and further training for ethics ambassadors. The QuestionLine was mainly a channel for asking questions as well as for any suspected issues that employees preferred not to report via management.

Case Study 30: Aligning Ethical Objectives and Behaviour

In 2015, Johnson Matthey put in place a Code of Ethics based on two simple principles: 'do the right thing' and 'speak up'. The document illustrates applications of those two principles in various business situations. Whilst the document is like many other corporate statements on mission, compliance or ethics, its introduction was a result of extensive discussions by groups of staff in the company and across the world, and is underpinned by a network of ethics ambassadors who are responsible for spreading the message and helping employees understand their responsibilities. It is helping to achieve that social element of trust that is critical to the success of statements made by business leaders. A subsequent evaluation showed that the approach has engendered internal enthusiasm and genuine ownership by employees all around the world. The ethics ambassadors are a key part of Johnson Matthey's ability to reach far into the organisation and embed the Code.

A 2010 review of codes of ethics in finance found that they are built on seven core principles or values: integrity, objectivity, competence, fairness, confidentiality, professionalism and diligence.[16] According to the IBE, the most commonly used value words in the FTSE 100 are: Integrity, Safety, Excellence, Customer Focus, Accountability, Respect, Innovation, Team/Teamwork, Trust and Openness.[17]

Statements of corporate goals and ethics have both external and internal value. The IBE points out that codes are an effective way of showing investors, customers and staff as well as other stakeholders that the company takes the obligation to conduct the business responsibly seriously.[18]

The IBE rightly states: 'A code of ethics can clarify where lines are drawn and discretion ends or is limited. *Ultimately, it is the decisions of individuals at all levels of the organisation which will determine the ethical culture of the business*' (emphasis added).[19]

In addition to setting out core values-based policies, codes should guide the reader towards additional support and should encourage the positive behaviours that underpin a robust ethical culture. Wherever possible, the procedures established by the code should be integrated into the day-to-day business rather than constituting an additional burden.

Codes are a way of reminding employees of the importance of ethical behaviour. The more positive and linked to processes that support business rather than encumber it, the better the integration of the values and concepts they contain into the culture. No code will succeed without time and effort spent on training and raising awareness. We now discuss one of the most important types of training that can be used to help people use the code to support them in resolving issues and doing the right thing.

How Do We Know What the Right Thing to Do is?

How do we know what the 'right thing' to do is in any given situation? There is no one answer to this question. Often, the answer is clouded by another question—right for whom? We have seen that a system that answers this question solely by saying 'the shareholders' may make decisions that are not right for society or individuals. We argue that the question could often only be answered by looking at the interests of all stakeholders who will be affected by the decision. The famous dilemma of if you could save five people by pulling a switch and shunting a train onto a track where it would only kill one, would you do so shows that there are no absolutes. Thankfully, most decisions do not involve such terrible choices. However, many do require weighing up the impact on one group versus another. Therefore, it is helpful to have the possibility to talk with others about an ethical dilemma. Often a better decision can be reached through open, fair, informed engagement in discussions where various points of view are represented. Discussion is healthy, especially when it encompasses diverse perspectives. As discussed below, the use of ethical decision-making models can also help to determine what is the right thing to do in any situation. This does not mean that everyone will necessarily agree with the decision, but if it can be seen to be fair and to have been reached through a fair process of involvement, then acceptance will be supported. In addition, having a common set of core ethical values will make it easier to resolve issues. This is one of the main benefits of core values—they facilitate ethical decision-making in difficult situations.

States and organisations have processes to set laws or rules. The processes by which these rules are made and applied, as well as the substance of the rules, need to be demonstrably *fair*. The process of fair, open, informed discussion is critical. In the context of regulation, making the rules is only the start and the process of engagement must be continued on a constant basis. So, the relationship between regulator/enforcer and commercial business will be critical. Recognising widely differing views within the Church of England on human sexuality and priesthood, the Archbishop of Canterbury described the process of mediated dialogue that was adopted in 2016 not as reaching unanimous agreement, but as 'disagreeing well'. The philosopher Jürgen Habermas talks about people having an 'ideal speech situation', in which there is an equality of power and absence of deceit.[20]

Decisions and actions at any time do not necessarily need to be 'right'—the universal answer that is right for all time—or completely agreed upon by everyone. They must be considered by everyone involved to be fair in the circumstances at the time and to have been reached by fair processes.

A study by the IBE found that all major religions of the world are based on the same simple principle of treating others how you would wish them to treat you.[21] This is the opposite of selfishness. The theologian Hans Küng suggests that four 'directions' flow from the twin principles of treating others as you wish them to treat you and 'humanity': respect for life, speak and act truthfully, deal honestly and fairly, and respect and love one another.[22] This has strong echoes in the findings of Sisodia, Sheth and Wolfe that successful businesses are based on love, by which they mean an emotional attachment to all stakeholders and an altruistic commitment to see that those stakeholders' wishes and interests are respected.[23]

Ethical Dilemmas, Ethical Decision-Making Models and Scenario-Based Training

Rushworth Kidder suggested that most ethical dilemmas can be classified into four conflicts:

- truth versus loyalty;
- individual versus community;
- short term versus long term;
- justice versus mercy.[24]

We mention this to emphasise the point that most issues are not presented as good versus bad; rather, they involve grey areas, often caused by a clash of positive values, such as honesty versus loyalty. These dilemmas are difficult to resolve as the individual is pulled in two equally persuasive directions. Trying to determine the right thing to do can therefore be stressful and complicated, and it is good practice to prepare employees for such situations. Therefore, codes should not just contain information about values and business principles, but should also contain tools to help people work through examples of the application of ethical values to the real situations they may face in their own daily work. An important type of training involves facilitated analysis of these potential dilemmas, and discussions of how the values and principles contained in the code can assist in resolving them. Reliance on online training is unlikely to achieve the same goals.

People should be given opportunities to develop their minds and critical thinking. They should also be given ongoing opportunities to identify moral or unusual problems that need more than swift thought, and should then be encouraged to take time, and be allowed time, to think through the answers, through discussion with colleagues and outside thinkers whose moral reasoning and judgement is valued. This means ongoing training, involving discussion on solutions to applying morality to hard problems, rather than just cold learning of the principles alone.

Organisational structures, systems and culture should encourage us to think about what the right thing to do is in new (and even familiar) situations, to check and discuss decisions with others, and to seek feedback, evaluate, learn, apply and change how we do things (and then keep monitoring the changes to see if we have improved outputs and behaviour). It is critical to the success of ethical decision-making that we can recognise when we have an ethical dilemma and that we have people we can ask about it. Social pressure can assist us in doing the right thing, but we do need to check that the pressure and actions are ethical.

Scenario-based training has been shown to be the most effective type of training as it exposes people to situations which they are likely to encounter and allows them to practise how they should respond. This is most likely because scenarios are essentially stories, and human beings are curious, so stories can pique our curiosity. Given that time pressure can narrow our focus and result in a failure to see the ethical dimension, it is easy to understand why having thought things out prior to being confronted with an issue is helpful. And we know that many business decisions are made in stressful situations without the luxury of time to think things through carefully.

Good practice involves sourcing the scenario to be used in training from the very people who will be using them. Who is better placed than they are to know what problems may come up in their day-to-day work? There are many sources for training scenarios: the most important thing is to use scenarios that are relevant to the people being trained. It is therefore useful to set up a 'scenario bank' containing issues for discussion and suggestions for resolution and further information. Ethics ambassadors can be helpful in creating and augmenting a scenario bank.

However, we cannot anticipate every type of ethical dilemma that an employee will face; therefore, an ethical decision-making model that can be used to work through any issue that arises is a useful addition to the toolbox.

Figure 14.2 is an example of such a model, and further examples are contained in the Codes of Ethics of Borealis (www.borealisgroup.com/ethics) and Johnson

Matthey. (www.matthey.com/governance). Other examples can be seen in the IBE's *Good Practice Guide to Ethics in Decision-Making.*

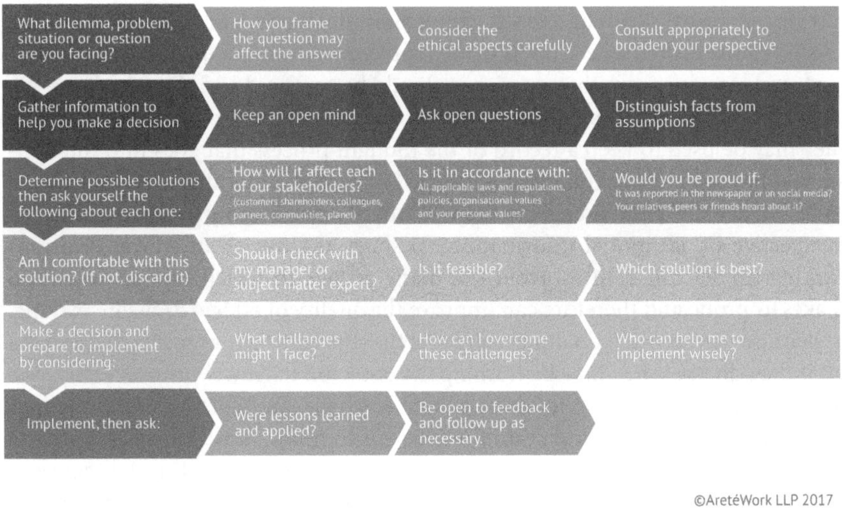

Figure 14.2: An ethical decision-making model

Ethical decision-making models are a response to the findings of behavioural psychology and other disciplines about how people make decisions when under stress and the observation that people trying to manage a crisis or an ethical issue 'free-style' make many preventable errors. They often miss important facts that were staring them in the face or make decisions based upon what they thought were facts, but which turned out to be assumptions. They may find it difficult to predict the ultimate consequences of initial decisions and therefore, as Palmer points out, 'find themselves facing decisions, contemplating options, and choosing alternatives that they did not foresee when they embarked on the series of decisions'. This may result in them doing something unethical that they would not have done had they had the correct or complete information.[25]

Ethical decision-making models can also be used in much the same way as Gawande uses checklists,[26] by asking questions to ensure that relevant (ethical) points are not inadvertently overlooked and that the issues are properly analysed. They constitute a process, a checklist or an aide memoire to ensure that all aspects of the situation are recognised and considered based on both 'fast and slow' systems in our brains, and that the decision is not made solely intuitively.

Ethical decision-making models should be short, visually attractive and intuitively simple to use. They must ask questions to provoke insights and remind people to ask themselves critical questions. The model above begins with the following question: 'What dilemma, problem, situation or question are you facing?' The reason for this is that people often miss the ethical implications of a particular workplace moment. Using this model during scenario-based training, we use this question to create the habit of thinking critically about one's actions on a regular basis. The horizontal flow within each colour in Figure 14.2 contains additional information and questions to ask oneself to improve decision-making, and following the arrows down on the left gives a short description of each step. The process is not over when a decision is made, implementation can often be the difficult part, and learning from the experience should be captured and shared.

Ethical decision-making models are not a record-keeping procedure (although they may be used to keep a record of the thought process that goes into the decision). They are most useful when employed as part of an inquiry with colleagues; to facilitate a debate that engages the wisdom of others who may have a different perspective or additional information. In short, the use of an ethical decision-making model can help to avoid the many pitfalls to which human cognition makes us prone and therefore can improve the quality of ethical decision-making.

Because people often do not even realise that they are facing an ethical dilemma or, if they do, that they may be framing the issue too narrowly or incorrectly, one of the goals of training is to teach people to challenge their own thinking and perspective. One of the most common errors is to frame something as a 'business decision', reducing it to a cost–benefit equation that ignores the ethical dimension. The famous case of the exploding petrol tanks on the Ford Pinto is an example of the consequences of cost-benefit thinking. The decision regarding whether to change the design of the car to make it safer was framed as the cost of adapting the vehicles versus the cost of damages for wrongful death and injury over the life of the vehicle model. Although there were other contributory causes for such a callous decision, the very fact that they even did the maths shows how ethical blindness can result.[27] More recently, similar flawed decision-making contributed to the VW emissions scandal.

Decisions and debates should guard against mis-framing and mis-representation of issues, so should encourage looking at issues from different perspectives and accepting constructive challenge as part of the process of reaching the best decision. If the issue is inaccurately framed, much of the analysis that follows may be faulty or inapplicable.

Mary Gentile reminds us that often people know what is the right thing to do, but lack the necessary strategies to achieve it.[28] Standing up against authority or speaking truth to power are difficult things to do even for relatively senior managers, let alone junior employees. Mary Gentile's *Giving Voice to Values* approach gives people strategies to help them bring their values to work and express them when necessary, and is therefore a good addition to any training programme. Gentile outlines strategies for developing 'scripts', and implementation plans for responding to commonly heard 'reasons and rationalizations' for questionable practices, and practising the delivery of those scripts. *Giving Voice to Values* is about 'building the skills, the confidence, the moral muscle, and, frankly, the *habit* of voicing our values'.

People tend to forget that the most difficult dilemmas involve conflicting positive values. Gentile points out that these are *conflicting* values rather than values versus a lack of values. So the first requirement in addressing the conflict is to realise that a conflict in fact exists before one can exercise judgement in balancing the competing values in the particular context. She identifies the following common reasons and 'professional rationalisations' that are heard in a workplace for *not* acting in accordance with one's values:

(a) Expected or standard practice: 'Everyone does this, so it's really standard practice. It's even expected.'
(b) Materiality: 'The impact of this action is not material. It doesn't really hurt anyone.'
(c) Locus of responsibility: 'This is not my responsibility; I'm just following orders here.'
(d) Locus of loyalty: 'I know this isn't quite fair to the customer but I don't want to hurt my reports/team/boss/company.'[29]

These are rationalisations and, as we know from Ariely, human beings will misbehave to the extent that they can rationalise bad behaviour, ie, cheat and still feel good about themselves. Therefore, the aim is to develop a culture where the ability to rationalise is reduced or eliminated. In addition, certain types of cultures—for example, those characterised by bullying, fear, strict hierarchy or secrecy—can increase the difficulty of implementing values-based decisions. Senior managers should be aware of any sub-cultures with these or similar characteristics and should work towards eliminating the source of the fear and changing the culture. In situations like these, additional training will make no difference.

Responding Ethically When under Stress: Time Matters

If ethical principles are to be successfully applied, it is important to provide sufficient time to consider their implications. For example, on well-run modern construction sites, a variety of tradesmen will be briefed at the start of each day on what work they should complete that day. Yet they know that if they encounter any safety issue or unexpected problem, they should not press on regardless, perhaps putting themselves or others at risk, and should instead stop and tell other relevant staff and managers. A solution can then be worked out through joint discussion, involving the relevant level of expertise. In other words, the instructions to complete a task within a set timeframe are subject to an overriding instruction to stop and consult if problems are encountered. Both their individual work contracts and the master construction contract should allow for time and funding to accommodate such unexpected issues. How often this happens in practise is unclear.

The Good Samaritan experiment conducted at the Princeton Theological Seminary in 1973 illustrated the importance of time in relation to ethical behaviour.[30] Subjects in this experiment were students at Princeton Theological Seminary. As each subject arrived, he was informed that he was to give a talk that would be recorded in another building. Along the way to the place for the talk, the subject encountered a 'victim' slumped in a doorway. The question was under what conditions would a subject stop to help the victim.

Half of the subjects were assigned to talk on the Parable of the Good Samaritan; the others were asked to discuss the employment prospects for divinity students after graduation. Some of the subjects were told they were late and should hurry; some were told they had just enough time to get to the recording room; and some were told they would arrive early. Judging by their responses to a questionnaire, they had different religious and moral orientations.

The only variable that made a difference in whether they stopped to help was how much of a hurry the subjects were in: 63% of subjects who were in no hurry stopped to help, 45% of those in a moderate hurry stopped and 10% of those that were in a great hurry stopped. Neither the assigned subject matter of the talk nor the subject's religious outlook made any difference. The most important factor was time or lack thereof—a factor derived entirely from the situation, not from their values or the proximity in time to thinking about the Parable of the Good Samaritan, as one might have expected.

The implications of the pace of business today are worrying in this regard. Decisions are made quickly and without the benefit of consultation, often in different time zones and cultures. This underscores the importance of values as the best guides in an ethical dilemma, as they are intrinsic, and of 'practising' ethical behaviour and exercising ethical decision-making muscles through scenario-based training.

'Time pressure reduces the cognitive resources available for decision makers and decreases the odds of their making the "should" choices.'[31] When we are in a hurry, we fall back on System 1 thinking, which is fast, automatic and emotional, as well as being prone to bias. System 2 is slow, deliberate, effortful and reason-based. 'When people are cognitively busy or tired, they rely on System 1, and they are more likely to engage in unethical behaviour'.[32]

Cultural change is not a time-limited project; it is an ongoing process. People come and go in organisations and when there is change at the top, it is particularly important to ensure that new management is committed to the core ethical values of the organisation. These values should form the basis of the recruitment process for all employees, but most importantly for those who will be the role models for the entire organisation. For that reason, one cannot be complacent when it comes to organisational culture. Values must be a constant and never-ending focus of senior leaders. As the risk climate changes, so too should the amount and quality of communication regarding the importance of ethical decision-making and behaviour increase.

Resources of Information, Education and Advice

Since decisions are made on a day-to-day basis at many levels in an organisation, people must have access to information and assistance to enable them to make these decisions correctly. It is not just senior managers who make decisions about their businesses. Often misconduct is caused in part by excessive secrecy, lack of access to information and/or an atmosphere where admitting ignorance is frowned upon. This is why culture is paramount and access to relevant information is important.

Internally, the most common sources of information will be company codes, policies and procedures on topics relevant to the business and industry. Anti-corruption, competition law, avoidance of conflicts of interest, modern slavery, anti-money laundering, gifts and entertainment and many other issues will usually be the subject of internal policies and procedures. However, it is not always easy to keep up with relevant changes in the law on these topics and not every organisation can afford to have a legal and/or compliance department responsible for churning out updated internal requirements. (On the other hand, businesses cannot afford *not* to have someone doing this!) One of the pitfalls of too much compliance is over-complicating the issues. Many anti-corruption training programmes go into detail about the differences between the US FCPA and the UK Bribery Act. For the vast majority of people in the organisation, it is sufficient to say 'do not, under any circumstances, pay a bribe'. For a small group of individuals, more specialist knowledge will be required, and a simple risk assessment will identify who they are.

Sources of information can be both internal and external. For example, large companies in supply chains can improve the skills and processes of smaller businesses through auditing and advice, such as accredited supplier agreements.[33]

Businesses use many different sources of information and advice in complying with regulation. A 2012 study found that around half of businesses surveyed had used trade associations, government department websites, insurance companies and accountants to help them comply with regulation. A total of 4 out of 10 mentioned the Businesslink website in relation to advice on regulatory requirements, whilst one-third mentioned their local council and around a quarter mentioned direct contact with a government department.[34] Many businesses (70%) used external agents as a source of information and advice in complying with regulation.[35]

A 2010 study for the then OFT found that a number of different relationships with third parties were important in supporting compliance with consumer protection law.[36] The source of improvement in understanding how to observe does not have to be an inspector or an official; it can be anyone who has expertise and respect. First, membership of trade associations or other collective bodies provided accurate, up-to-date and sector-specific information and support (such as standard terms and conditions) to traders on their obligations.[37] They appeared to offer to smaller businesses some of the advantages available to larger businesses—such as access to expert legal advice and helplines—that they could not otherwise afford. Trade associations were also seen as a way of pushing rogue or illegal traders out of a sector by allowing members to distinguish themselves from other businesses. Second, a relationship with local authority Trading Standards Services

(TSS) was generally regarded in a positive light where it existed, since TSS were able to offer authoritative advice (though some concerns do exist for a minority in this area), impartial adjudication and (for larger businesses with networks of outlets) a coordinated way of dealing with multiple TSS contacts.[38] Third, larger businesses were able to utilise external legal advice, which was perceived as a high-quality and reliable resource of expert opinion.[39] Fourth, in some sectors, companies monitored the behaviour of competitors and initiated complaints or action against each other.[40] Larger businesses were also able to build processes for addressing consumer protection law issues in their organisation, for example, through training, guidance and escalation procedures. These processes did exist in smaller businesses, but tended to be less formal.[41]

However, more could be done to help businesses. A 2013 report that examined business approaches towards consumer rights and complaints found that only about one-third (31%) reported that they had ever sought advice on complying with consumer rights from other organisations such as trade bodies. Larger businesses were more likely to have done so and to have done so more frequently. Only around a quarter of businesses that had used such advice reported that they had paid for it (27%), although large businesses were more likely to have paid.[42]

An organisation's visibility increases as its size increases. Hence, its exposure to external pressure also rises. Social legitimacy expectations have a greater impact on large firms due to them being more visible to the pressures that induce ethical behaviour.[43] In addition, it is likely that they will be exposed to greater risk and therefore must dedicate proportionately greater resources to tackling it. Complex, large corporations typically maintain extensive legal, compliance, audit and risk functions, employing in-house and outside consultants, who operate as 'shadow regulators'. Such 'gatekeepers' often have firm commitments to the basic regulatory norms they work with every day and refer to in their discussions with operations departments.[44] A recent survey of Scottish businesses noted that influencing business behaviour can be easier in larger businesses than smaller businesses:

> The survey research has also revealed notable differences between businesses of different sizes. Small businesses are influenced most by the personal views or beliefs of the business leader (owner). Medium and large businesses are significantly more influenced by both the interests of employees and customer/public opinion, together with issues such as business image.[45]

In any event, employees must be given adequate support to ensure that they know what laws and regulations apply to their jobs and how to get additional advice or assistance when it is needed. It is not credible to provide little or no guidance or support and then blame a 'rogue employee' for behaving unethically. More often than not, it is the barrel, not the apple that is rotten or at least negligent in providing assistance and ensuring the employee has the skills and knowledge to confront the risks that he or she is facing in his or her day-to-day work.

Promoting an Open Culture and Speaking up

Providing information, education and instructions on what to do or not do, and opportunities for people to ask questions is essential, but it is not enough. We have seen that people might not think about what they are going to do before doing it, and might underestimate risk for a variety of reasons. They might not realise that a decision or action raises ethical considerations. They may have other things on their minds, such as keeping their job or meeting targets. They may be inhibited from asking questions, for example, because they are afraid of attracting ridicule or blame.[46] So, it is important to provide a culture within which people feel free to ask questions like 'Have we got all the relevant information?', 'Should we be doing this?', 'Is this right?' and 'Is this in accordance with our values?' People will only do this if they feel safe. This constant checking and questioning is commonplace in the best safety-critical environments, such as aviation and construction sites.

Behaviours can be reinforced and will tend to increase in frequency when recognised, rewarded, given airtime and incentivised, and will bring personal gratification in financial or reputational currencies.[47] Thus, behaviours that are desired should be reinforced accordingly; behaviours that are not so enforced will fade. In order to change organisational behaviour, it is necessary to adopt strategies that involve issuing information, training or a communications cascade, and also to engage the social influence and support of small groups of 'people like me' affinities.[48]

Receiving constant feedback, especially positive feedback, assists learning. This means that people should feel able to raise and question issues, without fear of adverse consequences, including where they themselves have done something wrong or stupid. Repression of information will not assist group or individual learning, nor will a tendency to make decisions on inadequate information, in view of the tendency to infer the general from the particular. Feedback can be arranged from colleagues, customers and third parties such as ombudsmen, suppliers, investors, regulators and others. Reliance on external support is likely to be critical.

Organisations should have people available to whom anyone can talk, or to ask questions, at various levels of accessibility or seniority. These may be local ethics ambassadors, ethics committees, legal departments, integrity departments, consumer panels, workers' committees, suppliers' forums, directors' committees and so on.

Case Study 31: Contrasting Stories of a Culture of Checking

In the operating theatre of a well-known provincial hospital in 2015, a trainee doctor asked the consultant surgeon: 'Are you sure you are taking out the correct kidney?' The senior male consultant shouted at the junior female, ridiculing her, and continued what he was doing. No one else present said anything further or checked the position, but the junior was correct, and the healthy kidney was removed whilst the diseased one was left untouched.

On a long flight in 2015, Hodges asked a middle-ranking pilot if 'just culture' was really observed in airlines. The pilot confirmed that all pilots are free to fly a large commercial airliner virtually in any way they see fit, but their decisions are supported by highly sophisticated information technology systems, operating parameters and reminders, and monitors. Crucially, it is expected that any pilot of any seniority can question, and check with, a colleague of whatever seniority, and this would not be taken as criticism, but as normal and expected behaviour. Language would be used on both sides that is low key and non-critical. The exchange could operate as a learning opportunity for a junior person or an opportunity for a more senior person to review and justify an action. The prevailing culture was regarded as the critical component. The pilot said that when he went home and went out with his wife in the car, and he asked her, when she was driving, why she had taken a certain route, the same language would be taken as criticism. He said that the language we use to frame questions, and the context in which they are asked, is really important.

Case Study 32: The Support of Trusted Ethical Colleagues

In the 1980s, the senior management of the UK subsidiary of a pharmaceutical company headquartered in another European state decided to withdraw a licenced product since it appeared that the information that was filtering in from practitioners (in various countries) about its use indicated that it probably gave rise to an unexpected but serious adverse risk. At that stage, the pharmacovigilance system was not as sophisticated as it has since become in many respects, including the extent of the involvement of regulators, but the basic situation was that the drug was clearly effective for the condition for which it was licensed but data had begun to emerge that it might not be adequately safe. Interpretation of the available data was at that stage a matter of sophisticated technical judgement. The UK management discussed it with the global headquarters (located in a European state), which initially disagreed with the UK managers' views. The senior management of the US office also disagreed, since, after a long struggle, the drug was about to be licenced in the US. The commercial implications of withdrawing the drug were significant for the company. There was a major internal battle between senior managers. The views of the UK management prevailed, as they insisted that they were responsible for drug safety in the UK and it was their decision that the drug should be withdrawn in the UK. It was therefore withdrawn worldwide, which provoked many objections from doctors and patients. Why did the UK management prevail in this decision? First, the UK management comprised three individuals, who were all medically qualified and formed the same professional view on the safety issue. As a 'gang of three', they supported each other and formed a combined and unmoveable front with more senior colleagues abroad. As medical professionals, they felt that the ethical values that had been instilled throughout their professional lives were fundamental and non-negotiable, and trumped the commercial considerations of their employment. Such values were supported by a peer group of colleagues, which was then emerging as the Faculty of Pharmaceutical Physicians, in which it was no accident that the three of them played a prominent role. Their reputations, and those of the company, were enhanced by their 'difficult' decision.

Case Study 33: Ethics Ambassadors at Spectris

Like many other proactive companies, Spectris plc conducted a review of its approach to ethics and compliance in response to the implementation of the UK Bribery Act and in 2011 undertook a refresh of its Code of Ethics, basing the revised code firmly on its core values. Spectris also created a group-wide network of ethics officers from amongst existing employees in each of its operating companies, whose first task was to help ensure that communication and training about the Code was consistent across the group. These ethics officers were brought together at a conference—not only for training, but also to give them a chance to discuss the new role, meet each other, and understand the background and importance of the Code and the topics it covered. While the primary responsibility for doing the right thing remains with senior leaders, the ethics officers are there to support them. In addition to providing information about the relevant laws and policies, Spectris has focused on engaging employees as part of the process of integrating ethics and values into the everyday life of their businesses.

Cultures in which people feel inhibited from speaking up can foster extensive problems. The Equality and Human Rights Commission's inquiry into cleaning businesses found poor treatment of workers going unchallenged where people feared risking their jobs by raising problems:

> [O]n the whole, respondents' attitudes to their current jobs are best characterised as stoical and largely uncomplaining; conditioned perhaps by their low expectations of the industry set against a backdrop of perceived limited choices. Respondents often said that they felt they had either to endure any problems they encountered at work or leave ...[49]

> A substantial number of respondents said it would not be a problem to raise issues with their supervisor/manager. Some had done so, but generally these had not been serious issues such as a bad relationship with a particular supervisor. The most common view among respondents with serious problems at work was that they had to put up with them or leave their job. Several reported instances where they had complained about an aspect of their work only to get a response from the supervisor or manager that indicated: if they did not like it, someone who was prepared to do their job instead could easily be found. This was sometimes implied or said indirectly. There were no reports of specific threats of reprisals, such as the sack, for raising serious concerns but serious concerns were generally not raised. The overall sense of job insecurity and powerlessness probably means specific threats are not necessary to ward off complaints whereas in most cases, the general sense of economic reality is an effective block on individual negotiations for improved pay and conditions.[50]

A similar inquiry in the meat and poultry processing industry also suggested that the large-scale use in that sector of agency workers led to some people tolerating significant abuse because of the possibility of converting from 'temp to perm' employment status and not wishing to jeopardise that option.[51]

When All Else Fails, External Whistleblowing

In recent years, a considerable amount of effort has been put into creating pathways for people to blow the whistle on bad things that were occurring in their organisations but were being ignored by management. Serious examples that concerned people were in the NHS, financial services, and bribery and human rights abuses. The communication is usually about an issue that the communicator feels cannot be raised through normal internal management channels, so is raised by some external or other route, which the corporation may regard as a breach of internal procedures, duties of employment or discipline.[52]

It is important to protect individual whistleblowers, since there is clear evidence that a whistleblower can suffer at the hands of managers or colleagues for 'letting the side down'. Companies creating whistleblowing lines emphasise that retaliation will not be tolerated for concerns raised in good faith, and must be vigilant to ensure that it does not occur when the identity of the whistleblower is known. There are frequent references to the problem that individuals do not report concerns because of the fear of adverse personal consequences, such as serious examples in the NHS[53] and in banking; the Parliamentary Commission on Banking Standards was 'shocked by the evidence it heard that so many people turned a blind eye to misbehaviour and failed to report it'.[54] Research for the IBE has shown that while a quarter of workers are aware of misconduct at work, more than half (52%) of those stay silent.[55] However, it may be that a significant amount of traffic in whistleblowing channels that should by nature be anonymous and retaliation-free is in fact unreliable and emanates from individuals who have other problems or motivations; careful handling of information is therefore particularly important.[56] Therefore, it is important that proper investigation techniques are used and that confidentiality is respected. Reputations can be unjustifiably damaged by individuals seeking to use the system to destroy a rival or retaliate for some perceived unfair treatment.

It is good practice for any organisation to have both internal and external speak-up pathways for people to raise concerns. Blowing the whistle, either through the press, social media or through third-party whistleblowing organisations, is a clear indication of a cultural failure. A series of channels in which concerns may be escalated if they do not receive a satisfactory response should be established. An individual should have the option of raising issues with managerial superiors, suggestions boxes, human relations staff, senior management and directors, as well as externally to company-provided speak-up lines, regulators or other specialist support functions. Cultivating speaking-up and whistleblowing policies can lead to an increased level of trust within organisations.[57] But if an adequate response is not given when an issue is raised, the frustration at not being 'heard' and the associated fall in trust that this generates can turn someone into an external whistleblower.

It is also important to recognise that speaking up and/or whistleblowing can have negative connotations in various European countries, due to experiences during the Second World War and in countries that experienced totalitarian regimes. In order to be effective, cultural sensitivities must be considered. For this reason, Borealis called its 'speak-up channel' 'QuestionLine', promoting it and using it primarily as a place to get advice and assistance.

A business with an open, ethical culture will not need to rely heavily on a speak-up mechanism, but it should have one. The ideal in an ethical organisation is that there is constant spontaneous discussion and sharing of information, so that the ability to speak up anonymously or outside the normal management chain and external whistleblowing is a rare occurrence, and is only needed as a fail-safe mechanism. An organisation should not expect to see much activity that could be described as 'whistleblowing' if everyone is openly sharing information and is not afraid to speak up. An open culture should minimise the risk of wrongdoing not being identified. The number, frequency and subject matter of all concerns should be monitored and the handling of such concerns should be regularly reviewed by senior managers. The metrics that will be generated through this regular monitoring will provide good external evidence of the culture of an organisation. The absence of complaints should not be taken as evidence that none exist without further investigation and insight into the culture. In an analogy to safety, an increased reporting of ethical 'near misses' should be seen as a good thing, as it shows a developing ethical awareness.

The most important purpose of a whistleblowing system is to identify cultures where there is a problem that is invisible to the outside world or through other metrics. In its 2012 Report, the Association of Certified Fraud Examiners reported that 50.9% of reported fraud within organisations is identified by tip-offs from employees or contractors.[58] In 2014, the Association calculated that three times as many frauds are discovered by tip-offs than by any other method.[59] Feldman and Lobel's research also found that workers are most likely to report their co-workers when they witnessed localised employee theft than environmental illegality, sexual harassment, corporate financial fraud and safety issues.[60] People believe that they themselves will report more frequently than other people, and that others are motivated by different rationales compared to themselves. Women are more likely to report corporate misconduct and are motivated to report by different factors from men. Generally, people prefer to confront illegal behaviour from within their organisation rather than reporting it externally, as long as they believe that internal reporting will be effective. That is the ideal situation, as it indicates an open culture. This is not always the case, of course, hence the need for other means of surfacing issues. The existence of a duty to report can make a huge difference.[61]

Monitoring, Measuring and Reporting

In addition to the measurement of culture discussed in previous chapters, there are numerous metrics that can be obtained through monitoring issues raised through all of the various channels in the organisation, such as exit interviews and speak-up lines. These can help management to keep its finger on the pulse and contribute to external reporting. In addition, adherence to instruments such as the Global Reporting Initiative (GRI) significantly increases transparency and stimulates an organisation to review ethics, integrity and governance, as well as other aspects related to sustainability.[62]

Conclusions

1. Regulators, principally those from the US, have driven the development of compliance departments and compliance programmes, including lengthy and complicated policies, procedures and systems.
2. Despite these measures, unethical behaviour has continued and numerous high-profile ethical standards have brought about the realisation that compliance will fail if it is not underpinned by a strong ethical culture.
3. Companies have adopted one of two diverse approaches orientated either towards compliance or values.
4. An orientation based upon values is more likely to achieve the desired outcome of better ethical decision-making and will be beneficial to the company in other ways as well.
5. In this chapter, we set out our ideas about the components of a values-oriented framework, based around the cornerstone of an ethical practice code founded on the company's core ethical values.
6. Another important aspect of the framework is competent ethical decision-making, achieved in part through scenario-based training and the use of ethical decision-making models.
7. We must be mindful of the fact that numerous factors can affect ethical behaviour, even in people with strong values and good intentions. Some of these are the pressure of time, social pressure to conform, and the fast and slow systems that are involved in human decision-making.
8. Another essential element of such a framework is an open culture, where people are encouraged to speak up without fear of retaliation. Many channels should exist for this purpose, including, as a last resort, a so-called speak-up line. An employee going to the press or an unrelated whistle-blowing institution is a sign of a failure in the culture.

APPENDICES

> When you tug at a single thing in nature, you find it attached to the rest of the world.
>
> John Muir

Appendix 1: EBP in Organisations

We set out suggested checklists on how to establish and nurture EBP. The first is a list of general questions that leaders of organisations might ask themselves to enable them to support EBP in their organisations. The second is a list of the types of evidence that external stakeholders might take into consideration in making their judgement as to whether an organisation can be trusted.

Best practice as to what constitutes EBP generally, and in specific sectorial contexts, will evolve. It is important that the achievement of EBP is not regarded as a 'tick-box' or administrative exercise. It is essential that ethical culture and behaviour are at the centre of the concept, and drive all activities and decisions by the organisation. The EBP concept should cover a 'law-abiding' approach to regulatory performance and compliance, but it would include acceptance that not every action might be perfect. Things sometimes go wrong, but the key issues would be whether this was not intentional and whether failure was acknowledged, things were put right, and lessons were learned and applied.

Questions to Assist Leaders in Implementing EBP

This list consists of some important challenges that leaders may ask themselves (and others) when developing EBP in their organisations. Some of these points may appear to overlap, but it is sometimes important to look at a situation from different angles:

- Have we defined the essential ethical purpose of our organisation?
- Have we identified and consistently championed ethical values?
- Do our systems result in the right people being 'on the bus' and in the right jobs?
- Are our leaders and board members able to challenge each other and themselves, and hold each other to account?
- Are we supporting people to make ethical decisions and behave ethically, minimising the ability to rationalise unethical behaviour?

- Do we incentivise, reward or require people to meet targets or perform in ways that inevitably raise ethical conflicts or risk unethical conduct?
- Are we producing constant reliable evidence that those contributing to and/or working on behalf of our organisation can be trusted?
- Are we producing constant reliable evidence that the organisation itself can be trusted?
- What training are we doing to develop people's ethical awareness and facilities, including their ability to spot an ethical issue, analyse it properly and implement their decision?
- Are we developing a sense of internal cohesion, involving everyone across the entire organisation?
- Do we have enough and appropriate resources to support our people to identify and do the right thing?
- Are we ensuring that our leaders in particular are open to multiple influencers to ensure sufficient challenge?
- Do all the elements of our organisation, including people, processes and systems, contribute to the maintenance of a strong ethical culture that supports ethical decision-making and behaviour?
- How have we reduced the risk that decisions are influenced by unethical considerations and context?
- Do our employees consistently rate our organisation as a good place to work?

Examples of the Types of Evidence That May Be Provided to Support EBP/EBR

This is a long list of *possible evidence* and it is very important that it is not treated as a definitive list that can be 'ticked' so as to award or withhold recognition of EBP. First, it is the nature and extent of the underlying *evidence* that will be important to evaluate in order to form a judgment. Second, organisations can be considered to operate on the basis of EBP even if something goes wrong. It will always be important to consider evidence *over time* and to note the direction of travel, such as whether improvements are being made (in which case the organisation should be encouraged) or not.

The Foundation

1. Evidence of a belief that ethics is everyone's responsibility.
2. An articulated and inspirational social purpose for the organisation.
3. Evidence of thoughtfully identified core ethical values, whose meanings are clear to all employees, and continuous communication and training for all (including the board) to reinforce these values.

4. Evidence of a public commitment to EBP by all leaders and managers, including public statements of adherence to EBP, similar to the Partnering Against Corruption Initiative (which the CEO signs personally) or the UN Global Compact and active pursuit of the relevant responsibilities, especially active involvement in these programmes.
5. Evidence of employing ethical decision-making models and other structures for checking business decisions against wider ethical principles and the expectations of all stakeholders.
6. Evidence demonstrating an understanding of the fair and legitimate needs of all internal and external stakeholders, and of discussing, agreeing and reviewing how these may fairly be achieved.
7. Evidence of continually developing means for demonstrating the extent to which EBP exists and therefore that trust can be placed in the firm, including that appropriate actions and improvements are made in response to feedback.

Ethical Culture

8. Evidence of holistic support for EBP by all aspects of the business structure and systems, including strategy, objectives, performance management and operational culture, and of the removal of any impediments or disincentives to its achievement.
9. Results of regularly conducted ethical risk assessments demonstrating that management is aware of the various types of ethical (and compliance) risks to which the company is exposed, including through their internal culture.
10. Evidence of obtaining external feedback from customers and stakeholders. Feedback from consumers would include active engagement, such as through all front-line staff and supported by a customer service function, and by membership of an Ombudsman scheme. Feedback from suppliers would include the relevant use of communication by direct and independent means.
11. Anecdotal evidence of adherence to the organisation's ethical values in practice, through actions, decisions and discussions at all levels. Is this a place where good people want to work?

People and Ethos

12. Evidence of the use of the core values to ensure that people are hired who share these values—for example, recruitment procedures focusing on more than just skills and experience in the hiring process. Looking for candidates who have demonstrated high standards of integrity and trustworthiness. When recruiting senior managers, consider ethical leadership skills and be vigilant for traits that would potentially cause dysfunction or lack of alignment with the organisation's ethical values.
13. Providing evidence of recognition, reward, remuneration and advancement based on performance in accordance with the organisation's ethical values

and associated objectives rather than only on commercial targets. Evidence of how performance management take into consideration how results are achieved as well as what is achieved.

14. Evidence of a commitment to continuous improvement in management and leadership (personal development, employee fulfilment, leadership programmes). Evidence of the provision of reasonable opportunities for employees to improve their skills and contribute to the development of the business.
15. Evidence that leaders are fully committed to ethical values and understand their role in creating an ethical culture, and set a strong, positive example.
16. Evidence of employee involvement and engagement in fostering EBP, such as using ethics ambassadors.
17. Evidence of management with the personalities and skills required to promote the conditions in which EBP can flourish, such as openness, transparency, fairness, accountability and empowerment.
18. Evidence that groups are designed in terms of size and links that support and do not inhibit discussions on decisions, and reaching ethical decisions.
19. Evidence of a collaborative atmosphere, working across functions, business units and cultures with curiosity and respect, and the ability to learn lessons and continuously improve.
20. Evidence of tolerance for, and encouragement of, constructive conflict without fear of reprisals for raising difficult issues.
21. Evidence that constructive challenge and discussion on what is right and fair in different circumstances is encouraged.
22. Evidence of supporting a culture of thinking, checking and engaging with others on whether actions are ethical, and that decisions counter mental shortcuts, underestimating risk, thinking that people have all the necessary information and cheating a bit.
23. Evidence that people respond to adverse situations fairly and openly, assisting in identifying the root cause(s) and taking corrective action.

Aligned Systems and Processes

24. Evidence that processes and systems are in alignment with ethical values and supporting EBP, and are embedded in the business rather than separate from it.
25. Performance management systems and incentive schemes that reward good leadership and ethical behaviours, not just results, and that do not foster unethical behaviour.
26. Evidence of the provision of clear and adequate information and professional assistance to support all aspects of EBP.
27. Evidence of periodic auditing of the extent to which EBP can be demonstrated and the development and/or application of various relevant metrics.

28. Evidence of honest measurement and monitoring to enable the organisation to demonstrate the existence of a strong ethical culture.

Frameworks

29. A written Code of Ethical Business Practice, developed from within, based upon the organisation's values and aligned with the culture, forming the cornerstone of the organisation's approach to ethics and compliance.
30. Regular ethical/anti-corruption risk assessments, done by the business, with expert support as needed and the implementation of mitigation measures in response to risks identified.
31. Clear, succinct policies and procedures that are easily accessible and kept updated.
32. Evidence of a regular pattern of communications at all levels of management, including regarding demonstrable behaviour in line with ethical principles and publicised sensitively.
33. Evidence of training aimed at informing those doing business on behalf of the organisation as to what is expected of them, mainly conducted face to face and supplemented by training delivered online or by other technological means, such as apps.
34. A network of employee ethics ambassadors to assist in embedding ethical values, communications and training.
35. Evidence of development of ethical decision-making skills, including how to recognise and resolve ethical dilemma and how to effectively implement solutions once these are determined. This would include ethical decision-making models and scenario-based training using realistic scenarios developed internally (scenario bank).
36. Evidence of adequate resources, including people to develop and deliver the necessary materials for training and awareness raising, to carry out proper investigations of ethical lapses and to capture and communicate the lessons learned.
37. Evidence of the effective due diligence of third parties, conducted by the business, with support as needed.
38. Evidence of the involvement of relevant third parties and strategic partners in the commitment to ethical business practice, including the supply chain and anyone acting on behalf of the organisation.
39. An appropriate mechanism for speaking up, catering to the language and cultural characteristics of the organisation, supported by a skilled approach to investigations and discipline, as well as a climate of 'psychological safety' in which to do so.[1]
40. Evidence of monitoring, measuring, tracking and reporting elements of ethical business practice by various means.

Incentives

41. Evidence that financial, performance, organisational and other incentives support EBP, the identification of ethical conflicts and their ethical resolution.
42. Evidence of competing with oneself, and the organisation's own record, to improve performance.

Spreading EBR

43. Evidence of supporting the adoption of EBP amongst stakeholders, including staff, suppliers, customers, regulators, local communities and society. Evidence that entities understand their supply chain. The extent of due diligence and engagement in EBP will depend on the level of risk and resources available to the parties. A higher-level example would be requiring and supporting suppliers to adopt ethical values and support structures, and to provide evidence of this.
44. Agreement of protocols with relevant stakeholders in relation to EBP.

Appendix 2: Actions to Support EBR

We summarise here suggested actions to incentivise organisations to adopt meaningful ethical policies and build ethical cultures, and to remove barriers to achieving and sustaining EBR. We set out two lists for actions to be taken by regulatory authorities and governments respectively.

The intention is for actions by public bodies to remove barriers to businesses acting ethically, to encourage businesses to operate EBP and to respond to those who provide satisfactory evidence that they operate based on EBP by recognising this commitment. In effect, the public sector should engage with organisations that operate EBP and meet them halfway.

The basic principles are as follows:

(a) The adoption of EBP should be a *voluntary* behaviour by an individual business and its staff, in which they earn recognition.
(b) Regulators and enforcers should *recognise* when a firm has acted ethically, giving credit for this in their relationships and interactions.
(c) Regulators and enforcers can take steps to *incentivise and promote* wider and deeper adoption of EBP within the business community and in markets.
(d) Government and international organisations (the OECD, the World Bank, the IMF, the UN and others) should support regulators and enforcers, and other governments.

Much of what is suggested can build on existing structures and practice, such as co-regulatory systems, the existence in some firms of ethical mission statements and corporate responsibility goals, and the shifts that have been identified above in UK regulatory and enforcement practice. Larger companies will have elements of EBP without necessarily calling it that. In some cases, they may already do almost everything we have previously suggested. We have set out in chapters 13 and 14, and in these Appendices, some general guidance that we believe an organisation could refer to on its way towards achieving EBP. However, we wish to emphasise that there is no one-size-fits-all ethical culture and the leaders of each organisation contemplating EBP (or for that matter wishing to ensure that their culture is ethical) should make their own decisions about the actions required to achieve it. If we, or anyone else, become too prescriptive, we will have only created 'compliance' by the back door, and that is not the goal.

In some sectors, both firms and regulators may find the adoption of EBP/EBR a straightforward next step that requires little change. However, other sectors may need to undergo significant re-adjustment. In achieving such change, it will be essential that appropriate leadership is shown by politicians, business leaders and officials, and appropriate incentives are in place and legislative and cultural barriers are removed. Piloting the approach in some sectors and practice can be anticipated to illuminate and assist change more widely. Regulators may have to look at their own internal cultures to determine whether there are barriers to adoption and what changes may need to be made to support them in operating EBR.

Actions by Regulatory and Enforcement Bodies

1. Regulatory and enforcement authorities should review their cultures, objectives, enforcement strategies and policies to enable individual businesses to engage the entire regulatory community on an EBR protocol.
2. The ideal is to enshrine a trusting relationship between businesses and authorities in an EBR protocol, which states the basis of the agreement. Those authorities that have enforcement powers without an *ex ante* regulatory system may still enter into an EBR protocol, for example, with businesses that operate in sectors where there is a high risk of non-compliance and that wish to 'do the right thing'.
3. Businesses should be able to commit individually or collectively to an EBR protocol with all regulatory authorities that is 'recognised' by an external body and includes agreement on which (a) regulatory control activities and systems will be performed by which organisations (for example, within co-regulatory structures that contain different 'tiers'), and (b) evidence will be offered to demonstrate their ongoing adherence to ethical commerce.
4. EBR protocols should cover:
   a. commitment to supporting ethical behaviour;
   b. commitment to work collaboratively;
   c. details on how outputs are to be delivered and monitored;
   d. means of visible compliance;

   e. means of monitoring performance, including the facility for receiving and demonstrating response to complaints;
   f. protocols on approach to identification of problems, and means of agreement of holistic responses to addressing problems;
   g. commitment to identifying causes of unethical behaviour and implementing means of supporting rectification and redress.
5. Demonstrating the achievement of EBP should be encouraged and rewarded by regulators. Hence, enforcement policies and sentencing guidelines should be revised and should specify an appropriate cooperative response to those who demonstrably observe EBR protocols.
6. To ensure a consistent and proportionate response to business and to similar behaviours, there should be a mechanism for the harmonisation of approaches between different regulators and enforcers, so that businesses are treated similarly by all the public bodies with which they may interact.
7. Sufficiently wide adherence to EBP, since it would justify a reliable co-regulatory approach, should trigger a comprehensive better regulation review of the regulatory system so as to reallocate responsibilities to the appropriate level of actor, whilst ensuring transparency and verification of practice.
8. Bodies responsible for enforcement should have a wide-ranging toolbox of powers, including inspecting, verifying, obtaining relevant information, initiating and approving actions aimed at reducing future risk and making redress for harm caused, and initiating the imposition of proportionate sanctions.
9. The response to adverse events should, where proportionate, focus on identifying the cause of the problem, identifying an effective means of reducing the risk of reoccurrence, making demonstrably fair remedial and redress measures, and finally considering what marking or sanctioning should apply.
10. In imposing sanctions, the behaviour of individuals and the systems and controls of an organisation should be considered separately and in context. Thus, individuals' actions may be seen to be perhaps either a mistake or criminal, viewed in the context of what the organisation has done to support individuals to operate in a compliant way.
11. The approach to enforcement strategy should:
   a. set out the circumstances in which powers will or will not be considered for use;
   b. be based on principles of predictability, fairness, proportionality, reducing risk and encouraging improved performance;
   c. investigate the causes of serious or potentially systemic non-compliance, so that potential options for reducing the risk of reoccurrence of non-compliance, whether by an infringer or others, can be decided upon and implemented;
   d. evaluate the impact on victims, so that risk-based remedial action can be identified and taken;
   e. encourage those businesses and individuals that have demonstrated their trustworthiness to continue to operate on a fair, no-blame environment;

f. recognise that individuals are the root cause of both good and bad behaviour, whilst the behaviour of individuals and groups can be influenced by external factors, such as incentives, group culture, level of support, education, reminders;
g. support a virtuous business ethic;
h. give fair incentives to infringers to avoid, reduce, acknowledge, redress and mitigate the harm they cause;
i. recognise that problems will occur, irrespective of blame, and that most people in most businesses wish to do the right thing most of the time, and hence support them;
j. distinguish those whose motivations and actions are ethically unacceptable, to be sanctioned proportionately;
k. evaluate the moral seriousness of the motivation, actions and outcomes of actors who have broken the rules, and impose proportionate sanctions appropriately.

Actions by Government

1. Political leadership should explain and endorse the concepts of EBP and EBR as a national policy.
2. Official bodies should be empowered to support EBR in practice, including through arrangements to incentivise businesses to adopt EBR and to remove barriers to its achievement and recognition.
3. There should be a consistent approach by all public regulators to recognise ethical practice by firms, whether or not formal arrangements exist. That would involve review and alignment of the Regulators' Code (which would be made applicable to all enforcers) and of all relevant policy documents, including enforcers' mission statements and enforcement policies and the courts' Sentencing Guidelines, so as to ensure a consistent approach.
4. All regulatory and enforcement bodies should be able to encourage the adoption of EBP on the part of those they regulate, to support pilot schemes and to enter protocol arrangements, including adding an ethical component within Primary Authority arrangements where acceptable evidence supported this in particular cases.
5. There should be recognition that regulatory and business compliance systems should function as a more integrated system. Hence, the collaborative approach illustrated by the Primary Authority scheme should be extended to as many areas of business and regulated sectors as possible.
6. Government should facilitate a permanent forum for discussion involving representatives of all regulators, enforcers, firms and other stakeholders on what constitutes best practice in EBP (which may vary depending on sector or circumstances) and on how arrangements should evolve.

7. Government should take steps to facilitate the spread of ethical values, and discussion on their content and how they apply in practical situations. This would involve the inclusion of ethics in formal educational and skills teaching, accreditation and or training provided by educational, commercial and professional organisations.
8. Political statements and information on EBP should be made to explain the rationale for not responding to every adverse event with a punitive response ('Who is to blame? Who is going to be punished?'), since lessons would otherwise not be learned and applied, and improvements would not be achieved in performance and reduction of risk.
9. Government should review the statutory basis and mandates of regulators to ensure they can and will encourage EBR. This would involve:
   - revision of competency provisions (training and assessment) to ensure front-line officials are equipped professionally and culturally to support EBR;
   - ensuring performance of regulation is based on how far they recognise and respond to compliance demonstrated, for example, through EBP.
   - reviewing resources and intra-regulatory cooperation, including cross-government leadership.
10. Government should consider whether and how the adoption of EBP might be encouraged under public procurement arrangements and supply chain integrity.

Appendix 3. The US Department of Justice's Evaluation of Corporate Compliance Programs: Sample Topics and Questions

1. Analysis and Remediation of Underlying Misconduct

— *Root Cause Analysis*—What is the company's root cause analysis of the misconduct at issue? What systemic issues were identified? Who in the company was involved in making the analysis?

— *Prior Indications*—Were there prior opportunities to detect the misconduct in question, such as audit reports identifying relevant control failures or allegations, complaints, or investigations involving similar issues? What is the company's analysis of why such opportunities were missed?

— *Remediation*—What specific changes has the company made to reduce the risk that the same or similar issues will not occur in the future? What specific remediation has addressed the issues identified in the root cause and missed opportunity analysis?

2. Senior and Middle Management

— *Conduct at the Top*—How have senior leaders, through their words and actions, encouraged or discouraged the type of misconduct in question? What concrete actions have they taken to demonstrate leadership in the company's compliance and remediation efforts? How does the company monitor its senior leadership's behavior? How has senior leadership modelled proper behavior to subordinates?
— *Shared Commitment*—What specific actions have senior leaders and other stakeholders (e.g., business and operational managers, Finance, Procurement, Legal, Human Resources) taken to demonstrate their commitment to compliance, including their remediation efforts? How is information shared among different components of the company?
— *Oversight*—What compliance expertise has been available on the board of directors? Have the board of directors and/or external auditors held executive or private sessions with the compliance and control functions? What types of information have the board of directors and senior management examined in their exercise of oversight in the area in which the misconduct occurred?

3. Autonomy and Resources

— *Compliance Role*—Was compliance involved in training and decisions relevant to the misconduct? Did the compliance or relevant control functions (e.g., Legal, Finance, or Audit) ever raise a concern in the area where the misconduct occurred?
— *Stature*—How has the compliance function compared with other strategic functions in the company in terms of stature, compensation levels, rank/title, reporting line, resources, and access to key decision-makers? What has been the turnover rate for compliance and relevant control function personnel? What role has compliance played in the company's strategic and operational decisions?
— *Experience and Qualifications*—Have the compliance and control personnel had the appropriate experience and qualifications for their roles and responsibilities?
— *Autonomy*—Have the compliance and relevant control functions had direct reporting lines to anyone on the board of directors? How often do they meet with the board of directors? Are members of the senior management present for these meetings? Who reviewed the performance of the compliance function and what was the review process? Who has determined compensation/bonuses/raises/hiring/termination of compliance officers? Do the compliance and relevant control personnel in the

field have reporting lines to headquarters? If not, how has the company ensured their independence?

— *Empowerment*—Have there been specific instances where compliance raised concerns or objections in the area in which the wrongdoing occurred? How has the company responded to such compliance concerns? Have there been specific transactions or deals that were stopped, modified or more closely examined as a result of compliance concerns?
— *Funding and Resources*—How have decisions been made about the allocation of personnel and resources for the compliance and relevant control functions in light of the company's risk profile? Have there been times when requests for resources by the compliance and relevant control functions have been denied? If so, how have those decisions been made?
— *Outsourced Compliance Functions*—Has the company outsourced all or part of its compliance functions to an external firm or consultant? What has been the rationale for doing so? Who has been involved in the decision to outsource? How has that process been managed (including who oversaw and/or liaised with the external firm/consultant)? What access level does the external firm or consultant have to company information? How has the effectiveness of the outsourced process been assessed?

4. Policies and Procedures

a. Design and Accessibility

— *Designing Compliance Policies and Procedures*—What has been the company's process for designing and implementing new policies and procedures? Who has been involved in the design of policies and procedures? Have business units/divisions been consulted prior to rolling them out?
— *Applicable Policies and Procedures*—Has the company had policies and procedures that prohibited the misconduct? How has the company assessed whether these policies and procedures have been effectively implemented? How have the functions that had ownership of these policies and procedures been held accountable for supervisory oversight?
— *Gatekeepers*—Has there been clear guidance and/or training for the key gatekeepers (e.g., the persons who issue payments or review approvals) in the control processes relevant to the misconduct? What has been the process for them to raise concerns?
— *Accessibility*—How has the company communicated the policies and procedures relevant to the misconduct to relevant employees and third parties? How has the company evaluated the usefulness of these policies and procedures?

b. Operational Integration

— *Responsibility for Integration*—Who has been responsible for integrating policies and procedures? With whom have they consulted (e.g., officers, business segments)? How have they been rolled out? Do compliance personnel assess whether employees understand the policies?
— *Controls*—What controls failed or were absent that would have detected or prevented the misconduct? Are they there now?
— *Payment Systems*—How was the misconduct in question funded (e.g., purchase orders, employee reimbursements, discounts, petty cash)? What processes could have prevented or detected improper access to these funds? Have those processes been improved?
— *Approval/Certification Process*—How have those with approval authority or certification responsibilities in the processes relevant to the misconduct known what to look for, and when and how to escalate concerns? What steps have been taken to remedy any failures identified in this process?
— *Vendor Management*—If vendors had been involved in the misconduct, what was the process for vendor selection and did the vendor in question go through that process? See further questions below under Item 10, 'Third Party Management'.

5. Risk Assessment

— *Risk Management Process*—What methodology has the company used to identify, analyze, and address the particular risks it faced?
— *Information Gathering and Analysis*—What information or metrics has the company collected and used to help detect the type of misconduct in question? How has the information or metrics informed the company's compliance program?
— *Manifested Risks*—How has the company's risk assessment process accounted for manifested risks?

6. Training and Communications

— *Risk-Based Training*—What training have employees in relevant control functions received? Has the company provided tailored training for high-risk and control employees that addressed the risks in the area where the misconduct occurred? What analysis has the company undertaken to determine who should be trained and on what subjects?
— *Form/Content/Effectiveness of Training*—Has the training been offered in the form and language appropriate for the intended audience? How has the company measured the effectiveness of the training?

— *Communications about Misconduct*—What has senior management done to let employees know the company's position on the misconduct that occurred? What communications have there been generally when an employee is terminated for failure to comply with the company's policies, procedures, and controls (e.g., anonymized descriptions of the type of misconduct that leads to discipline)?
— *Availability of Guidance*—What resources have been available to employees to provide guidance relating to compliance policies? How has the company assessed whether its employees know when to seek advice and whether they would be willing to do so?

7. Confidential Reporting and Investigation

— *Effectiveness of the Reporting Mechanism*—How has the company collected, analyzed, and used information from its reporting mechanisms? How has the company assessed the seriousness of the allegations it received? Has the compliance function had full access to reporting and investigative information?
— *Properly Scoped Investigation by Qualified Personnel*—How has the company ensured that the investigations have been properly scoped, and were independent, objective, appropriately conducted, and properly documented?
— *Response to Investigations*—Has the company's investigation been used to identify root causes, system vulnerabilities, and accountability lapses, including among supervisory manager and senior executives? What has been the process for responding to investigative findings? How high up in the company do investigative findings go?

8. Incentives and Disciplinary Measures

— *Accountability*—What disciplinary actions did the company take in response to the misconduct and when did they occur? Were managers held accountable for misconduct that occurred under their supervision? Did the company's response consider disciplinary actions for supervisors' failure in oversight? What is the company's record (e.g., number and types of disciplinary actions) on employee discipline relating to the type(s) of conduct at issue? Has the company ever terminated or otherwise disciplined anyone (reduced or eliminated bonuses, issued a warning letter, etc.) for the type of misconduct at issue?
— *Human Resources Process*—Who participated in making disciplinary decisions for the type of misconduct at issue?
— *Consistent Application*—Have the disciplinary actions and incentives been fairly and consistently applied across the organization?
— *Incentive System*—How has the company incentivized compliance and ethical behavior? How has the company considered the potential negative

compliance implications of its incentives and rewards? Have there been specific examples of actions taken (e.g., promotions or awards denied) as a result of compliance and ethics considerations?

9. Continuous Improvement, Periodic Testing and Review

— *Internal Audit*—What types of audits would have identified issues relevant to the misconduct? Did those audits occur and what were the findings? What types of relevant audit findings and remediation progress have been reported to management and the board on a regular basis? How have management and the board followed up? How often has internal audit generally conducted assessments in high-risk areas?
— *Control Testing*—Has the company reviewed and audited its compliance program in the area relating to the misconduct, including testing of relevant controls, collection and analysis of compliance data, and interviews of employees and third-parties? How are the results reported and action items tracked? What control testing has the company generally undertaken?
— *Evolving Updates*—How often has the company updated its risk assessments and reviewed its compliance policies, procedures, and practices? What steps has the company taken to determine whether policies/procedures/practices make sense for particular business segments/subsidiaries?

10. Third Party Management

— *Risk-Based and Integrated Processes*—How has the company's third-party management process corresponded to the nature and level of the enterprise risk identified by the company? How has this process been integrated into the relevant procurement and vendor management processes?
— *Appropriate Controls*—What was the business rationale for the use of the third parties in question? What mechanisms have existed to ensure that the contract terms specifically described the services to be performed, that the payment terms are appropriate, that the described contractual work is performed, and that compensation is commensurate with the services rendered?
— *Management of Relationships*—How has the company considered and analyzed the third party's incentive model against compliance risks? How has the company monitored the third parties in question? How has the company trained the relationship managers about what the compliance risks are and how to manage them? How has the company incentivized compliance and ethical behavior by third parties?
— *Real Actions and Consequences*—Were red flags identified from the due diligence of the third parties involved in the misconduct and how were they resolved? Has a similar third party been suspended, terminated, or

audited as a result of compliance issues? How has the company monitored these actions (e.g., ensuring that the vendor is not used again in case of termination)?

11. Mergers and Acquisitions (M&A)

— *Due Diligence Process*—Was the misconduct or the risk of misconduct identified during due diligence? Who conducted the risk review for the acquired/merged entities and how was it done? What has been the M&A due diligence process generally?

— *Integration in the M&A Process*—How has the compliance function been integrated into the merger, acquisition, and integration process?

— *Process Connecting Due Diligence to Implementation*—What has been the company's process for tracking and remediating misconduct or misconduct risks identified during the due diligence process? What has been the company's process for implementing compliance policies and procedures at new entities?

NOTES

1. Why Do People Conform to Rules or Break Them?

1 *Behavioral Insights Toolkit* (Internal Revenue Service, 2017), https://www.irs.gov/pub/irs-utl/17rpirsbehavioralinsights.pdf.

2 D Palmer, *Normal Organizational Wrongdoing: A Critical Analysis of Theories of Misconduct in and by Organizations* (Oxford University Press, 2012).

3 D Kahneman, *Thinking, Fast and Slow* (Allen Lane, 2011).

4 MH Banaji and AG Greenwald, *Blindspot: Hidden Biases of Good People* (Bantam Books, 2016).

5 C Chabris and D Simons, *The Invisible Gorilla* (Crown Books, 2010).

6 E Pronin, T Gilovich et al, 'Objectivity in the Eye of the Beholder: Divergent Perceptions of Bias in Self versus Others' (2004) 111(3) *Psychological Review* 781.

7 M Heffernan, *Wilful Blindness: Why We Ignore the Obvious at Our Peril* (Simon & Schuster, 2011), 11.

8 A Gawande, *The Checklist Manifesto: How to Get Things Right* (Profile Books, 2010).

9 M Gladwell, *Outliners: The Story of Success* (Little Brown, 2008).

10 AHK Fudickar, J Wiltfang and B Bein, 'The Effect of the WHO Surgical Safety Checklist on Complication Rate and Communication' (2012) 109 *Deutsches Ärzteblatt International* 6; RJ Kearns, V Uppal, J Bonner et al, 'The Introduction of a Surgical Safety Checklist in a Tertiary Referral Obstetric Centre' (2011) 20 *BMJ Quality & Safety* 818, L Nilsson, O Lindberget, A Gupta et al, 'Implementing a Pre-operative Checklist to Increase Patient Safety: A 1-Year Follow-up of Personnel Attitudes' (2010) 54 *Acta Anaesthesiologica Scandinavica* 76; RSK Takala, SL Pauniaho, A Kotkansalo et al, 'A Pilot Study of the Implementation of WHO Surgical Checklist in Finland: Improvements in Activities and Communication' (2011) 55 *Acta Anaesthesiologica Scandinavica* 1206.

11 AB Böhmer, P Kindermann, U Schwanke U et al, 'Long-Term Effects of a Perioperative Safety Checklist from the Viewpoint of Personnel' (2013) 57 *Acta Anaesthesiologica Scandinavica* 150.

12 AB Böhmer, F Wappler, T Tinschmann et al, 'The Implementation of a Perioperative Checklist Increases Patients' Perioperative Safety and Staff Satisfaction' (2012) 56 *Acta Anaesthesiologica Scandinavica* 332; P Helmiö, K Blomgren, A Takala et al, 'Towards Better Patient Safety: WHO Surgical Safety Checklist in Otorhinolaryngology' (2011) 36 *Clinical Otolaryngology* 242.

13 AB Haynes, TG Weiser, WR Berry et al, 'Changes in Safety Attitude and Relationship to Decreased Postoperative Morbidity and Mortality Following Implementation of a Checklist-Based Surgical Safety Intervention' (2011) 20 *BMJ Quality & Safety* 102.

14 A Steinar Haugen, E Søfteland, SK Almeland, N Sevadalis, B Vonen, GE Eide, MW Nortvedt and S Harthug, 'Effect of the World Health Organization Checklist on Patient Outcomes' (2015) 261(5) *Annals of Surgery* 821.

15 Gawande (n 8).

16 D Ariely, *Predictably Irrational: The Hidden Forces That Shape Our Decisions* (HarperCollins, 2008).

17 MH Bazerman and AE Tenbrunsel, *Blind Spots: Why We Fail to Do What's Right and What to Do about it* (Princeton University Press, 2011) 70.

18 See generally D Kahneman and S Frederick, 'Representativeness Revisited: Attribute Substitution in Intuitive Judgment' in T Gilovich, D Griffin and D Kahneman (eds), *Heuristics and Biases: The Psychology of Intuitive Judgment* (Cambridge University Press, 2002) 49; ND Weinstein, 'Unrealistic Optimism about Susceptibility to Health Problems: Conclusions from a Community-Wide Sample' (1987) 10 *Journal of Behavioral Medicine* 481, 494; A Tversky and D Kahneman, 'Availability: A Heuristic for Judging Frequency and Probability' (1973) 5 *Cognitive Psychology* 207, 221.

19 GF Loewenstein et al, 'Risk as Feelings' (2001) 127 *Psychological Bulletin* 267, 280; Y Rottenstreich and CK Hsee, 'Money, Kisses, and Electric Shocks: On the Affective Psychology of Risk' (2001) 12 *Psychological Science* 185, 185. For a demonstration that probability is often neglected with respect to things, but not with respect to money (without, however, emphasising the role of emotions), see AP McGraw, E Shafir and A Todorov, 'Valuing Money and Things: Why a $20 Item Can Be Worth More and Less than $20' (2010) 56 *Management Science* 816, 827. For a discussion of emotions and risk, see generally P Slovic (ed), *The Feeling of Risk: New Perspectives on Risk Perception* (Earthscan, 2010).

20 See www.engineering.com/Library/ArticlesPage/tabid/85/ArticleID/166/Ford-Pinto.aspx; LS Paine, *Vale Shift. Why Companies Must Merge Social and Financial Imperatives to Achieve Superior Performance* (McGraw-Hill, 2003) 220.

21 J Haidt, *The Righteous Mind: Why Good People are Divided by Politics and Religion* (Penguin Books, 2012).

22 Ibid.

23 Ariely (n 16); D Ariely, *The (Honest) Truth about Dishonesty: How We Lie to Everyone—Especially Ourselves* (HarperCollins, 2012).

24 Ariely, *The (Honest) Truth about Dishonesty* (n 23) ch 2.

25 Ariely (n 16) 203.

26 A Bandura, 'Moral Disengagement in the Perpetration of Inhumanities' (1999) 3(3) *Personality and Social Psychology Review* (Special Issue on Evil and Violence) 193.

27 Y Feldman and HE Smith, 'Behavioral Equity' [2014] 170 *Journal of Institutional and Theoretical Economics* 137.

28 C Moore, JR Detert, LK Treviño, VL Baker and DM Mayer, 'Employees Do Bad Things: Moral Disengagement and Unethical Organizational Behavior' (2012) 65(1) *Personnel Psychology* 1.

29 BE Ashforth and V Anand, 'The Normalization of Corruption in Organizations' in RM Kramer and BM Staw (eds), *Research in Organizational Behavior* (Jai Press, 2003) vol 25, 1.

30 E Haisley and RA Weber, 'Self-Serving Interpretations of Ambiguity in Other-Regarding Behavior' (2010) 68(2) *Games and Economic Behavior* 634.

31 CK Hsee, 'Elastic Justification: How Tempting But Task-Irrelevant Factors Influence Decisions' (1995) 62(3) *Organizational Behavior and Human Decision Processes* 330.

32 Y Feldman and D Teichman, 'Are All Legal Probabilities Created Equal?' (2009) 84(4) *New York University Law Review* 980; Y Feldman, 'The Complexity of Disentangling Intrinsic and Extrinsic Compliance Motivations: Theoretical and Empirical Insights from the Behavioral Analysis of Law' (2011) 35 *Washington University Journal of Law & Policy* 11; Y Feldman, 'Bounded Ethicality and the Law: A Proposed Framework for the Incorporation of Ethical Decision Making Research into Behavioral Law and Economics' in E Zamir and D Teichman (eds), *The Oxford Handbook of Behavioral Economics and the Law* (Oxford University Press, 2014).

33 Heffernan (n 7).

34 D Johnson, *Ethics at Work: 2015 Survey of Employees. Main Findings and Themes* (Institute of Business Ethics, 2015).

35 M Syed, *Black Box Thinking: Marginal Gains and the Secrets of High Performance* (John Murray, 2015) 80.

36 Marshall Report, *Economic Instruments and the Business Use of Energy: Report to the Chancellor of the Exchequer* (HM Treasury, 1998).

37 NetRegs, *SME-nvironment 2006* (Environment Agency, 2006).

38 I Worthington and D Patton, 'Researching the Drivers of SME Environmental Behaviour: A Study of the UK Screen-Printing Sector' (2005) 12(5) *Business Strategy and the Environment* 352.

39 S Arora and T Cason, 'Why Do Firms Volunteer to Exceed Environmental Regulations? Understanding Participation in EPA's 3/50 Program' (1996) 72(4) *Land Economics* 413.

40 R Fairman and C Yapp, *Making an Impact on SME Compliance Behaviour: An Evaluation of the Effect of Interventions upon Compliance with Health and Safety Legislation in Small and Medium-Sized Enterprises* (Health and Safety Executive, 2005), Research Report 366.

41 *The Anderson Review of Government Guidance on Regulation. Business Perspectives of Government Guidance. Research Study Conducted for Department for Business, Enterprise and Regulatory Reform. Final Report* (Ipsos MORI, 2008).

42 However, treating 'employing' SMEs as a sub-group, discounting those without staff, employment was considered the second most time-consuming (26%) and *the most* expensive (40%). SMEs felt much better placed to deal with health and safety regulation than employment (87% and 53% respectively said they were very or fairly well equipped to comply). A quarter (25%) said they were not well equipped for employment regulation, compared to one in eight (13%) for health and safety.

43 *Factors Affecting Compliance with Consumer Law and the Deterrent Effect of Consumer Enforcement Prepared for the Office of Fair Trading by IFF Research* (Office of Fair Trading, 2010) OFT1228.

44 ibid para 1.6.

45 ibid paras 1.71.9.

46 ibid para 1.12.

47 ibid para 1.13. Businesses perceived they had been disadvantaged by competitors breaching regulations inhibiting a level playing field (29%), acting dishonestly with customers (22%) and using misleading advertising (19%).

48 ibid para 1.15.

49 *Complying with Regulation—Business Perceptions Survey* (National Audit Office, 2009).

50 *Drivers of Compliance and Non-compliance with Consumer Protection Law: A Report by Ipsos MORI Commissioned by the OFT* (Office of Fair Trading, 2010) OFT1225a, para 1.41.

51 *Consumer Rights and Business Practices* (IFF Research, 2013).

52 *Competition Law Compliance Survey. Prepared for the Office of Fair Trading by Synovate (UK) Ltd* (Office of Fair Trading, 2011).

53 *The Impact of Competition Interventions on Compliance and Deterrence* (Office of Fair Trading, 2011), OFT1391, para 1.15.

54 ibid, para 1.16.

55 *Lightening the Load: The Regulatory Impact on UK's Smallest Businesses* (Department for Business Innovation & Skills, 2010).

56 ibid para 2.16.

57 MW Toffel and JL Short, 'Coming Clean and Cleaning up: Does Voluntary Self-Reporting Indicate Effective Self-Policing?' (2011) 54(3) *Journal of Law and Economics* 609; AA Pfaff and W Sanchirico, 'Big Field, Small Potatoes: An Empirical Assessment of EPA's Self-Audit Policy' (2004) 23(3) *Journal of Policy Analysis and Management* 415.

58 *Report of a Senior Practitioners' Workshop on Identifying Indicators of Corporate Culture* (International Corporate Governance Network, IBE, Institute of Chartered Secretaries and Administrators, held on 17 December 2015).

59 W Buffett and D Clark, *Warren Buffett's Management Secrets: Proven Tools for Personal and Business Success* (Simon & Schuster, 2009).

60 DJ Simons and CF Chabris, 'Gorillas in Our Midst: Sustained Inattentional Blindness for Dynamic Events' (1999) 28(9) *Perception* 1059; following U Neisser, 'The Control of Information Pickup in Selective Looking' in AD Pick (ed), *Perception and its Development: A Tribute to Eleanor Gibson* (Erlbaum, 1979).

61 SL Grover and C Hui, 'How Job Pressures and Extrinsic Rewards Affect Lying Behaviour' (2005) 16(3) *International Journal of Conflict Management* 287.

62 CB Cadsby, F Song and F Tapon, 'Are You Paying Your Employees to Cheat? An Experimental Investigation' (2010) 10(1) *Journal of Economic Analysis and Policy* 1.

63 Y Minisha, BJ Dykes, ES Block and TG Pollocy, 'Why "Good" Firms Do Bad Things: The Effects of High Aspirations, High Expectation, and Prominence on the Incidence of Corporate Illegality' (2010) 53(4) *Academy of Management Journal* 701.

64 D Gentilin, *The Origins of Ethical Failures. Lessons for Leaders* (Routledge, 2016) 90.

65 F Nietzsche, *Beyond Good and Evil* (Penguin Books, 1886).

66 Donelson Forsyth.

67 MH Banaji and AG Greenwald, *Blindspot: Hidden Biases of Good People* (Bantam Books, 2016) 130.

68 J Jost and M Banaji, 'The Role of Stereotyping in System-Justification and the Production of False Consciousness' (1994) 33 *British Journal of Social Psychology* 1.

69 H Tajkel, MG Billig, RP Bundy and C Flament, 'Social Categorization and Intergroup Behaviour' (1971) 1(2) *European Journal of Social Psychology* 149.

70 F Gino and MJ Bazerman, 'When Misconduct Goes Unnoticed: The Acceptability of Gradual Erosion in Others' Unethical Behaviour' (2009) 45 *Journal of Experimental Social Psychology* 708.

71 D Chugh, 'Societal and Managerial Implications of Implicit Social Cognition: Why Milliseconds Matter' (2004) 17 *Social Justice Research* 2013.

72 O Sezer, F Gino and MH Bazerman, 'Ethical Blind Spots: Explaining Unintentional Unethical Behavior' (2015) 6 *Current Opinion In Psychology* 77.

73 *Report of a Senior Practitioners' Workshop* (n 58).

74 See IL Janis and M Mann, *Decision Making* (Free Press, 1977), 423, where, however, it is also pointed out that there are some studies that an initially dominant risk-averse viewpoint within a group may shift an individual away from risk.

75 B Fisse and J Braithwaite, *Corporations, Crime and Accountability* (Cambridge University Press, 1993).

76 Nietzsche (n 65).

77 Press release, 'FCA Fines Five Banks £1.1 Billion for FX Failings and Announces Industry-Wide Remediation Programme', 12 November 2014.

78 'GSK Announces Changes to its Global Sales and Marketing Practices to Further Ensure Patient Interests Come First', press release, 17 December 2013, available at http://us.gsk.com/en-us/media/press-releases/2013/gsk-announces-changes-to-its-global-sales-and-marketing-practices-to-further-ensure-patient-interests-come-first.

79 ibid, Sir Andrew Whitty.

80 R Steinholtz with N Dando, *IBE Good Practice Guide to Performance Management for an Ethical Culture* (Institute for Business Ethics, 2015)

81 RR Faulkner, ER Cheney, GA Fisher and WE Baker, 'Crime by Committee: Conspirators and Company Men in the Illegal Electrical Industry Cartel' (2003) 41 *Criminology* 511.

82 JM Connor, *Global Price Fixing*, 2nd edn (Berlin, Springer-Verlag, 2008).

83 H Hovenkamp, *The Antitrust Enterprise: Principle and Execution* (Harvard University Press, 2005) 66.

84 For instance, 'budget meetings' in the Vitamin cartel, European Commission, Case COMP/E-1/37.512 *Vitamins* [2001] OJ L6/1.

85 European Commission, Case COMP/F/38.899 *Gas Insulated Switchgear* [2007] OJ C75/19.

86 European Commission, Case COMP/38354 *Industrial Bags* [2005] OJ L282/41.

87 See DC Klawiter and JM Driscoll, 'Antitrust Compliance in the Age of Multi-jurisdictional Leniency: New Ideas and New Challenges' [2009] *Global Competition Review Supplement* 24.

88 E Goffman, *Strategic Interaction* (Basil Blackwell, 1970).

89 RA Robson, 'Crime and Punishment: Rehabilitating Retribution as a Justification for Organizational Criminal Activity' (2010) 47 *American Business Law Journal* 109. This finding supported the view that senior management are central to the formation of cartels: Faulkner et al (n 80). It contradicted a view that cartels are mostly led by more junior employees: J Sonnenfeld and PR Lawrence, 'Why Do Companies Succumb to Price Fixing?' (1978) 56 *Harvard Business Review* 145.

90 JK Ashton and AD Pressey, 'Who Manages Cartels? The Role of Sales and Marketing Managers within International Cartels: Evidence from the European Union 1990–2009' (2012) CCP Working Paper 12-11. One British businessman imprisoned for a cartel in the US commented that 'it doesn't seem right that by dumping everybody else in the mud you can get away with it. Especially when, clearly in some of these incidents, the people that have gone to the authorities in the first place were by far the most culpable participants in this illegal activity'. See M O'Kane, 'Does Prison Work for Cartelists? The View from behind Bars. An Interview with Bryan Allison' (2011) 56(2) *Antitrust Bulletin* 483, 490–91.

91 G Mars, *Cheats at Work: An Anthropology of Workplace Crime* (Unwin Paperbacks, 1982).

92 D Bush and BD Gelb. 'When Marketing Practices Raise Antitrust Concerns' (2005) 46 *MITSloan Management Review* 73; DT Le Clair, 'Marketing Planning and the Policy Environment in the European Union' (2000) 17 *International Marketing Review* 193.

93 HS Schwartz, 'Anti-social Actions of Committed Organizational Participants: An Existential Psychoanalytic Perspective' (1987) 8 *Organization Studies* 327.

94 SS Simpson and CS Koper, 'The Changing of the Guard: Top Management Characteristics, Organizational Strain and Antitrust Offending' (1997) 13 *Journal of Quantitative Criminology* 373.

95 WE Baker and RR Faulkner, 'The Social Organization of Conspiracy: Illegal Networks in the Heavy Electrical Equipment Industry' (1993) 58 *American Sociological Review* 837.

96 SS Simpson and CS Koper, 'The Changing of the Guard: Top Management Characteristics, Organizational Strain and Antitrust Offending' (1997) 13 *Journal of Quantitative Criminology* 373.

97 *Better Business Better Scotland* (Social Value Lab, 2015).

98 *A Duty to Care? Evidence of the Importance of Organisational Culture to Effective Governance and Leadership* (Chartered Institute of Personnel and Development, 2016).

2. Characteristics to Build on

1 EO Wilson, *The Social Conquest of Earth* (Liveright Publishing, 2012).

2 ibid 57 and 241.

3 J Haidt, *The Righteous Mind: Why Good People are Divided by Politics and Religion* (Penguin Books, 2012).

4 F Laloux, *Reinventing Organizations: A Guide to Creating Organizations Inspired by the Next Stage of Human Consciousness* (Nelson Parker, 2014).

5 AH Maslow, *Motivation and Personality* (HarperCollins, 1987); *Toward a Psychology of Being*, 2nd edn (New York, Van Nostrand Reinhold, 1968); *The Farther Reaches of Human Nature* (Penguin/Arkana, 1993).

6 R Kegan and L Lahey, *Immunity to Chance* (Harvard Business School Publishing, 2009).

7 E Jacques and SD Clement, *Executive Leadership: A Practical Guide to Managing Complexity* (Malden, MA, Blackwell Business, 1991).

8 R Barrett, *What My Soul Told Me* (Fulfilling Books, 2012) 94.

9 R Barrett, *The Values-Driven Organization: Cultural Health and Employee Well-Being as a Pathway to Sustainable Performance*, 2nd edn (Routledge, 2017) 63.

10 ibid 67.

11 F Trompenaars, *Riding the Waves of Culture: Understanding Diversity in Global Business* (Irwin, 1993) 156.

12 C Mills, 'Navigating the Tension between Global and Local: A Communication Perspective' in J Buckingham and V Nilakant (eds), *Managing Responsibly: Alternative Approaches to Corporate Management and Governance* (Gower, 2012).

13 J Darley, TR Tyler and K Bilz, 'Enacting Justice: The Interplay of Individual and Institutional Perspectives' in M Hogg and J Cooper (eds), *The SAGE Handbook of Social Psychology* (Sage, 2003); JT Jost and B Major (eds), *The Psychology of Legitimacy* (Cambridge University Press, 2001); TR Tyler, *Why People Obey the Law* (Yale University Press, 2006); TR Tyler and SL Blader, *Cooperation in Groups: Procedural Justice, Social Identity, and Behavioral Engagement* (Psychology Press, 2000); TR Tyler and SL Blader, 'Can Businesses Effectively Regulate Employee Conduct? The Antecedents of Rule Following in Work Settings' (2005) 48 *Academy of Management Journal* 1143; J Jackson, B Bradford, M Hough, A Myhill, P Quinton and TR Tyler, 'Why Do People Comply with the Law? Legitimacy and the Influence of Legal Institutions' (manuscript, 2013).

14 TR Tyler and HJ Smith, 'Social Justice and Social Movements' in DT Gilbert, ST Fiske and G Lindzey (eds), *The Handbook of Social Psychology*, 4th edn, vol II (Oxford University Press, 1998); TR Tyler and P Degoey, 'Trust in Organizational Authorities: The Influence of Motive Attributions on Willingness to Accept Decisions' in RM Kramer and TR Tyler (eds), *Trust in Organizational Authorities* (Sage, 1996); K Murphy, '"Trust Me, I'm the Taxman": The Role of Trust in Nurturing Compliance' (2002) *Centre for Tax System Integrity Working Paper No 43*, 1–31.

15 J Braithwaite and T Makkai, 'Trust and Compliance' (1994) 4(1) *Policing and Society* 1; K Aoki, L Axelrad, and RA Kagan, 'Industrial Effluent Control in the United States and Japan' in RA Kagan and L Axelrad, *Regulatory Encounters* (University of California Press, 2000); M Wenzel, 'The Impact of Outcome Orientation and Justice Concerns on Tax Compliance: The Role of Taxpayers' Identity' (2002) 87(4) *Journal of Applied Psychology* 629; M Wenzel, 'Principles of Procedural Fairness in Reminder Letters: A Field-Experiment' (2002) *Centre for Tax System Integrity Working Paper No 42*; K Murphy, 'Procedural Justice and Tax Compliance' (2003) 38(3) *Australian Journal of Social Issues* 379.

16 TR Tyler and SL Blader, *Cooperation in Groups: Procedural Justice, Social Identity, and Behavioral Engagement* (Psychology Press, 2000); TR Tyler and SL Blader, 'The Group Engagement Model: Procedural Justice, Social Identity, and Cooperative Behaviour' (2003) 7 *Personality and Social Psychology Review* 349 (finding that over 80% of compliance decisions are driven by the credibility of the organisation's leadership message and congruence of organisational and personal values, and less than 20% are driven by formal rewards and punishments).

17 D Thornton, RA Kagan and N Gunningham, 'General Deterrence and Corporate Environmental Behaviour' (2005) 27 *Law & Policy* 266.

18 TR Tyler and J Jackson, 'Popular Legitimacy and the Exercise of Legal Authority: Motivating Compliance, Cooperation and Engagement' (2014) 20(1) *Psychology, Public Policy and Law* 78.

19 M Hough, J Jackson and B Bradford, 'Legitimacy, Trust and Compliance' in J Tankebe and A Liebling (eds), *Legitimacy in Criminal Justice* (Oxford University Press, 2013).

20 Also found in TR Tyler and YJ Huo, *Trust in the Law: Encouraging Public Cooperation with the Police and Courts* (Russell-Sage Foundation, 2001).

21 K Murphy, TR Tyler and A Curtis, 'Nurturing Regulatory Compliance: Is Procedural Justice Effective When People Question the Legitimacy of the Law?' (2009) 3 *Regulation & Governance* 3; TR Tyler and JM Darley, 'Building a Law-Abiding Society: Taking Public Views about Morality and the Legitimacy of Law into Account When

Formulating Substantive Law' (2000) 28 *Hofstra Law Review* 707; TR Tyler, J Dienhart and T Thomas, 'The Ethical Commitment to Compliance: Building Value-Based Cultures' (2008) 5 *California Management Review* 31.

22 KM Carlsmith, JM Darley and PH Robinson, 'Why Do We Punish? Deterrence and Just Deserts as Motives for Punishment' (2002) 83(2) *Journal of Personality and Social Psychology* 284; JM Darley, KM Carlsmith and PH Robinson, 'Incapacitation and Just Deserts as Motives for Punishment' (2000) 24 *Law and Human Behaviour* 659.

23 M Aalders and T Wilthagen, 'Moving beyond Command-and-Control: Reflexivity in the Regulation of Occupational Safety and Health and the Environment' (1997) 19 *Law & Policy* 415; N Gunningham and J Rees, 'Industry Self-Regulation: An Institutional Perspective' (1997) 19 *Law & Policy* 363; A King and M Lenox, 'Industry Self-Regulation without Sanctions: The Chemical Industry's Responsible Care Program' (2000) 43 *Academy of Management Journal* 698; C Rechtschaffen, 'Deterrence vs. Cooperation and the Evolving Theory of Environmental Enforcement' (1998) 71 *Southern California Law Review* 1181.

24 *How Your Business Can Achieve Compliance: Guidance* (Office of Fair Trading, 2010), OFT1278; *Drivers of Compliance and Non-compliance with Competition Law: An OFT Report* (Office of Fair Trading, 2010), OFT1227.

25 A Mehta and K Hawkins, 'Integrated Pollution Control and its Impact: Perspectives from Industry' (1998) 10 *Journal of Environmental Law* 61; M Vandenbergh, 'Beyond Elegance: A Testable Typology of Social Norms in Corporate Environmental Compliance' (2003) 22 *Stanford Environmental Law Journal* 55.

26 *Business Perceptions Survey 2012* (IFF Research, 2012) para 1.7. This comprised 2,294 15-minute telephone interviews with senior business decision-makers covering four areas of regulation: company law, employment law, health & safety law and planning law.

27 ibid para 1.15.

3. The Traditional Way of Enforcing the Law: Deterrence

1 AI Solzhenitsyn, *The Gulag Archipelago* (Harper & Row, 1973).

2 F Parisi, B Luppi and I Fargnoli, 'Deterrence of Wrongdoing in Ancient Law' (2014) *Minnesota Legal Studies Research Paper* No 14-38; G Williams, 'The Aims of Tort Law' (1951) 4 *Current Legal Problems* 137; T Brooks, *Punishment* (Routledge, 2012).

3 AC Pigou, *The Economics of Welfare* (Macmillan, 1920) 169–71; G Becker, 'Crime and Punishment: An Economic Approach' (1968) 76 *Journal of Political Economy* 169; GJ Stigler, 'The Theory of Economic Regulation' (1971) 2 *Bell Journal of Economics and Management Science* 3; R Kagan and J Scholz, 'The "Criminology of the Corporation" and Regulatory Enforcement Styles' in K Hawkins and J Thomas (eds), *Enforcing Regulation* (Kluwer-Nijhoff, 1984); M Allingham, *Rational Choice* (St Martin's Press, 1999); MS Archer and JQ Tritter, *Rational Choice Theory: Resisting Colonization* (Routledge, 2001); M Faure, A Ogus and N Philipsen, 'Curbing Consumer Financial Losses: The Economics of Regulatory Enforcement' (2009) 31 *Law & Policy* 161.

4 Kagan and Scholz (n 3).

5 Allingham (n 3); Archer and Tritter (n 3).

6 AC Pigou, *The Economics of Welfare* (Macmillan, 1920) 168–71.

7 Becker (n 3); Stigler (n 3); Faure, Ogus and Philipsen (n 3).

8 D Dewees, D Duff and M Trebilcock, *Exploring the Domain of Accident Law: Taking the Facts Seriously* (Oxford University Press, 1996); WJ Cardi, R Penfield and A Yoon, 'Does Tort Law Deter?' (2011) *Wake Forest University Legal Studies Paper* No 1851383.

9 PH Robinson and J Darley, *Justice, Liability and Blame* (Westview, 1995); D Nagin, 'Criminal Deterrence Research at the Outset of the Twenty-First Century' in M Tonry (ed), *Crime and Justice: A Review of Research* (University of Chicago Press, 1998). See the summary in A Bottoms and A von Hirsch, 'The Crime-Preventive Impact of Penal Sanctions' in P Cane and HM Kritzer (eds), *The Oxford Handbook of Empirical Legal Research* (Oxford University Press, 2010) 104.

10 LS Beres and TD Griffith, 'Habitual Offender Statutes and Criminal Deterrence' (2001) 34 *Connecticut Law Review* 55, 59; see also I Ehrlich, 'Crime, Punishment, and the Market for Offenses' (1996) 10 *Journal of Economic Perspectives* 43, 55–63; PW Greenwood et al, *Three Strikes and You're Out: Estimated Benefit and Cost of California's Mandatory New Sentencing Laws* (RAND Corporation, 1994) 16. But see D Kessler and SD Levitt, 'Using Sentence Enhancements to Distinguish between Deterrence and Incapacitation' (1999) 42 *Journal of Law & Economics* 343.

11 U Gneezy and A Rustichini, 'A Fine is a Price' (2000) XXIX *Journal of Legal Studies* 1; see also John List and Uri Gneezy, 'What Makes People Do What They Do?' *Freakanomics Blog*, 21 October 2013, https://www.behavioraleconomics.com/why-do-people-behave-the-way-they-do.

12 D Awrey and D Kershaw, 'Toward a More Ethical Culture in Finance: Regulatory and Governance Strategies' in N Morris and D Vines (eds), *Capital Failure; Rebuilding Trust in Financial Services* (Oxford University Press, 2014).

13 R Ellickson, *Order without Law: How Neighbors Settle Disputes* (Harvard University Press, 1994); L Bernstein, 'Opting out of the Legal System: Extralegal Contractual Relations in the Diamond Industry' (1992) 21(1) *Journal of Legal Studies* 115; L Bernstein, 'Private Commercial Law in the Cotton Industry: Creating Cooperation through Rules, Norms and Institutions' (2001) 99 *Michigan Law Review* 1724; A Greif, 'Contract Enforceability and Economic Institutions in Early Trade: The Maghribi Traders' Coalition' (1993) 83 *American Economic Review* 525.

14 RA Kagan, N Gunningham and D Thornton, 'Fear, Duty, and Regulatory Compliance: Lessons from three Research Projects' in C Parker and VL Nielsen (eds), *Explaining Compliance: Business Responses to Regulation* (Edward Elgar, 2012) 40.

15 R Miles, *Conduct Risk Management: Using a Behavioural Approach to Protect Your Board and Financial Services Business* (Kogan Page, 2017) ch 6.

16 *Positive Impact 10/11—Consumer Benefits from the OFT's Work*, July 2011, OFT1354, para 4.59.

17 *An Assessment of Discretionary Penalties Regimes. Final Report. A Report Prepared for the Office of Fair Trading by London Economics* (Office of Fair Trading, 2009), OFT1132, para 1.15.

18 ibid para 1.27.

19 ibid para 1.4.

20 At the EU level, see Commission Notice on Immunity from fines and reduction of fines in cartel cases [2006] OJ C207/4-6. In the UK, see *Applications for Leniency and No-Action in Cartel Cases. OFT's Detailed Guidance on the Principles and Process* (Competition and Markets Authority, 2013), OFT1495.

21 Bribery Act 2010, s 7(2).

22 Fines totalling £1,114,918,000 were imposed on five banks for failing to control business practices in their G10 spot foreign exchange (FX) trading operations: Citibank NA £225,575,000 ($358 million), HSBC Bank plc £216,363,000 ($343 million), JP Morgan Chase Bank NA £222,166,000 ($352 million), Royal Bank of Scotland plc £217,000,000 ($344 million) and UBS AG £233,814,000 ($371 million): Press release, 'FCA Fines Five Banks £1.1 Billion for FX Failings and Announces Industry-Wide Remediation Programme', 12 November 2014.

23 M Carney, 'The Future of Financial Reform', 2014 Monetary Authority of Singapore Lecture, 17 November 2014.

24 Occasional Paper 24, *Behaviour and Compliance in Organisations* (FCA, December 2016).

25 US Department of Justice Memorandum, 'Individual Accountability for Corporate Wrongdoing', September 9, 2015.

26 S Quillian Yates, 'Remarks at New York University School of Law Announcing New Policy on Individual Liability in Matters of Corporate Wrongdoing', 10 September 2015, available at www.justice.gov/opa/speech/deputy-attorney-general-sally-quillian-yates-delivers-remarks-new-york-university-school.

27 *Trends in Regulatory Enforcement in UK Financial Markets: 2015/16 Year-End Report* (NERA, 2016).

28 See *Annual Report and Accounts 2014/15* (Care Quality Commission, 2015); *CQC's Strategy 2016–2021: Shaping the Future: Consultation Document* (Care Quality Commission, 2016).

29 'Capital Punishment in America: Who Killed the Death Penalty?' *The Economist*, 15 December 2015.

30 *Modern Crime Prevention Strategy March 2016* (Home Office, 2016).

31 ibid, Introduction.

32 A Braga, AV Papachristos and DM Hureau, 'The Effects of Hot Spots Policing on Crime: An Updated Systematic Review and Meta-analysis' (2012) 31 *Justice Quarterly* 4; B Taylor, C Koper and D Woods, 'A Randomized Controlled Trial of Different Policing Strategies at Hot Spots of Violent Crime' (2011) 7(2) *Journal of Experimental Criminology* 149.

33 SN Durlauf and DS Nagin, 'The Deterrent Effect of Imprisonment' in *Controlling Crime: Strategies and Tradeoffs* (University of Chicago Press, 2010) 43; *Modern Crime Prevention Strategy* (n 30) section 4.

34 RT Guerette and KJ Bowers, 'Assessing the Extent of Crime Displacement and Diffusion of Benefits: A Review of Situational Crime Prevention Evaluations' (2009) 47(4) *Criminology* 1333.

35 ME Wolfgang, 'Delinquency in Two Birth Cohorts' in KT van Dusen and SA Mednick (eds), *Prospective Studies of Crime and Delinquency* (Springer, 1983) 7; TE Moffitt, 'Adolescence-Limited and Life-Course Persistent Antisocial Behavior: A Developmental Taxonomy' (993) 100 *Psychological Review* 674.

36 *Modern Crime Prevention Strategy* (n 30) section 3.

37 ibid.

38 POH Wikström, D Oberwittler, K Treiber and B Hardie, *Breaking Rules: The Social and Situational Dynamics of Young People's Urban Crime* (Oxford University Press, 2012).

39 D Jolliffe and DP Farrington, 'Empathy and Offending: A Systematic Review and Meta-analysis' (2004) 9(5) *Aggression and Violent Behaviour* 441.

40 TE Moffitt, R Poulton and A Caspi, 'Lifelong Impact of Early Self-Control' (2003) 101(5) *American Scientist* 352; L Levy, D Santhakumaran and R Whitecross, *What Works to Reduce Crime?: A Summary of the Evidence* (Justice Analytical Services, Scottish Government, 2014).

41 See POH Wikström and K Treiber, 'Social Disadvantage and Crime: A Criminological Puzzle' (2016) *American Behavioral Scientist*, http://dx.doi.org/10.1177/0002764216643134.

42 ER Kimonis, B Cross, A Howard and K Donoghue, 'Maternal Care, Maltreatment and Callous-Unemotional Traits among Urban Male Juvenile Offenders' (2013) 42(2) *Journal of Youth and Adolescence* 165; KM Kitzmann, NK Gaylord, AR Holt and ED Kenny, 'Child Witnesses to Domestic Violence: A Meta-analytic Review' (2003) 71(2) *Journal of Consulting and Clinical Psychology* 339; A Leschied, D Chiodo, E Nowicki and S Rodger, 'Childhood Predictors of Adult Criminality: A Meta-analysis Drawn from the Prospective Longitudinal Literature' (2008) 50(4) *Canadian Journal of Criminology and Criminal Justice* 435; E McCrory, SA De Brito, and E Viding, 'Research Review: The Neurobiology and Genetics of Maltreatment and Adversity' (2010) 51(10) *Journal of Child Psychology and Psychiatry* 1079.

43 Indeed, studies are clear that inherited crime propensity is likely to be modified by environmental effects. See, eg, CR Cloninger, S Sigvardsson, M Bohman and A-L Von Knorring, 'Predisposition to Petty Criminality in Swedish Adoptees: II. Cross-fostering Analysis of Gene-Environment Interaction' (1982) 39(11) *Archives of General Psychiatry* 1242; TE Moffitt, 'The New Look of Behavioral Genetics in Developmental Psychopathology: Gene-Environment Interplay in Antisocial Behaviors' (2005) 131(4) *Psychological Bulletin* 533.

44 A Caspi and BW Roberts, 'Personality Development across the Life Course: The Argument for Change and Continuity' (2001) 12(2) *Psychological Inquiry* 49; L Konicar, R Veit, H Eisenbarth, B Barth, P Tonin, U Strehl, and N Birbaumer, 'Brain Self-Regulation in Criminal Psychopaths' (2015) *Scientific Reports* 5.

45 The reference in the Home Office document was: 'Wikstrom et al (forthcoming)'. See P-OH Wikström and K Treiber, 'Social Disadvantage and Crime: A Criminological Puzzle' (2016) 60(10) *American Behavioural Scientist* 1232; and P-OH Wikström, 'Why Crime Happens: A Situational Action Theory' in G Manzo (ed), *Analytical Sociology: Actions and Networks* (John Wiley & Sons, 2014).

46 G Dawson, SB Ashman and LJ Carver, 'The Role of Early Experience in Shaping Behavioral and Brain Development and its Implications for Social Policy' (2000) 12(4) *Development and Psychopathology* 695; O Doyle, CP Harmon, JJ Heckman and RE Tremblay, 'Investing in Early Human Development: Timing and Economic Efficiency' (2009) 7(1) *Economics & Human Biology* 1.

47 On development of self-control in adults, see: M Muraven, 'Building Self-Control Strength: Practicing Self-Control Leads to Improved Self-Control Performance' (2010) 46(2) *Journal of Experimental Social Psychology* 465. On development of empathy in adults, see, for example, H Riess, JM Kelley, RW Bailey, EJ Dunn and M Phillips, 'Empathy Training for Resident Physicians: A Randomized Controlled Trial of a Neuroscience-Informed Curriculum' (2012) 27(10) *Journal of General Internal Medicine* 1280.

48 P Cane, *Atiyah's Accidents, Compensation and the Law*, 8th edn (Cambridge University Press, 2013) 477.

49 Lord Bingham of Cornhill, 'The Uses of Tort' (2010) 1 *Journal of European Tort Law* 3.

50 AZ Roisman et al, 'Preserving Justice: Defending Toxic Tort Litigation' (2004) 15 *Fordham Environmental Law Review* 191 (tort liability changes the behaviour of others); AF Popper, 'In Defense of Deterrence' (2012) 75(1) *Albany Law Review* 101. The impact or quantum force of messaging—the deterrent value—is difficult to calculate. 'My fundamental conclusion is that modern American negligence law regulates activity levels to a considerably greater extent than has previously been recognized.' SG Gilles, 'Rule-Based Negligence and the Regulation of Activity Levels' (1992) 21 *Journal of Legal Studies* 319, 320.

51 WK Viscusi (ed), *Regulation through Litigation* (Brookings Institution Press, 2002).

52 G Calabresi, 'Some Thoughts on Risk Distribution and the Law of Torts' (1961) 70 *Yale Law Journal* 499; S Shavell, *Foundations of Economic Analysis of Law* (2004), 261; P O'Malley, 'Fines, Risks and Damages: Money Sanctions and Justice in Control Societies' (2010) *Sydney Law School Research Paper No 10/40*; R Merkin and J Steele, *Insurance and the Law of Obligations* (Oxford University Press, 2013); R Merkin, 'Tort, Insurance and Ideology: Further Thoughts' (2012) 75(3) *Modern Law Review* 301

53 *Factors Affecting Compliance with Consumer Law and the Deterrent Effect of Consumer Enforcement Prepared for the Office of Fair Trading by IFF Research* (Office of Fair Trading, 2010), OFT1228, para 1.19; *Drivers of Compliance and Non-compliance with Competition Law. An OFT Report* (Office of Fair Trading, 2010), OFT1227, para 1.10; *Consumer Law and Business Practice. Drivers of Compliance and Non-compliance* (Office of Fair Trading, 2010), OFT1225.

54 *The Impact of Competition Interventions on Compliance and Deterrence* (Office of Fair Trading, 2011), OFT1391. The survey comprised 501 responses from large firms and 308 from small firms, with responses from two business organisations and 27 telephone interviews with professionals.

55 JC Bosch and EW Eckard, 'The Profit of Price Fixing: Evidence from Stock Market Reaction to Federal Indictments' (1991) 73(2) *Review of Economics and Statistics* 309; A Gunster and MA van Dijk, 'The Impact of European Antitrust Policy: Evidence from the Stock Market', Working Paper (2011).

56 See, eg, *A World Class Competition Regime* (Department of Trade and Industry, 2001); and S Calkin, 'Corporate Compliance and the Antitrust Agencies' Bi-modal Penalties' (2007) 60(3) *Law and Contemporary Problems* 127.

57 *The Deterrent Effect of Competition Enforcement by the OFT*, report prepared for the OFT by Deloitte, (Office of Fair Trading, 2007), OFT962, para 6.10: 'Our survey suggests that at present the threat of private actions is not seen as a serious deterrent in comparison to the possibility of public enforcement action.'

58 ibid, para 6.14, referring to Deloitte and Touche, *The Deterrent Effect of Competition Enforcement by the OFT* (Office of Fair Trading, 2007).

59 *Factors Affecting Compliance with Consumer Law* (n 54) para 1.10.

60 *Director Leadership of Health and Safety, Report No HSL/2005/21* (Health & Safety Laboratory, 2005) 14, referencing A Hopkins, *Making Safety Work: Getting Management Committed to Occupational Health and Safety* (Allen & Unwin, Australia, 1995). See www.hse.gov.uk/research/hsl_pdf/2005/hsl0521.pdf.

61 P May, 'Regulation and Compliance Motivations: Marine Facilities and Water Quality' in *Corporate Environmental Behaviour and the Effectiveness of Government Interventions: Proceedings of a Workshop Sponsored by the US EPA*, 26–27 April 2004.

62 See www.hse.gov.uk/enforce/prosecutions.htm.

63 A Griffin, *New Strategies for Reputation Management* (Kogan Page, 2008) 154; R Moss Kanter, *SuperCorp: How Vanguard Companies Create Innovation, Profits, Growth and Social Growth* (Crown Business, 2009); S Zadek, *The Civil Corporation: The New Economy of Corporate Citizenship* (Earthscan Publications, 2003); C Parker, *The Open Corporation: Effective Self-Regulation and Democracy* (Cambridge University Press, 2002); T O'Callaghan, *Reputation Risk and Globalisation: Exploring the Idea of a Self-Regulating Corporation* (Edward Elgar, 2016).

64 See JM Karpoff and JR Lott, Jr, 'The Reputational Penalty Firms Bear from Committing Fraud' (1993) 36 *Journal of Law and Economics* 757; JM Karpoff, DS Lee and GS Martin, 'Cost to Firms of Cooking the Books' (2008) 43 *Journal of Financial and Quantitative Analysis* 581; L Bai, JD Cox and RS Thomas, 'Lying and Getting Caught: An Empirical Study of the Effect of Securities Class Action Settlements on Targeted Firms' (2010) 158 *University of Pennsylvania Law Review* 1877; SP Ferris and AC Pritchard, 'Stock Price Reactions to Securities Fraud Class Actions under the Private Securities Litigation Reform Act', Michigan Law and Economics Research Paper, No 01-009, 2001, available at http://papers.ssrn.com/sol3/papers.cfm?abstract_id=288216; see also S Bhagat, J Bizjak and JL Coles 'The Shareholder Wealth Implications of Corporate Lawsuits' (1998) 27 *Financial Management* 5, 6–7.

65 Summarised in the following seminal work: I Ayres and J Braithwaite, *Responsive Regulation: Transcending the Deregulation Debate* (Oxford University Press, 1992).

66 K Hawkins, *Environment and Enforcement: Regulation and the Social Definition of Pollution* (Clarendon Press, 1984); K Hawkins, *Law as Last Resort* (Oxford University Press, 2003).

67 H Genn, 'Business Responses to the Regulation of Health and Safety in England' (1993) 15 *Law and Policy* 219; BM Hutter, *Compliance: Regulation and Environment* (Clarendon Press, 1997); BM Hutter, *Regulation and Risk: Occupational Health and Safety on the Railways* (Oxford University Press, 2001).

68 P Grabosky, 'Beyond the Regulatory State' (1994) 27(2) *Australian and New Zealand Journal of Criminology* 192; P Grabosky, 'Green Markets: Environmental Regulation by the Private Sector' (1994) 16(4) *Law and Policy* 419; N Gunningham and P Grabosky, *Smart Regulation. Designing Environmental Policy* (Oxford University Press, 1998).

69 F Haines, *Corporate Regulation: Beyond 'Punish or Persuade'* (Clarendon Press, 1997).

70 F Haines, 'Regulatory Reform in Light of Regulatory Character: Assessing Industrial Safety Change in the Aftermath of the Kader Toy Factory Fire in Bangkok, Thailand' (2003) 12 *Social and Legal Studies* 461; reprinted in F Haines (ed), *Crime and Regulation* (Ashgate, 2007).

71 BM Hutter and C Jones, 'From Government to Governance: External Influences on Business Risk Management' (2007) 1 *Regulation & Governance* 27.

72 J Braithwaite and P Grabosky, *Of Manners Gentle: Enforcement Strategies of Australian Business Regulatory Agencies* (Oxford University Press, 1987).

73 PJ May and S Winter, 'Regulatory Enforcement and Compliance: Examining Danish Agro-environmental Policy' (1999) 18(4) *Journal of Policy Analysis and Management* 625.

74 J Black and R Baldwin, 'Really Responsive Regulation' (2008) 71(1) *Modern Law Review* 59.

75 *Civil Aviation Authority Regulatory Enforcement Policy* (Civil Aviation Authority, October 2012)

76 MA Delmas and MW Toffel, 'Organizational Responses to Environmental Demands: Opening the Black Box' (2008) 29 *Strategic Management Journal* 1027; C Coglianese and J Nash, *Leveraging the Private Sector: Management-Based Strategies for Improving Environmental Performance* (Resources for the Future, 2006); A Prakash and M Potoski, *The Voluntary Environmentalists: Green Clubs, ISO 14001, and Voluntary Environmental Regulations* (Cambridge University Press, 2006); A Prakash, *Greening the Firm: The Politics of Corporate Environmentalism* (Cambridge University Press, 2000).

77 J Rees, 'Development of Communitarian Regulation in the Chemical Industry' (1997) 19 *Law & Policy* 477; J Rees, *Hostages of Each Other: The Transformation of Nuclear Safety since Three Mile Island* (University of Chicago Press, 1994); N Gunningham and D Sinclair, 'Organizational Trust and the Limits of Management-Based Regulation' (2009) 43 *Law & Society Review* 865.

78 N Gunningham, RA Kagan and D Thornton, *Shades of Green: Business, Regulation and Environment* (Stanford: Stanford University Press, 2003) 20–40; Prakash (n 76); S Konar and M Cohen, 'Information as Regulation: The Effect of Community Right to Know Laws on Toxic Emissions' (1997) 32 *Journal of Environmental Economics and Management* 109.

79 Greenstreet Berman Ltd, *Research Results: What is the Value in Regulators Sharing Information?* (Better Regulation Delivery Office, 2013).

80 LS Beres and TD Griffith, 'Habitual Offender Statutes and Criminal Deterrence' (2001) 34 *Connecticut Law Review* 55, 59; see also I Ehrlich, 'Crime, Punishment, and the Market for Offenses' (1996) 10 *Journal of Economic Perspectives* 43, 55–63 (surveying the research on the question); PW Greenwood et al, *Three Strikes and You're Out: Estimated Benefit and Cost of California's Mandatory New Sentencing Laws* (RAND Corporation, 1994) 16. But see D Kessler and SD Levitt, 'Using Sentence Enhancements to Distinguish Between Deterrence and Incapacitation' (1999) 42 *Journal of Law & Economics* 343. *Association studies*: DP Farrington, PA Langan and P-O Wikström, 'Changes in Crime and Punishment in America, England and Sweden between the 1980s and 1990s' (1994) 3 *Studies in Crime and Crime Prevention* 104; D Nagin, 'Criminal Deterrence Research at the Outset of the Twenty-First Century' in M Tonry (ed), *Crime and Justice: A Review of Research* (University of Chicago Press, 1998). *Meta-analysis*: TC Pratt, FT Cullen, KR Blevins, LE Daigle and TD Madensen, 'The Empirical Status of Deterrence Theory: A Meta-analysis' in FT Cullen, JP Wright and KR Blevins (eds), *Taking Stock: The Status of Criminological Theory* (Transaction Publishers, 2006).

81 See generally T Brooks (ed), *Deterrence* (Ashgate, 2014) (debates continue over whether it is even possible); DS Nagin, 'Criminal Deterrence Research at the Outset of the Twentieth Century' (1998) 23 *Crime and Justice* 1 (review of the literature); M Tonry, 'Learning from the Limitations of Deterrence Research' (2008) 37 *Crime & Justice* 279.

82 Pratt et al (n 80) 385. See also P-O Wikström, 'Deterrence and Deterrent Experiences: Preventing Crime through the Threat of Punishment' in SG Shoham, O Beck and M Kett (eds), *International Handbook of Penology and Criminal Justice* (CRC Press, 2008); M Tonry, 'Learning from the Limitations of Deterrence Research' in M Tonry (ed), *Crime and Justice: A Review of Research* (University of Chicago Press, 2009) 37, 279.

83 I Vilares, MJ Wesley, W-Y Ahn, RJ Bonnie, M Hoffman, OD Jones, SJ Morsem, G Yaffe, T Lohrenz and PR Montague, 'Predicting the Knowledge-Recklessness Distinction in the Human Brain' (2017), www.pnas.org/cgi/doi/10.1073/pnas.1619385114.

84 MR Ginther, RJ Bonnie, MB Hoffman, FX Shen, KW Simons, OD Jones and R Marois, 'Parsing the Behavioral and Brain Mechanisms of Third-Party Punishment' (2016) 36 *Journal of Neuroscience* 9420.

85 A recent overview is A Bottoms and A von Hirsch, 'The Crime-Preventive Impact of Penal Sanctions' in P Cane and HM Kritzer (eds), *The Oxford Handbook of Empirical Legal Research* (Oxford University Press, 2010), 104; FH Easterbrook, 'Criminal Procedure as a Market System' (1983) 12 *Journal of Legal Studies* 289, 295 and fn 7; R MacCoun, 'Drugs and the Law: A Psychological Analysis of Drug Prohibition' (1993) 113 *Psychological Bulletin* 497; DP Farrington, PA Langan and P-O Wikström, 'Changes in Crime and Punishment in America, England and Sweden between the 1980s and 1990s' (1994) 3 *Studies in Crime and Crime Prevention* 104; PH Robinson and J Darley, *Justice, Liability and Blame* (Westview, 1995); PH Robinson and J Darley, 'The Utility of Desert' (1997) 91 *Northwestern University Law Review* 453; D Nagin, 'Criminal Deterrence Research at the Outset of the Twenty-First Century' in M Tonry (ed), *Crime and Justice: A Review of Research* (University of Chicago Press, 1998); PA Langan and DP Farrington, *Crime and Justice in the United States and England and Wales, 1981–96* (Bureau of Justice Statistics, 1998); HL Ross, *Deterring the Drinking Driver* (Lexington Books, 1982); PH Robinson and JM Darley, 'The Role of Deterrence in the Formulation of Criminal Law Rules: At its Worst When Doing its Best' (2003) 91 *Georgetown Law Journal* 949, 953–56; A Blumstein, 'Prisons' in JQ Wilson and J Petersilia (eds), *Crime* (Institute for Contemporary Studies Press, 1995) 387, 408–09. See also M Miller, *Director Leadership of Health and Safety* (Health & Safety Laboratory, 2005) iv.

86 *Modern Crime Prevention Strategy* (n 30).

87 Durlauf and Nagin (n 33).

88 *Behavioural Insights and Public Policy. Lessons from around the World* (OECD, 2017).

89 *Mind, Society and Behavior* (World Bank Group, 2015).

90 B Hutter, 'Regulating Employers and Employees: Health and Safety in the Workplace' (1983) 20 *Journal of Law and Society* 452; B Hutter, *Regulation and Risk: Occupational Health and Safety on the Railways* (Oxford University Press, 2001).

91 M Glennie, *The Balkans: Nationalism, War and the Great Powers, 1804–1999* (Penguin Books, 1999); M Glennie, *The Rebirth Of History: Eastern Europe in the Age of Democracy* (Penguin Books, 1990); D Galligan and M Kurkchiyan, *Law and Informal Practices: The Post-communist Experience* (Oxford University Press, 2003), T Judt, *Postwar: A History of Europe since 1945* (William Heinemann, 2005).

4. Fair and Proportionate Measures

1 I Ayres and J Braithwaite, *Responsive Regulation: Transcending the Deregulation Debate* (Oxford University Press, 1992); N Gunningham and P Grabosky, *Smart Regulation: Designing Environmental Policy* (Oxford University Press, 1998); see also N Gunningham, 'Enforcement and Compliance Strategies' in M Cave, R Baldwin and M Lodge (eds), *The Oxford Handbook of Regulation* (Oxford University Press, 2010); J Black, 'Critical Reflections on Regulation' (2002) 27 *Australian Journal of Legal Philosophy* 1; C Parker, *The Open Corporation: Effective Self-Regulation and Democracy* (Cambridge University Press, 2002); J Black and R Baldwin, 'Really Responsive Regulation' (2008) 71(1) *Modern Law Review* 59.

2 See MHRA Press Release, 8 April 2009.

3 'Skin Lightener Campaign Prosecution Results', London Trading Standards, press release, 3 May 2016.

4 See 'FCA Fines Five Banks £1.1 Billion for FX Failings and Announces Industry-Wide Remediation Programme', press release, 12 November 2014; 'FCA Fines Barclays £294,432,000 for Forex Failings', press release, 20 May 2015; *The Economist*, 23 May 2015, 6.

5 'Leeds Businessman Receives Record Jail Sentence over £2.2m Recycling Fraud', Environment Agency, press release, 18 July 2016.

6 Information Commissioner's Office, 'Cold Call Crooks Hit with £10k a Day in Fines by Regulator', Information Commissioner, news release, 24 August 2016.

7 'NHS Fined £40,000 after Pensioner Falls to His Death Whilst Riding a Mobility Scooter' *The Guardian*, 15 January 2016.

8 E Reyes, '£6m Payment Agreed in Second Deferred Prosecution' *Law Society Gazette*, 8 July 2016.

9 'Thames Water Fined £1 Million for Pollution to Grand Union Canal', Environment Agency for England and Wales, 5 January 2016, available at: www.gov.uk/government/news/thames-water-fined-1-million-for-pollution-to-grand-union-canal.

10 'Putting the Corporate Manslaughter Sentencing Guidelines to the Test', Corker Binning, www.corkerbinning.com/wp-content/uploads/2016/07/Putting-the-corporate-manslaughter-sentencing-guidelines-to-the-test-1-1.pdf.

11 'FCA Fines RBS, NatWest and Ulster Bank Ltd £42 Million for IT Failures', Financial Conduct Authority, press release, 20 November 2014.

12 'Notice of Intention to Impose a Financial Penalty Pursuant to Section 30A(3) of the Gas Act and 27A(3) of the Electricity Act 1989', Gas and Electricity Markets Authority, 18 December 2015.

13 Decision Notice AJT01247, 8 July 2016, https://www.fca.org.uk/sites/default/files/andrew-tinney.pdf.

14 *Serious Fraud Office v Rolls-Royce plc and Rolls-Royce Energy Systems Inc*, Judgment of Sir Brian Leveson P, 17 January 2017, available at: https://www.judiciary.gov.uk/wp-content/uploads/2017/01/sfo-v-rolls-royce.pdf.

15 See https://www.sfo.gov.uk/cases/rolls-royce-plc,

16 See https://iconewsblog.wordpress.com/2017/07/03/four-lessons-nhs-trusts-can-learn-from-the-royal-free-case.

17 See https://ico.org.uk/about-the-ico/news-and-events/news-and-blogs/2017/07/royal-free-google-deepmind-trial-failed-to-comply-with-data-protection-law.

5. The Need for Cooperation

1 CI Barnard, *The Functions of the Executive* (The President and Fellows of Harvard, 1938) 4.

2 D Black, *The Behaviour of Law* (Emerald Group Publishing, 1976, special edition 2010); W Ulrich and N McWhorter, *Business Architecture: The Art and Practice of Business Transformation* (Meghan-Kiffer Press, 2011) 63. A 'collectivity of people without organization is not a group': A Cohen, *Two Dimensional Man* (Routledge & Kegan Paul, 1974) 66.

3 J Collins and JI Porras, *Built to Last: Successful Habits of Visionary Companies*, 12th edn (HarperCollins, 2005).

4 LS Paine, *Vale Shift. Why Companies Must Merge Social and Financial Imperatives to Achieve Superior Performance* (McGraw-Hill, 2003) 183.

5 F Laloux, *Reinventing Organizations: A Guide to Creating Organizations Inspired by the Next Stage of Human Consciousness* (Nelson Parker, 2014) 74–83.

6 M Crozier, *The Bureaucratic Phenomenon* (University of Chicago Press, 1964; revised edn Transaction Press, 2010).

7 This summary draws on the Introduction to the 2010 edition of Crozier (n 6) by E Friedberg.

8 ibid.

9 P Sedgwick, *The Enterprise Culture* (SPCK, 1992) 4.

10 AS Bachmann, 'Melting Pot or Tossed Salad? Implications for Designing Effective Multicultural Workgroups' (2006) 26(6) *Management International Review* 721, 722.

11 JE McLean and RD Lewis, 'Communicating across Cultures: Management Matters' (2010) *Summer British Journal of Administrative Management* 30.

12 T Peters and RH Waterman, Jr, *In Search of Excellence: Lessons from America's Best-Run Companies* (Harper & Row, 1982); this summary is from M Parker, *Organizational Culture and Identity* (SAGE Publications, 2000).

13 BJ Schoordijk, 'Risk management alshoeksteen van corporate governance' in SHA Dumoulinea (ed), *Tussen Themis en Mercurius* (Kluwer, 2005); DAMHW Strik, 'Deel II—Aansprakelijkheidvoorfalendrisicomanagement' in *Ondernemingsbestuur en risicobeheersing op de drempel van eennieuw decennium: eenondernemingsrechtelijkeanalyse* (Kluwer, 2009); J Eijsbouts, 'Corporate Responsibility, beyond Voluntarism. Regulatory Options to Reinforce the Licence to Operate' (Inaugural lecture, Maastricht University, 2011).

14 Directive 2001/83/EC on the Community code relating to medicinal products for human use. Extensive guidelines can be found in Volume 9A of the Rules Governing Medicinal Products in the European Union: Guidelines on Pharmacovigilance for Medicinal Products for Human Use, which includes guidelines for competent authorities and the EMEA in Part II.

15 Regulation (EC) No 765/2008 of the European Parliament and of the Council of 9 July 2008 setting out the requirements for accreditation and market surveillance relating to the marketing of products and repealing Regulation (EEC) No 339/93.

16 Decision No 768/2008/EC, Annex I, art R32.

17 Report from the Commission to the European Parliament, the Council and the European Economic and Social Committee on the implementation of Regulation (EC) No 765/2008 of the European Parliament and of the Council of 9 July 2008

setting out the requirements for accreditation and market surveillance relating to the marketing of products and repealing Regulation (EEC) No 339/93, COM (2013) 77, 13 February 2013, para 2.3.

18 The Reporting of Injuries, Diseases and Dangerous Occurrences Regulations 2013, SI 2013/1471.

19 DG INFSO *Consultation about a Code for Effective Open Voluntarism* (2012).

20 Greenstreet Berman Ltd, Research Results: *What is the Value in Regulators Sharing Information?* (Better Regulation Delivery Office, 2013).

21 *Better Business Compliance Partnerships: Programme Evaluation* (Department for Communities and Local Government, 2016).

22 *Overcoming Cultural Barriers to Information Sharing within Regulatory Services* (BRDO, 2016).

23 *Learning from Mistakes: How Complaints Can Drive Improvements to Public Services* (Citizens Advice, 2016). The Complaints Survey by Populus used a weighted sample of 1,719 adults resident in England, surveyed in December 2015, and the Civic Life Survey by Boxclever Consulting surveyed 2,025 UK adults in December 2014.

24 J Tallberg, 'Paths to Compliance: Enforcement, Management, and the European Union' (2002) 56(3) *International Organization* 609.

25 *The Transformation to Performance-Based Regulation* (Civil Aviation Authority, 2014) 1.

26 Directive 2001/83/EC on the Community code relating to medicinal products for human use.

27 Regulation (EC) No 765/2008 of the European Parliament and of the Council of 9 July 2008 setting out the requirements for accreditation and market surveillance relating to the marketing of products and repealing Regulation (EEC) No 339/93, art 1.2 and ch III.

28 Commission Implementing Regulation (EU) No 520/2012, ch II.

29 Commission Implementing Regulation (EU) No 520/2012, recital 2.

30 Commission Implementing Regulation (EU) No 520/2012, arts 20–24.

31 Regulation (EU) No 726/2004, art 27.

32 Commission Implementing Regulation (EU) No 520/2012, recital 9.

33 ibid, ch IV.

34 Information kindly supplied by Eric Klassen.

35 Communication from the Commission to the Council and the European Parliament. Setting up an Aviation Safety Management System for Europe, COM (2011) 670, 25 October 2011, p 3.

36 AJ Stolzer, CD Halford and JJ Goglia, 'Introduction' in AJ Stolzer, CD Halford and JJ Goglia (eds), *Implementing Safety Management Systems in Aviation* (Ashgate, 2011) xlviii.

37 *The Transformation to Performance-Based Regulation* (n 25) 1; D McCune, C Lewis and D Arendt, 'Safety Culture in Your Safety Management System' in AJ Stolzer, CD Halford and JJ Goglia (eds) (n 36) 138; S Dekker, *Just Culture. Balancing Safety and Accountability* (Ashgate, 2007) ix; *Building a Culture of Candour: A Review of the Threshold for the Duty of Candour and of the Incentives for Care Organisations to Be Candid* (Royal College of Surgeons of London, 2014).

38 See *Regulation and Growth* (BRDO, 2016), https://view.pagetiger.com/Regulation-and-Growth/Spring-2016; *Primary Authority Handbook* (Regulatory Delivery, 2016); *Primary Authority Changes 2017: Unlocking the Potential* (Regulatory Delivery, 2017).

39 See recommendations on providing good guidance in *The Good Guidance Guide: Taking the Uncertainty out of Regulation* (Better Regulation Executive, 2009).

40 ibid 5.

41 Directive 89/391/EEC on the introduction of measures to encourage improvements in the safety and health of workers at work.

42 ibid art 7.

43 *Reducing Risks, Protecting People—HSE's Decision-Making Process* (Health and Safety Executive, 2001), available at: www.hse.gov.uk/risk/theory/r2p2.pdf.

44 *Enforcement Policy Statement* (Health & Safety Executive, 2009), 02/09, para 1.

45 ibid para 2.

46 See www.hse.gov.uk/enforce/emm.pdf.

47 Every improvement notice contains a statement that in the opinion of an inspector an offence has been committed. Information about Notices is available at: www.hse.gov.uk/enforce/enforcementguide/notices/notices-intro.htm. Improvement and prohibition notices, and written advice, may be used in court proceedings. A prohibition notice stops work in order to prevent serious personal injury. The HSE may use these powers even when the duty-holder has voluntarily undertaken to do, or is already doing, what the Notice specifies as the HSE's requirements: see *Smallwood* v *Railtrack* [2001] All ER (D) 103 (Jan).

48 A simple caution is a statement by an inspector, which is accepted in writing by the duty-holder, that the duty-holder has committed an offence for which there is a realistic prospect of conviction. A simple caution may only be used where a prosecution could be properly brought. 'Simple cautions' are entirely distinct from a caution given under the Police and Criminal Evidence Act 1984 by an inspector before questioning a suspect about an alleged offence. Enforcing authorities should take account of current Home Office guidelines when considering whether to offer a simple caution. The use of simple cautions appears to be very rare.

49 *Enforcement Policy Statement* (n 44) para 4.

50 *Involving Your Workforce in Health and Safety: Guidance for All Workplaces* (Health & Safety Executive, 2015).

51 *National Local Authority Enforcement Code. Health and Safety at Work. England, Scotland & Wales* (Health and Safety Executive, 2013), www.hse.gov.uk/lau/national-la-code.pdf. The Code is given legal effect as HSE guidance to LAs under s 18(4)(b) of the HSW Act 1974 and applies to England, Wales and Scotland. Enforcement of health and safety is split between the HSE and approximately 382 LAs in accordance with the Enforcing Authority (Health & Safety) Regulations 1998.

52 *National Local Authority Enforcement Code* (n 51) para 4.

53 ibid paras 30 and 34.

54 ie, excluding Northern Ireland.

55 www.hse.gov.uk/statistics/history/histfatals.xls. The rate of fatal injuries to workers fell by 38% between 1999/2000 and 2009/10: *Progress in Health and Safety Outcomes since 2000* (Health and Safety Executive, 2010), www.hse.gov.uk/statistics/history/progress-since-2000.pdf.

56 Comments by Lord Grocott in Parliament in 2007, www.publications.parliament.uk/pa/ld200708/ldhansrd/text/80704-0001.htm#08070478000003, quoted in *Reclaiming Health and Safety for All: An Independent Review of Health and Safety Legislation* (R Löfstedt, 2011).

57 M Webster and H Bolt (Frontline Consultants), *The Effectiveness of HSE's Regulatory Approach: The Construction Example* (Health & Safety Executive, 2016) RR1082.

58 This was based on earlier successful pioneering projects in the 1990s, such as the engagement with parties in charge of steelwork erection which led to the recognition of the safety benefits of using nets and the elimination of deaths and serious injuries from related falls.

59 F Blanc, *From Chasing Violations to Managing Risks: Origins, Challenges and Evolutions in Regulatory Inspections* (Edward Elgar, forthcoming).

6. Trust within and in Organisations

1 O O'Neill, *A Question of Trust* (Cambridge University Press, 2002).

2 F Fukuyama, *Trust: The Social Virtues and the Creation of Prosperity* (Penguin Books, 1995) 27.

3 SE Asch, 'Effects of Group Pressure upon the Modification and Distortion of Judgments' in H Guetzkow (ed), *Groups, Leadership and Men* (Carnegie Press, 1951).

4 DJ Brass, KD Butterfield and BC Skaggs, 'Relationships and Unethical Behaviour: A Social Network Perspective' (1998) 23 *Academy of Management Review* 14.

5 D Palmer and C Moore, 'Social Networks and Organizational Wrongdoing in Context' in D Palmer, K Smith-Crowe and R Greenwood (eds), *Organizational Wrongdoing: Key Perspectives and New Directions* (Cambridge University Press, 2016).

6 See the discussion in LK Treviño and GR Weaver, *Managing Ethics in Business Organizations* (Stanford Business Books, 2003) chs 1–3.

7 K Polanyi, *The Great Transformation: The Political and Economic Origins of Our Time*, 2nd edn (Beacon Press, 2001); B Lange, F Haines and D Thomas (eds), *Regulatory Transformations: Rethinking Economy-Society Interactions* (Hart Publishing, 2015).

8 M Ridley, *Origins of Virtue* (London, Penguin Science, 1998) 250.

9 O O'Neill, 'Trust, Trustworthiness, and Accountability' in N Morris and D Vines (eds), *Capital Failure; Rebuilding Trust in Financial Services* (Oxford University Press, 2014) 178.

10 TM Jones, 'Ethical Decision Making by Individuals in Organizations: An Issue-Contingent Model' (1991) 16(2) *Academy of Management Review* 366.

11 O'Neill (n 1) 4.

12 N Gold, 'Trustworthiness and Motivations' in Morris and Vines (n 9) 135.

13 O'Neill (n 9) 178.

14 A Baier, 'Trust and Antitrust' (1986) 96(2) *Ethics* 231, 234.

15 O'Neill (n 13).

16 K Hawley, 'Trust, Distrust and Commitment' (2012) 48(1) *Noûs* 1.

17 ibid.

18 O'Neill (n 1) 64.

19 ibid 25.

20 Fukuyama (n 2) 27–28.

21 D Awrey and D Kershaw, 'Toward a More Ethical Culture in Finance: Regulatory and Governance Strategies' in Morris and Vines (n 9).

22 R Ellickson, *Order without Law: How Neighbors Settle Disputes* (Harvard University Press, 1994); L Bernstein, 'Opting out of the Legal System: Extralegal Contractual Relations in the Diamond Industry' (1992) 21(1) *Journal of Legal Studies* 115; L Bernstein, 'Private Commercial Law in the Cotton Industry: Creating Cooperation through Rules, Norms and Institutions' (2001) 99 *Michigan Law Review* 1724; A Greif, 'Contract Enforceability and Economic Institutions in Early Trade: The Maghribi Traders' Coalition' (1993) 83 *American Economic Review* 525.

23 See multiple references cited by P Nichols and P Dowden, 'Improving Ethical Culture by Measuring Stakeholder Trust', 10 April 2017 by SCCE, http://complianceandethics.org.

24 G Dietz and N Gillespie, *The Recovery of Trust: Case Studies of Organisational Failures and Trust Repair* (Institute of Business Ethics, 2012). The organisations were: Siemens, Mattel, Toyota, the BBC, BAE Systems and Severn Trent Water.

25 O'Neill (n 9) 178; Jones (n 10).

26 H Sants, 'Delivering Intensive Supervision and Credible Deterrence', speech delivered at the Reuters Newsmaker Event, London, 12 March 2009: 'a principles-based approach does not work with people who have no principles'.

27 R Steinholtz, 'Ethics Ambassadors: Getting under the Skin of the Business' (2014) *Business Compliance* 16.

28 CA Heimer, 'Explaining Variation in the Impact of Law: Organizations, Institutions, and Professions' (1996) 15 *Studies in Law, Politics and Society* 29, 37.

29 ibid.

30 RC Mayer, JH Davis and D Schoorman, 'An Integrative Model of Organizational Trust' (1995) 20(3) *Academy of Management Review* 709; G Dietz and D Den Hartog, 'Measuring Trust inside Organisations' (2006) 35(5) *Personnel Review* 557.

31 University of Bath School of Management, *Cultivating Trustworthy Leaders* (Chartered Institute of Professional Development, 2014).

32 Communication, A renewed EU strategy 2011–14 for Corporate Social Responsibility COM (2011) 681, 25 October 2011; J Ruggie, *The Special Representative of the Secretary-General, Report of the Special Representative of the Secretary-General on the issue of human rights and transnational business corporations and other business enterprises, Guiding Principles on Business and Human Rights: Implementing the United Nations 'Protect, Respect and Remedy' Framework*, A/HRC/17/31, 21 March 2011. See JL Campbell, 'Why Would Corporations Behave in Socially Responsible Ways? An Institutional Theory of Corporate Social Responsibility' (2007) 32(2) *Academy of Management Review* 946; J Eijsbouts, 'Corporate Responsibility, beyond Voluntarism. Regulatory Options to Reinforce the Licence to Operate' (Inaugural lecture, Maastricht University, 2011).

33 *Corporate Responsibility. Good for Business and Society: Government Response to Call for Views on Corporate Responsibility* (Department for Business Innovation & Skills, 2014).

34 *Mission-Led Business Review: Call for Evidence* (Cabinet Office, 2016). This states the key characteristics of a mission-led business are that it: can fully distribute its profits; identifies an intention to have a positive social impact as a central purpose of its business; makes a long-term or binding commitment to deliver on that intention through its business and operations; and reports on its social impact to its stakeholders.

35 *Cultivating Trustworthy Leaders* (Chartered Institute of Personnel and Development, 2014); *Experiencing Trustworthy Leaders* (Chartered Institute of Personnel and Development, 2014).

36 M Heffernan, 'Aberrant Personalities Abound in Business' *Financial Times*, 15 July 2017.

37 Gold (n 12) 146.

38 J Haidt, *The Righteous Mind: Why Good People are Divided by Politics and Religion* (Penguin Books, 2012) 72.

39 RD Hare, 'Psychopathy: A Clinical Construct Whose Time Has Come' (1996) 23(1) *Criminal Justice and Behavior* 25.

40 P Babiak and RD Hare, *Snakes in Suits: When Psychopaths Go to Work* (Harper Collins, 2009); P Babiak, CS Neumann and RD Hare, 'Corporate Psychopathy: Talking the Walk' (2010) 28(2) *Behavioral Sciences and the Law* 174; BJ Board and K Frtizon, 'Disordered Personalities at Work' (2005) 11(1) *Psychology, Crime & Law* 17.

41 Gold (n 12) 146.

42 M Gentile, 2013, *Giving Voice to Values in the Workplace: A Practical Approach to Building Moral Competence* (Information Age Publishing, 2009).

43 Babiak and Hare (n 40).

44 J Collins and JI Porras, *Built to Last: Successful Habits of Visionary Companies*, 12th edn (HarperCollins, 2005).

45 ibid.

46 J Collins, *Good to Great* (Harper Business, 2001).

47 J Collins, *How the Mighty Fall: And Why Some Companies Never Give in* (HarperCollins, 2009).

48 ibid.

49 R Sisodia, J Sheth and D Wolfe, *Firms of Endearment: How World-Class Companies Profit from Passion and Purpose*, 2nd edn (Pearson Education, 2014).

50 R Barrett, *The Values-Driven Organization: Cultural Health and Employee Well-Being as a Pathway to Sustainable Performance*, 2nd edn (Routledge, 2017).

51 eg, LS Paine, *Vale Shift. Why Companies Must Merge Social and Financial Imperatives to Achieve Superior Performance* (McGraw-Hill, 2003); LK Treviño and GR Weaver, *Managing Ethics in Business Organizations* (Stanford Business Books, 2003); J Mackey and R Sisoda, *Conscious Capitalism: Liberating the Heroic Spirit of Business* (Harvard Business Review Press, 2014); F Laloux, *Reinventing Organizations* (Nelson Parker, 2014); T O'Callaghan, *Reputation Risk and Globalisation: Exploring the Idea of a Self-Regulating Corporation* (Edward Elgar, 2016).

7. How to Learn and Improve Performance

1 D Gentilin, *The Origins of Ethical Failures: Lessons for Leaders* (Routledge, 2016).

2 M Syed, *Black Box Thinking: Marginal Gains and the Secrets of High Performance* (John Murray, 2015).

3 D McCune, C Lewis and D Arendt, 'Safety Culture in Your Safety Management System' in AJ Stolzer, CD Halford and JJ Goglia (eds), *Implementing Safety Management Systems in Aviation* (Ashgate, 2011) 138.

4 S Dekker, *Just Culture. Balancing Safety and Accountability* (Ashgate, 2007) ix.

5 C Duhigg, 'What Google Learned from its Quest to Build the Perfect Team' *New York Times*, 25 February 2016.

6 *The Transformation to Performance-Based Regulation* (Civil Aviation Authority, 2014), 1; McCune et al (n 3) 138; Dekker (n 4) ix; *Building a Culture of Candour: A Review of the Threshold for the Duty of Candour and of the Incentives for Care Organisations to Be Candid* (Royal College of Surgeons of London, 2014).

7 RF Baumeister et al, 'Bad is Stronger than Good' (2001) 5 *Review of General Psychology* 323.

8 V Braithwaite, 'Is Reintegrative Shaming Relevant to Tax Evasion and Avoidance?' in H Elffers, P Verboon and W Huisman (eds), *Managing and Maintaining Compliance* (Boom Legal Publishers, 2006).

9 BJ Schoordijk, 'Risk management alshoeksteen van corporate governance' in SHA Dumoulinea (ed), *Tussen Themis en Mercurius* (Kluwer, 2005); DAMHW Strik, 'Deel II—Aansprakelijkheidvoorfalendrisicomanagement' in *Ondernemingsbestuur en risicobeheersing op de drempel van eennieuw decennium: eenondernemingsrechtelijkeanalyse* (Kluwer, 2009); J Eijsbouts, 'Corporate Responsibility, beyond Voluntarism: Regulatory Options to Reinforce the Licence to Operate' (Inaugural lecture, Maastricht University, 2011).

10 DA Lucas, 'Organisational Aspects of Near Miss Reporting' in TW van der Schaaf, DA Lucas and AR Hale (eds), *Near Miss Reporting as a Safety Tool* (Butterworths-Heinemann, 1991).

11 *NHS Complaints Reform: Making Things Right* (Department of Health, 2003); *Independent Inquiry into Care Provided by Mid Staffordshire NHS Foundation Trust January 2005—March 2009. Volume I. Chaired by Robert Francis QC*, HC375-I (2010); A Clwyd and T Hart, *A Review of the NHS Hospitals Complaints System: Putting Patients Back in the Picture* (Department of Health, 2013); *Building a Culture of Candour* (n 6); *A Review into the Quality of NHS Complaints Investigations Where Serious or Avoidable Harm Has Been Alleged* (Parliamentary and Health Service Ombudsman, 2015).

12 *Learning from Mistakes: How Complaints Can Drive Improvements to Public Services* (Citizens Advice, 2016). The Complaints Survey by Populus used a weighted sample of 1,719 adults resident in England surveyed in December 2015, and the Civic Life Survey by Boxclever Consulting surveyed 2,025 UK adults in December 2014.

13 *Report on Legal and Cultural Issues in Relation to ATM Safety Occurrence Reporting in Europe: Outcome of a Survey Conducted by the Performance Review Unit in 2005–2006* (Brussels, Eurocontrol Performance Review Commission, 2006).

14 Dekker (n 4) 103.

15 Proposal for a Regulation of the European Parliament and of the Council on occurrence reporting in civil aviation amending Regulation (EU) No 996/2010 and repealing Directive No 2003/42/EC, Commission Regulation (EC) No 1321/2007 and Commission Regulation (EC) No 1330/2007, COM(2012) 776, 18 December 2012, recital 35.

16 RL Helmreich, 'Building Safety on the Three Cultures of Aviation' in *Proceedings if the IATA Human Factors Seminar* (Bangkok, 1999) 39–43; McCune et al (n 3).

17 Dekker (n 4) 10, 53.

18 HS Becker, *Outsiders: Studies in the Sociology of Deviance* (London, Free Press of Glencoe, 1963); Dekker (n 4) 73.

19 Dekker (n 4).
20 A Hidden, *Clapham Junction Accident Investigation Report* (London, HMSO, 1989).
21 Dekker (n 4) 9.
22 Syed (n 2).
23 E Tarnow, 'Self-Destructive Obedience in the Airplane Cockpit and the Concept of Obedience Optimization' in T Blass (ed), *Obedience to Authority: Current Perspectives on the Milgram Paradigm* (Erlbaum Associates, 2000).
24 M Heffernan, *Wilful Blindness: Why We Ignore the Obvious at Our Peril* (Simon & Schuster, 2011) ch 6.
25 M Tamuz, 'The Impact of Computer Surveillance on Air Safety Reporting' (1987) *Columbia Journal of World Business* 69.
26 A possible interpretation of this is that the more analytical 'slow' brain was being forced to engage.
27 M Tamuz, 'The Impact of Computer Surveillance on Air Safety Reporting' (1987) *Columbia Journal of World Business* 69.
28 S Griffith, 'American Airlines ASAP', paper presented at the Global Analysis and Information network (GAIN) Workshop, Cambridge, MA, 1996.
29 Two US Federal Aviation Authority (FAA) systems had a dual mission (enforce and learn). The other system (Aviation Safety Reporting System (ASRS)), operated by NASA, focused solely on learning and could not enforce: it was voluntary and confidential.
30 US FAA, Office of Aviation Safety, 'Near Midair Collisions in the U.S.' (unpublished statistics, 1987).
31 M Tamuz, 'Learning Disabilities for Regulators: The Perils of Organizational Learning in the Air Transportation Industry' (2001) 33(3) *Administration & Society* 276, Figure 3, adapted from M Tamuz, 'The Impact of Computer Surveillance on Air Safety Reporting' (1987) 22(1) *Journal of World Business* 66. By permission of Elsevier Science; US Federal Aviation Administration, the Office of Aviation Policy and Planning (1999) and the US Federal Aviation Administration Office of Aviation Safety (1987). Data was missing for 1966 to 1967.
32 Tamuz (n 31) Figure 2, citing original source as adaptation from the US Federal Aviation Administration, the Office of Aviation Policy and Planning (1999) and the U.S. Federal Aviation Administration Office of Aviation Safety (1987). Data was missing for 1966 to 1967.
33 ibid 5.
34 JG March, LS Sproull and M Tamuz, 'Learning from Samples of One or Fewer' (1991) 2(1) *Organizational Science* 1.
35 Regulation (EU) No 996/2010, recital 4. Even in 1994, it was provided that a safety recommendation shall in no case create a presumption of blame or liability for an accident or incident: Directive 94/56/EC, art 10.
36 Regulation (EU) No 996/2010, recital 22.
37 ibid recital 24.
38 ibid recital 25.
39 Defined in Commission Regulation (EU) No 691/2010 of 29 July 2010 laying down a performance scheme for air navigation services and network functions and amending Regulation (EC) No 2096/2005 laying down common requirements for the provision of air navigation services, art 2(k).

40 Communication from the Commission to the Council and the European Parliament. Setting up an Aviation Safety Management System for Europe, COM (2011) 670, 25 October 2011, 5.

41 Commission Regulation (EU) No 691/2010 of 29 July 2010 laying down a performance scheme for air navigation services and network functions and amending Regulation (EC) No 2096/2005 laying down common requirements for the provision of air navigation services, art 2(k).

42 Dekker (n 4) 15.

43 McCune et al (n 3) 195.

44 'Simply stated, a regulatory "compliant" airline is not necessarily a safe airline.' B Yantis, 'SMS Implementation' in Stolzer et al (n 3).

45 The first *IOSA Standards Manual* was published in 2002; see *ICAO Safety Management Manual*, 2nd edn (International Civil Aviation Organization, 2009). See also *Safety Management Manual* (International Business Aircraft Council, 2006).

46 ICAO Annex 19.

47 *The Transformation to Performance-Based Regulation* (n 6) 1.

48 *Keeping the Aviation Industry Safe: Safety Intelligence and Safety Wisdom. 16 Aviation Industry Senior Executives Reflect on How They Run a Safe Business in a Commercial Environment. A Future Sky Safety White Paper* (European Commission, 2016).

49 Committee on Standards of Public Life, 'Getting the Balance Right: Implementing Standards in Public Life', Tenth Report of the Committee on Standards in Public Life, 2005, para 4.31.

50 *Leading Health and Safety at Work: Leadership Actions for Directors and Board Members* (Institute of Directors and HSE, 2011).

51 See Helmreich (n 16) 39; McCune et al (n 3).

52 The following points are taken from the *Safety Management Manual* of British Airways.

53 *Organisational Culture: Evolving Approaches to Embedding and Assurance* (Chartered Institute of Internal Auditors, 2016).

54 ibid.

55 *Culture and the Role of Internal Audit: Looking below the Surface* (Chartered Institute of Internal Auditors, 2014); *Organisational Culture* (n 53).

56 *An Organization with a Memory* (Department of Health, 2000); *The NHS Plan: A Plan for Investment, a Plan for Reform* (Department of Health, 2000); *Building a Safer NHS for Patients: Implementing an Organization with a Memory* (Department of Health, 2001).

57 *Learning from Bristol: The Department of Health's Response to the Report of the Public Inquiry into Children's Heart Surgery at the Bristol Royal Infirmary 1984–1995* (2002) Cm 5363, i and 367.

58 Sir Liam Donaldson, *Call for Ideas* (Department of Health, 2001); *Making Amends: A Consultation Paper Setting out Proposals for Reforming the Approach to Clinical Negligence in the NHS. Report by the Chief Medical Officer* (Department of Health, 2003).

59 Dr B Kirkup CBE, *The Report of the Morecambe Bay Investigation* (Department of Health, 2015) para 11.

60 ibid para 8.3.

61 J Andrews and M Butler, *Trusted to Care: An Independent Review of the Princess of Wales Hospital and Neath Port Talbot Hospitals at ABMU* (Dementia Services Development Centre and The People Organisation, 2014) para 5.1.

62 *Building a Culture of Candour* (n 6). The authors recommended that the duty of candour should be extended from the initial limitation to events that caused death or serious injury to include harm defined as moderate: the issue had been disputed.

63 ibid para 1.29.

64 Reference from original text. For the impact of a lack of an enabling environment for candour/open disclosure, see K Mazor et al, 'Communicating with Patients about Medical Errors' (2004) 164 *Archives of Internal Medicine* 1690; C Vincent, 'Understanding and Responding to Adverse Events' (2003) 348(11) *New England Journal of Medicine* 1051; *Building a Culture of Candour* (n 6) para 1.32.

65 *Sir R Francis QC, Freedom to Speak up: An Independent Review into Creating an Open and Honest Reporting Culture in the NHS* (Department of Health, 2015).

66 Public Administration Select Committee—Sixth Report, *Investigating Clinical Incidents in the NHS*, 24 March 2015, para 74. The Public Administration Select Committee noted an academic paper that had argued that: 'Investigations should be focused on learning and improvement. They should not attribute blame or liability for the causation of safety issues and there should be clear agreements that punitive proceedings will not be taken against staff based on findings of any safety investigation.' See C Macrae and C Vincent, 'Learning from Failure: The Need for Independent Safety Investigation in Healthcare' (2014) 107(11) *Journal of the Royal Society of Medicine* 439.

67 See *Learning Not Blaming: The Government Response to the Freedom to Speak up Consultation, the Public Administration Select Committee Report 'Investigating Clinical Incidents in the NHS', and the Morecambe Bay Investigation* (Department of Health, 2015), Cm 9113; *NHS England Serious Incident Framework (2015); Report of the Expert Advisory Group: Healthcare Safety Investigation Branch* (Department of Health, 2016).

68 Rt Hon Jeremy Hunt MP, Speech at Global Patient Safety Summit, Lancaster House, 10 March 2016, https://www.gov.uk/government/speeches/from-a-blame-culture-to-a-learning-culture.

69 *Report of the Expert Advisory Group: Healthcare Safety Investigation Branch* (Department of Health, 2016), 21

70 ibid 25, 26.

71 National Advisory Group on the Safety of Patients in England, *A Promise to Learn—A Commitment to Act* (Department of Health, 2013).

72 ibid 32.

73 Directive 2013/11/EU on consumer ADR. See C Hodges, I Benöhr and N Creutzfeldt-Banda, *Consumer ADR in Europe* (Hart Publishing, 2012); J Zekoll, M Bälz and I Amelung (eds), *Dispute Resolution: Alternatives to Formalization—Formalization of Alternatives?* (Brill, 2014); P Cortes, *The New Regulatory Framework for Consumer Dispute Resolution* (Oxford University Press, 2016).

74 Widely found in Nordic states and currently being investigated more widely.

75 The US Committee of Sponsoring Organizations of the Treadway Commission, which is aided by supported by five supporting organisations, including the Institute of Management Accountants (IMA), the American Accounting Association (AAA), the American Institute of Certified Public Accountants (AICPA), the Institute of Internal Auditors (IIA) and Financial Executives International (FEI).

8. Why Should We Be Ethical?

1 P Nichols, Joseph S Kolodny Professor of Social Responsibility in Business, Professor of Legal Studies and Business Ethics, the Wharton School, University of Pennsylvania and P Dowden, President and CEO, Center for Business Ethics and Corporate Governance, 'Improving Ethical Culture by Measuring Stakeholder Trust', 10 April 2017, http://complianceandethics.org/author/doug-stupca.

2 Warren Buffett, letter to shareholders, Annual Report (Berkshire Hathaway, 2010).

3 T Donaldson, *Corporations and Morality* (Prentice Hall, 1982). See also SC de Hoo, 'In Pursuit of Corporate Sustainability and Responsibility: Past Cracking Perceptions and Creating Codes' (Inaugural lecture, Maastricht University, 2011) 11, referring to the principle of reciprocity and also a corporate social contracts-based approach.

4 The presumption of justice as fairness: J Rawls, *A Theory of Justice* (Belknap Press, 1971).

5 See A Sen, *The Idea of Justice* (Allen Lane, 2009) 361–64 on human rights.

6 N Gunningham and P Grabosky, *Smart Regulation: Designing Environmental Policy* (Oxford University Press, 1998).

7 M Carney, 'The Future of Financial Reform', 2014 Monetary Authority of Singapore Lecture, 17 November 2014: 'A trusted system can retain its social licence to support the real economy in innovative and efficient ways.'

8 AV Joseph, 'Successful Examples of Corporate Social Responsibility' (2009) 44(3) *Indian Journal of Industrial Relations* 402, 403.

9 Rapport van de CommissieBurgmans over de verhouding MVO en corporate governance, uitgebracht op 6 november 2008 aan de Staatssecretaris van EconomischeZaken (www.ez.nl).

10 See https://www.unglobalcompact.org; *Guide to Corporate Sustainability: Shaping a Sustainable Future* (United Nations, 2000, revised 2003). See *Impact. Transforming Business, Changing the World. The United Nations Global Compact* (United Nations DNV GL, 2015).

11 See www.oecd.org/daf/inv/mne.

12 See www.iso.org/iso/home/standards/iso26000.htm.

13 See www.ilo.org/empent/Publications/WCMS_094386/lang--en/index.htm.

14 J Ruggie, *The Special Representative of the Secretary-General, Report of the Special Representative of the Secretary-General on the Issue of Human Rights and Transnational Business Corporations and Other Business Enterprises. Guiding Principles on Business and Human Rights: Implementing the United Nations 'Protect, Respect and Remedy' Framework*, A/HRC/17/31, 21 March 2011.

15 *Guide to Corporate Sustainability* (n 10).

16 See https://www.unglobalcompact.org/what-is-gc/mission/principles.

17 C Hodges, *Law and Corporate Behaviour: Integrating Theories of Regulation, Enforcement, Culture and Ethics* (Hart Publishing, 2015) ch 20.

18 *Corporate Responsibility. Good for Business and Society: Government Response to Call for Views on Corporate Responsibility* (BIS, March 2014).

19 ibid para 2.1.

20 ibid para 1.2.

21 *SDGs Mean Business: How Credible Standards Can Help Companies Deliver the 2030 Agenda* (World Wildlife Fund, 2017).

22 J Collins, *Good to Great* (Harper Business, 2001); J Collins and JI Porras, *Built to Last: Successful Habits of Visionary Companies*, 12th edn (HarperCollins, 2005).

23 R Barrett, *The Values-Driven Organization* (Routledge, 2014).

24 F Taylor, *The Principles of Scientific Management* (Harper Brothers, 2011).

25 A Edmans, 'Does the Stock Market Fully Value Intangibles? Employee Satisfaction and Equity Prices' (2011) 101 *Journal of Financial Economics* 621.

26 A Maslow, 'A Theory of Human Motivation' (1943) 50 *Psychological Review* 370; F Hertzberg, *The Motivation to Work* (John Wiley & Sons, 1959); D McGregor, The Human Side of Enterprise (McGraw-Hill, 1960).

27 Edmans (n 25). The results were that a value-weighted portfolio of stock returns of the '100 Best Companies to Work for in America' earned a four-factor alpha of 0.29% per month from 1984 to 2009, or 3.5% per year from 1984 to 2009, and 2.1% above industry benchmarks.

28 See multiple references cited by Nichols and Dowden (n 1) fns iii–v.

29 L Guiso, P Sapienza and L Zingales, 'The Value of Corporate Culture' (2015) 117(1) *Journal of Financial Economics* 60.

30 ibid.

31 *Organisational Culture: Evolving Approaches to Embedding and Assurance* (Chartered Institute of Internal Auditors, 2016).

32 *A Duty to Care? Evidence of the Importance of Organisational Culture to Effective Governance and Leadership* (Chartered Institute of Personnel and Development, 2016).

33 C Hampden-Turner and F Trompenaars, *Riding the Waves of Culture: Understanding Diversity and Global Business* (McGraw-Hill, 1997); JR Katzenbach and Z Khan, *Leading Outside the Lines: How to Mobilize the Informal Organization, Energize Your Team, and Get Better Results* (Jossey-Bass, 2010).

34 *Employee Engagement: What's Your Engagement Ratio?* (Gallup Consulting, 2009).

35 ON Godart, H Görg and A Hanley, 'Trust-Based Work-Time and Product Improvements: Evidence from Firm Level Data', Kiel Institute for the World Economy, Working Paper No 1914, 2014.

36 R Barrett, *The Values-Driven Organization: Cultural Health and Well-Being as a Pathway to Sustainable Performance* (Routledge, 2017).

37 LS Paine, *Vale Shift: Why Companies Must Merge Social and Financial Imperatives to Achieve Superior Performance* (McGraw-Hill, 2003).

38 ibid 141.

39 ibid; see also 54.

40 J Kay, *Obliquity* (Profile Books, 2010). See also 'Unilever: In Search of the Good Business' *The Economist*, 9 August 2014, 69.

41 C Mayer, *Firm Commitment: Why the Corporation is Failing Us and How to Restore Trust in it* (Oxford University Press, 2013) 167.

42 J Kay, *Obliquity* (Profile Books, 2010) 36.

43 J Buckingham and V Nilakant (eds), *Managing Responsibly: Alternative Approaches to Corporate Management and Governance* (Gower, 2012).

44 WH Erhard, MC Jensen and S Zaffron, 'Integrity: A Positive Model that Incorporates the Normative Phenomena of Morality, Ethics, and Legality', SSRN, 2007, https://papers.ssrn.com/sol3/papers.cfm?abstract_id=1542759.

45 R Sisodia, J Sheth and D Wolfe, *Firms of Endearment: How World-Class Companies Profit from Passion and Purpose*, 2nd edn (Pearson Education, 2014).

46 *Governing Culture: Practical Considerations for the Board and its Committees* (EY, 2016),

47 *EY Culture and Boards at a Glance 2016. Survey of 100 Board Members of FTSE 350 Companies* (EY, 2016).

48 *UK Customer Satisfaction Index* (Institute of Customer Service, January 2016).

49 D Barton, J Manyika, T Koller, R Palter, J Godsall and J Zoffer, *Measuring the Economic Impact of Short-Termism* (McKinsey & Company, 2017).

50 D Barton, J Manyika and S Keohane Williamson, 'The Data: Where Long-Termism Pays off' *Harvard Business Review*, May–June 2017, 67.

51 *Financial Times*, 21 January 2017.

52 A number of the largest fines imposed in this data set were imposed by the US government, with the US Department of Justice (DOJ) imposing 58% of the fines, followed by the US Federal Housing Finance Agency (which oversees the secondary mortgage markets in the US and applied large sanctions after the financial crisis) with 17% and the EU General Directorate of Competition with 11%. The US DOJ statistics also show a path towards more frequent imprisonment and longer sentences for individuals involved in these violations, as the agency sees that holding managers accountable is an effective way to deter and punish misconduct. See the US DOJ 2015 Antitrust Division Criminal Enforcement Update, available at www.justice.gov/atr/division-update/2015/division-update-spring-2015.

53 See Global Investigation Review's annually updated Enforcement Scorecard Database for a full methodological description, available at http://globalinvestigationsreview.com/enforcement-scorecard.

54 *Corporate Governance and Business Integrity: A Stocktaking of Corporate Practices* (OECD, 2015).

55 This chapter recognises that risks faced by the financial sector are often not the same as those faced by companies operating in other sectors. 'In the context of financial institutions, the focus naturally tends to be on financial risks, such as credit, liquidity or market risks, although there is also an increasing emphasis on operational risk. In the case of non-financial institutions, the same risks will also be present, although not always to the same extent as in financial institutions … Risk governance rules and practices appropriate for financial institutions therefore may not be directly applicable to non-financial institutions. At the same time, some more general lessons can probably be learned from risk management failures in the financial sector.' See OECD, *Risk Management and Corporate Governance, Corporate Governance* (OECD Publishing, 2014), available at http://dx.doi.org/10.1787/9789264208636-en.

56 These remedial actions included: (i) its suspension from the dollar clearing through the New York branch for high-risk clients at its Hong Kong subsidiary; (ii) its exiting high-risk client relationship with certain business lines at its branches in the United Arab Emirates; (iii) not accepting new dollar-clearing clients or accounts across its operations without prior approval from the New York State Department of Financial Services; (iv) the appointment of 'a competent and responsible' executive reporting directly to the CEO for the oversight of remedies; and (v) the implementation of a series of enhanced due diligence and know-your-customer requirements, among others. See Thomson Reuters-Accelus, 'The Rising Cost of Non-compliance: From the End of a Career to the End of a Firm', November 2014, http://info.accelus.thomsonreuters.com/Cost-Of-Non-Compliance?cid=Blog.

57 'The size of any potential fine is unquantifiable, so this represents an unquantifiable risk. Nevertheless, a substantial fine could hamper (the company's) ability to grow its dividend, in my view. I have therefore sold the fund's position in (the company), reinvesting the proceeds into parts of the portfolio in which I have greater conviction.' Neil Woodford, head of investment, Woodford Funds blog, September 2014, https://woodfordfunds.com/bank-withdrawal.

58 For example: 'BNP Paribas pleaded guilty in New York State Supreme Court to falsifying business records and conspiring to falsify business records. BNPP also agreed to a cease and desist order and to pay a civil monetary penalty of $508 million to the Board of Governors of the Federal Reserve System. The New York State Department of Financial Services announced that BNPP agreed to, among other things, terminate or separate from the bank 13 employees, including the Group Chief Operating Officer and other senior executives.' See the US DOJ Press Release, 1 May 2015, available at www.justice.gov/opa/pr/bnp-paribas-sentenced-conspiring-violate-international-emergency-economicpowers-act-and.

9. The Status of Corporate Governance

1 M Heffernan, *Wilful Blindness: Why We Ignore the Obvious at Our Peril* (Walker Publishing Company, 2011).

2 AA Berle and GC Means, *The Modern Corporation and Private Property* (Harcourt, Brace & World, 1923); M Friedman, *Capitalism and Freedom* (University of Chicago Press, 1962); RE Freeman, *Strategic Management: A Stakeholder Approach* (Pitman/Ballinger, 1984); A Sen, *On Ethics and Economics* (Blackwell, 1987); JR Boatright, 'Business Ethics and the Theory of the Firm' (1996) 34(2) *American Business Law Journal* 217; JE Stiglitz, 'Evaluating Economic Change' (2004) 133(3) *Daedalus* 18; T Donaldson and LE Preston, 'The Stakeholder Theory of the Corporation: Concepts, Evidence, and Implications' (1995) 20(1) *Academy of Management Review* 65; AL Friedman and S Miles, 'Developing Stakeholder Theory' (2002) 39(1) *Journal of Management Studies* 1; TM Jones, W Felps and GA Bigley, 'Ethical Theory and Stakeholder-Related Decisions: The Role of Stakeholder Culture' (2007) 32(1) *Academy of Management Review* 137; RK Mitchell, BR Agle and DJ Wood, 'Toward a Theory of Stakeholder Identification and Salience: Defining the Principle of Who and What Really Counts' (1997) 22(4) *Academy of Management Review* 853.

3 W Werner, 'Management, Stock Market and Corporate Reform: Berle and Means Reconsidered' (1977) 77(3) *Columbia Law Review* 388; A Kaufman, L Zacharias and M Karson, *Managers vs Owners: The Struggle for Corporate Control in American Democracy* (Oxford University Press, 1995); WW Bratton, 'Berle and Means Reconsidered at the Century's Turn' (2001) 26 *Journal of Corporation Law* 737.

4 J Schumpeter, *Capitalism, Socialism and Democracy* (Harper & Row, 1943). See also N Gold, 'Trustworthiness and Motivations' in N Morris and D Vines (eds), *Capital Failure; Rebuilding Trust in Financial Services* (Oxford University Press, 2014), who argues that this was a misinterpretation of what Adam Smith had said: see A Smith, *Theory of Moral Sentiments* (1759).

5 FY Edgeworth, *Mathematical Physics: An Essay on the Application of Mathematics to the Moral Sciences* (Kegan Paul, 1881), 12.

6 SB Lewin, 'Economics and Psychology: Lessons for Our Own Day from the Early Twentieth Century' (1996) 34(3) *Journal of Economic Literature* 1293; M Mandler, 'A Difficult Choice in Preference Theory: Rationality Implies Completeness or Transitivity But Not Both' in E Millgram (ed), *Varieties of Practical Reasoning* (MIT Press, 2001).

7 Werner (n 3); Kaufman et al (n 3); Bratton (n 3).

8 FA von Hayek, *The Constitution of Liberty* (Routledge & Kegan Paul, 1960).

9 J Rawls, *A Theory of Justice* (Harvard University Press, 1971).

10 P Sedgwick, *The Enterprise Culture* (SPCK, 1992) 126.

11 S Jaffer, N Morris, E Sawbridge and D Vines, 'How Changes to the Financial Services Industry Eroded Trust' in Morris and Vines (n 4).

12 L Stout, *The Shareholder Value Myth* (Berrett-Koehler Publishers, 2012); C Mayer, *Firm Commitment* (Oxford University Press, 2012).

13 R Sandler, *Medium and Long-Term Retail Savings in the UK: A Review* (HM Treasury, 2002).

14 IH Cheng, H Hong and J Scheinkman, 'Yesterday's Heroes: Compensation and Creative Risk Taking', unpublished working paper, Princeton University, 2009, cited in H Davies, *The Financial Crisis: Who is to Blame?* (Polity Press, 2010).

15 Stout (n 12); Mayer (n 12).

16 S Baiman, 'Agency Research in Managerial Accounting: A Survey' (1982) 1 *Journal of Accounting Literature* 154; JL Bradach and R Eccles, 'Price, Authority, and Trust' (1989) 15 *Annual Review of Sociology* 97; L Donaldson, 'The Ethereal Hand: Organizational Economics and Management Theory' (1990) 15(3) *Academy of Management Review* 369; L Donaldson, *American Anti-management Theories of Organization: A Critique of Paradigm Proliferation* (Cambridge University Press, 1995); KM Eisenhardt, 'Agency Theory: An Assessment and Review' (1989) 14(1) *Academy of Management Review* 57; EF Fama and MC Jensen, 'Agency Problems and Residual Claims' (1983) 26 *Journal of Law and Economics* 327; M Jensen and W Meckling, 'Theory of the Firm: Managerial Behaviour, Agency Costs and Ownership Structure' (1976) 3 *Journal of Financial Economics* 305; F Lafontaine, 'Agency Theory and Franchising: Some Empirical Results' (1992) 23(2) *RAND Journal of Economics* 263; D Levinthal, 'A Survey of Agency Models of Organizations' (1998) 9 *Journal of Economic Behaviour and Organization* 153; J Pfeffer, *New Directions for Organization Theory: Problems and Prospects* (Oxford University Press, 1997)

17 A Kleanthous, 'Putting a Price on Value' in C MacFarland (ed), *The Virtue of Enterprise: Responsible Business for a New Economy* (ResPublica, 2013).

18 J Armour and JN Gordon, 'Systemic Harms and the Limits of Shareholder Value' in Morris and Vines (n 4). For an absence of voice in corporate environmental responsibility, see C Bradshaw, 'The Environmental Business Case and Unenlightened Shareholder Value' (2012) 1 *Legal Studies* 141.

19 J Buckingham and V Nilakant, 'Introduction: Globalizing Corporate Social Responsibility—Challenging Western Neo-liberal Management Theory' in J Buckingham and V Nilakant (eds), *Managing Responsibly. Alternative Approaches to Corporate Management and Governance* (Gower, 2012).

20 CC Manz and HP Simms, *Business without Bosses* (John Wiley, 1993).

21 JL Bower and LS Paine, 'The Error at the Heart of Corporate Leadership' *Harvard Business Review*, May–June 2017, 50.
22 ibid 56.
23 ibid 54.
24 ibid 57.
25 Companies Act 2006, s 172.
26 Mayer (n 12) 167.
27 ibid.
28 ibid 246. See also 'Family Firms: Business in the Blood' *The Economist*, 9 August 2014, 55.
29 Mayer (n 12) 8.
30 See particularly P Montagnon, *Ethics, Risk and Governance* (Institute of Business Ethics, 2014); F Coffey, *The Role and Effectiveness of Ethics and Compliance Practitioners* (Institute of Business Ethics, 2014); L Tansey Martens, *Globalising a Business Ethics Programme* (Institute of Business Ethics, 2012);
31 D Palmer, *Normal Organizational Wrongdoing: A Critical Analysis of Theories of Misconduct in and by Organizations* (Oxford University Press, 2012).
32 J Mackey and R Sisoda, *Conscious Capitalism: Liberating the Heroic Spirit of Business* (Harvard Business Review Press, 2014).
33 *G20/OECD Principles of Corporate Governance. OECD Report to G20 Finance Ministers and Central Bank Governors* (OECD, 2015).
34 *Corporate Governance and Business Integrity: A Stocktaking of Corporate Practices* (OECD, 2015).
35 *Toward Effective Governance of Financial Institutions* (G30, 2012).
36 ibid 14.
37 ibid, section 7.
38 *A New Paradigm: Financial Institution Boards and Supervisors* (G30, October 2013).
39 ibid.
40 *Toward Effective Governance of Financial Institutions* (n 35); *A New Paradigm* (n 38); *The FCA's Approach to Advancing its Objectives* (FCA, 2013); *The Salz Review of Barclays' Business Practices Report to the Board of Barclays PLC* (2013); *Report of the Collective Engagement Working Group* (Collective Engagement Working Group, 2013).
41 *Report on The Lord Mayor's Conference on Trust and Values*, November 2011; *Investing in Integrity. The Lord Mayor's Conference on Trust and Values* (City Values Forum, October 2012); *A Report on the Culture of British Retail Banking* (New City Agenda and Cass Business School, 2014).
42 Companies Act 2006, s 172.
43 *Investing in Integrity* (n 41).
44 Report of the Committee on *Financial Aspects of Corporate Governance* (1992), para 3.2, at www.ecgi.org/codes/documents/cadbury.pdf.
45 Walker Review, *A Review of Corporate Governance in UK Banks and Other Financial Industry Entities—Final Recommendations* (HM Treasury, 2009).
46 *Combined Code on Corporate Governance* (Financial Reporting Council, 2010).
47 *The UK Corporate Governance Code* (Financial Reporting Council, October 2012). By the end of 2013, compliance was reported to be high: *Developments in Corporate Governance 2013: The Impact and Implementation of the UK Corporate Governance and Stewardship Codes* (Financial Reporting Council, 2013). See also *The Accountancy Regulations* (Financial Reporting Council, 2014); *The Actuarial Scheme* (Financial Reporting Council, 2014); *Sanctions Guidance* (Financial Reporting Council, 2014).

48 *The UK Corporate Governance Code* (Financial Reporting Council, October 2014).

49 ibid, Preface, paras 3 and 4.

50 Financial Reporting Council, *The UK Stewardship Code* (Financial Reporting Council, 2010); *Developments in Corporate Governance 2013: The Impact and Implementation of the UK Corporate Governance and Stewardship Codes* (FRC, December 2013) (finding that companies were responding in a positive manner to the changes introduced in October 2012, but with less uptake of new reporting recommendations on the activities of audit committees).

51 *Corporate Governance Policy and Voting Guidelines* (National Association of Pension Funds, November 2013).

52 *Comply or Explain: Investor Expectations and Current Practices* (Association of British Insurers, December 2012), available at www.abi.org.uk/content/contentfilemanager.aspx?contentid=65367.

53 *The Kay Review of UK Equity Markets and Long-Term Decision Making: Final Report* (BIS, July 2012). See also JA McCahery and EPM Vermeulen, 'Understanding the Board of Directors after the Financial Crisis: Some Lessons for Europe' (2014) 41(1) *Journal of Law and Society* 121, who argue for the remuneration criterion of value creation through sustainable growth and innovation, and the ongoing involvement on boards of venture capitalists.

54 *The UK Corporate Governance Code* (Financial Reporting Council, 2014).

55 ibid para 4.

56 ibid para 5.

57 *Impact: Transforming Business, Changing the World. The United Nations Global Compact* (DNV GL, 2015).

58 Committee on Standards in Public Life, *Standards Matter: A Review of Best Practice in Promoting Good Behaviour in Public Life*, Cm 8519, 2013.

59 Investment Association, 'Supporting UK Productivity with Long-Term Investment', March 2016.

60 *Corporate Culture and the Role of Boards: Report of Observations* (Financial Reporting Council, 2016). See also *Governing Values: Risk and Opportunity—A Guide to Board Leadership in Purpose Values and Culture* (City Values Forum with Tomorrow's Company, 2016); *A Duty to Care? Evidence of the Importance of Organisational Culture to Effective Governance and Leadership* (Chartered Institute of Personnel and Development, 2016).

61 *G20/OECD Principles of Corporate Governance: OECD Report to G20 Finance Ministers and Central Bank Governors* (OECD, 2015).

62 *The Values Most Valued by UK plc* (Maitland, 2015), available at www.maitland.co.uk/news/business/the-values-most-valued-by-uk-plc.

63 D Johnson, *Ethics at Work. 2015 Survey of Employees: Main Findings and Themes* (Institute of Business Ethics, 2015).

64 *The 2016 Good Governance Report: The Great Governance Debate Continued* (Institute of Directors, 2016).

65 The Chartered Institute of Internal Auditors' report cites Michael Lewis, 'Why Only Britain's Bankers Can Save the World from Another Big Short' *The Times*, 23 January 2016: 'It seems to me that the problem in 2008 was so systematic that putting people in jail was almost beside the point. We need to change the system. It isn't that you had a couple of bad guys, You had a whole system that was rotten; thousands and thousands of people behaving very badly because the system basically instructed them to do it.'

66 Kamal Ahmed, 'UBS Rogue trader: "It Could Happen Again"' *BBC News*, 1 August 2016, www.bbc.co.uk/news/correspondents/kamalahmed.

67 J Collins and JI Porras, *Built to Last: Successful Habits of Visionary Companies*, 12th edn (HarperCollins, 2005); J Collins, *Good to Great* (Harper Business, 2001); R Barrett, *The Values-Driven Organisation: Unleashing Human Potential for Performance and Profit* (Routledge, 2015); C Hodges, *Law and Corporate Behaviour: Integrating Theories of Regulation, Enforcement, Culture and Ethics* (Hart Publishing, 2015); C Hodges, *Ethical Business Regulation: Understanding the Evidence* (Department for Business Innovation & Skills, Better Regulation Delivery Office, 2016).

68 R Sisodia, J Sheth and D Wolfe, *Firms of Endearment. How World-Class Companies Profit from Passion and Purpose*, 2nd edn (Pearson Education, 2014); Barrett (n 67); Barrett, *The Values-Driven Organization: Cultural Health and Employee Well-Being as a Pathway to Sustainable Performance*, 2nd edn (Routledge, 2017).

69 P Montagnon, *Stakeholder Engagement Values, Business Culture and Society* (Institute of Business Ethics, 2016).

70 *The Future of Governance: One Small Step …* (Grant Thornton, 2016).

71 *The Values Most Valued by UK* plc (n 62).

72 *Corporate Culture and the Role of Boards* (n 60) 36.

73 JR Graham, CR Harvey, J Popadak and S Rajgopal, 'Corporate Culture: Evidence from the Field', https://papers.ssrn.com/sol3/papers.cfm?abstract_id=2805602; Deloitte, *Global Human Capital Trends 2016: The New Organisation, Different by Design* (Deloitte, 2016), https://www2.deloitte.com/content/dam/Deloitte/global/Documents/HumanCapital/gx-dup-global-human-capital-trends-2016.pdf; *PWC 2013 Culture and Change Management Survey* (Katzenbach Center at Strategy&), https://www.strategyand.pwc.com/culture-and-change; *EY Culture and Boards Survey 2016* (EY, 2016), www.ey.com/uk/en/services/assurance/ey-is-your-board-yet-to-realise-the-true-value-of-culture; *Korn Ferry Institute Global Survey 2014* (2014), https://www.kornferry.com/press/15195.

74 Montagnon (n 69).

75 *Corporate Governance and Business Integrity* (n 34).

76 *Corporate Misconduct—Individual Consequences: Global Enforcement Focuses the Spotlight on Executive Integrity* (EY, 2016).

77 *Global Business Ethics Survey: Measuring Risk and Promoting Workplace Integrity* (Ethics and Compliance Initiative, 2016).

78 House of Commons International Development Committee, *DFID's use of private sector contractors*, Eighth Report of Session 2016–17, 36.

79 House of Commons' Business, Energy and Industrial Strategy Committee, *Corporate Governance*. Third Report of Session 2016–17, HC 702.

80 ibid paras 44–55.

81 *The 2014 Global Workforce Study: Driving Engagement through a Consumer-Like Experience* (Towers Watson, 2014).

82 *The 2012 Global Workforce Study* (Towers Watson, 2012).

83 B Rayton, T Dodge and G D'Analeze, *Employee Engagement Task Force: 'Nailing the Evidence' Workgroup* (University of Bath School of Management, 2012) ii.

84 *Building Our Industrial Strategy. Green Paper* (HM Government, 2017).

85 See www.valuescentre.com.

86 *Promoting Integrity by Creating Opportunities for Responsible Businesses* (B20 Cross-Thematic Group, 2017), www.b20germany.org/priorities/responsible-business-conduct-anti-corruption/rbcac-recommendations.

10. The Status of Regulatory Policy

1 C Mayer, *Firm Commitment: Why the Corporation is Failing Us and How to Restore Trust in it* (Oxford, Oxford University Press, 2013) ch 4.

2 ibid 144.

3 K Polanyi, *The Great Transformation: The Political and Economic Origins of Our Time*, 2nd edn (Beacon Press, 2001); B Lange, F Haines and D Thomas (eds), *Regulatory Transformations: Rethinking Economy–Society Interactions* (Hart Publishing, 2015).

4 E Costa, K King, R Dutta and F Algate, *Applying Behavioural Insights to Regulated Markets* (Behavioural Insights Team for Citizens Advice, 2016).

5 RH Thaler and CR Sunstein, *Nudge* (Yale University Press, 2008).

6 *Behavioural Insights and Public Policy: Lessons from Around the World* (OECD, 2017).

7 *Toward Effective Governance of Financial Institutions* (G30, 2012); *Investing in Integrity: The Lord Mayor's Conference on Trust and Values* (City Values Forum, October 2012); *A New Paradigm: Financial Institution Boards and Supervisors* (G30, 2013); C Adamson, 'The Importance of Culture in Driving Behaviours of Firms and How the FCA Will Assess This', speech by Director of Supervision at the CFA Society UK Professionalism Conference, 19 April 2013; *The Salz Review of Barclays' Business Practices Report to the Board of Barclays plc* (2013), para 2.4; *A Report on the Culture of British Retail Banking* (New City Agenda and Cass Business School, 2014); M Carney, 'The Future of Financial Reform', 2014 Monetary Authority of Singapore Lecture, 17 November 2014; J Shipton, 'Integrity in Financial Markets—Challenges from Asia', Speech to the FCA International Regulators' Seminar, London, 24 November 2014.

8 *OECD Best Practice Principles for Regulatory Policy: Regulatory Enforcement and Inspections* (OECD, 2014).

9 *Risk and Regulatory Policy: Improving the Governance of Risk* (OECD, 2010).

10 The shift was noted from *Consultation on Public Consultation Best Practice Principles for Improving on Enforcement and Inspections* (OECD, June 2013) to *OECD Best Practice Principles for Regulatory Policy: Regulatory Enforcement and Inspections* (OECD, 2014).

11 P Lunn, *Regulatory Policy and Behavioural Economics* (OECD, 2014) 10.

12 ibid 11.

13 ibid, quoting *OECD Best Practice Principles for the Governance of Regulators* (OECD, 2013).

14 *Behavioural Insights and Public Policy* (n 6).

15 See C Hodges, *Law and Corporate Behaviour. Integrating Theories of Regulation and Enforcement* (Hart Publishing, 2015) ch 9.

16 Communication from the Commission, Better Regulation for Better Results—An EU Agenda, COM (2015) 215 final, 19 May 2015.

17 *Drivers of Compliance and Non-compliance with Consumer Protection Law: A Report by Ipsos MORI Commissioned by the OFT* (Office of Fair Trading, 2010), OFT1225a, para 1.34.

18 R Fairman and C Yapp, *Making an Impact on SME Compliance Behaviour: An Evaluation of the Effect of Interventions upon Compliance with Health and Safety Legislation in Small and Medium-Sized Enterprises* (Health and Safety Executive, 2005), Research Report 366; *The Anderson Review of Government Guidance on Regulation: Business Perspectives of Government Guidance. Research Study Conducted for Department for*

Business, Enterprise and Regulatory Reform. Final Report (Ipsos MORI, 2008); *The Anderson Review. Summary of Views from Meetings with Small and Medium-Sized Enterprises (SMEs)* (Department for Business, Enterprise and Regulatory Reform, 2009); *How Your Business Can Achieve Compliance: Guidance* (Office of Fair Trading, 2010) OFT1278.

19 *Delivering Regulatory Reform: Report by the Comptroller and Auditor General* (National Audit Office, 2011).

20 P Hampton, *Reducing Administrative Burdens: Effective Inspection and Enforcement* (HM Treasury, 2005).

21 R Macrory, *Regulatory Justice: Making Sanctions Effective* (HM Treasury, 2006); reprinted in R Macrory, *Regulation, Enforcement and Governance in Environmental Law* (Hart Publishing, 2010). Implementation was in the Regulatory Enforcement and Sanctions Act 2008. Subsequent codification occurred in the Consumer Rights Act 2015.

22 See the Legislative and Regulatory Reform (Regulatory Functions) Order 2007, SI 2007/3544, which specified various bodies, including 27 national regulatory agencies such as the Civil Aviation Authority, the Environment Agency, the Financial Services Authority, the Food Standards Agency, the Health and Safety Commission, the Health and Safety Executive, the Office of Fair Trading (other than any regulatory function under competition or merger law) and the Pensions Regulator. See subsequent amendments in the Legislative and Regulatory Reform (Regulatory Functions) (Amendment) Order 2009, SI 2009/2981, the Legislative and Regulatory Reform (Regulatory Functions) (Amendment) Order 2010, SI 2010/3028, and the Legislative and Regulatory Reform (Regulatory Functions) (Amendment) Order 2014, SI 2014/860 (adding the Groceries Code Adjudicator, Monitor and the Regulator of Community Interest Companies, and omitting three others). An order may not specify *regulatory* functions in relation to the Gas and Markets Authority, the Office of Communications, the Office of Rail Regulation, the Postal Services Commission and the Water Services Regulatory Authority, since these are specified in primary legislation: Legislative and Regulatory Reform Act 2006, s 24(5).

23 Legislative and Regulatory Reform Act 2006, s 21. The government later claimed that the principles of good regulation were 'a widely accepted definition of best practice': S Vadera, *Government Response to the House of Lords Select Committee on Regulators: Report on UK Economic Regulators* (Department for Business Enterprise & Regulatory Reform, 2008) para 1.2.

24 Regulatory Enforcement and Sanctions Act ss 72, 73(3)–(6).

25 The Regulators' Code 2014. Introduced as the *Regulators' Compliance Code: Statutory Code of Practice for Regulators* (Department for Business Enterprise and Regulatory Reform, 2007), made under s 22(1)of the Legislative and Regulatory Reform Act 2006.

26 Regulators' Code, provisions 1 and 5.

27 Criminal Law Act 2003, s 142.

28 Legal Aid, Sentencing and Punishment of Offenders Act 2012, s 63.

29 Proceeds of Crime Act 2002; Civil Recovery Orders under the Crime and Courts Act 2013, s 266.

30 *Modern Crime Prevention Strategy March 2016* (Home Office).

31 A Braga, AV Papachristos and DM Hureau, 'The Effects of Hot Spots Policing on Crime: An Updated Systematic Review and Meta-analysis' (2012) 31(4) *Justice Quarterly* 633; B Taylor, C Koper and D Woods, 'A Randomized Controlled Trial of

Different Policing Strategies at Hot Spots of Violent Crime' (2011) 7(2) *Journal of Experimental Criminology* 149.

32 ME Wolfgang, 'Delinquency in Two Birth Cohorts' in KT van Dusen and AA Mednick (eds), *Prospective Studies of Crime and Delinquency* (Springer Netherlands, 1983); TE Moffitt, 'Adolescence-Limited and Life-Course Persistent Antisocial Behavior: A Developmental Taxonomy' (1993) 100 *Psychological Review* 674; *Modern Crime Prevention Strategy March 2016* (Home Office) part 3.

33 C Hodges, 'Mass Collective Redress: Consumer ADR and Regulatory Techniques' (2015) 23 *European Review of Private Law* 829.

34 Consumer Rights Act 2015, sch 5.

35 Section 213 of the Enterprise Act 2002 provides for categories of enforcer: general (the Competition and Markets Authority, Trading Standards Services in Great Britain and the Department of Enterprise, Trade and Investment in Northern Ireland); designated (see SI 2003/1399 as amended by SI 2005/917 and SI 2013/478: the Civil Aviation Authority, Director General of Electricity Supply for Northern Ireland, Director General of Gas for Northern Ireland, Ofcom, the Water Services Regulation Authority, the Gas and Electricity Markets Authority, the Information Commissioner, the Office of Road and Rail (ORR), the Consumers' Association and the Financial Conduct Authority); community (a qualified entity for the purposes of the Injunctions Directive EC 98/27); and EU Consumer Protection Cooperation (various bodies designated as national contract points under Regulation (EC) 2006/2004 on Consumer Protection Cooperation).

36 Consumer Rights Act 2015, s 79 and sch 7.

37 *Enhancing Consumer Confidence through Effective Enforcement: Consultation on Consolidating and Modernising Consumer Law Enforcement Powers* (Department for Business Innovation & Skills, March 2012), available at www.bis.gov.uk/assets/biscore/consumer-issues/docs/e/12-543-enhancing-consumer-confidence-effective-enforcement-consultation.pdf.

38 ibid, Foreword by Norman Lamb MP, Minister for Employment Relations, Consumer and Postal Affairs.

39 ibid para 4.

40 See Hodges (n 15) ch 13.

41 *Decision Procedure and Penalties (DEPP) Manual* (Financial Conduct Authority); *OFT's Guidance as to the Appropriate Amount of a Penalty* (Office of Fair Trading, 2012); *Administrative Penalties: Statement of Policy on the CMA's Approach* (Competition & Markets Authority, 2014).

42 Previous policies illustrating former approaches are noted in Hodges (n 15).

43 P Lunn, *Regulatory Policy and Behavioural Economics* (OECD, 2014), 11; *OECD Best Practice Principles for the Governance of Regulators* (OECD, 2013); *Standards of Conduct: Treating Customers Fairly. Findings from the 2014 Challenge Panel* (Ofgem, March 2015); *Food We Can Trust: Regulating the Future* (Food Standards Authority, 2016); *Keeping the Aviation Industry Safe: Safety Intelligence and Safety Wisdom. 16 Aviation Industry Senior Executives Reflect on How They Run a Safe Business in a Commercial Environment. A Future Sky Safety White Paper* (European Commission, 2016).

44 *Corporate Governance and Business Integrity: A Stocktaking of Corporate Practices* (OECD, 2015); *Final Draft: The UK Corporate Governance Code* (Financial Reporting Council, 2016); *Corporate Culture and the Role of Boards: Report of Observations* (Financial Reporting Council, 2016); P Montagnon, *Stakeholder Engagement Values, Business Culture & Society* (Institute of Business Ethics, 2016).

45 P Babiak and RD Hare, *Snakes in Suits: When Psychopaths Go to Work* (HarperCollins, 2006).

46 Costa et al (n 4).

47 F Vibert, *The New Regulatory Space* (Edward Elgar, 2014).

48 N Gunningham and P Grabosky, *Smart Regulation: Designing Environmental Policy* (Oxford University Press, 1998); see also N Gunningham, 'Enforcement and Compliance Strategies' in M Cave, R Baldwin and M Lodge (eds), *The Oxford Handbook of Regulation* (Oxford University Press, 2010).

49 J Black, 'Critical Reflections on Regulation' (2002) 27 *Australian Journal of Legal Philosophy* 1, reprinted in F Haines (ed), *Crime and Regulation* (Ashgate, 2007).

50 C Parker, *The Open Corporation: Effective Self-Regulation and Democracy* (Cambridge University Press, 2002).

51 C Coglianese and D Lazer, 'Management-Based Regulation: Prescribing Private Management to Achieve Public Goals' (2003) 37 *Law & Society Review* 691–730.

52 World Business Council for Sustainable Development *A Vision for Sustainable Consumption: Innovation, Collaboration and the Management of Choice* (2011).

53 A Kleanthous, 'Putting a Price on Value' in C MacFarland (ed), *The Virtue of Enterprise: Responsible Business for a New Economy* (ResPublica, 2013).

54 BJ Richardson, 'Mandating Environmental Liability Insurance' (2001) 12 *Duke Environmental Law and Policy Forum* 293.

55 RH Kraakman, 'Gatekeepers: The Anatomy of a Third-Party Enforcement Strategy' (1986) 2 *Journal of Law, Economics and Organization* 53.

56 DJ Ventry, 'Whistleblowers and Qui Tam for Tax' (2008) 61(2) *Tax Lawyer* 357.

57 M Foucault, *The History of Sexuality: An Introduction*, vol 1 (Random House, 1990) 93.

58 F Cafaggi and H Muir Watt (eds), *The Regulatory Function of European Private Law* (Edward Elgar, 2009).

F Cafaggi, *The Challenge of Transnational Private Regulations: Conceptual and Constitutional Debates* (Wiley-Blackwell 2011); F Cafaggi, 'New Foundations of Transnational Private Regulation' (2011) 38(1) *Journal of Law and Society* 1; F Cafaggi, *Enforcement of Transnational Regulation: Ensuring Compliance in a Global World* (Edward Elgar, 2012); F Cafaggi, 'Transnational Governance by Contract: Private Regulation and Contractual Networks in Food Safety' in J Swinnen, J Wouters, M Maertens and A Marx (eds), *Private Standards and Global Governance: Economic, Legal and Political Perspectives* (Edward Elgar, 2012).

59 H Collins, *Regulating Contracts* (Oxford University Press, 2002).

60 S Peltzman, 'The Effects of FTC Advertising Regulation' (1981) 24 *Journal of Law & Economics* 405; G Jarrell and S Peltzman, 'The Impact of Product Recalls on the Wealth of Sellers' (1985) 93 *Journal of Political Economy* 512; ML Mitchell and MT Maloney, 'Crisis in the Cockpit? The Role of Market Forces in Promoting Air Travel Safety' (1989) 32 *Journal of Law & Economics* 329; JM Karpoff and, JR Lott, Jr, 'The Reputational Penalty Firms Bear from Committing Criminal Fraud' (1993) 36 *Journal of Law & Economics* 757; CR Alexander, 'On the Nature of the Reputational Penalty for Corporate Crime: Evidence' (1999) 42 *Journal of Law & Economics* 489; JM Karpoff, D Scott Lee and GS Martin, 'The Cost to Firms of Cooking the Books' (2008) 43 *Journal of Financial and Quantitative Analysis* 581; J Armour, C Mayer and A Polo, 'Regulatory Sanctions and Reputational Damage in Financial Markets' (2010) Oxford Legal Studies Research Paper No 62/2010.

61 JR Graham, Si Li and Jiaping Qiu, 'Corporate Misreporting and Bank Loan Contracting' (2008) 89 *Journal of Financial Economics* 44.

62 Summarized in S Oded, 'Inducing Corporate Proactive Compliance: Liability Controls & Corporate Monitors' (PhD thesis, Erasmus Universiteit Rotterdam, 2012).

63 N Shover, D Clelland and J Lynxwiler, *Enforcement or Negotiation: Constructing a Regulatory Bureaucracy* (State University of New York Press, 1986).

64 BM Hutter, *Compliance: Regulation and Environment* (Clarendon Press, 1997).

65 JT Scholz, 'Cooperation, Deterrence, and the Ecology of Regulatory Enforcement' (1984) 18 *Law and Society Review* 179; EA Bardach and RA Kagan, *Going by the Book: The Problem of Regulatory Unreasonableness* (Temple University Press, 1982).

66 J Baggs, B Silverstein and M Foley. 'Workplace Health and Safety Regulations: Impact of Enforcement and Consultation on Workers' Compensation Claims Rates in Washington State' (2003) 43(5) *American Journal of Industrial Medicine* 483.

67 R Baldwin and M Cave, *Understanding Regulation: Theory, Strategy, and Practice* (Oxford University Press, 1999); SP Huntington, 'The Marasmus of the ICC: The Commission, the Railroads, and the Public Interest' (1952) 61(4) *Yale Law Journal* 467; GJ Stigler, 'The Theory of Economic Regulation' (1971) 3 *Bell Journal of Economics and Management Science* 3; ME Levine and JL Forrence, 'Regulatory Capture, Public Interest, and the Public Agenda: Toward a Synthesis' (1990) 6(1) *Journal of Law, Economics, & Organization* 167; J-J Laffont and J Tirole, 'The Politics of Government Decision-Making: A Theory of Regulatory Capture' (1991) 106(4) *Quarterly Journal of Economics* 1089; PJ May and S Winter, 'Regulatory Enforcement and Compliance: Examining Danish Agro-environmental Policy' (1999) 18(4) *Journal of Political Analysis and Management* 625.

68 *Striking the Balance: Upholding the Seven Principles of Public Life in Regulation* (Committee on Standards in Public Life, 2016).

69 *Regulatory Futures Review* (Cabinet Office, 2017), https://www.gov.uk/government/uploads/system/uploads/attachment_data/file/582283/Regulatory_Futures_Review.pdf.

70 Deregulation Act 2015, s 108.

71 *Growth Duty: Statutory Guidance. Statutory Guidance under Section 110(6) of the Deregulation Act 2015* (Department for Business, Energy & Industrial Strategy, 2017) para 2.2.

72 ibid para 3.3.

73 P Kurer, *Legal and Compliance Risk: A Strategic Response to a Rising Threat for Global Business* (Oxford University Press, 2015).

74 *Smarter Regulation: Strengthening the UK Economy with Fit for Purpose Regulation of Our Financial Services* (CBI, 2016).

11. Ethical Business Regulation

1 *Report of a Senior Practitioners' Workshop on Identifying Indicators of Corporate Culture* (International Corporate Governance Network, IBE, Institute of Chartered Secretaries and Administrators, 17 December 2015).

2 House of Commons' Business, Energy and Industrial Strategy Committee, *Corporate Governance*. Third Report of Session 2016–17, HC 702.

3 JR Graham, CR Harvey, J Popadak and S Rajgopal, 'Corporate Culture: Evidence from the Field', https://papers.ssrn.com/sol3/papers.cfm?abstract_id=2805602.

4 *Corporate Culture and the Role of Boards: Report of Observations* (Financial Reporting Council, 2016).

5 The primary authority scheme was created under the Regulatory Enforcement and Sanctions Act 2008 and was amended by s 67 of the Enterprise and Regulatory Reform Act 2013. It commenced on 6 April 2009 under the Regulatory Enforcement and Sanctions Act 2008 (Commencement No 1) Order 2008, SI 2371/2008. The primary focus is on provision of advice and guidance to businesses. Inspection plans may also be developed by the primary authority, which is required to consult the business, and the plan takes effect after it has been approved by the Better Regulation Delivery Office, under ss 67 and 68 of the Enterprise and Regulatory Reform Act 2013. Trade associations can provide assistance to their members, thereby playing significant self-regulatory roles in the architecture of the scheme: see the Enterprise Bill.

6 *OECD Best Practice Principles for the Governance of Regulators* (OECD, 2013).

7 *Corporate Plan June 2015–March 2018* (Revenue Scotland) 9.

8 Recent examples include the Food Standards Agency's 'Food We Can Trust' initiative, which includes the principle that 'Businesses doing the right thing for consumers should be recognised; action will be taken against those that do not'; and Ofgem's emphasis on a culture of treating customers fairly. See *Consultation: The Future of Retail Market Regulation* (Ofgem, 2015).

9 *The Anderson Review of Government Guidance on Regulation: Business Perspectives of Government Guidance. Research Study Conducted for Department for Business, Enterprise and Regulatory Reform. Final Report* (Ipsos MORI, 2008).

12. Developing Examples of Ethical Regulation

1 *Civil Aviation Authority Regulatory Enforcement Policy* (Civil Aviation Authority, October 2012).

2 *Regulation and Growth* (BRDO, 2016), https://view.pagetiger.com/Regulation-and-Growth/Spring-2016.

3 Enterprise Act 2016, s 20 and sch 3.

4 *Primary Authority Changes 2017: Unlocking the Potential* (Regulatory Delivery, 2017).

5 *What You Can Expect of Regulatory Delivery* (Department for Business, Energy & Industrial Strategy, Regulatory Delivery, 2017), www.gov.uk/government/uploads/system/uploads/attachment_data/file/605699/rd-service-standards.pdf.

6 R Freeman, *Strategic Management: A Stakeholder Approach* (MIT Press, 1994).

7 J Rowe and R Enticott, 'Evaluating the Links between Locality and Environmental Performance of SMEs: Some Observations from Survey and Partnership Programmes in the Greater Bristol Area' (1998) 5(3) *Eco-Management and Auditing* 112; D Williamson and G Lynch-Wood, 'A New Paradigm for SME Environmental Practice' (2001) 13(6) *International Journal of Total Quality Management* 424; G Lynch-Wood and D Williamson, 'The Social Licence as a Form of Regulation for Small and Medium Enterprises' (2007) 34(3) *Journal of Law and Society* 321.

8 D Williamson, G Lynch-Wood and J Ramsey, 'Drivers of Environmental Behaviour in Manufacturing SMEs and the Implications for CSR' (2006) 67 *Journal of Business Ethics* 317; R Lewicki, D Saunders and J Minton, *Negotiation* (McGraw-Hill, 1999).

9 H Croall, 'Combating Financial Crime: Regulatory versus Crime Control Approaches' (2003) 11 *Journal of Financial Crime* 45, reprinted in F Haines (ed), *Crime and Regulation* (Ashgate, 2007).

10 *Food We Can Trust: Regulating the Future* (FSA, 2016).

11 See www.food.gov.uk/enforcement/regulation/regulating-our-future.

12 'Regulating Our Future Audit Data Research Published', press release, Food Standards Agency, 2017; Y Robinson and D Thomson, *Report on the Regulating Our Future Pilot to Test the Consistency between Local Authority Interventions and First and Second Party Audit Processes* (Bristol City Council, Food Standards Agency, Mitchells & Butlers, NSF, 2017); F Kirby and Y Robinson, *Report on Pilot Study: Sharing of Industry Audit Data to Inform the Local Authority Interventions* (Food Standards Agency and Tesco, 2017).

13 'Latest Figures Reveal Decline in Cases of Campylobacter', press release, Food Standards Agency, 14 March 2017. The trend continued: 'Survey Shows Further Reduction in Levels of Campylobacter in Chicken', press release, Food Standards Agency, 14 June 2017.

14 *Leading Health and Safety at Work: Leadership actions for Directors and Board Members* (Institute of Directors and HSE, 2011), www.hse.gov.uk/pubns/indg417.pdf.

15 C Lekka, *A Review of the Literature on Effective Leadership Behaviours for Safety* (Health & Safety Executive, 2012), Research Report 952.

16 This is from Ruth Steinholtz's personal experience.

17 See *Consultation: The Future of Retail Market Regulation* (Ofgem, 2015).

18 *Forward Work Programme 2017–18* (Ofgem, 2017).

19 *Allocation of Voluntary Redress Payments in the Context of Enforcement Cases* (Ofgem, June 2016), figure on p 12.

20 *Enforcement Overview 2014/15* (Ofgem, 2015). See M Canto-Lopez, 'Ofgem's Recent Trends in Enforcement: Settlements, Redress and the Consumer's Interest' (2016) 21(2) *Utilities Law Review* 66.

21 *Meat and Poultry Processing Inquiry Review: Report of the Findings and Recommendations* (Equality and Human Rights Commission, 2012).

22 *Innovation and Collaboration: Future Proofing the Water Industry for Customers. Methodology for the Strategic Review of Charges 2021–2027* (WICS, 2017), www.watercommission.co.uk/UserFiles/Documents/SRC21_Innovation%20and%20Collaboration_Methodology_WICS_amended.pdf.

23 This section has kindly been contributed by Laura McGlynn of the Scottish government.

24 See https://press.which.co.uk/whichpressreleases/scottish-cities-top-the-table-for-nuisance-calls.

25 *The Bribery Act 2010. Guidance about Procedures which Relevant Commercial Organisations Can Put in Place to Prevent Persons Associated with Them from Bribing (Section 9 of the Bribery Act 2010)* (Ministry of Justice, 2011).

26 *Brief Factual Summary of the Public Consultation on Enforcement and Compliance* (European Commission, 30 January 2017).

27 J Luyendijk, *Swimming with Sharks: Inside the World of the Bankers* (Guardian Books, 2015) 175.

28 *Report of the Inquiry into the Supervision of the Bank of Credit and Commerce International* (2991) HC 192.

29 Strong criticism of the Bank of England was made in *A New Approach to Regulating and Developing Singapore's Financial Sector* (Monetary Authority of Singapore, 1997); Board of Banking Supervision, *Report of the Board of Banking Supervision Inquiry into the Circumstances of the Collapse of Barings* (Bank of England, 1995).

30 The Equitable Life Payments Scheme and various progress reports, at www.gov.uk/government/collections/equitable-life-payment-scheme-documents; *Administering the Equitable Life Payment Scheme* (NAO, April 2013).

31 N Moloney, 'The Legacy Effects of the Financial Crisis on Regulatory Design in the EU' in E Ferran, N Moloney, JG Hill and JC Coffee, Jr, *The Aftermath of the Global Financial Crisis* (Cambridge University Press, 2012). See *Guidance Consultation. Assessing Suitability* (FSA, 2011), which outlines failures to assess the risks that consumers are prepared to sustain.

32 J Black and R Nobles, 'Personal Pensions Misselling: The Causes and Lessons of Regulatory Failure' (1998) *Modern Law Review* 789.

33 P McConnell and K Blacker, 'Systemic Operational Risk: The UK Payment Protection Insurance Scandal' (2012) 7 *Journal of Operational Risk* 79; E Ferran, 'Regulatory Lessons from the Payment Protection Insurance Mis-selling Scandal on the UK' (2012) 13 *European Business Organization Law Review* 247. See recently *Finalised Guidance. Payment Protection Products. FSA/OFT Joint Guidance* (FSA/OFT, 2013), FG13/02/OFT1474; *Payment Protection Insurance Customer Contact Letters (PPI CCLs)—Fairness, Clarity and Potential Consequences: Guidance Consultation* (FSA, March 2012); 'Press Release: Commitment to Help Consumers Agreed at PPI Summit', BBA, 23 April 2012; 'Treasury Committee Publishes Correspondence with FSA and FOS on Mis-selling', House of Commons Select Committees, 23 May 2012; *Payment Protection Insurance Customer Contact Letters (PPI CCLs)—Fairness, Clarity and Potential Consequences* (FG12/17: FSA, July 2012); *PPI Complaint Handling—FSA Fine*, 4 January 2013; *Assessing the Quality of Investment Advice in the Retail Banking Sector. A Mystery Shopping Review* (FSA, February 2013); *TR13/7— Payment Protection Insurance Complaints: Report on the Fairness of Medium-Sized Firms' Decisions and Redress* (FCA, August 2013); 'Rogue PPI Claim Companies Targeted by Fines and Toughened Regulations', Ministry of Justice, 21 November 2013; *Financial Services Mis-selling: Regulation and Redress: Forty-First Report of Session 2015–16* (HC Paper No 847: House of Commons Committee of Public Accounts, May 2016).

34 J Gray, 'The Legislative Basis of Systematic Review and Compensation for the Mis-selling of Retail Financial Services and Products' (2004) 25 *Statute Law Review* 196; *Dealing Fairly with Interest-Only Mortgage Customers Who Risk Being Unable to Repay Their Loan* (Financial Conduct Authority, May 2013.

35 *Consumer Market Study on Advice within the Area of Retail Investment Services-Final Report* (Synovate Ltd, 2011).

36 *Interest Rate Hedging Products: Pilot Findings* (FSA, 31 January 2013); letter from Clive Adamson to anonymous banks on Interest Rate Hedging Products Review and associated agreements, 29 January 2013, available at www.parliament.uk/business/committees/committees-a-z/commons-select/treasury-committee/news/treasury-committee-publishes-agreement-between-fca-and-banks-on-irhp-review/.

37 S Miller, 'The Libor Scandal: Culture, Corruption and Collective Action Problems in the Global Banking Sector' in J O'Brien and G Gilligan (eds), *Integrity, Risk and Accountability in Capital Markets. Regulating Culture* (Hart Publishing, 2013) (referring to institutional corruption). See *LIBOR, Public Inquiries and FSA Disciplinary Powers* (House of Commons Library, SN/BT/6376, July 2012); *The Wheatley Review of LIBOR: Initial Discussion Paper* (HM Treasury, August 2012); *Fixing LIBOR: Some Preliminary Findings* (House of Commons Treasury Select Committee—HC 481-I, August 2012), Volume I: Report, together with formal minutes and Volume II: Oral evidence; *The Wheatley Review of LIBOR: Final Report* (Martin Wheatley, September 2012); *Wheatley Review of LIBOR—Written Ministerial Statement* (HM Treasury, October 2012); *LIBOR, Public Inquiries and FSA Disciplinary Powers—Commons Library Note* (SN/BT/6376: House of Commons Library, November 2012); *Internal Audit Report: A Review of the Extent of Awareness within the FSA of Inappropriate LIBOR Submissions* (FSA, March 2013); 'LIBOR Becomes a Regulated Activity', press release, BBA, 2 April 2013.

38 *The Salz Review of Barclays' Business Practices Report to the Board of Barclays plc* (April 2013)

39 *Independent Lending Review. Terms of Reference* (RBS, 2013); Sir A Large and Oliver Wyman, *Independent Lending Review* (25 November 2013); 'Press Release: RBS to Act on SME Lending Review Findings', 1 November 2013; L Tomlinson, *Banks' Lending Practices: Treatment of Businesses in Distress* (December 2013).

40 *Final Notice to Lloyds TSB Bank plc and Bank of Scotland plc, 10 December 2013* (FCA), www.fca.org.uk/static/documents/final-notices/lloyds-tsb-bank-and-bank-of-scotland.pdf.

41 *Eurobarometer 74, Autumn 2010, Europeans, the EU and the Crisis* (European Commission, 2010).

42 ST Omarova, 'Wall Street as a Community of Fate: Toward Financial Industry Self-Regulation' (2011) 159(2) *University of Pennsylvania Law Review* 411.

43 JV Rees, *Hostages of Each Other: The Transformation of Nuclear Safety since Three Mile Island* (University of Chicago Press, 1994); JV Rees, 'Development of Communitarian Regulation in the Chemical Industry' (1997) 19 *Law & Policy* 477.

44 See *Report on The Lord Mayor's Conference on Trust and Values*, November 2011; *Investing in Integrity. The Lord Mayor's Conference on Trust and Values*, City Values Forum, October 2012; *Toward Effective Governance of Financial Institutions* (G30, 2012); *A New Paradigm: Financial Institution Boards and Supervisors* (G30, 2013); *The FCA's Approach to Advancing its Objectives* (FCA, 2013); *The Salz Review* (n 38); *Report of the Collective Engagement Working Group* (Collective Engagement Working Group, 2013); *A Report on the Culture of British Retail Banking* (New City Agenda and Cass Business School, 2014).

45 C Mayer, *Firm Commitment: Why the Corporation is Failing Us and How to Restore Trust in it* (Oxford University Press, 2013); N Morris and D Vines (eds), *Capital Failure: Rebuilding Trust in Financial Services* (Oxford University Press, 2014); F Vibert, *The New Regulatory Space* (Edward Elgar, 2014).

46 *Financial Services Mis-selling* (n 33).

47 *The FCA's Approach to Advancing its Objectives* (FCA, July 2013).

48 C Adamson, 'The Importance of Culture in Driving Behaviours of Firms and How the FCA Will Assess This', speech by Director of Supervision at the CFA Society UK Professionalism Conference, 19 April 2013, www.fca.org.uk/news/regulation-professionalism.

49 *The Salz Review* (n 38) para 2.4.
50 ibid paras 2.5 and 2.7.
51 ibid para 2.13.
52 ibid para 2.21.
53 ibid para 2.25.
54 ibid para 2.32.
55 ibid para 2.34.
56 J Black, 'Seeing, Knowing, and Regulating Financial Markets: Moving the Cognitive Framework from the Economic to the Social', LSE Legal Studies Working Paper No 24/2013.
57 *Report of the Collective Engagement Working Group* (Collective Engagement Working Group, December 2013), available at www.investmentuk.org/assets/files/press/2013/20131203-cewginvestorforum.pdf.
58 *A Report on the Culture of British Retail Banking* (New City Agenda and Cass Business School, 2014). The founders of New City Agenda were Lord McFall of Alcluith, David Davis MP and Lord Sharkey.
59 Andrew Bailey, Deputy Governor, Prudential Regulation, Bank of England and Chief Executive Officer, Prudential Regulatory Authority, 'Culture in Financial Services—A Regulator's Perspective', speech at City Week Conference, 9 May 2016.
60 *Changing Banking for Good: Report of the Parliamentary Commission on Banking Standards: Volume I: Summary, and Conclusions and Recommendations HC Paper No.27-I, II* Parliamentary Commission on Banking Standards, June 2013; *Government Response to Parliamentary Commission on Banking Standards* (HM Treasury and Department for Business Innovation & Skills, 2013), Cm 8661; *Banking Reform: A New Structure for Stability and Growth* (HM Treasury and Department for Business, Innovation and Skills, 2013); *Bank of England Response to the Final Report of the Parliamentary Commission on Banking Standards* (Bank of England, 2013); *The FCA's Response to the Parliamentary Commission on Banking Standards* (FCA, 2013).
61 ibid para 1.3.
62 Senior persons are required to formally accept a written Statement of Responsibilities that sets out their role. This will allow deposit-taking institutions and regulators to ensure that a named individual is accountable for each key risk in their businesses, and will help regulators hold these individuals to account in the event of failure. Senior persons are pre-approved by regulators before taking up a new post. Approvals may be subject to conditions, for example, where it is felt that individuals need to acquire a specific skill to carry out the job well. The Senior Persons Regime only includes the most senior individuals within deposit-taking institutions. The previously existing Approved Persons Regime continues to apply to all non-deposit-taking entities. Individuals holding posts that oversee both deposit-taking and non-deposit-taking institutions within a banking group may be subject to both the new Senior Persons Regime and the Approved Persons Regime. Sections 59 (functions for which approval is required), 59ZA (senior management functions), 60 (statements of responsibilities) and 60A (vetting of relevant authorised persons) of the Financial Services and Markets Act 2000, introduced by the Financial Services (Banking Reform) Act 2013. New 'threshold conditions' for persons: Financial Services and Markets Act (Threshold Conditions) Order 2013/555. See *Regulatory Reform: the PRA and FCA Regimes for Approved Persons* (FSA, October 2012), CP12/2.

63 Introduced in s 36 of the Financial Services (Banking Reform) Act 2013 as taking, or agreeing to the taking of, a decision as the way in which the business is to be carried on, or failing to take steps that could prevent such a decision, while being aware of a risk that the implementation of the decision may cause the failure of the group institution, such conduct falling far below what could reasonably be expected of a person in that position, and implementation of the decision causes the failure of the institution.

64 *The FCA's Approach to Advancing its Objectives* (n 47); *The FCA's Response to the Parliamentary Commission on Banking Standards* (n 60). The latter referred to enforcement against individuals as 'cutting through the 'accountability firewall' and imposing tough penalties': para 6. See also *Consultation Paper. Strengthening Accountability in Banking: A New Regulatory Framework for Individuals* (PRA and FCA, 2014), FCA CP14/13 PRA CP 14/14.

65 Speech, Tracey McDermott, acting chief executive, FCA, 7 June 2016.

66 *Sanctioning the Directors of Failed Banks. Response to Consultation* (Law Society, 2012).

67 Meeting of the Law and Ethics in Finance Project, Bank of England, 20 January 2015.

68 K Ahmed, 'UBS Rogue Trader: "It Could Happen Again"' *BBC*, 1 August 2016.

69 Luyendijk (n 27).

70 C Hodges, 'Mass Collective Redress: Consumer ADR and Regulatory Techniques' (2015) 23 *European Review of Private Law* 829; C Hodges, *Law and Corporate Behaviour: Integrating Theories of Regulation, Enforcement, Compliance, Culture and Ethics* (Hart Publishing, 2015) 274–301; R Money-Kyrle, 'Collective Enforcement of Consumer Rights in the United Kingdom' in Martin Schmidt-Kessel, Christoph Strünck and Malte Kramme (eds), *Im Namen der Verbraucher? Kollektive Rechtsdurchsetzung in Europa* (Schriften zu Verbraucherrecht und Verbraucherwissenschaften, Band 5 Jenaer Wissenschaftliche Verlagsgesellschaft, 2015).

71 *Financial Services Mis-selling: Regulation and Redress* (National Audit Office, 2016), HC Paper No 851. The figure excludes an interest rate hedging products scheme and other schemes which were established in 2013.

72 *Annual Review 2016–2017* (Banking Standards Board, 2017).

73 M Shafik, 'From "Ethical Drift" to "Ethical Lift": Reversing the Tide of Misconduct in Global Financial Markets', Bank of England, 2016, available at www.bankofengland.co.uk/publications/Documents/speeches/2016/speech930.pdf.

74 This is the critical problem with both the Senior Managers Regime and the Central Bank of the Netherlands' approach of requiring an appropriate culture to exist in banks by inspecting boards: *Supervision of Behaviour and Culture: Foundations, Practice & Future Development* (DeNederloandscheBank, 2015).

75 *Regulatory Sandbox* (Financial Conduct Authority, 2015); *Industry Sandbox. Sandbox Consultation. Finding Preview* (Innovate Finance, 2017); 'Financial Conduct Authority Provides Update on Regulatory Sandbox', press release, Financial Conduct Authority, 16 June 2017.

76 *Supervision of Behaviour and Culture* (n 74).

77 *Credit Card Market Study: Final Findings Report* (FCA, 2016), MS14/6.3.

78 *Annual Business Plan 2017–18* (FCA, 2017) 72.

79 *FX Global Code* (Bank of International Settlements, 2017), available at www.globalfxc.org/docs/fx_global.pdf.

80 From 1 January 2016 to 31 July 2016, the Environment Agency oversaw payment of £403,000 to environment charities by 10 businesses voluntarily and 7 after discussion with the Agency in the shadow of its powers under the Environmental Civil Sanctions (England) Order 2010: 'Enforcement Undertakings Accepted by the Environment Agency', Environment Agency, 2016.

81 *Annual Review 2015/2016* (Banking Standards Board, 2016).

82 M Sparro, *The Regulatory Craft: Controlling Risks, Solving Problems, and Managing Compliance* (Brookings Institution Press, 2000); K Yeung, *Securing Compliance: A Principled Approach* (Hart Publishing, 2004); WPJ Wils, *Principles of European Antitrust Enforcement* (Hart Publishing, 2005); B Morgan and K Yeung, *An Introduction to Law and Regulation* (Cambridge University Press, 2007).

83 *OECD Guidelines for Multinational Enterprises*, 2011 edn, para 7.

84 C Hodges, *Ethical Business Regulation: Understanding the Evidence* (Department for Business Innovation and Skills, 2016).

85 *Opportunity Now: Europe's Mission to Innovate* (European Commission, 2016).

86 Competition and Consumer Policy, *Delivering Better Outcomes for Consumers and Businesses in Scotland* (Scottish Government, 15 December 2016), www.gov.scot/Publications/2016/12/5688; *Report of the Working Group on Consumer and Competition Policy for Scotland: Scottish Government Response* (Scottish Government, 2016) 16.

87 *Draft Manual on Consumer Protection* (UNCTAD, 2016) ch 6.

88 *Striking the Balance: Upholding the Seven Principles of Public Life in Regulation* (Committee on Standards in Public Life, 2016) 62, 69–70. The associated annex is available at https://www.gov.uk/government/uploads/system/uploads/attachment_data/file/550542/Prof_Christopher_Hodges_-_Ethics_for_regulators.pdf.

89 *Regulatory Futures Review* (Cabinet Office, 2017), https://www.gov.uk/government/uploads/system/uploads/attachment_data/file/582283/Regulatory_Futures_Review.pdf.

90 Hodges (n 70); Hodges (n 84); *Striking the Balance* (Committee on Standards in Public Life, 2016) Annex.

13. The Cultural and Leadership Framework for Ethical Business Practice in Organisations

1 Warren Buffett, letter to shareholders, Annual Report, Berkshire Hathaway, 2010.

2 LV Gerstner Jr, *Who Says Elephants Can't Dance?: Inside IBM's Historic Turnaround* (HarperCollins, 2002).

3 P-O Karlsson, D Aguirre and K Rivera, 'Are CEOs Less Ethical Than in the Past?' (2017) 87 *Strategy & Leadership*.

4 JR Graham, CR Harvey, J Popadak and S Rajgopal, 'Corporate Culture: Evidence from the Field', https://papers.ssrn.com/sol3/papers.cfm?abstract_id=2805602.

5 C O'Reilly and J Chatman, 'Culture as a Social Control: Corporations, Cults and Commitment' in B Staw and L Cummings (eds), *Research in Organizational Behavior* (JAI Press, 1996).

6 Graham et al (n 4) 5.

7 E Schein, *Organizational Culture and Leadership* (Jossey-Bass, 1985).
8 JP Kotter and JL Heskett, *Corporate Culture and Performance* (Free Press, 1992) 4.
9 ibid.
10 R Barrett, *The Values-Driven Organization* (Routledge, 2014) 11.
11 R Barrett, *The Values-Driven Organization: Cultural Health and Employee Well-Being as a Pathway to Sustainable Performance*, 2nd edn (Routledge, 2017) 32.
12 M Parker, *Organizational Culture and Identity* (Sage, 2000) 231.
13 E Jacques, *The Changing Culture of a Factory* (Tavistock, 1951) 251.
14 M Parker, *Organizational Culture and Identity* (Sage, 2000) 220, 231.
15 L Hoecklin, *Managing Cultural Differences: Strategies for Competitive Advantage* (Wokingham, Addison-Wesley, 1995) 4 (rather than embracing a standardised way of behaving, the company's French, German and British managers 'had values and behaviours more French, more German and more British than those of their compatriots working for local, domestic companies').
16 J Shipton, 'Integrity in Financial Markets—Challenges from Asia', Speech to the FCA International Regulators' Seminar, London, 24 November 2014.
17 S Mandis, *What Happened to Goldman Sachs: An Insider's Story of Organizational Drift and its Unintended Consequences* (Harvard Business Review Press, 2013).
18 Schein (n 7) 14.
19 ibid.
20 Kotter and Heskett (n 8) 11.
21 Graham et al (n 4) 6.
22 ibid.
23 ibid 9.
24 ibid 22.
25 ibid 23.
26 ibid 30.
27 P Drucker, *The Practice of Management* (Butterworth Heinemann, 1954).
28 W Edwards Deeming, *The New Economics for Industry, Government, Education*, 2nd edn (MIT Press, 2000).
29 M Parker, *Organizational Culture and Identity* (Sage, 2000) 226.
30 See www.valuescentre.com.
31 Barrett (n 11) 16.
32 ER Lawrence and KM Kacmar, 'Exploring the Impact of Job Insecurity on Employees' Unethical Behavior' (2017) 27(1) *Business Ethics Quarterly* 39.
33 *Management of Risk in Government. A Framework for Boards and Examples of What Has Worked in Practice: A Non-executives' Review*, 2017.
34 R Barrett, 'Building a Winning Organisational Culture', www.valuescentre.com/sites/default/files/uploads/article_building_a_winning_organizational_culture.pdf.
35 J Collins and JI Porras, *Built to Last: Successful Habits of Visionary Companies*, 12th edn (HarperCollins, 2005).
36 ibid xxii.
37 Barrett (n 11) 32.
38 K Evans, *'Using the Gift of Complaints': A Review of Concerns (Complaints) Handling in NHS Wales* (Welsh Government, 2014).
39 Collins and Porras (n 35) xix.
40 Barrett (n 11).

41 W Buffett and D Clark, *Warren Buffett's Management Secrets: Proven Tools for Personal and Business Success* (Simon & Schuster, 2009).
42 www.groucho-marx.com. Quoted in LS Paine, *Value Shift: Why Companies Must Merge Social and Financial Imperatives to Achieve Superior Performance* (McGraw-Hill, 2003) 284.
43 J Kay, *Obliquity* (Profile Books, 2010) 174.
44 *IBE Response to Corporate Governance Consultation* (IBE, 2017).
45 Collins and Porras (n 35) 47. The authors cite a number of company credos and ideologies, such as that of Johnson & Johnson (at 59–71).
46 Kay (n 43) 154.
47 A study in 1982 found that only 18 out of 80 companies had clearly articulated sets of qualitative (non-financial) beliefs: T Deal and A Kennedy, *Corporate Cultures: The Rites and Rituals of Corporate Life* (Addison-Wesley, 1982).
48 J Mackey and R Sisoda, *Conscious Capitalism: Liberating the Heroic Spirit of Business* (Harvard Business Review Press, 2014), 47
49 F Laloux, *Reinventing Organizations: A Guide to Creating Organizations Inspired by the Next Stage of Human Consciousness* (Nelson Parker, 2014).
50 JS Mill, inaugural address to the University of St Andrews, 1867.
51 Buffett (n 1).
52 D Gentilin, *The Origins of Ethical Failures: Lessons for Leaders* (Routledge, 2016), quoting DM Mayer, S Nurmohamed, LK Treviño, DL Shapiro and M Schminke, 'Encourage Employees to Report Unethical Conduct Internally: It Takes a Village' (2013) 121 *Organizational Behavior and Human Decision Processes* 89.
53 S Killingsworth, 'Modeling the Message: Communicating Compliance through Organizational Values and Culture' (2012) 25 *Georgetown Journal of Legal Ethics* 961.
54 B Rayton, T Dodge and G D'Analeze, *Employee Engagement Task Force: 'Nailing the Evidence' Workgroup* (Bath, University of Bath School of Management, 2012).
55 *Compliance and Ethics Leadership Roundtable, 2007.* Corporate Executive Board research; M Griffin and T Davis, *Corporate Executive Board Research Alert, Sourcing Competitive Advantage from Organizational Integrity: The Hidden Cost of Misconduct*; Ethics Resource Center, *National Business Ethics Survey*, 2 (2007), www.ethics.org/resource/2007-national-business-ethics-survey.
56 M Bovens, *The Quest for Responsibility: Accountability and Citizenship in Complex Organizations* (Cambridge University Press, 1998).
57 Business Ethics Briefing, *Ethics Ambassadors: Promoting Ethics on the Front Line* (IBE, April 2017) Issue 57.
58 J Elkington and S Fennel, 'Partners for Sustainability' in J Bendell (ed), *Terms for Endearment: Business, NGOs and Sustainable Development* (Greenleaf Books, 2000); CL Hartman and ER Stafford, 'Green Alliances: Building New Business with Environmental Groups' (1997) 30(2) *Long Range Planning* 184; JW Selsky and B Parker, 'Cross-sector Partnerships to Address Social Issues: Challenges to Theory and Practice' (2005) 31(6) *Journal of Management* 1; J Alexander, 'Cultivating Character: The Challenge of Business Ethics Education' in J Buckingham and V Nilakant (eds), *Managing Responsibly: Alternative Approaches to Corporate Management and Governance* (Gower, 2012).
59 AL George, *Presidential Decision Making in Foreign Policy: The Effective Use of Information and Advice* (Westview, 1980) 191–208; J Habermas, 'Political Communication

in Media Society: Does Democracy Still Enjoy an Epistemic Dimension? The Impact of Normative Theory on Empirical Research' (2006) 16 *Communication Theory* 411.

60 IL Janis, *Groupthink*, 2nd edn (Wadsworth, 1982).

61 J Dryzek, *Deliberative Democracy and Beyond: Liberals, Critics, Contestations* (Oxford University Press, 2000); HS Richardson, *Democratic Autonomy: Public Reasoning about the Ends of Policy* (Oxford University Press, 2002).

62 *Corporate Culture and the Role of Boards: Report of Observations* (Financial Reporting Council, 2016).

63 D Kipnis, 'Does Power Corrupt?' (1972) 24(1) *Journal of Personality and Social Psychology* 33.

64 AD Galinsky, DH Gruenfeld and JC Magee, 'From Power to Action' (2003) 85(3) *Journal of Personality and Social Psychology* 453.

65 I Martin, *Making it Happen: Fred Goodwin, RBS and the Men Who Blew up the British Economy* (Simon & Schuster, 2013).

66 J Ewing, *Faster, Higher, Farther: The Inside Story of the Volkswagen Scandal* (Bantam Press, 2017).

67 ibid ch 22.

68 J Collins, *Good to Great* (Harper Business, 2001).

69 N Gold, 'Trustworthiness and Motivations' in N Morris and D Vines (eds), *Capital Failure; Rebuilding Trust in Financial Services* (Oxford, Oxford University Press, 2014).

70 M Bacharach, G Guerra and DJ Zizzo, 'The Self-Fulfilling Property of Trust: An Experimental Study' (2007) 63(4) *Theory and Decision* 349.

71 P-O Karlsson, D Aguirre and K Rivera, 'Are CEOs Less Ethical Than in the Past?' (2017) 87 *Strategy & Leadership*, at www.strategy-business.com/feature/Are-CEOs-Less-Ethical-Than-in-the-Past?gko=50774.

72 R Sisodia, J Sheth and D Wolfe, *Firms of Endearment: How World-Class Companies Profit from Passion and Purpose*, 2nd edn (Pearson Education, 2014).

73 JA Autry, *Love and Profit: The Art of Caring Leadership* (Avon Books, 1991).

74 Sisodia et al (n 72) 9–10.

75 See also *Developments in Corporate Governance and Stewardship 2015* (FRC, January 2016).

76 *Corporate Culture and the Role of Boards: Report of Observations* (FRC, 2016) 52.

77 Companies Act 2006, s 172.

78 P Montagnon, *Stakeholder Engagement Values, Business Culture and Society* (Institute of Business Ethics, 2016).

79 *Building Relationships with the Local Community* (Association of Convenience Stores, 2016).

80 *OECD Foreign Bribery Report: An Analysis of the Crime of Bribery of Foreign Public Officials* (OECD, 2014).

81 M Heffernan, *Wilful Blindness: Why We Ignore the Obvious at Our Peril* (Walker Publishing Company, 2011).

82 I Larkin and L Pierce, 'Compensation and Employee Misconduct: The Inseparability of Productive and Counterproductive Behaviour in Firms' in D Palmer, K Smith-Crowe and R Greenwood (eds), *Organizational Wrongdoing: Key Perspectives and New Directions* (Cambridge University Press, 2016) 270.

83 R Steinholtz with N Dando, *Performance Management for an Ethical Culture, Good Practice Guide* (Institute of Business Ethics, 2014).

84 G Jacobs, FD Belshak and DN Den Hartog, '(Un)Ethical Behavior and Performance Appraisal: The Role of Affect, Support, and Organizational Justice' (2014) 121 *Journal of Business Ethics* 63.

85 This refers to Wells Fargo's goal of having customers sign up for eight products per household: see MP Regan, 'Eight Rhymes with Separate for Wells Fargo' *Bloomberg Gadfly*, 20 September 2016, www.bloomberg.com/gadfly/articles/2016-09-20/eight-rhymes-with-separate-for-critics-of-wells-fargo.

86 Gentilin (n 52).

87 D Ariely, U Gneezy, G Lowenstein and N Mazar, 'Large Stakes and Big Mistakes' (2009) 76(2) *Review of Economic Studies* 451; DH Pink, *Drive: The Surprising Truth about What Motivates Us* (Riverhead Books, 2009).

88 T Noe and HP Young, 'The Limits to Compensation in the Financial Services Sector' in Morris and Vines (n 69).

89 M Dorff, *Indispensable and Other Myths: Why the CEO Pay Experiment Failed and How to Fix it* (University of California Press, 2014).

90 JC Coffee, Jr, 'Understanding Enron: It's the Gatekeepers, Stupid' (2002) 57 *Business Lawyer* 1403; JC Coffee, Jr, *Gatekeepers: The Professions and Corporate Governance* (Oxford University Press, 2004).

91 See, eg, S Bhagat, BJ Bolton and R Romano, 'Getting Incentives Right: Is Deferred Bank Executive Compensation Sufficient?', European Corporate Governance Institute (ECGI)—Law Working Paper No 241/2014 Yale Law & Economics Research Paper No 489, which argues retaining equity-based incentive pay, reforming bank capital structure to reduce the probability of a tail event, and the mandatory issuance of contingent convertible capital debt that converts to equity under specified adverse states of the world.

92 E Pikulina, L Renneboog, J Ter Horst and P Tobler, 'Bonus Schemes and Trading Activity' TILEC Discussion Paper No 2013-007.

93 J-M Hitz and S Müller-Bloch, 'Market Reactions to the Regulation of Executive Compensation', http://papers.ssrn.com/sol3/papers.cfm?abstract_id=2434580, which reports weak evidence of an average negative reaction to proposed legislation in Germany, and negative stock price reactions on the most exposed firms.

94 V Cable, 'Responsible Capitalism', speech to National Association of Pension Funds, November 2012.

95 'Peter Mandelson Gets Nervous about People Getting "Filthy Rich"' *The Guardian*, 26 January 2012.

96 Montagnon (n 78).

97 *Performance-Related Pay: What Does Business Think?* (High Pay Centre, 2014).

98 *The Power and Pitfalls of Executive Reward: A Behavioural Perspective* (Chartered Institute of Personnel and Development, 2015).

99 Cable (n 94).

100 SA Bank, BR Cheffins and H Wells, 'Executive Pay: What Worked?' *Journal of Corporation Law*, UCLA School of Law, Law-Econ Research Paper No 16-11, University of Cambridge Faculty of Law Research Paper No 38/2016.

101 AJ Mayo and N Nohria, *In Their Time: The Greatest Business Leaders of the Twentieth Century* (Harvard Business School Press, 2005) 258.

102 Large and Medium-sized Companies and Groups (Accounts and Reports) Regulations 2008, sch 8.

103 *Your Guide—Directors' Remuneration in FTSE 100 and 250 Companies* (Deloitte, 2015).
104 ibid.
105 *Directors' Remuneration Reporting Guidance 2016* (GC100 and Investor Group, 2016).
106 *Executive Remuneration Working Group Issues Interim Report* (Investment Management Association, 21 April 2016).
107 *Executive Remuneration Working Group: Final Report* (Investment Association, 2016).
108 *The Investment Association Principles of Remuneration* (Investment Association, 2016); see also 'Open Letter to Remuneration Committee Chairmen', Investment Association, 2016.
109 *Corporate Governance Reform: Green Paper* (Department for Business, Energy and Industrial Strategy, 2016).
110 C Philp, *Restoring Responsible Ownership: Ending the Ownerless Corporation and Controlling Executive Pay* (High Pay Centre, 2016).
111 House of Commons' Business, Energy and Industrial Strategy Committee, *Corporate Governance*. Third Report of Session 2016–17, HC 702.
112 ibid para 75.
113 ibid para 99.
114 L Noonan, 'Credit Suisse Executives Agree 40% Cut to Bonuses' *Financial Times*, 15 April 2017.
115 TT Selvarajan and R Sardessai, 'Appraisal of Ethical Performance: A Theoretical Model' (2010) 26(3) *Journal of Applied Business Research* 1.
116 *Incentivising Ethics: Managing Incentives to Encourage Good and Deter Bad Behaviour* (Transparency International, 2016).
117 D Cable and V Freek, 'Stop Paying Executives for Performance' *Harvard Business Review*, 23 February 2016,. See also a 2011 blog by Knowledge at the Wharton Business School: http://knowledge.wharton.upenn.edu/article/the-problem-with-financial-incentives-and-what-to-do-about-it.

14. The Ethics and Compliance Framework

1 R Steinholtz, 'Ethics Ambassadors: Getting under the Skin of the Business' (2014) 3–4 *Business Compliance* 16.
2 Lord Thomas of Cwmgiedd, 'Worthy of Trust? Law, Ethics and Culture in Banking', speech at the Bank of England, 21 March 2017.
3 See C Parker and S Gilad, 'Internal Corporate Compliance Management Systems: Structure, Culture and Agency' in C Parker and V Lehmann Nielsen (eds), *Explaining Compliance: Business Responses to Regulation* (Edward Elgar, 2012) ch 8.
4 Many studies and official statements support this: J Braithwaite, *To Punish or Persuade: Enforcement of Coal Mine Safety* (State University of New York Press, 1985) 61; DP McCaffrey and DW Hart, *Wall Street Policies Itself: How Securities Firms Manage the Legal Hazards of Competitive Pressures* (Oxford University Press, 1998), 174; J Rees, *Hostages of Each Other: The Transformation of Nuclear Safety Since Three Mile Island* (University of Chicago Press, 1994); *How Your Business Can Achieve Compliance*

(OFT, 2005), OFT 424, 10; KS Desai, 'Antitrust Compliance Programmes' (2006) GCR Nov Supp (European Antitrust Review) 15–21; Joshua, 'Antitrust Compliance Programmes for Multinational Companies [2001] *International Financial Law Review Supplement* (Competition and Antitrust, 2001); ABA, *Antitrust Compliance*, 2005, 81.

5 M Weait, 'The Role of the Compliance Officer in Firms Carrying on Investment Business' (1994) 9(8) *Butterworth's Journal of International Banking and Financial Law* 381.

6 J Braithwaite, *Corporate Crime in the Pharmaceutical Industry* (Routledge & Kegan Paul, 1984) 359; V Braithwaite, 'The Australian Government's Affirmative Action Legislation: Achieving Social Change through Human Resource Management' (1993) 15 *Law & Policy* 327; Rees (n 4) 92, 98–99, 108; S Taylor, *Making Bureaucracies Think: The Environmental Impact Statement Strategy of Administrative Reform* (Stanford University Press, 1984).

7 A Newton, *The Handbook of Compliance: Making Ethics Work in Financial Services* (Prentice Hall, 1998) 74.

8 US Department of Justice, Criminal Division, Fraud Section, *Evaluation of Corporate Compliance Programs*, 8 February 2017, available at www.justice.gov/criminal-fraud/page/file/937501/download.

9 Presentation by Florian Beranek, UNIDO, 'Regional Business Integrity Conference: Culture of Business Integrity: Pathways to Sustainability and Success', Singapore, 6 March 2017.

10 D Johnson, *Ethics at Work. 2015 Survey of Employees: Main Findings and Themes* (Institute of Business Ethics, 2015).

11 LK Treviño and GR Weaver, 2003, *Managing Ethics in Business Organisations* (Stanford University Press, 2003) 193.

12 Steinholtz, (n 1).

13 Cited in the Appendix to *FRC Culture Report: Corporate Culture and the Role of Boards* (FRC, 2016).

14 A Edmondson, 'Psychological Safety and Learning Behaviour in Working Teams' (1999) 44(2) *Administrative Science Quarterly* 350.

15 D Ariely, *Predictably Irrational: The Hidden Forces that Shape Our Decisions* (HarperCollins, 2008) 135.

16 JA Ragatz and RF Duska, 'Financial Codes of Ethics' in J Boatright (ed), *Finance Ethics: Critical Issues in Theory and Practice* (John Wiley, 2010).

17 *Codes of Business Ethics: A Guide to Developing and Implementing an Effective Code* (Institute for Business Ethics, 2016) 15.

18 ibid 11.

19 ibid 34.

20 J Habermas, *The Philosophical Discourse of Modernity* (Polity, 1987).

21 S Webley, *Towards Ethical Norms in International Business Transactions* (Institute of Business Ethics, 2014).

22 H Küng, 'The World's Religions: Common Ethical Values', speech, 2005. See also H Küng, *Global Responsibility: In Search of a New World Ethic* (Crossroad Publishing Company, 1991).

23 R Sisodia, J Sheth and D Wolfe, *Firms of Endearment: How World-Class Companies Profit from Passion and Purpose*, 2nd edn (Pearson Education, 2014).

24 R Kidder, *Moral Courage: Taking Action When Your Values Are Put to the Test* (William Morrow, 2005).

25 D Palmer, *Normal Organizational Wrongdoing: A Critical Analysis of Theories of Misconduct in and by Organizations* (Oxford University Press, 2012) 106.

26 A Gawande, *The Checklist Manifesto: How to Get Things Right* (Profile Books, 2010).

27 MH Bazerman and AE Tenbrunsel, *Blind Spots: Why We Fail to Do What's Right and What to Do About It* (Princeton University Press, 2011).

28 MC Gentile, *Giving Voice to Values* (Yale University Press, 2010).

29 ibid 179.

30 JM Darley and CD Batson, 'From Jerusalem to Jericho: A Study of Situational and Dispositional Variables in Helping Behavior' (1973) 27 *Journal of Personality and Social Psychology* 100.

31 Bazerman and Tenbrunsel (n 27) 165.

32 O Sezer, F Gino and M Bazerman, 'Ethical Blind Spots: Explaining Unintentional Unethical Behavior' (2015) 6 *Current Opinion In Psychology* 77.

33 ibid. A telephone survey of 506 SMEs (10–249 employees) was conducted alongside a further 49 in-depth interviews with SMEs to explore issues around supply chains and other types of relationships with large businesses and how they impact on SME growth.

34 *Business Perceptions Survey 2012* (IFF Research, 2012) para 1.26.

35 ibid para 1.27. This was up from 64% in the 2010 survey. Businesses were more likely to use external agents as a source of information in cases of employment law (86%) and company law (81%), and were less likely to use agents for food safety (44%) and fire safety (55%).

36 *Drivers of Compliance and Non-compliance with Consumer Protection Law: A Report by Ipsos MORI Commissioned by the OFT* (Office of Fair Trading, 2010), OFT1225a.

37 ibid para 1.12.

38 ibid para 1.13.

39 ibid para 1.14.

40 ibid para 1.15.

41 ibid para 1.17.

42 *Consumer Rights and Business Practices* (IFF Research, March 2013). The survey found that 27% of businesses reported that existing consumer rights legislation was 'not very' or 'not at all easy' to understand; medium and large businesses were more likely to report this (37% and 38% respectively). The survey was based on 1,000 20-minute telephone interviews with senior decision-makers of businesses which sell goods, services or digital content to consumers, and 60 completed 'cost sheets' from businesses between September 2012 and January 2013.

43 P DiMaggio and W Powell, 'The Iron Cage Revisited: Institutional Isomorphism and Collective Rationality' in W Powell and P DiMaggio (eds), *The New Institutionalism on Organizational Analysis* (University of Chicago Press, 1991); D Wood, 'Corporate Social Performance Revisited' (1991) 16(4) *Academy of Management Review* 691; D Greening and B Gray, 'Testing a Model of Organizational Response to Social and Political Issues' (1994) 37(3) *Academy of Management Journal* 467; R Marshall, M Cordano and M Silverman, 'Exploring Individual and Institutional Drivers of proactive Environmentalism in the US Wine Industry' (2005) 14(2) *Business Strategy and the Environment* 92.

44 RH Kraakman, 'Gatekeepers: The Anatomy of a Third-Party Enforcement Strategy' (1986) 2 *Journal of Law, Economics and Organization* 53; C Parker and VL Nielsen, 'Corporate Compliance Systems: Could They Make Any Difference?' (2009) 41 *Administration and Society* 3; CJ Coffee, Jr, *Gatekeepers: The Professions and Corporate Governance* (Oxford University Press, 2006).
45 *Better Business Better Scotland* (Social Value Lab, 2015).
46 Edmondson (n 14).
47 L Herrero, *Homo Imitans: The Art of Social Infection:* Viral ChangeTM *in Action* (meetingminds, 2011) 61.
48 ibid.
49 W Sykes, C Groom, P Desai and J Kelly, *Coming Clean: The Experience of Cleaning Operatives* (Equality and Human Rights Commission, 2014) 16.
50 ibid 80.
51 *Inquiry into Recruitment and Employment in the Meat and Poultry Processing Sector: Report of the Findings and Recommendations* (Equality and Human Rights Commission, 2010).
52 *The Whistleblowing Commission: Report on the Effectiveness of Existing Arranges for Workplace Whistleblowing in the UK* (Whistleblowing Commission, November 2013) para 2.
53 *Report of the Mid Staffordshire NHS Foundation Trust Public Inquiry*, HC 947, Public Inquiry, chaired by Robert Francis QC, February 2013.
54 *Parliamentary Commission on Banking Standards, 'Changing Banking for Good'* (June 2013) para 142.
55 British Standards Institution, *Whistleblowing Arrangements Code of Practice*, PAS 1998: 2008, July 2008.
56 P Kurer, *Legal and Compliance Risk: A Strategic Response to a Rising Threat for Global Business* (Oxford University Press, 2015) 243; D Gentilin, *The Origins of Ethical Failures: Lessons for Leaders* (Routledge, 2016) 57.
57 *Effective Speak-up Arrangements for Whistleblowers* (Association of Chartered Certified Accountants, 2016).
58 *Report to the Nation on Occupational Fraud Abuse: 2012 Global Fraud Study* (Association of Certified Fraud Examiners, 2012).
59 Schumpeter, 'The Enemy within: Fraud within Companies is a Risk That Can Never Be Eliminated, Just Managed' *The Economist*, 1 March 2014, 73.
60 See the summary in Y Feldman and O Lobel, 'Individuals as Enforcers: The Design of Employee Reporting Systems' in C Parker and VL Nielsen (eds), *Explaining Compliance: Business Reponses to Regulation* (Edward Elgar, 2011).
61 *The Whistleblowing Commission* (n 52) para 2.
62 Global Reporting Initiative, https://www.globalreporting.org/Pages/default.aspx.

Appendices

1 A Edmondson, 'Psychological Safety and Learning Behaviour in Working Teams' (1999) 44(2) *Administrative Science Quarterly* 350.

INDEX

NB: Page numbers in **bold** refer to information in tables, and those in *italics* refer to information in figures